# Third Workshop on Arabic Natural Language Processing (WANLP 2017)

Co-located with EACL 2017

Valencia, Spain
3 April 2017

ISBN: 978-1-5108-3874-1

# Preface

Welcome to the Third Arabic Natural Language Processing Workshop held at EACL 2017 in Valencia, Spain.

A number of Arabic NLP (or Arabic NLP-related) workshops and conferences have taken place in the last few years, both in the Arab World and in association with international conferences. The Arabic NLP workshop at EACL 2017 follows in the footsteps of these previous efforts to provide a forum for researchers to share and discuss their ongoing work. This particular workshop is the third in a series, following the First Arabic NLP workshop held at EMNLP 2014 in Doha, Qatar; and the Second Arabic NLP workshop held at ACL 2015 in Beijing, China.

We received 47 submissions and selected 22 (47% acceptance rate) for presentation in the workshop. All papers were reviewed by three reviewers on average. The number of submissions is over twice that of the previous workshop in Beijing, which also had a higher acceptance rate (65%). Ten papers will be presented orally and 12 as part of a poster session. The presentation mode is independent of the ranking of the papers. The papers cover a diverse set of topics from Maltese and Arabic dialect processing to models of semantic similarity and credibility analysis, advances in Arabic treebanking, and error annotation for dyslexic texts.

The quantity and quality of the contributions to the workshop are strong indicators that there is a continued need for this kind of dedicated Arabic NLP workshop.

We would like to acknowledge all the hard work of the submitting authors and thank the reviewers for the valuable feedback they provided. We hope these proceedings will serve as a valuable reference for researchers and practitioners in the field of Arabic NLP and NLP in general.

Nizar Habash, General Chair, on behalf of the organizers of the workshop.

# Organizers

**General Chair**
Nizar Habash, New York University Abu Dhabi

**Program Chairs**
Mona Diab, The George Washington University
Kareem Darwish, Qatar Computing Research Institute
Wassim El-Hajj, American University of Beirut, Lebanon
Hend Al-Khalifa, King Saud University
Houda Bouamor, Carnegie Mellon University in Qatar

**Publication Chairs**
Nadi Tomeh, LIPN, Université Paris 13, Sorbonne Paris Cité
Mahmoud El-Haj, Lancaster University

**Publicity Chairs**
Fethi Bougares, University of Le Mans
Wajdi Zaghouani, Carnegie Mellon University-Qatar

**Program Committee:**
Ahmed Abdelali, Qatar Computing Research Institute, Qatar
Nora Al-Twairesh, King Saud University, Saudi Arabia
Areeb Alowsiheq, Imam University, KSA
Salha Alzahrani, Taif University, Saudi Arabia
Almoataz B. Al-Said, Cairo University, Egypt
Alberto Barrón-Cedeño, Qatar Computing Research Institute, Qatar
Fethi Bougares, Le Mans University, France
Tim Buckwalter, University of Maryland, USA
Violetta Cavalli-Sforza, Al Akhawayn University, Morocco
Abeer Dayel, King Saud University, Saudi Arabia
Tamer Elsayed, Qatar University, Qatar
Ossama Emam, IBM, USA
Ramy Eskander, Columbia University, USA
Nizar Habash, New York University Abu Dhabi, UAE
Bassam Haddad, University of Petra, Jordan
Hazem Hajj, American University of Beirut, Lebanon
Maha Jarallah Althobaiti, Taif University, Saudi Arabia
Azzeddine Mazroui, University Mohamed I, Morocco
Karine Megerdoomian, The MITRE Corporation, USA
Ghassan Mourad, Université Libanaise, Lebanon
Hamdy Mubarak, Qatar Computing Research Institute, Qatar
Preslav Nakov, Qatar Computing Research Institute, Qatar

Alexis Nasr, University of Marseille, France
Kemal Oflazer, Carnegie Mellon University Qatar, Qatar
Eshrag Refaee, Jazan University, Saudi Arabia
Mohammad Salameh, Carnegie Mellon University, Qatar
Hassan Sawaf, eBay Inc., USA
Khaled Shaalan, The British University in Dubai, UAE
Khaled Shaban, Qatar University, Qatar
Otakar Smrž, Džám-e Džam Language Institute, Czech Republic
Wajdi Zaghouani, Carnegie Mellon University, Qatar
Imed Zitouni, Microsoft Research, USA

**Invited Speaker:**

Stephan Vogel, Qatar Computing Research Institute (QCRI), Qatar

# Table of Contents

# Workshop Program

**Monday April 3, 2017**

**09:00–11:30    Session AAA: Session**

09:00–09:10    *Opening Remarks*
Nizar Habash

09:10–10:00    *Keynote*
Stephan Vogel

10:00–10:20    *Identification of Languages in Algerian Arabic Multilingual Documents*
Wafia Adouane and Simon Dobnik

10:20–10:40    *Arabic Diacritization: Stats, Rules, and Hacks*
Kareem Darwish, Hamdy Mubarak and Ahmed Abdelali

10:40–11:00    *Semantic Similarity of Arabic Sentences with Word Embeddings*
El Moatez Billah Nagoudi and Didier Schwab

**11:00–11:30    *Coffee Break***

**11:30–12:50    Session BBB: Session**

11:30–11:50    *Morphological Analysis for the Maltese Language: The challenges of a hybrid system*
Claudia Borg and Albert Gatt

11:50–12:10    *A Morphological Analyzer for Gulf Arabic Verbs*
Salam Khalifa, Sara Hassan and Nizar Habash

12:10–12:30    *A Neural Architecture for Dialectal Arabic Segmentation*
Younes Samih, Mohammed Attia, Mohamed Eldesouki, Ahmed Abdelali, Hamdy Mubarak, Laura Kallmeyer and Kareem Darwish

12:30–12:50    *Sentiment Analysis of Tunisian Dialects: Linguistic Ressources and Experiments*
Salima Medhaffar, Fethi Bougares, Yannick Estève and Lamia Hadrich-Belguith

**12:50–14:30    *Lunch Break***

**Monday April 3, 2017 (continued)**

**14:30–16:30**   **Session CCC: Session**

14:30–14:50   *CAT: Credibility Analysis of Arabic Content on Twitter*
Rim El Ballouli, Wassim El-Hajj, Ahmad Ghandour, Shady Elbassuoni, Hazem Hajj
and Khaled Shaban

14:50–15:10   *A New Error Annotation for Dyslexic texts in Arabic*
Maha Alamri and William J Teahan

15:10–15:30   *An Unsupervised Speaker Clustering Technique based on SOM and I-vectors for
Speech Recognition Systems*
Hany Ahmed, Mohamed Elaraby, Abdullah M. Mousa, Mostafa Elhosiny, Sherif
Abdou and Mohsen Rashwan

**15:30–16:00**   ***Poster Boaster ( 2 min each for 12 papers)***

**16:00–16:30**   ***Coffee Break***

**16:30–18:00**   **Session DDD: Session**

*SHAKKIL: An Automatic Diacritization System for Modern Standard Arabic Texts*
Amany Fashwan and Sameh Alansary

*Arabic Tweets Treebanking and Parsing: A Bootstrapping Approach*
Fahad Albogamy, Allan Ramsay and Hanady Ahmed

*Identifying Effective Translations for Cross-lingual Arabic-to-English User-
generated Speech Search*
Ahmad Khwileh, Haithem Afli, Gareth Jones and Andy Way

*A Characterization Study of Arabic Twitter Data with a Benchmarking for State-of-
the-Art Opinion Mining Models*
Ramy Baly, Gilbert Badaro, Georges El-Khoury, Rawan Moukalled, Rita Aoun,
Hazem Hajj, Wassim El-Hajj, Nizar Habash and Khaled Shaban

*Robust Dictionary Lookup in Multiple Noisy Orthographies*
Lingliang Zhang, Nizar Habash and Godfried Toussaint

*Arabic POS Tagging: Don't Abandon Feature Engineering Just Yet*
Kareem Darwish, Hamdy Mubarak, Ahmed Abdelali and Mohamed Eldesouki

# Identification of Languages in Algerian Arabic
# Multilingual Documents

**Wafia Adouane and Simon Dobnik**
CLASP, Department of FLoV
University of Gothenburg, Sweden
{wafia.adouane,simon.dobnik}@gu.se

## Abstract

This paper presents a language identification system designed to detect the language of each word, in its context, in a multilingual documents as generated in social media by bilingual/multilingual communities, in our case speakers of Algerian Arabic. We frame the task as a sequence tagging problem and use supervised machine learning with standard methods like HMM and Ngram classification tagging. We also experiment with a lexicon-based method. Combining all the methods in a fall-back mechanism and introducing some linguistic rules, to deal with unseen tokens and ambiguous words, gives an overall accuracy of 93.14%. Finally, we introduced rules for language identification from sequences of recognised words.

## 1 Introduction

Most of the current Natural Language Processing (NLP) tools deal with one language, assuming that all documents are monolingual. Nevertheless, there are many cases where more than one language is used in the same document. The present study seeks to fill in some of the needs to accommodate multilingual (including bilingual) documents in NLP tools. The phenomenon of using more than one language is common in multilingual societies where the contact between different languages has resulted in various language (code) mixing like code-switching and borrowings. Code-switching is commonly defined as the use of two or more languages/language varieties with fluency in one conversation, or in a sentence, or even in a single word. Whereas borrowing is

used to refer to the altering of words from one language into another.

There is no clear-cut distinction between borrowings and code-switching, and scholars have different views and arguments. We based our work on (Poplack and Meechan, 1998) where the authors consider borrowing as the adaptation of lexical items, with a phonological and morphological integration, from one language to another. Otherwise, it is a code-switching, at single lexical item, phrasal or clausal levels, either the lexical item/phrase/clause exists or not in the first language.[1] We will use "language mixing" as a general term to refer to both code-switching and borrowing.

We frame the task of identifying language mixing as a segmentation of a document/text into sequences of words belonging to one language, i.e. segment identification or chunking based on the language of each word. Since language shifts can occur frequently at each point of a document we base our work on the isolated word assumption as referred to by (Singh and Gorla, 2007) wherein the authors consider that it is more realistic to assume that every word in a document can be in a different language rather than a long sequence of words being in the same language. However, we are also interested in identifying the boundaries of each language use, sequences of words belonging to the same language, which we address by adding rules for language chunking.

This paper's main focus is the detection of language mixing in Algerian Arabic texts, written in Arabic script, used in social media while its contribution is to provide a system that is able to detect the language of each word in its context. The paper is organized as follows: in Section 2, we give a brief overview of Algerian Arabic which is

---

[1] Refers to the first language the speakers/users use as their mother tongue.



*Proceedings of The Third Arabic Natural Language Processing Workshop (WANLP)*, pages 1–8,
Valencia, Spain, April 3, 2017. ©2017 Association for Computational Linguistics

a well suited, and less studied, language for detecting language mixing. In Section 3, we present our newly built linguistic resources, from scratch, and we motivate our choices in annotating the data. In Section 4, we describe the different methods used to build our system. In Section 5, we survey some related work, and we conclude with the main findings and some of our future directions.

## 2 Algerian Arabic

Algerian Arabic is a group of North African Arabic dialects mixed with different languages spoken in Algeria. The language contact between many languages, throughout the history of the region, has resulted in a rich complex language comprising words, expressions, and linguistic structures from various Arabic dialects, different Berber varieties, French, Italian, Spanish, Turkish as well as other Mediterranean Romance languages. Modern Algerian Arabic is typically a mixture of Algerian Arabic dialects, Berber varieties, French, Classical Arabic, Modern Standard Arabic, and a few other languages like English. As it is the case with all North African languages, Algerian Arabic is heavily influenced by French where code-switching and borrowing at different levels could be found.

Algerian Arabic is different from Modern Standard Arabic (MSA) mainly phonologically and morphologically. For instance, some sounds in MSA are not used in Algerian Arabic, namely the interdental fricatives 'ث' /θ/, 'ذ' /ð/ and the glottal fricative 'ه' /h/ at a word final position. Instead they are pronounced as aspirated stop 'ت' /t/, dental stop 'د' /d/ and bilabial glide 'و' /w/ respectively. Hence, the MSA word ذهب /*hb/ "gold" is pronounced/written as 'دهب' /dhb/ in Algerian Arabic. Souag (2000) gives a detailed description of the characteristics of Algerian Arabic and describes at length how it differs from MSA. Compared to the rest of Arabic varieties, Algerian Arabic is different in many aspects (vocabulary, pronunciation, syntax, etc.). Maybe the main common characteristics between them is the use on non-standard orthography where people write according to their pronunciation.

## 3 Corpus and Lexicons

In this section, we describe how we collected and annotated our corpus and explain the motivation behind some annotation decisions. We then describe how we build lexicons for each language and provide some statistics about each lexicon.

### 3.1 Corpus

We automatically collected content from various social media platforms that we knew they use Algerian Arabic. We included texts of various topics, structures and lengths. In total, we collected 10,597 documents. On this corpus we ran an automatic language identifier which is trained to distinguish between the most popular Arabic varieties (Adouane et al., 2016). Afterwards, we only consider the documents that were identified as Algerian Arabic which gives us 10,586 documents (215,843 tokens).[2] For robustness, we further pre-processed the data where we removed punctuation, emoticons and diacritics, and then we normalized it. In social media users do not use punctuation and diacritics/short vowels in a consistent way, even within the same text. We opt for such normalization because we assume that such idiosyncratic variation will not affect language identification.

Based on our knowledge of Algerian Arabic and our goal to distinguish between borrowing and code-switching at a single lexical item, we decided to classify words into six languages: Algerian Arabic (ALG), modern standard Arabic (MSA), French (FRC), Berber (BER)[3], English (ENG) and Borrowings (BOR) which includes foreign words adapted to the Algerian Arabic morphology. Moreover, we grouped all Named Entities in one class (NER), sounds and interjections in another (SND). Our choice is motivated by the fact that these words are language independent. We also keep digits to keep the context of words and grouped them in a class called DIG.

In total, we have nine separate classes. First, three native speakers of Algerian Arabic annotated the first 1,000 documents (22,067 words) from the pre-processed corpus, following a set of annotation guidelines which takes into account the above-mentioned linguistic differences between

---

[2] We use *token* to refer to lexical words, sounds and digits (excluding punctuation and emoticons) and *word* to refer only to lexical words.

[3] Berber is an Afro-Asiatic language used in North Africa and which is not related to Arabic.

Algerian Arabic and Modern Standard Arabic. To assess the quality of the data annotation, we computed the inter-annotator agreement using the Cohen's kappa coefficient ($\kappa$), a standard metric used to evaluate the quality of a set of annotations in classification tasks by assessing the annotators' agreement (Carletta, 1996). The $\kappa$ on the human annotated 1,000 documents is 89.27%, which can be qualitatively interpreted as "really good".

Next, we implemented a tagger based on Hidden Markov Models (HMM) and the Viterbi algorithm, to find the best sequence of language tags over a sequence of words. The assumption is that the context of the surrounding words and their language tags will predict the language for the current word. We apply smoothing – we assign an equal low probability (estimated from the training data) for unseen words – during training to estimate the emission probability and compute the transmission probabilities. We trained the HMM tagger on the human annotated 1,000 documents. We divided the remaining corpus (non-annotated data) into 9 parts (each part from 1-8 includes 1,000 documents and the last part includes 1,586 documents). We first used the trained tagger to automatically annotate the first part, then manually checked/corrected the annotation. After that, we added the checked annotated part to the already existing training dataset and used that to annotate the following part. We performed the same bootstrapping process until we annotated all the parts.

The gradual bootstrapping annotation of new parts of the corpus helped us in two ways. First, it speeded up the annotation process which took five weeks for three human annotators to check and correct the annotations in the entire corpus compiled so far. It would take them far longer if they started annotation without the help of the HMM tagger. Second, checking and correcting the annotation of the automatic tagger served us to analyse the errors the tagger was making. The final result is a large annotated corpus with a human annotation quality which is an essential element for learning useful language models. Table 1 shows some statistics about the current annotated corpus.

| Category | ALG | MSA | FRC | BOR | NER | ENG | BER | DIG | SND |
|---|---|---|---|---|---|---|---|---|---|
| # Words | 118,942 | 82,114 | 6,045 | 4,025 | 2,283 | 254 | 99 | 1,394 | 687 |

Table 1: Statistics about the annotated corpus.

## 3.2 Lexicons

We asked two other Algerian Arabic native speakers to collect words for each included language from the web excluding the platforms used to build the above-described corpus. We cleaned the newly compiled word lists and kept only one occurrence for each word, and we removed all ambiguous words: words that occur in more than one language. Table 2 gives some statistics about the final lexicons that are lists of words that unambiguously occur in a given language, one word per line in a `.txt` file. Effectively, we see the role of dictionaries as stores for exceptions, while for ambiguous words we work towards a disambiguation mechanism.

| Category | ALG | MSA | FRC | BOR | NER | ENG | BER |
|---|---|---|---|---|---|---|---|
| # Types | 42,788 | 94,167 | 3,206 | 2,751 | 1,945 | 157 | 21,789 |

Table 2: Statistics about the lexicons.

## 4 Experiments and Results

In this section, we describe the methods and the different experimental setups we used to build our language identification tool. We analyze and discuss the obtained results. We start identifying language at a word level and then we combine words to identify the language of sequences. We approach the language identification at the word level by taking into account the context of these words. We supplement the method with a lexicon lookup approach and manually constructed rules.

To evaluate the performance of the system, we divided the final human annotated dataset into two parts: the training dataset which contains 10,008 documents (215,832 tokens) and the evaluation dataset which contains 578 documents (10,107 tokens). None of the documents included in the evaluation dataset were used to compile the lexicons previously described.

### 4.1 Identifying words

### 4.1.1 HMM Tagger

In Section 3.1 we describe an implementation of a tagger based on Hidden Markov Models (HMM) used as a helping tool to bootstrap data annotation. Now, having an annotated corpus we are interested in the performance of the tagger on our final fully annotated corpus which we discuss here. We train the HMM tagger on the training data and evaluate it on the evaluation data. Table 3 shows the performance of the tagger.

| Category | Precision (%) | Recall (%) | F-score (%) |
|---|---|---|---|
| ALG | 87.10 | 89.96 | 88.50 |
| BER | 100 | 18.18 | 30.77 |
| BOR | 97.71 | 40.38 | 57.14 |
| DIG | 100 | 94.74 | 97.30 |
| ENG | 100 | 24.14 | 38.89 |
| FRC | 82.28 | 63.87 | 71.92 |
| MSA | 84.03 | 88.04 | 85.99 |
| NER | 84.07 | 61.69 | 71.16 |
| SND | 100 | 85.71 | 92.31 |

Table 3: Performance of the HMM tagger.

The overall accuracy of the tagger is 85.88%. This quite high performance gives an idea about how useful and helpful was the use of the HMM tagger to annotate the data before the human checking. The tagger also outperforms the majority baseline (#majority class / #total tokens) which is 55.10%. From Table 3 we see that the HMM tagger is good at identifying ALG and MSA words, given an F-score of 88.50% and 85.99% respectively.[4] However, this performance dropped with other categories, it is even lower than the majority baseline for BER and ENG.

The confusion matrix of the tagger (omitted here due to space constraints) shows that all categories are confused either with ALG or MSA. This can be explained by the fact that ALG and MSA are the majority classes which means that both emission and transmission probabilities are biased to these two categories. The analysis of the most frequent errors shows that errors can be grouped into two types. The first type includes ambiguous words. For example, in the sentence

الماتش مشري حارس خلا البيت يدخل

/AlmAt\$ m\$ry HArs xlA Albyt ydxl/

"the football match is bought, the goal keeper allowed the (goal) ball to enter", the word 'البيت' is "the goal" in French, the same word means "the house" in MSA and "the room" in ALG. Also the following word 'يدخل' which means " to enter" is

used with all the possible meanings of 'البيت' (enter a house/ a room and ball enters). The second type of errors relates to unseen words in the training data. Because of the smoothing we used, the HMM tagger does not return 'unseen word'. Instead, another tag is assigned, mostly ALG and MSA. We could identify such words by setting manually some thresholds, but it is not clear what these should be.

The Precision is high for all unambiguous tokens, however the Recall is very low. To overcome the limitation of the HMM tagger in dealing with unseen words, we decided to explore other methods. Moreover, we want to reduce the uncertainty of our tagger deciding what is an unseen word. We found it difficult to set any threshold that is not data-dependent. Therefore, we introduced a new category called unknown UNK which is inspired from *active learning* (Settles, 2009). We believe that this should be used in all automatic systems instead of returning a simple guess based on its training model.

### 4.1.2 Lexicon-based Tagger

We devised a simple algorithm that performs a lexicon look-up and returns for each word the language of the lexicon it appears in (note that lexicons contain only unambiguous words). For SND, we created a list of most common sounds like '

بفف' "pff", 'هه' "hh". For digits, we used the isdigit method built-in Python. In the case where a word does not appear in any lexicon, the unknown UNK category is returned. This method does not require training, but it requires good quality lexicons with a wide coverage. We evaluated the lexicon-based tagger on the same evaluation dataset and the results are shown in Table 4.

| Category | Precision (%) | Recall (%) | F-score (%) |
|---|---|---|---|
| ALG | 97.39 | 81.55 | 88.77 |
| BER | 100 | 63.64 | 77.78 |
| BOR | 98.52 | 83.91 | 90.63 |
| DIG | 100 | 100 | 100 |
| ENG | 100 | 55.17 | 71.11 |
| FRC | 96.30 | 84.85 | 90.21 |
| MSA | 97.69 | 82.43 | 89.42 |
| NER | 97.46 | 74.68 | 84.56 |
| SND | 100 | 100 | 100 |

Table 4: Performance of the lexicon tagger.

The overall accuracy of the tagger is 81.98%. From comparing the results shown in Table 4 and

---

[4]We ignore the DIG and SND categories because we are interested in lexical words. As explained above, we kept them to keep the context of each word.

Table 3, it is clear that the Recall has increased for all categories except for ALG and MSA. The reason is that now we have the UNK category where among the 10,107 tokens used for evaluation, 1,610 words are tagged as UNK instead of ALG or MSA. We examined the UNK words and found that these words do not exist in the lexicons. Either they are completely new words or they are different spellings of already covered words (which count as different words).

The confusion matrix of the lexicon-based tagger (omitted here) shows that the most frequent errors are between all categories and the UNK category. The tagger often confuses between ALG/MSA and MSA/ALG. It also occasionally confuses between ALG/FRC and ALG/NER. These errors could be explained by the fact that the context of a word is ignored.
For example, in the sentence

حطولنا بلا بقلاوا بلا ميقطعوه حرنا كيفاش نكلوه

/HTwlnA blA bqlAwA blA myqTEwh HrnA kyfA$ nklwh/ "they served us a dish of Baklava without cutting it, we did not know how to eat it", the first "بلا" means "dish" in French and the second "بلا" means "without" in MSA. In the sentence

وجدنا كلشي بلقيس لي قالولنا عليه

/wjdnA kl$y blqys ly qAlwlnA Elyh/ "we prepared everything according to the measures they (gave) told us", the word "بلقيس" means "with the measure" in ALG and it is a female name (NER). Analysing the tagging errors indicates that using lexicon-based tagger is not effective in dealing with ambiguous words because it ignores the context of words, and as known, the context is the main means of ambiguity resolution.

### 4.1.3 n-gram Tagger

Our goal is to build a language tagger, at a word level, which takes into account the context of each word in order to be able to properly deal with ambiguous words. At the same time, we want it to be able to deal with unseen words. Ideally we want it to return UNK for each word it did not see before. This is because we want to analyse the words the tagger is not able to identify and appropriately update our dictionaries.

The Natural Language Toolkit (NLTK) n-gram POS tagger (Steven et al., 2009) is well suited for further experimentation. First, the tagging principle is the same and the only difference is the set of tags. Secondly, the NLTK Ngram tagger offers the possibility of changing the context of a word up to trigrams as well as the possibility of combining taggers (unigram, bigram, trigram) with the back-off option. It is also possible to select a single category, for example the most frequent tag or UNK, as a default tag in case all other options fail. This combination of different taggers and the back-off option leads to the optimization of the tagger performance. We start with the method involving most knowledge/context, if it fails we back off progressively to a simpler method. Table 5 summarizes the results of different configurations. We train and evaluate on the same training and evaluation sets as before.

| Tagger | Accuracy (%) |
|---|---|
| Unigram | 74.89 |
| Bigram | 12.27 |
| Trigram | 07.97 |
| BackOff(Trigram, Bigram, Unigram, ALG) | 87.12 |
| BackOff(Trigram, Bigram, Unigram, UNK) | 74.95 |
| Default (ALG) | 52.12 |

Table 5: Performance of different n-gram tagger configurations.

The use of bigram and trigram taggers alone has a very little effect because of the data sparsety. It is unlikely to find the same word sequences (bigram, trigram) several times. However, chaining the taggers has a positive effect on the overall performance. Notice also that tagging words with the majority class ALG performs less than the majority baseline, 52.12% compared to 55.10%. In Table 6, we show the performance of the BackOff(Trigram, Bigram, Unigram, UNK) tagger in detail.

| Category | Precision (%) | Recall (%) | F-score (%) |
|---|---|---|---|
| ALG | 96.17 | 75.27 | 84.44 |
| BER | 100 | 27.27 | 42.86 |
| BOR | 99.24 | 41.01 | 58.04 |
| DIG | 100 | 94.74 | 97.30 |
| ENG | 100 | 20.69 | 34.29 |
| FRC | 97.38 | 60.61 | 74.71 |
| MSA | 97.45 | 79.48 | 87.55 |
| NER | 94.69 | 69.48 | 80.15 |
| SND | 100 | 85.71 | 92.31 |

Table 6: Performance of the BackOff(Trigram, Bigram, Unigram, UNK) tagger.

Compared to the previous tagger, this tagger suffers mainly from the unseen words where 2,279 tokens were tagged as UNK. This could account for the low Recall obtained for all categories. There is also some confusion between MSA/ALG, ALG/MSA and FRC/ALG.

### 4.1.4 Combining n-gram taggers and lexicons

The unknown words predicted by the Back-Off(Trigram, Bigram, Unigram, UNK) tagger can be replaced with words from our dictionaries. First, we run the BackOff(Trigram, Bigram, Unigram, UNK), and then we run the lexicon-based tagger to catch some of the UNK tokens. Table 7 summarizes the results.

| Category | Precision (%) | Recall (%) | F-score (%) |
|---|---|---|---|
| ALG | 96.47 | 92.88 | 94.64 |
| BER | 100 | 81.82 | 90.00 |
| BOR | 99.28 | 86.44 | 92.41 |
| DIG | 100 | 100 | 100 |
| ENG | 100 | 90.91 | 95.24 |
| FRC | 98.95 | 88.08 | 93.20 |
| MSA | 98.42 | 93.64 | 95.97 |
| NER | 96.05 | 94.81 | 95.42 |
| SND | 100 | 100 | 100 |

Table 7: Performance of the tagger combining n-gram and lexicons.

Combining information from the training data and the lexicons increases the performance of the language tagging for all categories, giving an overall accuracy of 92.86%. Still there are errors that are mainly caused by unseen and ambiguous words. Based on the confusion matrix of this tagger (omitted here) the errors affect the same language pairs as before.

All language tags are missing words that are tagged as UNK words (in total 476 words). We found that these words are neither seen in the training data nor covered by any existing lexicons new words or different (even as spelling variants of the existing words). Keeping track of the unseen words, by assigning them the UNK tag, allows us to extend the lexicons to ensure a wider coverage.

To test how data-dependent is our system, we cross-validated it, and all the accuracies were close to the reported overall accuracy of the system, combining n-grams and lexicons, evaluated on the evaluation data.

### 4.1.5 Adding rules

We analysed the lexicons and manually extracted some features that would help us identify the language, for instance the starting and the final sequence of characters of a word. The application of these rules improved the performance of the system, given an overall accuracy of 93.14%, by catching some unseen vocabulary (the number of UNK dropped to 446). As shown in Table 8, this hybrid tagger is still unable to deal with unseen words in addition to confusing some language pairs due to lexical ambiguity.

| | Misclassified languages | | | | | | | | | |
|---|---|---|---|---|---|---|---|---|---|---|
| | ALG | BER | BOR | DIG | ENG | FRC | MSA | NER | SND | UNK |
| ALG | [illegible] | 0 | 0 | 0 | 0 | 4 | 56 | 1 | 0 | 295 |
| BER | 1 | [illegible] | 0 | 0 | 0 | 0 | 0 | 0 | 0 | 1 |
| BOR | 1 | 0 | [illegible] | 0 | 0 | 5 | 1 | 0 | 0 | 30 |
| DIG | 0 | 0 | 0 | [illegible] | 0 | 0 | 0 | 0 | 0 | 0 |
| ENG | 1 | 0 | 0 | 0 | [illegible] | 0 | 0 | 0 | 0 | 0 |
| FRC | 28 | 0 | 0 | 0 | 0 | [illegible] | 0 | 0 | 0 | 16 |
| MSA | 134 | 0 | 1 | 0 | 0 | 1 | [illegible] | 5 | 0 | 101 |
| NER | 6 | 0 | 2 | 0 | 0 | 0 | 8 | [illegible] | 0 | 3 |
| SND | 0 | 0 | 0 | 0 | 0 | 0 | 0 | 0 | [illegible] | 0 |

(Row labels are under "Correct languages.")

Table 8: Confusion matrix of the Hybrid Tagger.

## 4.2 Identifying sequences of words

Now that we have a model that predicts the category of each token in a text, we added rules to label also non-linguistic words (punctuation (PUN) and emoticons (EMO)). This helps us to keep the original texts as produced by users as well as PUN and EMO be might be useful for other NLP tasks like sentiment and opinion analysis. Based on this extended annotation, we designed rules to identify the language of a specific segment of a text. The output of the system is a chunked text (regardless of its length) identifying language boundaries. It is up to the user how to chunk language independent categories, i.e. NER, DIG and SND, either separately or include them in larger segments based on a set of rules. For instance, the sentence

واش ندير يا ناااااس راني راني توجور روطاااار الرفاي
نتاعي مينوضنيش مام نريقليه ماشي لا فوط نتاعي 😊 😊

/wA\$ ndyr yA nAs rAny twjwr rwtAr AlrAfAy ntAEy mynwDny\$/ mAm nryqlyh mA\$y lA fwT ntAEy/ " what should I do people, I am always late my alarm clock does not wake me up even I set it , it is not my fault" is chunked as follows:

6

[واش ندير]ALG [يا ناس]MSA [راني]ALG [تّوجور روطار]FRC
[الرفاي]BOR [نتاعي مينوضنيش]ALG [مام]FRC [نريقليه]BOR
[ماشي]ALG [لا فوط]FRC [نتاعي]ALG [☺ ☺]EMO

Chunking text segments based on the language is entirely based on the identification of the language of each word in the segment. One of the open questions is what to do when words tagged as UNK are encountered. We still do not have a good way to deal with this situation, so we leave them as separate chunks UNK. Extending the training dataset and the coverage of the current lexicons would help to solve the problem.

## 5 Related Work

There is an increasing need to accommodate multilingual documents in different NLP tasks. Most work focuses on detecting different language pairs in multilingual texts, among others, Dutch-Turkish (Nguyen and Doğruöz, 2013), English-Bengali and English-Hindi (Das and Gambäck, 2013), English-French (Carpuat, 2014), Swahili-English (Piergallini et al., 2016). Since 2014, a Shared Task on Language Identification in Code-Switched Data is also organized (Solorio et al., 2014).

Detecting language mixing in Arabic social media texts has also attracted the attention of the research community. (Elfardy et al., 2013) propose an automatic system to identify linguistic code switch points between MSA and dialectal Arabic (Egyptian). The authors use a morphological analyser to decide whether a word is in MSA or DA, and they compare the performance of the system to the previous one (Elfardy and Diab, 2012) where they used unsupervised approach based on lexicons, sound-change rules, and language models. There is also work on detecting language mixing in Moroccan Arabic (Samih and Maier, 2016). In contrast to the previous work on Arabic, our annotation scheme and the system make a distinction between code-switching and borrowing which they do not consider. We also detect words in their contexts and do not group them in a Mixed category. To the best of our knowledge, we are not aware of any similar system which identifies language mixing in Algerian Arabic documents.

## 6 Conclusions and Future Work

We have presented a system for identifying the language at word and long sequence levels in multilingual documents in Algerian Arabic. We described the data and the different methods used to train the system that is able to identify language of words in their context between Algerian Arabic, Berber, English, French, Modern Standard Arabic and mixed languages (borrowings). The system achieves a very good performance, with an overall accuracy of 93.14% against a baseline of the majority class of 55.10%.

We discussed the limitations of the current system and gave insights on how to overcome them. The system is also able to identify language boundaries, i.e. sequence of tokens, including digits, sounds, punctuation and emoticons, belonging to the same language/category. Moreover, it performs also well in identifying Named Entities. Our system trained on a multilingual data from multiple domains handles several tasks, namely context sensitive language identification at a word level (borrowing or code-switching), language identification at long sequence level (chunking) and Named Entity recognition.

In the future, we plan to evaluate the automatic lexicon extension, as well as use the system in tasks such as error correction, Named Entity categorization(Person, Location, Product, Company), topic identification, sentiment analysis and textual entailment. We are currently extending our corpus and annotating it with other linguistic information.


## References

Wafia Adouane, Nasredine Semmar, Richard Johansson, and Victoria Bobicev. 2016. Automatic detection of Arabicized Berber and Arabic varieties. In *Proceedings of the Third Workshop on NLP for Similar Languages, Varieties and Dialects*, pages 63–72.

Jean Carletta. 1996. Assessing agreement on classification tasks: the kappa statistic. *Computational Linguistics*, 2(22):249–254.

Marine Carpuat. 2014. Mixed-language and code-switching in the canadian hansard. In *Proceedings of The First Workshop on Computational Approaches to Code Switching*, pages 107–115.

Amitava Das and Björn Gambäck. 2013. Code-mixing in social media text: The last language identification frontier? *Traitement Automatique des Langues*, 54(3):41–64.

Heba Elfardy and Mona Diab. 2012. Token level identification of linguistic code switching. In *COLING*, pages 287–296.

Heba Elfardy, Mohamed Al-Badrashiny, and Mona Diab. 2013. Code switch point detection in arabic.

In *Proceedings of the 18th International Conference on Application of Natural Language to Information Systems (NLDB2013)*.

Dong Nguyen and A. Seza Doğruöz. 2013. Word level language identification in online multilingual communication. In *Proceedings of the 2013 Conference on Empirical Methods in Natural Language Processing*, pages 18–21.

Mario Piergallini, Rouzbeh Shirvani, Gauri S. Gautam, and Mohamed Chouikha. 2016. Word-level language identification and predicting code-switching points in swahili-english language data. In *Proceedings of the Second Workshop on Computational Approaches to Code Switching*, pages 21–29.

Shana Poplack and Marjory Meechan. 1998. How languages fit together in codemixing. *The International Journal of Bilingualism*, 2(2):127–138.

Younes Samih and Wolfgang Maier. 2016. Detecting code-switching in moroccan arabic. In *Proceedings of SocialNLP @ IJCAI-2016*.

Burr Settles. 2009. Active learning literature survey. Computer Sciences Technical Report 1648, University of Wisconsin–Madison.

Anil Kumar Singh and Jagadeesh Gorla. 2007. Identification of languages and encodings in a multilingual document. In *Building and Exploring Web Corpora (WAC3-2007): Proceedings of the 3rd Web as Corpus Workshop, Incorporating Cleaneval*.

Thamar Solorio, Elizabeth Blair, Suraj Maharjan, Steven Bethard, Mona Diab, Mahmoud Ghoneim, Abdelati Hawwari, Fahad AlGhamdi, Julia Hirschberg, Alison Chang, and Pascale Fung. 2014. Overview for the first shared task on language identification in code-switched data. In *Proceedings of The First Workshop on Computational Approaches to Code Switching*, pages 62–72.

Lameen Souag. 2000. *Grammar of Algerian Darja*. Retrieved from `https://goo.gl/p2EmVH`.

Bird Steven, Ewan Klein, and Edward Loper. 2009. *Natural Language Processing with Python*. O'Reilly Media.

# Arabic Diacritization: Stats, Rules, and Hacks


**Kareem Darwish**    **Hamdy Mubarak**    **Ahmed Abdelali**

Qatar Computing Research Institute,
HBKU, Doha, Qatar

{kdarwish,hmubarak,aabdelali}@hbku.edu.qa



## Abstract

In this paper, we present a new and fast state-of-the-art Arabic diacritizer that guesses the diacritics of words and then their case endings. We employ a Viterbi decoder at word-level with back-off to stem, morphological patterns, and transliteration and sequence labeling based diacritization of named entities. For case endings, we use Support Vector Machine (SVM) based ranking coupled with morphological patterns and linguistic rules to properly guess case endings. We achieve a low word level diacritization error of 3.29% and 12.77% without and with case endings respectively on a new multi-genre free of copyright test set. We are making the diacritizer available for free for research purposes.


## 1  Introduction

Modern Standard Arabic (MSA) text is typically written without diacritics (short vowels). During reading, Arabic readers need to reintroduce diacritics to disambiguate words and to sound them correctly given their context. Diacritics play two main roles depending on their position in the word. The final vowel in a word – case ending – which typically appears on the last letter of the stem indicates its syntactic role; while diacritics on the rest of the letters indicate the lexical choice. The role of diacritics is crucial for some applications such as text-to-speech (TTS) and can be beneficial in other Arabic processing steps such as part-of-speech (POS) tagging and word sense disambiguation. A single word can have multiple meaning given the different diacritized forms. The word "Elm"[1] could be viewed as a homo-

graph for different lexical items. The word can be diacritized in the following ways: "Eilom" (knowledge/science), "Ealam" (flag), "Ealima" (he knew), "Eulima" (it was known), "Eal~ama" (he taught), etc. Beginners learning Arabic get accustomed to diacritics and gradually learn to disambiguate the text without them. For final diacritics, they can help disambiguate the syntactic roles of words in sentences. Consider the syntactically ambiguous sentence: "r>Y AlmElm Altlmy*". It most likely means: "The teacher saw the student" resulting in the diacritized version "ra>Y AalomuEal~imu Aalt~ilomy*a", because Arabic prefers placing the subject ahead of the object. However, Arabic allows subjects and objects to switch positions, and hence the meaning might be "The student saw the teacher" with diacritized form "r>Y AalomuEal~ima Aalt~ilomy*u".

In this paper we present a new state-of-the-art Arabic diacritizer. The diacritizer works in two cascaded steps: First, it guesses the diacritics for the core of words – disambiguating lexical choice; and then it guesses case endings – disambiguating syntactic roles. For the first step, we employ a Viterbi decoder at word-level with back-off to stem, morphological patterns, and transliteration and sequence labeling based diacritization of named entities. For the second, we employ SVM-based ranking coupled with morphological patterns and linguistic rules to properly guess case endings.

The contributions of this work is as follows:

- We introduce a back-off scheme where OOV words are diacritized using their morphological patterns (a.k.a stem templates)

- We use transliteration mining coupled with sequence labeling to guess diacritics on Arabic words based on how the words are transliterated in English.

---

[1]Buckwalter encoding is used exclusively in the paper.

9


*Proceedings of The Third Arabic Natural Language Processing Workshop (WANLP)*, pages 9–17,
Valencia, Spain, April 3, 2017. ©2017 Association for Computational Linguistics

- We employ SVM-based ranking to guess the appropriate cased endings.

- We use morphological patterns and linguistic rules to better guess case endings.

- We offer a new copyright-free multi-genre test set to measure diacritization accuracy.

- We offer a state-of-the-art Arabic diacritizer that is coded entirely in Java and can be used freely for research purposes.

## 2 Background

### 2.1 Arabic Diacritization

Significant research has addressed diacritic restoration/recovery or diacritization for Arabic and some other Semitic languages which are typically written without short vowels. Diacritization is essential for a variety of applications such as TTS as well as educational tools for language learners.

In earlier attempts for automatic diacritization, Gal (2002) used a Hidden Markov Model for diacritics restoration, tested on the Quran text, and achieved 14% word error rate (WER). Vergyri and Kirchhoff (2004) used acoustic features in conjunction with morphological and contextual constrains to train a diacritizer. They evaluated their automatic diacritization system on two corpora, namely FBIS and LDC CallHome ECA, and reported a 9% diacritics error rate (DER) without case ending, and 28% DER with case endings. The difference between WER and DER is that the latter measures the percentage of letters with incorrect diacritics. Consequently, DER values are typically lower than WER values. Nelken and Shieber (2005) used a cascade of probabilistic finite state transducers trained on the LDCs Arabic treebank news stories (Part 2). The corpus consists of 501 news stories collected from Al-Hayat newspaper with a total of 144,199 words. The cascade included a word-based language model, a letter-based language model, and a morphological model. This combination of probabilistic models achieved an accuracy of 7.33% and 23.61% WER without and with case ending respectively. Zitouni et al. (2006) trained a maximum entropy model for sequence classification to restore diacritics for each character in a word. For training, they used the LDCs Arabic Tree-bank (Part 3, version 1.0) diacritized corpus, which includes complete vocalization (full diacritics including case ending) for each word. The corpus is composed of 600 documents from the An-Nahar Newspaper with a total of 340,281 words. The maxEnt system achieved 5.5% DER and 18% WER on words without case ending. Habash and Rambow (2007) presented "MADA-D" a system that combines a tagger and a lexeme language model. The system showed that the morphological tagger along with a 3-gram language model were able to achieve the best performance of 5.5% and 14.9% WER respectively for diacritized words without and with case ending. We compare to their system in our paper. Rashwan et al. (2009) introduced a two layers stochastic system to automatically diacritize Arabic text. The system combines both morphological knowledge and the word full form features. These information is exploited through a maximum marginal probability on the full form supplemented with linguistic factorization model based on morphological analysis and POS tagging. While the first is fast, the second one used as a fall back is more accurate as it exploits more inner knowledge from the word parts and the context. Later work by Rashwan et al. (2015) used deep learning to improve diacritization accuracy and they reported a WER of 3.0% without case ending and 9.9% WER for guessing case ending. We compare to their system in our paper. Recent work by Abandah et al. (2015) uses recurrent neural networks to improve diacritization, and they report results that are better than those of MADA. Bebah et al. (2014) developed a hybrid approach that utilizes the output of the open source morphological Analyzer AlKhalil Morpho System (Mohamed Ould Abdallahi Ould et al., 2011) which outputs all possible diacritization for each word analyzed out of context. These outputs were then fed to an HMM to guess the correct diacritized form. The system was trained on a large body of text consisting of 2,463,351 vowelized words divided between NEMLAR corpus (460,000 words), Tashkeela corpus (780,000 words), and RDI corpus (1,223,351 words). The training was carried out with 90% of a corpus and the remaining 10% composed of 199,197 words was used for testing. The system achieved 9.93% WER.

For more indepth survey on relevant work on Arabic diacritization, Azmi and Almajed (2015) provide a comprehensive survey. To the exception of Belinkov and Glass (2015) which performed lower than the state-of-the-art when

using a recurrent neural network for diacritization, traditionally, works on diacritic restoration
rely on linguistic features and tools. MADA
(Morphological Analysis and Disambiguation for
Arabic) (Habash et al., 2009) and its successor
MADAMIRA (Pasha et al., 2014) are among the
few available tools for diacritization. The core of
MADA – MADAMIRA as well – utilizes morpho
syntactic features to select a proper analysis from
a list of potential analyses provided by the Buckwalter Arabic Morphological Analyzer (BAMA)
(Buckwalter, 2004). Using a set of SVMs trained
on the Arabic Penn Treebank, MADAMIRA
selects the most probable features. The analysis
MADAMIRA selects consists of the diacritized
form along with other features such as its lexeme,
its morphological features, and English glossary.

## 2.2 ATB

The availability of diacritized text for training is
crucial. Much of the previous work on diacritization relied on using the Arabic Penn Treebank
(ATB). Though ATB is invaluable for many tasks
such as POS tagging and parsing, it is sub-optimal
for diacritization for the following reasons:
1. ATB is limited in terms of size with less than
570k tokens and in terms of diversity with 87,160
unique surface forms (excluding numerals). In
comparison, the AFP news corpus has approximately 765,890 unique tokens (Cole et al., 2001).
These limitation would lead to poor coverage.
2. ATB often uses inconsistent diacritizations.
For example the word "<nh" appears 27 as
"<in~ahu" and 37 as "<inhu" where the first is
the correct one. Also, the diacritic sukon "o" is
sometimes omitted in ATB (ex. "kwbnhAgn" is
diacritized as: "kuwbinohAgin"); and default diacritics preceding long vowels are optionally used.
We thus used a large diacritized corpus that we
describe in Section 3.1. When comparing with
systems that were trained on the ATB, some preprocessing is required, as we show later, to make
sure that we are not unfairly penalizing them.

## 3 Our Diacritizer

The diacritizer has two main components. The
first component recovers the diacritics for the core
word (i.e. word without case ending), and the second only recovers the case ending. In this section we describe: the training and test corpora we
used and how we processed them; the training of
our system that diacritizes core-words and guesses

case ending; and our results compared to those of
other systems that are described in the literature,
and some relaxations we applied during evaluation
to insure fair comparison.

### 3.1 Training and Test Corpora

For this work, we acquired a diacritized corpus from a commercial vendor containing more
than 9.7 million tokens with approximately 194k
unique surface forms (excluding numbers and
punctuation marks). The corpus is composed
mostly of modern standard Arabic (approximately
7 million words) and covers many genres including politics, economics, sports, science, etc., and
the remaining 2.7 million words are mostly religious text in classical Arabic. Thus the corpus is
well balanced and is considerably larger than the
ATB. We manually checked random samples from
the corpus and we estimate diacritization errors
to be less than 1%, and diacritization is thorough
with no omissions of sukon or optional diacritics.
We used the corpus to build several resources as
we describe in Section 3.2.

For testing, we used a new test set composed
of 70 WikiNews articles (majority are from 2013
and 2014) that cover a variety of themes, namely:
politics, economics, health, science and technology, sports, arts, and culture. The articles are
evenly distributed among the different themes (10
per theme). The articles contain 18,300 words. We
compare our results to three different systems that
are described in the literature, where the authors
were kind enough to either diacritize our test set
or provide a working system. The systems were
those of Rashwan et al. (2015), Belinkov and
Glass (2015), and MADAMIRA (Habash et al.,
2009; Pasha et al., 2014). The first two are recent systems and MADAMIRA is a popular tool
for processing Arabic.

### 3.2 Data Preparation

Given a word in the diacritized corpus, we produce multiple representations of it. To illustrate
the representations, we use the word "wakitAbihimo" (and their book) as our running example.
1. diacritized surface form ("wakitAbihimo"). 2.
diacritized surface form without case ending. To
remove case endings, we segment each word in
the corpus to its underlying clitics using the Farasa
segmenter (Darwish and Mubarak, 2016). For example, given the diacritized word "wakitAbihimo"
(and their book), it would be segmented to the prefix "wa", stem "kitAbi", and suffix "himo". The

case ending which is attached in this case to the stem is removed, leading to "kitAb" and the full surface form "wakitAbhimo". A few things are noteworthy here, namely that diacritized suffixes are often affected by the case-ending (ex. if the case ending in the this example was "u", the suffix would have been "humo"), and the case ending may be on the attached noun suffix (ex. "p" or "At") and not on the last letter in the stem.

3. diacritized stem with and without case ending, which would be 'kitAbi' and 'kitAb' respectively for our example. If the surface form had a noun suffix, then it was considered as part of the stem. For example, the word "kitAbAt" (writings) is segmented as "kitAb+At", where "At" is the noun suffix indicating feminine plural marker. In this example, the noun suffix is treated as if it is a part of the stem.

4. diacritized template of surface form. This step involves obtaining the root from which the word is derived and the stem template. Arabic words are typically derived from a set of a few thousand roots by fitting the roots into stem templates. For example, the word "kitAb" is derived by fitting the root "ktb" into the template "fiEAl". In our example, the surface form template is "wafiEAlihimo" and "wafiEAlhimo" with and without case ending respectively. We again used the Farasa to obtain the roots and stem templates.

5. diacritized stem template with and without case ending. As shown before for the example, the stem template is "fiEAl" and "fiEAli" with and without case ending respectively.

Based on different representations, we created the following dictionaries and language models:

1. surface form dictionary, which contained surface forms without diacritics and seen diacritized forms without case ending. For example, the undiacritized word "wktAbhm" has two seen diacritized forms, namely "wakitAbhimo" and "wakitAbhumo". In this example, the diacritized form of the suffix actually depends on the case ending. We have a module that corrects for this when placing the case ending.

2. stem dictionary, which contains the stem without diacritics and seen diacritized forms without case ending. From our example, the stem "ktAb" has the diacritized forms "kitAb" and "kut~Ab".

3. surface form and stem templates without diacritics along with the most common (based on statistics on the training corpus) diacritized tem-

plates. In our example, the template "wfEAlhm" would be mapped to "wafiEAlihimo" and the tempalte "fEAl" to "fiEAl".

4. a bigram surface form langauge model and a unigram stem language model. Both are without case ending.

## 3.3 Core word diacritization

For core-word diacritic recovery, our basic system uses a bigram word model with back-off to a stem unigram model, stem template-based diacritization, and a sequence labeling based stem diacritization model. We experimented with a trigram language model instead of a bigram model, and the bigger model did not yield any gain.

### 3.3.1 Baseline System

In our baseline system, we used the bigram language model using the word surface forms without case endings. When given a sentence to diacritize, we would build a lattice with all previously seen diacritized forms for a word by consulting the previously constructed dictionary. If a word is not seen before, it is left as is without any diacritics. Then we use our bigram model and the Viterbi algorithm to find the most likely path in the lattice.

In the following setups, different back-offs are used when a word is not found in the dictionary.

### 3.3.2 Back-off to Stem

For a surface form that is not found in the surface form dictionary, the surface form is segmented and the stem is extracted. Then we search for the stem in the stem dictionary, and we use the most probable stem diacritization using the stem unigram language model. If found, then the prefixes are diacritized and attached to the stem. If not, the input surface form is used. To attach the prefixes and suffixes to the stems, some affixes have one form (namely "w" (and), "f" (then), "s" (will), "b" (with), and "l" (to)) and others change form depending on the stem and the case ending. Those that depend on the case ending (some attached pronouns) are diacritized properly after we determine the case ending. One prefix that changes form and affects the diacritic of the first letter in the word is "Al" (the). Arabic has so-called *lam qamariyya* (literally meaning "moon *l*") and *lam shamsiyyah* ("sun *l*"), where the former is pronounced normally and the later is not pronounced with the first letter after it being stressed with a "~" (*shaddah*). An example of both are the words "Aloqamar" (the moon) pronounced as *alqamar* and "Al\$~amos" (the sun) pronounced as *ashams*.

In the case of lam qamariyyah, it receives a "o" diacritic, and the lam shamsiyyah case it is left bare.

### 3.3.3 Back-off based on Template

If the surface form and stem do not appear in our dictionaries, we attempt to diacritize using word and stem templates. To do so, we generate the equivalent undiacritized template for the surface form. For example, given the word "wsEAlhm" (and their coughing), we find that the underlying root is "sEl" with "wfEAlhm" and "fEAl" being the undiacritized surface form and stem templates respectively. If the surface form template is found in the previously constructed surface form template dictionary, the most likely diacritized template is used. In this example, this would be "wafiEAlhimo". If not, then we search the stem template dictionary and use the most likely diacritized template ("fiEAl" for our example).

### 3.3.4 Automatically Diacritized Transliterated Words

One of the important sources of words for which no diacritization candidates exist in our dictionaries and for which we can not obtain valid templates are foreign names. We devised a scheme to automatically diacritize transliterated words using transliteration mining and sequence labeling. The intuition for automatic diacritization draws from the fact that while short vowels are generally omitted in Arabic text, English vowels are often explicit. For example, the name "klntn" is written in English as "Clinton". The vowels on the English side imply that the proper Arabic diacritization is "kolinotun".

The automatic diacritization process has multiple steps. First, we need Arabic and English transliterations, which we could obtain from Wikipedia cross-lingual links. To do so, we used the Arabic Wikipedia snapshot from September 28, 2012 that has 348,873 titles including redirects, which are alternative names to articles. Of these articles, 254,145 have cross-lingual links to English Wikipedia. To find which words in English and Arabic titles would be transliterations, we used a transliteration miner akin to that of El-Kahky et al. (2011) that was trained using 3,452 parallel Arabic-English transliteration pairs. We aligned the word-pairs at character level using GIZA++ and the phrase extractor and scorer from the Moses machine translation package (Koehn et al., 2007). The alignment produced mappings between English letter sequences and Arabic letter sequences with associated mapping probabilities. Given a word in the Arabic title, we produced all its possible segmentations along with their associated mappings into English letters. We retained valid target sequences that produced a word in the corresponding English title. We further filtered out pairs where the transliteration probability was less than 0.1, obtaining 125k transliterated pairs.

Second, we trained a sequence labeler that would automatically assign the proper diacritic for each Arabic letter in a name given its English rendition. We constructed a training set of 500 Arabic-English transliteration pairs, where the Arabic is fully diacritized. For each pair, we used our transliteration miner to automatically map each Arabic letter to one or more English letters. Then given these mappings, we trained a conditional random fields (CRF) model using the CRF++ implementation (Kudo, 2005) using the following features: Arabic Letter, English mapping, is first letter in word, is last letter in word, and English is all vowels. The label was the observed diacritic.

Third, given all the transliterations we found from Wikipedia titles, we used the trained CRF model to automatically diacritize the Arabic words. In doing so, we were able to automatically diacritize more than 68k Arabic transliterations. We were not able to diacritize all of them because the transliteration miner was not able to fulfill the requirement that each Arabic letter was to be mapped to one or more English letters. An example diacritized name is "rAwlobinody" (Rawalpindi), which does not exist in the diacritization dictionary. We took a sample of 200 words that were automatically diacritized in this fashion and the accuracy of diacritization was 79%. Perhaps in the future we can utilize more training data to further improve the accuracy.

### 3.3.5 Word Look-up

Another method that we employed entails building a dictionary of words that we reckoned had only one possible diacritization or one that dominated all others. An example of this is the word "En", which has two diacritized forms namely "Eano" (about) and "Ean~a" (appeared). The second diacrized form, though possible, is archaic. We constructed a dictionary of such words using two methods. First, we manually constructed a set of about 393 Arabic prepositions, particles, and pronouns with and without prefixes and suffixes. Example entries in the dictionary include "fy" (in), "wfy" (and in), "fyhm" (in them), and "wfyh" (and in it). In the second, we collected statistics on the training corpus, and any word appearing at least 10 times with a diacritized form being used more than 90% of the time, we added the word and the dominating diacritized form to our dictionary. Picking the dominant form is mostly safe particularly in case such as words that start with prepositions. In other cases such as "gzp" (Gaza), the dominant form is "gaz~apa", while we know that it is possible for it to be diacritized as "gaz~apu" (with a different case ending). However, what we observed in our corpus is that it overwhelmingly appears as part of the collocation "qTAE gzp" (Gaza Strip), and the collocations forces "gzp" to have a specific diacritized form.

### 3.3.6 Results

Table 1 shows the results for the baseline system, the baseline with different back-off schemes, and the baseline with back-off and word look-up. We used the two common evaluation measures, namely error rate at word level (WER) and error rate at character/diacritic level (DER). As the results show, backing-off to using stems and word or stem templates, using automatically diacritized words, and using word look-up all had a positive effect on diacritizing core words. The most improvement was achieved when backing-up to stems and using word look-up. Automatically diacritized words had a smaller effect than we expected, because foreign named entities frequently use long vowels that are inserted during transliteration instead of short vowels. For example, "John" is typically transliterated as "jwno" (with the long vowel "w") rather than "juno". Combining the different enhancements led to even greater drops of 50% and 56% in WER and DER respectively. Compared to systems in the literature, our core word diacritizer is far ahead of MADAMIRA and that of (Belinkov and Glass, 2015). However, we lag behind the system of Rashwan et al. (2015). When score the output of different systems, we performed some relaxations to account for differences in diacritization conventions. The relaxations involved: removing default diacritics on letters followed by long vowels as in "jwno" where putting the diacritic "u" after "j" would be redundant; assuming that a letter, that is not a long vowel, with no diacritic to be followed by "o"; and removing diacritics from the determiner "Al".

| System | % WER | % DER |
|---|---|---|
| B | 6.64 | 2.40 |
| S | 4.69 | 1.44 |
| T | 5.96 | 1.90 |
| TSL | 6.56 | 2.39 |
| WL | 4.54 | 1.75 |
| S+T+TSL | 4.51 | 1.35 |
| **S+T+TSL+WL** | **3.29** | **1.06** |
| MADAMIRA | 6.73 | 1.91 |
| *Rashwan et al. (2015)* | *3.04* | *0.95* |
| Belinkov and Glass (2015) | 14.87 | 3.89 |

Table 1: Core word diacritization results for Baseline (B) and with back-off to Stem (S), Template based diacritization (T), and Transliteration and Sequence Labeling based diacritization (TSL), and Word look-up (WL).

### 3.4 Recovering Case Endings

Though the case ending of some words or word types might be fixed, such as prepositions and past tense verbs, case ending often depends on the role a word plays in the sentence. Consider the following examples: "*ahaba muHam~adN" (Muhammad went) and "*ahaba >lY muHam~adK" (he went to Muhammad). The name "muHam~ad" is assigned the case "N" (nominative) when it is a subject and "K" (genitive) when it is preceded by a preposition ">lY". Ascertaining case endings for simple prepositional phrases may be easy, however determining if a word is a subject or an object may be much hard. Though parsing can help determine the role of words in a sentence, it is typically very slow and hence impractical for some real life applications such as TTS.

To determine case endings, we use a linear SVM ranking (SVM$^{rank}$) model that is trained on a variety of lexical, morphological, and syntactic features. The advantage of an SVM$^{rank}$ model is that it is very fast, and it has been shown to be accurate for a variety of ranking problems (Joachims, 2006). For training, we use the implementation of Joachims (2006) with default parameter values. We also employ heuristics that include/exclude possible/impossible case ending to be considered by the SVM$^{rank}$ model. In the following, we describe our ranking model and how we determine which case endings to consider.

### 3.4.1 SVM$^{rank}$ Model

Here we describe the features we used for SVM$^{rank}$ to determine the case endings of words.

We use the Farasa segmenter and POS tagger (Darwish and Mubarak, 2016) to determine some of the morphological, lexical, and syntactic features. To help explain the features, we use here the running example "jrY Abn AljyrAn fy AlmlEb" (the neighbors' son ran in the playground), where we will focus on assigning the case ending $C$ of the word "AljyrAn" (the neighbors), which is segmented as "Al+jyrAn" and POS tagged as "DET+NOUN$_{masculine,plural}$" by Farasa. All feature values are computed on our training corpus. Position "0" is the current position, with "1" and "-1" being the next and previous positions. The features are as follows:

- $P(C|word_0)$ and $P(C|stem_0)$: this captures the likelihood that case ending can appear with the current word or stem respectively (ex. $P(C|AljyrAn)$ and $P(C|jyrAn)$).

- $P(C|word_{-1})$, $P(C|stem_{-1})$, $P(C|word_1)$, and $P(C|stem_1)$: this captures the context of the word (ex. $P(C|Abn)$, $P(C|Abn)$, $P(C|fy)$, and $P(C|fy)$).

- $P(C|POS_{word_0})$ and $P(C|POS_{stem_0})$: some case endings are likely for some POS tags and nearly impossible for others. For example, "DET" precludes tanween {"N", "K", "F"} (ex. $P(C|POS_{DET+NOUN})$ and $P(C|POS_{NOUN})$)

- $P(C|POS_{word_{-1}})$, $P(C|POS_{stem_{-1}})$, $P(C|POS_{word_1})$, and $P(C|POS_{stem_1})$: this captures local contextual information that may help in detecting some syntactic constructs (ex. $P(C|POS_{DET+NOUN})$ and $P(C|POS_{NOUN})$)

- $p(C|gen/num_{word_0})$, $p(C|gen/num_{word_{-1}})$, and $p(C|gen/num_{word_1})$: gender and number agreement may indicate dependency within a sentence (ex. $p(C|masc\_pl)$, $p(C|masc\_sing)$, and $p(C|null)^2$).

- $p(C|prefix_0)$, $p(C|POS_{prefix_0})$, $p(C|suffix_0)$, and $p(C|POS_{suffix_0})$: prefixes and suffixes may force or preclude certain case endings (ex. $p(C|Al)$, $p(C|DET)$, $p(C|null)$, $p(C|null)$).

- $p(C|stem\_template_0)$: Some stem templates favor particular case endings over others. For example, the template "mfAEyl" (as in "msAHyq" (powders)) does not allow tanween (ex. $p(C|fElAn)$).

---

<sup>2</sup>prepositions don't have a gender or number

- $p(C|last\_letter_{word_0})$: the last letter in the word may force or preclude certain case endings. For example, "Y" does not accept any diacritics. For our running example, we compute $p(C|n)$.

- $p(C|POS_0, POS_{word_{-1}}, diacritic_{word_{-1}})$: case endings are affected by the diacritic of the previous word in the case of NOUN-ADJ constructs (ex. $p(C|DET+NOUN, NOUN, u)$).

- $p(C|word, word_{-1})$: this helps capture collocations or local constructs such as short prepositional phrases (ex. $p(C|AbnAljyrAn)$).

- $p(C|POS, POS_{word_{-1}}, POS_{word_1})$ and $p(C|POS, POS_{word_{-1}}, POS_{word_{-2}})$: this can help detect local constructs such as NOUN-DET+NOUN which is often an idafa construct (ex. $p(C|DET+NOUN, NOUN, PREP)$ and $p(C|DET+NOUN, NOUN, V)$).

### 3.4.2 Filtering Heuristics

Limiting the possible case endings that the model has to rank can improve accuracy by disallowing bad choices. We applied simple heuristics to limit possible case endings to be scored by SVM$Rank$. Some of these are based on Arabic grammar, and others are purely statistical.

- If a word or stem appears more than 1,000 times in the training corpus, then restrict possible case endings to those seen in the training corpus. Though the threshold would not preclude other cases, it is high enough to make other cases rare.

- If the POS of the stem is VERB then restrict to {a, o, u, ~a, ~u, or null}.

- If stem POS is VERB and VERB is not present tense, then restrict to {a, o, ~a, or null}.

- If first suffix is "wn" or "yn" (either plural noun suffix or plural pronoun), then restrict to {a}.

- If first suffix is "An" (dual noun suffix), then restrict to {i}.

- If stem POS is NOUN and more than 80% of time the case ending was "o" in the training corpus, then restrict to {o}. This is meant to capture foreign named entities, which by the convention in the training corpus always get a case ending of "o".

- If word diacritized using the aforementioned Transliteration mining and sequence labeling method, then it is assumed to be a foreign named entity and the case ending is restricted to {a} or {null} if it ends with a "A, y, w, or Y".

15

- If suffix POS is CASE, then restrict to {F, ~F}.

- If word contains non-Arabic letters, then restrict to {null}.

- If the last letter in the stem is a long vowel "A, y, w, or Y", then restrict to {null}.

- If last letter in the stem is not a long vowel and is not followed by a long vowel, then disallow {null} to insure a case ending is chosen.

- If prefix POS has DET, then disallow tanween {K, N, F, ~K, ~N, ~F}.

- If word or stem POS appeared in training more than 50 times, then restrict case ending to those seen for the POS during training.

- If word or stem template appeared in training, then restrict case ending to those seen for the template during training.

- If stem-template matches "fwAEl, mfAEyl, or mfAEl", then disallow tanween.

- If a bigram appeared more than 1,000 in training with a single case ending for both words in the bigram, then restrict to the seen case endings.

- If the prefix does not have a DET and the following word does, then assume an idafa construct and disallow tanween.

- If the word matches ">n, <n, or lkn", then restrict case ending to {o} only if followed by a verb, and to {~a} otherwise.

### 3.4.3 Results

Table 2 shows the results of full diacritization including case ending with and without filtering heuristics. As can be seen, filtering heuristics led to 4.3% and 11.1% relative reduction in word and character error rates respectively. We are doing better than the other three systems. Though the system of Rashwan et al. (2015) was more accurate at core-word level, our system was doing a better job in case ending recovery leading to better overall diacritization.

### 3.5 Error Analysis

For error analysis, we inspected 500 random errors from the WikiNews test set. The following are those constituting more than 5% of the errors:
1. Core word diacritization errors: (21%) wrong form – ex. "Eadol" (justice) instead of "Ead~al" (he adjusted); (8%) out of vocabulary – ex. "Eab~ady" (Abbady – proper name).
2. Case ending errors: (12%) wrong ADJ-NOUN attachment – ex. "wzArp AlSHp AlSEwdyp"

| System | % WER | % DER |
|---|---|---|
| $\text{SVM}^{Rank}$ | 13.38 | 3.98 |
| **$\text{SVM}^{Rank}$+Heuristics** | **12.76** | **3.54** |
| MADAMIRA | 19.02 | 5.42 |
| Rashwan et al. (2015) | 15.95 | 4.29 |
| Belinkov and Glass (2015) | 30.50 | 7.89 |

Table 2: Full word diacritization results of our system using $\text{SVM}^{Rank}$ only ($\text{SVM}^{Rank}$) and $\text{SVM}^{Rank}$ after using heuristics to include/exclude possible/impossible case endings ($\text{SVM}^{Rank}$+Heuristics).

(Saudi Health Ministry) where Saudi was attached to health instead of Ministry; (14%) misidentification of SUBJ or OBJ – ex. OBJ is mistaken for a SUBJ because SUBJ is omitted, or SUBJ appears several words after VERB; (11%) words following conjunctions where their dependency is not clear; (7%) appositions; (6%) substitution of tanween with kasra or damma with kasra and damma respectively {u ↔ N, i ↔ K}; (6%) attachments in NOUN phrases with multiple subsequent nouns; and (5%) the SUBJ of a nominal sentence switches place with the predicate.

### 3.6 Implementation and Speed

The diacritizer is implemented entirely in Java making it platform independent and is backwards compatible to JDK 1.5. The diacritizer is packaged as a single jar file that is 100 megabytes in size. It is able to diacritize a test set composed of 500k words on an Intel i7 laptop with 16 gigabytes of RAM in 3 minutes and 44 seconds (including 42 sec. loading time) with memory footprint of 2.2 gigabytes. The current implementation is single threaded, so it does not make use of the multiple cores. We are providing it for free for research purposes.

## 4 Conclusion

In this paper we present a new state-of-the-art publicly available Arabic diacritizer. It uses a Viterbi decoder for word-level diacritization with backoffs to stems and morphological patterns. It also uses transliteration mining in conjunction with sequence labeling to diacritize named entities for which we have English transliterations. For case ending, it uses $\text{SVM}^{Rank}$ coupled with filtering heuristics. The diacritizer achieves 12.76% WER and 3.54% DER on a new multi-genre free of copyright test set.

## References

Gheith A Abandah, Alex Graves, Balkees Al-Shagoor, Alaa Arabiyat, Fuad Jamour, and Majid Al-Taee. 2015. Automatic diacritization of arabic text using recurrent neural networks. *International Journal on Document Analysis and Recognition (IJDAR)*, 18(2):183–197.

Aqil M Azmi and Reham S Almajed. 2015. A survey of automatic arabic diacritization techniques. *Natural Language Engineering*, 21(03):477–495.

Mohamed Bebah, Chennoufi Amine, Mazroui Azzeddine, and Lakhouaja Abdelhak. 2014. Hybrid approaches for automatic vowelization of arabic texts. *arXiv preprint arXiv:1410.2646*.

Yonatan Belinkov and James Glass. 2015. Arabic diacritization with recurrent neural networks. In *Proceedings of the 2015 Conference on Empirical Methods in Natural Language Processing*, pages 2281–2285, Lisbon, Portugal.

Tim Buckwalter. 2004. Buckwalter arabic morphological analyzer version 2.0. ldc catalog number ldc2004l02, isbn 1-58563-324-0.

Andy Cole, David Graff, and Kevin Walker. 2001. Arabic newswire part 1 corpus (1-58563-190-6). *Linguistic Data Consortium (LDC)*.

Kareem Darwish and Hamdy Mubarak. 2016. Farasa: A new fast and accurate arabic word segmenter. In *Proceedings of the Tenth International Conference on Language Resources and Evaluation (LREC 2016)*, Paris, France, may. European Language Resources Association (ELRA).

Ali El-Kahky, Kareem Darwish, Ahmed Saad Aldein, Mohamed Abd El-Wahab, Ahmed Hefny, and Waleed Ammar. 2011. Improved transliteration mining using graph reinforcement. In *Proceedings of the Conference on Empirical Methods in Natural Language Processing*, pages 1384–1393.

Ya'akov Gal. 2002. An hmm approach to vowel restoration in arabic and hebrew. In *Proceedings of the ACL-02 workshop on Computational approaches to Semitic languages*, pages 1–7. Association for Computational Linguistics.

Nizar Habash and Owen Rambow. 2007. Arabic diacritization through full morphological tagging. In *Human Language Technologies 2007: The Conference of the North American Chapter of the Association for Computational Linguistics; Companion Volume, Short Papers*, pages 53–56. Association for Computational Linguistics.

Nizar Habash, Owen Rambow, and Ryan Roth. 2009. Mada+ tokan: A toolkit for arabic tokenization, diacritization, morphological disambiguation, pos tagging, stemming and lemmatization. In *Proceedings of the 2nd International Conference on Arabic Language Resources and Tools (MEDAR)*, Cairo, Egypt, pages 102–109.

Thorsten Joachims. 2006. Training linear svms in linear time. In *ACM SIGKDD-2006*, pages 217–226. ACM.

Philipp Koehn, Hieu Hoang, Alexandra Birch, Chris Callison-Burch, Marcello Federico, Nicola Bertoldi, Brooke Cowan, Wade Shen, Christine Moran, Richard Zens, et al. 2007. Moses: Open source toolkit for statistical machine translation. In *Proceedings of the 45th annual meeting of the ACL on interactive poster and demonstration sessions*, pages 177–180. Association for Computational Linguistics.

Taku Kudo. 2005. Crf++: Yet another crf toolkit. *Software available at http://crfpp. sourceforge. net*.

Bebah Mohamed Ould Abdallahi Ould, Abdellouafi Meziane, Azzeddine Mazroui, and Abdelhak Lakhouaja. 2011. Alkhalil morphosys. In *7th International Computing Conference in Arabic*, pages 66–73, Riyadh, Saudi Arabia.

Rani Nelken and Stuart M Shieber. 2005. Arabic diacritization using weighted finite-state transducers. In *Proceedings of the ACL Workshop on Computational Approaches to Semitic Languages*, pages 79–86. Association for Computational Linguistics.

Arfath Pasha, Mohamed Al-Badrashiny, Mona Diab, Ahmed El Kholy, Ramy Eskander, Nizar Habash, Manoj Pooleery, Owen Rambow, and Ryan M Roth. 2014. Madamira: A fast, comprehensive tool for morphological analysis and disambiguation of arabic. In *LREC-2014*, Reykjavik, Iceland.

Mohsen Rashwan, Mohammad Al-Badrashiny, Mohamed Attia, and Sherif Abdou. 2009. A hybrid system for automatic arabic diacritization. In *The 2nd International Conference on Arabic Language Resources and Tools*, pages 54–60.

Mohsen Rashwan, Ahmad Al Sallab, M. Raafat, and Ahmed Rafea. 2015. Deep learning framework with confused sub-set resolution architecture for automatic arabic diacritization. In *IEEE Transactions on Audio, Speech, and Language Processing*, pages 505–516.

Dimitra Vergyri and Katrin Kirchhoff. 2004. Automatic diacritization of arabic for acoustic modeling in speech recognition. In *Proceedings of the workshop on computational approaches to Arabic script-based languages, COLING'04*, pages 66–73, Geneva, Switzerland. Association for Computational Linguistics.

Imed Zitouni, Jeffrey S Sorensen, and Ruhi Sarikaya. 2006. Maximum entropy based restoration of arabic diacritics. In *Proceedings of the 21st International Conference on Computational Linguistics and the 44th annual meeting of the Association for Computational Linguistics*, pages 577–584. Association for Computational Linguistics.

# Semantic Similarity of Arabic Sentences with Word Embeddings


**El Moatez Billah Nagoudi**
LIM - Laboratoire d'Informatique et de
Mathématiques, Université Amar
Telidji de Laghouat, Algérie
e.nagoudi@lagh-univ.dz

**Didier Schwab**
LIG-GETALP
Univ. Grenoble Alpes
France
didier.schwab@imag.fr



## Abstract

Semantic textual similarity is the basis of countless applications and plays an important role in diverse areas, such as information retrieval, plagiarism detection, information extraction and machine translation. This article proposes an innovative word embedding-based system devoted to calculate the semantic similarity in Arabic sentences. The main idea is to exploit vectors as word representations in a multidimensional space in order to capture the semantic and syntactic properties of words. IDF weighting and Part-of-Speech tagging are applied on the examined sentences to support the identification of words that are highly descriptive in each sentence. The performance of our proposed system is confirmed through the Pearson correlation between our assigned semantic similarity scores and human judgments.


**Keywords:** Semantic Sentences Similarity, Word Embedding, Word Representations, Space Vector Model.

## 1 Introduction

Text Similarity is an important task in several application fields, such as information retrieval, plagiarism detection, machine translation, topic detection, text classification, text summarization and others. Finding similarity between two texts, paragraphs or sentences, is based on measuring, directly or indirectly, the similarity between words.

There are two known types of words similarity: lexical and semantic. The first one handles the words as a stream of characters: words are similar lexically if they share the same characters in the same order (Manning et al., 2008). There are many techniques of lexical similarity measures, the most known are : Damerau-Levenshtein (Levenshtein, 1966), Needleman Wunsch (Needleman and Wunsch, 1970), LCS (Chvatal and Sankoff, 1975), JaroWinkler (Winkler, 1999), etc.

The second type aims to quantify the degree to which two words are semantically related. As an example they can be, synonyms, represent the same thing or they are used in the same context. The classical way to measure this semantic similarity is by using linguistic resources, like Word-Net (Miller, 1995), HowNet (Dong and Dong, 2003), BabelNet (Navigli and Ponzetto, 2012) or Dbnary (Sérasset, 2015). However, the word embedding techniques can be a more effective alternative to these linguistic databases (Mikolov et al., 2013a).

In this article we focus our investigation on measuring the semantic similarity between short Arabic sentences using word embedding representations. We also consider the IDF weighting and Part-of-Speech tagging techniques in order to improve the identification of words that are highly descriptive in each sentence.

The rest of this article is organized as follows, the next section describes work related to word representations in vector space. In Section 3, we present three variants of our proposed word embedding-based system. Section 4 describes the experimental results of this study. Finally, our conclusion and some future research directions are drawn in Section 5.

## 2 Word Embedding Models

Words representations as vectors in a multidimensional space allows to capture the semantic and syntactic properties of the language (Mikolov et al., 2013a). These representations can serve as a fundamental building unit to many applications of




*Proceedings of The Third Arabic Natural Language Processing Workshop (WANLP)*, pages 18–24,
Valencia, Spain, April 3, 2017. ©2017 Association for Computational Linguistics

Natural Language Processing (NLP). In the literature, several techniques are proposed to build vectorized space representations.

For instance, Collobert and Weston (2008) have proposed a unified system based on a deep neural network architecture, and trained jointly with many well known NLP tasks, including: Chunking, Part of Speech tagging, Named Entity Recognition and Semantic Role Labeling. Their word embedding model is stored in a matrix $M \in R^{d*|D|}$, where $D$ is a dictionary of all unique words in the training data, and each word is embedded into a $d\text{-}dimensional$ vector. The sentences are represented using the embeddings of their forming words. A similar idea was independently proposed and used by Turian et al. (Turian et al., 2010).

Mnih and Hinton (2009) have proposed another form to represent words in vector space, named Hierarchical Log-Bilinear Model (HLBL). Like virtually all neural language models, the HLBL model represents each word with a real-valued feature vector. For n-gram word-based, HLBL concatenates the $n - 1$ first embedding words $(w_1..w_{n-1})$ and learns a neural linear model to predicate the last word $w_n$.

Mikolov et al. (Mikolov et al., 2013c) have used a recurrent neural network (RNN) (Mikolov et al., 2010) to build a neural language model. The RNN encode the context word by word and predict the next word. The weights of the trained network are used as the words embeddings vectors.

Mikolov et al. (Mikolov et al., 2013a) (Mikolov et al., 2013b) have proposed two other approaches to build a words representations in vector space. using a simplified version of Bengio et al. (Bengio et al., 2003) neural language mode. They replaced the hidden layer by a simple projection layer in order to boost performance. In their work, two models are presented: the continuous bag-of-words model (CBOW) (Mikolov et al., 2013a), and the skip-gram model (SKIP-G) (Mikolov et al., 2013b).

In the first one, the continuous bag of word model CBOW (Mikolov et al., 2013a), predicts a pivot word according to the context by using a window of contextual words around it. Given a sequence of words $S = w_1, w_2, ..., w_i$, the CBOW model learns to predict all words $w_k$ from their surrounding words $(w_{k-l}, ..., w_{k-1}, w_{k+1}, ..., w_{k+l})$. The second model SKIP-G, predicts surrounding words of the current pivot word $w_k$ (Mikolov et al., 2013b).

Pennington et al. (Pennington et al., 2014) proposed a Global Vectors (GloVe) to build a words representations model, GloVe uses the global statistics of word-word co-occurrence to build co-occurrence matrix $M$. Then, $M$ is used to calculate the probability of word $w_i$ to appear in the context of another word $w_j$, this probability $P(i/j)$ represents the relationship between words.

## 3 System Description

### 3.1 Model Used

In (Mikolov et al., 2013a), all the methods (Collobert and Weston, 2008), (Turian et al., 2010), (Mnih and Hinton, 2009), (Mikolov et al., 2013c) have been evaluated and compared, and they show that CBOW and SKIP-G are significantly faster to train with better accuracy compared to these techniques. For this reason, we have used the CBOW word representations for Arabic model[1] proposed by Zahran et al. (Zahran et al., 2015). To train this model, they have used a large collection from different sources counting more than 5.8 billion words :

- Arabic Wikipedia (WikiAr, 2006).
- BBC and CNN Arabic corpus (Saad and Ashour, 2010).
- The open parallel corpus (Tiedemann, 2012).
- Arabase Corpus (Raafat et al., 2013).
- Osac: Open source arabic corpora. (Saad and Ashour, 2010)
- MultiUN corpus (Chen and Eisele, 2012)
- AGC Arabic Gigaword Corpus.
- King Saud University corpus (ksucorpus, 2012).
- Meedan Arabic corpus (Meedan, 2012).
- LDC Arabic newswire.
- Raw Quran text (Quran, 2007).
- KDE4 localization files (Tiedemann, 2009).
- Khaleej and Watan 2004 (Khaleej, 2004).

Training the Arabic CBOW model require choice of some parameters affecting the resulting vectors. All the parameters used by Zahran et al. (Zahran et al., 2015) are shown in Table 1.

---

[1]https://sites.google.com/site/mohazahran/data

**The Arabic CBOW Model Parameters**

| Parameter | Value |
| --- | --- |
| Vector size | 300 |
| Window | 5 |
| Sample | $1e-5$ |
| Hierarchical Softmax | NO |
| Negative | 10 |
| Freq. thresh. | 100 |

Table 1: Training configuration parameters

Where:

- **Vector size:** dimensionality of the word vectors.
- **Window:** number of words considered around the pivot word (context).
- **Sample:** threshold for sub-sampling of frequent words.
- **Hierarchical Softmax:** approximation of the full softmax used to predict words during training.
- **Negative:** number of negative examples in the training.
- **Frequency threshold:** threshold to discard less frequent words.

### 3.2 Words Similarity

We used CBOW model in order to identify the near matches between two words $w_i$ and $w_j$ (e.g. synonyms, singular, plural, feminization or closely related semantically). The similarity between $w_i$ and $w_j$ is obtained by comparing their vector representations $v_i$ and $v_j$ respectively. The similarity between $v_i$ and $v_j$ can be evaluated using the cosine similarity, euclidean distance, Manhattan distance or any other similarity measure functions. For example: let "الجامعة" (university), "المساء" (evening) and "الكلية" (faculty) be three words. The similarity between them is measured by computing the cosine similarity between their vectors as follows:

$$sim(\text{المساء},\text{الجامعة}) = cos(V(\text{المساء}), V(\text{الجامعة})) = 0.13$$

$$sim(\text{الكلية},\text{الجامعة}) = cos(V(\text{الجامعة}), V(\text{الكلية})) = 0.72$$

That means that, the words "الكلية" (faculty) and "الجامعة" (university) are semantically closer than "المساء" (evening) and "الجامعة" (university).

### 3.3 Sentences similarity

Let $S_1 = w_1, w_2, ..., w_i$ and $S_2 = w'_1, w'_2, ..., w'_j$ be two sentences, their word vectors are $(v_1, v_2, ..., v_i)$ and $(v'_1, v'_2, ..., v'_j)$ respectively. We have used three methods to measure the similarity between sentences. Figure 1 illustrates an overview of the procedure for computing the similarity between two candidate sentences in our system.

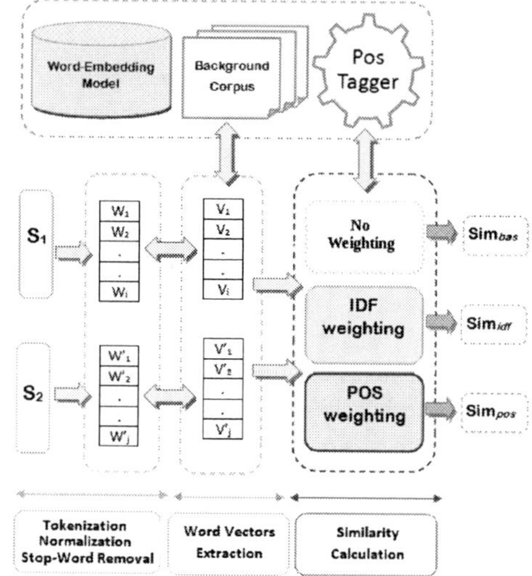


Figure 1: The architecture of the proposed system

In the following, we explain our proposed methods to compute the semantic similarity among sentences.

#### 3.3.1 No Weighting Method

A simple way to compare two sentences, is to sum their words vectors. In addition, this method can be applied to any size of sentences. The similarity between $S_1$ and $S_2$ is obtained by calculating the cosine similarity between $V_1$ and $V_2$, where:

$$\begin{cases} V_1 &= \sum_{k=1}^{i} v_k \\ V_2 &= \sum_{k=1}^{j} v'_k \end{cases}$$

For example, let $S_1$ and $S_2$ be two sentences:
$S_1 = $ "ذهب يوسف إلى الكلية" (*Joseph went to college*).
$S_2 = $ "يوسف يمضى مسرعا للجامعة" (*Joseph goes quickly to university*).

The similarity between S1 and S2 is obtained as follows:

**step 1: Sum of the word vectors**

20

$$V_1 = V(\text{الكلية}) + V(\text{يوسف}) + V(\text{ذهب})$$
$$V_2 = V(\text{للجامعة}) + V(\text{مسرعا}) + V(\text{يمضى}) + V(\text{يوسف})$$

**step 2: Calculate the similarity**

The similarity between $S_1$ and $S_2$ is obtained by calculating the cosine similarity between $V_1$ and $V_2$.

$$sim(S_1, S_2) = cos(V_1, V_2) = 0.71$$

In order to improve the similarity results, we have used two weighting functions based on the Inverse Document Frequency IDF (Salton and Buckley, 1988) and the Part-Of-Speech tagging (POS tagging) (Schwab, 2005) (Lioma and Blanco, 2009).

### 3.3.2 IDF Weighting Method

In this variant, the Inverse Document Frequency IDF concept is used to produce a composite weight for each word in each sentence. The IDF weighting of words (Salton and Buckley, 1988) is traditionally used in information retrieval (Turney and Pantel, 2010) and can be employed in our system. The *idf weight* serves as a measure of how much information the word provides, that is, whether the term that occurs infrequently is good for discriminating between documents (in our case sentences).

This technique uses a large collection of document (background corpus), generally the same genre as the input corpus that is to be semantically verified. In order to compute the *idf weight* for each word, we have used the BBC and CNN Arabic corpus[2] (Saad and Ashour, 2010) as a background corpus. In fact, the *idf* of each word is determined by using the formula:

$$idf(w) = log(\frac{S}{WS})$$

where $S$ is the total number of sentences in the corpus and $WS$ is the number of sentences containing the word $w$. The similarity between $S_1$ and $S_2$ is obtained by calculating the cosine similarity between $V_1$ and $V_2$, $cos(V_1, V_2)$ where:

$$\begin{cases} V_1 &= \sum_{k=1}^{i} idf(w_k) * v_k \\ V_2 &= \sum_{k=1}^{j} idf(w'_k) * v'_k \end{cases}$$

and $idf(w_k)$ is the weight of the word $w_k$ in the background corpus.

---

[2]https://sourceforge.net/projects/ar-text-mining/files/Arabic-Corpora/

**Example:** let's continue with the sentences of the previous example, and suppose that IDF weights of their words are:

| ذهب | يوسف | الكلية | يمضى | مسرعا | الجامعة |
|------|------|------|------|------|------|
| 0.27 | 0.37 | 0.31 | 0.29 | 0.22 | 0.34 |

**step 1: Sum of vectors with IDF weights**

$$V_1 = V(\text{الكلية}) * 0.31 + V(\text{يوسف}) * 0.37 + V(\text{ذهب}) * 0.27$$
$$V_2 = V(\text{الجامعة}) * 0.34 + V(\text{مسرعا}) * 0.22 + V(\text{يمضى}) * 0.29$$
$$+ V(\text{يوسف}) * 0.37$$

**step 2: Calculate the similarity**

The cosine similarity is applied to computed a similarity score between $V_1$ and $V_2$.

$$sim(S_1, S_2) = cos(V_1, V_2) = 0.78$$

We note that the similarity result between the two sentences is better than the previous method.

### 3.3.3 Part-of-speech weighting Method

An alternative technique is the application of the Part-of-Speech tagging (POS tag) for identification of words that are highly descriptive in each input sentence (Schwab, 2005) (Lioma and Blanco, 2009). For this purpose, we have used the POS tagger for Arabic language proposed by G. Braham et al. (Gahbiche-Braham et al., 2012) to estimate the part-of-speech of each word in sentence. Then, a weight is assigned for each type of tag in the sentence. For example, $verb = 0.4$, $noun = 0.5$, $adjective = 0.3$, $preposition = 0.1$, etc.

The similarity between S1 and S2 is obtained in three steps (Schwab, 2005) as follows:

**step 1: POS tagging**

In this step the POS tagger of G. Braham et al. (Gahbiche-Braham et al., 2012) is used to estimate the POS of each word in sentence.

$$\begin{cases} Pos\_tag(S_1) = Pos_{w_1}, Pos_{w_2}, ..., Pos_{w_i} \\ Pos\_tag(S_2) = Pos_{w'_1}, Pos_{w'_2}, ..., Pos_{w'_j} \end{cases}$$

The function $Pos\_tag(S_i)$ returns for each word $w_k$ in $S_i$ its estimated part of speech $Pos_{w_k}$.

**step 2: POS weighting**

At this point we should mention that, the weight of each part of speech can be fixed empirically. Indeed, we based on the training data of SemEval-

2017 (Task 1)[3] to fix the POS weights.

$$\begin{cases} V_1 & = & \sum_{k=1}^{i} Pos\_weight(Pos_{w_k}) * v_k \\ V_2 & = & \sum_{k=1}^{j} Pos\_weight(Pos_{w'_k}) * v'_k \end{cases}$$

where $Pos\_weight(Pos_{w_k})$ is the function which return the weight of POS tagging of $w_k$.

**step 3: Calculate the similarity**

Finally, the similarity between $S_1$ and $S_2$ is obtained by calculating the cosine similarity between $V_1$ and $V_2$ as follows:

$$sim(S_1, S_2) = cos(V_1, V_2)$$

**Example:** let us continue with the same example above.

$S_1 = $ "ذهب يوسف إلى الكلية" (*Joseph went to college*).

$S_2 = $ "يوسف يمضى مسرعا للجامعة" (*Joseph goes quickly to university*).

and suppose that POS weights are:

| $verb$ | $noun$ | $noun\_prop$ | $adj$ | $prep$ |
|--------|--------|--------------|-------|--------|
| 0.4 | 0.5 | 0.7 | 0.3 | 0.1 |

**step 1: Pos tagging**

The function $Pos\_tag(S_i)$ is applied to each sentence.

$$\begin{cases} Pos\_tag(S_1) & = & verb \; noun\_prop \; noun \\ Pos\_tag(S_2) & = & noun\_prop \; verb \; adj \; noun \end{cases}$$

**step 2: Sum of vectors with POS weighting**

$$V_1 = V(\text{الكلية}) * 0.5 + V(\text{يوسف}) * 0.7 + V(\text{ذهب}) * 0.4$$
$$V_2 = V(\text{يمضى}) * 0.5 + V(\text{مسرعا}) * 0.3 + V(\text{الجامعة}) * 0.4 + V(\text{يوسف}) * 0.7$$

**step 3: Calculate the similarity**

$$sim(S_1, S_2) = cos(V_1, V_2) = 0.82$$

## 4 Experiments And Results

### 4.1 Test Sample

In order to measure effectively the performances of our system, a large collection are necessary. In fact, we have used a dataset of 750 pairs of sentences drawn from publicly Microsoft Research

Video Description Corpus (MSR-Video) (MSR-video, 2016), and manually translated into Arabic. The sentence pairs have been manually tagged by four annotators, and the similarity score is the mean of the annotators. This score is a float number between "0" (indicating that the meaning of sentences are completely independent) to "1" (signifying meaning equivalence).

### 4.2 Preprocessing

In order to normalize the sentences for the semantic similarity step, a set of preprocessing are performed on the data set. All sentences went through by the following steps:

1. Stop-word removal.
2. Remove punctuation marks, diacritics and non letters.
3. We normalized أ ، إ ، آ to ا and ة to ه.
4. Replace final ى followed by ء with ئ.
5. Normalizing numerical digits to the token "$Num$".

### 4.3 Results

To evaluate the performance of our system, our three approaches were assessed based on their accuracy on the 750 sentences in the MSR-Video corpus. An example of our results is shown in Table 2.

| Sentence Pair | Hum. | Methods | | |
|---|---|---|---|---|
| | | No Weig. | IDF | POS |
| ذهب يوسف إلى الكلية<br>يوسف يمضى مسرعا للجامعة | 0.90 | 0.71 | 0.78 | 0.82 |
| إمرأة تتحدث على الهاتف<br>صبيان يتحدثان على الهاتف | 0.35 | 0.65 | 0.45 | 0.40 |
| رجل يصب المعكرونة في طبق<br>المتسابق في سيارة الإسعاف | 0.0 | 0.15 | 0.13 | 0.13 |
| إمرأة تضع الماكياج<br>إمرأة تضع المساحيق على وجهها | 0.92 | 0.55 | 0.67 | 0.72 |
| يزيل ترسبات السمكة<br>رجل يزيل الترسبات من السمكة | 1.0 | 0.85 | 0.92 | 0.94 |
| كلب يقرأ كتابا للطفل<br>يقرأ طفل كتابا عن الكلاب | 0.20 | 0.82 | 0.87 | 0.88 |

Table 2: Example of sentence similarity results

The sentence pairs in Table 2, were selected randomly from our dataset. It can be seen that the similarity estimation provided by our system are fairly consistent with human judgements. How-

[3]http://alt.qcri.org/semeval2017/task1/data/uploads/

ever, the similarity score is not good enough when two sentences share the same words, but with a totally different meaning, like in the last pair of sentences.

On the other hand, we calculate the Pearson correlation between our assigned semantic similarity scores and human judgements. The results are presented in Table 3.

| Approach | Correlation |
|---|---|
| Basic method | 72.33 % |
| IDF-weighting method | 78.20% |
| POS tagging method | 79.69% |

Table 3: Correlation results

These results indicate that when the no weighting method is used the correlation rate reached 72.33%. Both IDF-weighting and POS tagging approaches significantly outperformed the correlation to more than 78% (respectively 78.2% and 79.69%).

## 5   Conclusion and Future Work

In this article, we presented an innovative word embedding-based system to measure semantic relations between Arabic sentences. This system is based on the semantic properties of words included in the word-embedding model. In order to make further progress in the analysis of the semantic sentence similarity, this article showed how the IDF weighting and Part-of-Speech tagging are used to support the identification of words that are highly descriptive in each sentence. In the experiments we have shown how these techniques improve the correlation results. The performance of our proposed system was confirmed through the Pearson correlation between our assigned semantic similarity scores and human judgements. As future work, we can make more improvement in the semantic similarity results by a smart hybridisation between both IDF weighting and POS tagging techniques.

## References


Yoshua Bengio, Réjean Ducharme, Pascal Vincent, and Christian Jauvin. 2003. A neural probabilistic language model. *Journal of machine learning research*, 3(Feb):1137–1155.

Yu Chen and Andreas Eisele. 2012. Multiun v2: Un documents with multilingual alignments. In *LREC*, pages 2500–2504.

Václáv Chvatal and David Sankoff. 1975. Longest common subsequences of two random sequences. *Journal of Applied Probability*, 12(02):306–315.

Ronan Collobert and Jason Weston. 2008. A unified architecture for natural language processing: Deep neural networks with multitask learning. In *Proceedings of the 25th international conference on Machine learning*, pages 160–167. ACM.

Zhendong Dong and Qiang Dong. 2003. Hownet-a hybrid language and knowledge resource. In *Natural Language Processing and Knowledge Engineering, 2003. Proceedings. 2003 International Conference on*, pages 820–824. IEEE.

Souhir Gahbiche-Braham, Hélène Bonneau-Maynard, Thomas Lavergne, and François Yvon. 2012. Joint segmentation and pos tagging for arabic using a crf-based classifier. In *LREC*, pages 2107–2113.

Khaleej. 2004. Khaleej and watan corpus https://sites.google.com/site/mouradabbas9/corpora, (accessed january 20,2017).

ksucorpus. 2012. King saud university corpus, http://ksucorpus.ksu.edu.sa/ar/ (accessed january 20,2017).

Vladimir I Levenshtein. 1966. Binary codes capable of correcting deletions, insertions, and reversals. In *Soviet physics doklady*, volume 10, pages 707–710.

Christina Lioma and Roi Blanco. 2009. Part of speech based term weighting for information retrieval. In *European Conference on Information Retrieval*, pages 412–423. Springer.

Christopher D Manning, Prabhakar Raghavan, Hinrich Schütze, et al. 2008. *Introduction to information retrieval*, volume 1. Cambridge university press Cambridge.

Meedan. 2012. Meedan's open source arabic english, https://github.com/anastaw/meedan-memory, (accessed january 20,2017).

Tomas Mikolov, Martin Karafiát, Lukas Burget, Jan Cernockỳ, and Sanjeev Khudanpur. 2010. Recurrent neural network based language model. In *Interspeech*, volume 2, page 3.

Tomas Mikolov, Kai Chen, Greg Corrado, and Jeffrey Dean. 2013a. Efficient estimation of word representations in vector space. In *In: ICLR: Proceeding of the International Conference on Learning Representations Workshop Track*, pages 1301–3781.

Tomas Mikolov, Ilya Sutskever, Kai Chen, Greg S Corrado, and Jeff Dean. 2013b. Distributed representations of words and phrases and their compositionality. In *Advances in neural information processing systems*, pages 3111–3119.

Tomas Mikolov, Wen-tau Yih, and Geoffrey Zweig. 2013c. Linguistic regularities in continuous space word representations. In *Hlt-naacl*, volume 13, pages 746–751.

George A Miller. 1995. Wordnet: a lexical database for english. *Communications of the ACM*, 38(11):39–41.

Andriy Mnih and Geoffrey E Hinton. 2009. A scalable hierarchical distributed language model. In D. Koller, D. Schuurmans, Y. Bengio, and L. Bottou, editors, *Advances in Neural Information Processing Systems 21*, pages 1081–1088. Curran Associates, Inc.

MSR-video. 2016. Microsoft research video corpus, https://www.microsoft.com/en-us/download/details.aspx?id=52422, (accessed january 21,2017).

Roberto Navigli and Simone Paolo Ponzetto. 2012. Babelnet: The automatic construction, evaluation and application of a wide-coverage multilingual semantic network. *Artificial Intelligence*, 193:217–250.

Saul B Needleman and Christian D Wunsch. 1970. A general method applicable to the search for similarities in the amino acid sequence of two proteins. *Journal of molecular biology*, 48(3):443–453.

Jeffrey Pennington, Richard Socher, and Christopher D Manning. 2014. Glove: Global vectors for word representation. In *EMNLP*, volume 14, pages 1532–1543.

Quran. 2007. Raw quran text, http://tanzil.net/ download/, (accessed january 20,2017).

Hazem M Raafat, Mohamed A Zahran, and Mohsen Rashwan. 2013. Arabase-a database combining different arabic resources with lexical and semantic information. In *KDIR/KMIS*, pages 233–240.

Motaz K Saad and Wesam Ashour. 2010. Osac: Open source arabic corpora. In *6th ArchEng Int. Symposiums, EEECS*, volume 10.

Gerard Salton and Christopher Buckley. 1988. Term-weighting approaches in automatic text retrieval. *Information processing & management*, 24(5):513–523.

Didier Schwab. 2005. *Approche hybride-lexicale et thématique-pour la modélisation, la détection et lexploitation des fonctions lexicales en vue de lanalyse sémantique de texte*. Ph.D. thesis, Université Montpellier II.

Gilles Sérasset. 2015. Dbnary: Wiktionary as a lemon-based multilingual lexical resource in rdf. *Semantic Web*, 6(4):355–361.

Jörg Tiedemann. 2009. News from opus-a collection of multilingual parallel corpora with tools and interfaces. In *Recent advances in natural language processing*, volume 5, pages 237–248.

Jörg Tiedemann. 2012. Parallel data, tools and interfaces in opus. In *LREC*, volume 2012, pages 2214–2218.

Joseph Turian, Lev Ratinov, and Yoshua Bengio. 2010. Word representations: a simple and general method for semi-supervised learning. In *Proceedings of the 48th annual meeting of the association for computational linguistics*, pages 384–394. Association for Computational Linguistics.

Peter D Turney and Patrick Pantel. 2010. From frequency to meaning: Vector space models of semantics. *Journal of artificial intelligence research*, 37:141–188.

WikiAr. 2006. Arabic wikipedia corpus, http://linguatools.org/tools/corpora/wikipedia-monolingual-corpora/, (accessed january 21,2017).

William E Winkler. 1999. The state of record linkage and current research problems. In *Statistical Research Division, US Census Bureau*. Citeseer.

Mohamed A Zahran, Ahmed Magooda, Ashraf Y Mahgoub, Hazem Raafat, Mohsen Rashwan, and Amir Atyia. 2015. Word representations in vector space and their applications for arabic. In *International Conference on Intelligent Text Processing and Computational Linguistics*, pages 430–443. Springer.

# Morphological Analysis for the Maltese Language:
# The challenges of a hybrid system


**Claudia Borg**
Dept. A.I., Faculty of ICT
University of Malta
claudia.borg@um.edu.mt

**Albert Gatt**
Institute of Linguistics
University of Malta
albert.gatt@um.edu.mt



## Abstract

Maltese is a morphologically rich language with a hybrid morphological system which features both concatenative and non-concatenative processes. This paper analyses the impact of this hybridity on the performance of machine learning techniques for morphological labelling and clustering. In particular, we analyse a dataset of morphologically related word clusters to evaluate the difference in results for concatenative and non-concatenative clusters. We also describe research carried out in morphological labelling, with a particular focus on the verb category. Two evaluations were carried out, one using an unseen dataset, and another one using a gold standard dataset which was manually labelled. The gold standard dataset was split into concatenative and non-concatenative to analyse the difference in results between the two morphological systems.


## 1   Introduction

Maltese, the national language of the Maltese Islands and, since 2004, also an official European language, has a hybrid morphological system that evolved from an Arabic stratum, a Romance (Sicilian/Italian) superstratum and an English adstratum (Brincat, 2011). The Semitic influence is evident in the basic syntactic structure, with a highly productive non-Semitic component manifest in its lexis and morphology (Fabri, 2010; Borg and Azzopardi-Alexander, 1997; Fabri et al., 2014). Semitic morphological processes still account for a sizeable proportion of the lexicon and follow a non-concatenative, root-and-pattern strategy (or templatic morphology) similar to Arabic and Hebrew, with consonantal roots combined

with a vowel melody and patterns to derive forms. By contrast, the Romance/English morphological component is concatenative (i.e. exclusively stem-and-affix based). Table 1 provides an example of these two systems, showing inflection and derivation for the words *eżamina* 'to examine' taking a stem-based form, and *gideb* 'to lie' from the root $\sqrt{\text{GDB}}$ which is based on a templatic system. Table 2 gives an examply of verbal inflection, which is affix-based, and applies to lexemes arising from both concatenative and non-concatenative systems, the main difference being that the latter evinces frequent stem variation.

Table 1: Examples of inflection and derivation in the concatenative and non-concatenative systems

|  | **Derivation** | **Inflection** |
|---|---|---|
| **Concat.** | | |
| *eżamina* | *eżaminatur* | *eżaminatr-iċi*, sg.f |
| 'examine' | 'examiner' | *eżaminatur-i*, pl. |
| **Non-Con.** | | |
| *gideb* 'lie' | *giddieb* | *giddieb-a*, sg.f. |
| $\sqrt{\text{GDB}}$ | 'liar' | *giddib-in*, pl. |

Table 2: Verbal inflections for the concatenative and non-concatenative systems.

|  | *eżamina* 'examine' | *gideb* $\sqrt{\text{GDB}}$ 'lie' |
|---|---|---|
| 1SG | n-eżamina | n-igdeb |
| 2SG | t-eżamina | t-igdeb |
| 3SGM | j-eżamina | j-igdeb |
| 3SGF | t-eżamina | t-igdeb |
| 1PL | n-eżamina-w | n-igdb-u |
| 2PL | t-eżamina-w | t-igdb-u |
| 3PL | j-eżamina-w | j-igdb-u |

To date, there still is no complete morphological analyser for Maltese. In a first attempt at a




*Proceedings of The Third Arabic Natural Language Processing Workshop (WANLP)*, pages 25–34,
Valencia, Spain, April 3, 2017. ©2017 Association for Computational Linguistics

computational treatment of Maltese morphology, Farrugia (2008) used a neural network and focused solely on broken plural for nouns (Schembri, 2006). The only work treating computational morphology for Maltese in general was by Borg and Gatt (2014), who used unsupervised techniques to group together morphologically related words. A theoretical analysis of the templatic verbs (Spagnol, 2011) was used by Camilleri (2013), who created a computational grammar for Maltese for the Resource Grammar Library (Ranta, 2011), with a particular focus on inflectional verbal morphology. The grammar produced the full paradigm of a verb on the basis of its root, which can consist of over 1,400 inflective forms per derived verbal form, of which traditional grammars usually list 10. This resource is known as Ġabra and is available online[1]. Ġabra is, to date, the best computational resource available in terms of morphological information. It is limited in its focus to templatic morphology and restricted to the wordforms available in the database. A further resource is the lexicon and analyser provided as part of the Apertium open-source machine translation toolkit (Forcada et al., 2011). A subset of this lexicon has since been incorporated in the Ġabra database.

This paper presents work carried out for Maltese morphology, with a particular emphasis on the problem of hybridity in the morphological system. Morphological analysis is challenging for a language like Maltese due to the mixed morphological processes existing side by side. Although there are similarities between the two systems, as seen in verbal inflections, various differences among the subsystems exist which make a unified treatment challenging, including: (a) stem allomorphy, which occurs far more frequently with Semitic stems; (b) paradigmatic gaps, especially in the derivational system based on semitic roots (Spagnol, 2011); (c) the fact that morphological analysis for a hybrid system needs to pay attention to both stem-internal (templatic) processes, and phenomena occurring at the stem's edge (by affixation).

First, we will analyse the results of the unsupervised clustering technique by Borg and Gatt (2014) applied on Maltese, with a particular focus of distinguishing the performance of the technique on the two different morphological systems. Second, we are interested in labelling words with their morphological properties. We view this as a classification problem, and treat complex morphological properties as separate features which can be classified in an optimal sequence to provide a final complex label. Once again, the focus of the analysis is on the hybridity of the language and whether a single technique is appropriate for a mixed morphology such as that found in Maltese.

## 2 Related Work

Computational morphology can be viewed as having three separate subtasks — segmentation, clustering related words, and labelling (see Hammarström and Borin (2011)). Various approaches are used for each of the tasks, ranging from rule-based techniques, such as finite state transducers for Arabic morphological analysis (Beesley, 1996; Habash et al., 2005), to various unsupervised, semi- or fully-supervised techniques which would generally deal with one or two of the subtasks. For most of the techniques described, it is difficult to directly compare results due to difference in the data used and the evaluation setting itself. For instance, the results achieved by segmentation techniques are then evaluated in an information retrieval task.

The majority of works dealing with unsupervised morphology focus on English and assume that the morphological processes are concatenative (Hammarström and Borin, 2011). Goldsmith (2001) uses the minimum description length algorithm, which aims to represent a language in the most compact way possible by grouping together words that take on the same set of suffixes. In a similar vein, Creutz and Lagus (2005; 2007) use Maximum a Posteriori approaches to segment words from unannotated texts, and have become part of the baseline and standard evaluation in the Morpho Challenge series of competitions (Kurimo et al., 2010). Kohonen et al. (2010) extends this work by introducing semi- and supervised approaches to the model learning for segmentation. This is done by introducing a discriminative weighting scheme that gives preference to the segmentations within the labelled data.

Transitional probabilities are used to determine potential word boundaries (Keshava and Pitler, 2006; Dasgupta and Ng, 2007; Demberg, 2007). The technique is very intuitive, and posits that the

---

[1]http://mlrs.research.um.edu.mt/resources/gabra/

most likely place for a segmentation to take place is at nodes in the trie with a large branching factor. The result is a ranked list of affixes which can then be used to segment words.

Van den Bosch and Daelemans (1999) and Clark (2002; 2007) apply Memory-based Learning to classify morphological labels. The latter work was tested on Arabic singular and broken plural pairs, with the algorithm learning how to associate an inflected form with its base form. Durrett and DeNero (2013) derives rules on the basis of the orthographic changes that take place in an inflection table (containing a paradigm). A log-linear model is then used to place a conditional distribution over all valid rules.

Poon et al. (2009) use a log-linear model for unsupervised morphological segmentation, which leverages overlapping features such as morphemes and their context. It incorporates exponential priors as a way of describing a language in an efficient and compact manner. Sirts and Goldwater (2013) proposed Adaptor Grammars (AGMorph), a nonparametric Bayesian modelling framework for minimally supervised learning of morphological segmentation. The model learns latent tree structures over the input of a corpus of strings. Narasimhan et al. (2015) also use a log-linear model, and morpheme and word-level features to predict morphological chains, improving upon the techniques of Poon et al. (2009) and Sirts and Goldwater (2013). A morphological chain is seen as a sequence of words that starts from the base word, and at each level through the process of affixation a new word is derived as a morphological variant, with the top 100 chains having an accuracy of 43%. It was also tested on an Arabic dataset, achieving an F-Measure of 0.799. However, the system does not handle stem variation since the pairing of words is done on the basis of the same orthographic stem and therefore the result for Arabic is rather surprising. The technique is also lightly-supervised since it incorporates part-of-speech category to reinforce potential segmentations.

Schone and Jurafsky (2000; 2001) and Baroni et al. (2002) use both orthographic and semantic similarity to detect morphologically related word pairs, arguing that neither is sufficient on its own to determine a morphological relation. Yarowsky and Wicentowski (2000) use a combination of alignment models with the aim of pairing inflected

words. However this technique relies on part-of-speech, affix and stem information. Can and Manandhar (2012) create a hierarchical clustering of morphologically related words using both affixes and stems to combine words in the same clusters. Ahlberg et al. (2014) produce inflection tables by obtaining generalisations over a small number of samples through a semi-supervised approach. The system takes a group of words and assumes that the similar elements that are shared by the different forms can be generalised over and are irrelevant for the inflection process.

For Semitic languages, a central issue in computational morphology is disambiguation between multiple possible analyses. Habash and Rambow (2005) learn classifiers to identify different morphological features, used specifically to improve part-of-speech tagging. Snyder and Barzilay (2008) tackle morphological segmentation for multiple languages in the Semitic family and English by creating a model that maps frequently occurring morphemes in different languages into a single abstract morpheme.

Due to the intrinsic differences in the problem of computational morphology between Semitic and English/Romance languages, it is difficult to directly compare results. Our interest in the present paper is more in the types of approaches taken, and particularly, in seeing morphological labelling as a classification problem. Modelling different classifiers for specific morphological properties can be the appropriate approach for Maltese, since it allows the flexibility to focus on those properties where data is available.

## 3 Clustering words in a hybrid morphological system

The Maltese morphology system includes two systems, concatenative and non-concatenative. As seen in the previous section, most computational approaches deal with either Semitic morphology (as one would for Arabic or its varieties), or with a system based on stems and affixes (as in Italian). Therefore, we might expect that certain methods will perform differently depending on which component we look at. Indeed, overall accuracy figures may mask interesting differences among the different components.

The main motivation behind this analysis is that Maltese words of Semitic origin tend to have considerable stem variation (non-concatenative), whilst the word formation from Romance/English origin words would generally leave stems whole (concatenative)[2]. Maltese provides an ideal scenario for this type of analysis due to its mixed morphology. Often, clustering techniques would either be sensitive to a particular language, such as catering for weak consonants in Arabic (de Roeck and Al-Fares, 2000), or focus solely on English or Romance languages (Schone and Jurafsky, 2001; Yarowsky and Wicentowski, 2000; Baroni et al., 2002) where stem variation is not widespread.

The analysis below uses a dataset of clusters produced by Borg and Gatt (2014), who employed an unsupervised technique using several interim steps to cluster words together. First, potential affixes are identified using transitional probabilities in a similar fashion to (Keshava and Pitler, 2006; Dasgupta and Ng, 2007). Words are then clustered on the basis of common stems. Clusters are improved using measures of orthographic and semantic similarity, in a similar vein to (Schone and Jurafsky, 2001; Baroni et al., 2002). Since no gold-standard lexical resource was available for Maltese, the authors evaluated the clusters using a crowd-sourcing strategy of non-expert native speakers and a separate, but smaller, set of clusters were evaluated using an expert group. In the evaluation, participants were presented with a cluster which had to be rated for its quality and corrected by removing any words which do not belong to a cluster. In this analysis, we focus on the experts' cluster dataset which was roughly balanced between non-concatenative (NC) and concatenative (CON) clusters. There are 101 clusters in this dataset, 25 of which were evaluated by all 3 experts, and the remaining by one of the experts. Table 3 provides an overview of the 101 clusters in terms of their size.

Immediately, it is possible to observe that concatenative clusters tend to be larger in size than non-concatenative clusters. This is mainly due to the issue of stem variation in the non-concatenative group, which gives rise to a lot of false negatives. It is also worth noting that part of the difficulty here is that the vowel patterns in the non-concatenative process are unpredictable. For example *qsim* 'division' is formed from *qasam* 'to divide' $\sqrt{\text{QSM}}$, whilst *ksur* 'breakage' is formed from *kiser* 'to break' $\sqrt{\text{KSR}}$. Words are con-

---

<sup></sup>
[2]Concatenative word formations would always involve a recognisable stem, though in some cases they may undergo minor variations as a result of allomorphy or allophomy.

Table 3: Comparison of non-concatenative and concatenative clusters in expert group

| Size | NC | CON |
|---|---|---|
| <10 | 53% (25) | 26% (14) |
| 10–19 | 23% (11) | 37% (20) |
| 20–29 | 13% (6) | 15% (8) |
| 30–39 | 2% (1) | 9% (5) |
| >40 | 9% (4) | 13% (7) |
| Total | 47 | 53 |
| Evaluated by all experts | 13 | 13 |
| Evaluated by one expert | 34 | 40 |

structed around infixation of vowel melodies to form a stem, before inflection adds affixes. In the concatenative system there are some cases of allomorphy, but there will, in general, be an entire stem, or substring thereof, that is recognisable.

### 3.1 Words removed from clusters

As an indicator of the quality of a cluster, the analysis looks at the number of words that experts removed from a cluster — indicating that the word does not belong to a cluster. Table 4 gives the percentage of words removed from clusters, divided according to whether the morphological system involved is concatenative or non-concatenative. The percentage of clusters which were left intact by the experts were higher for the concatenative group (61%) when compared to the non-concatenative group (45%). The gap closes when considering the percentage of clusters which had a third or more of their words removed (non-concatenative at 25% and concatenative at 20%). However, the concatenative group also had clusters which had more than 80% of their words removed. This indicates that, although in general the clustering technique performs better for the concatenative case, there are cases when bad clusters are formed through the techniques used. The reason is usually that stems with overlapping substrings are mistakenly grouped together. One such cluster was that for *ittra* 'letter', which also got clustered with *ittraduċi* 'translate' and *ittratat* 'treated', clearly all morphologically unrelated words. However, these were clustered together because the system incorrectly identified *ittra* as a potential stem in all these words.

Table 4: Number of words removed, split by concatenative and non-concatenative processes

| By Percentage | NC | CON |
|---|---|---|
| 0% | 45% (33) | 61% (49) |
| 1–5% | 1% (1) | 1% (1) |
| 5–10% | 7% (5) | 4% (3) |
| 10–20% | 5% (4) | 11% (9) |
| 20–30% | 17% (12) | 4% (3) |
| 30–40% | 8% (6) | 4% (3) |
| 40–60% | 7% (5) | 3% (2) |
| 60–80% | 10% (7) | 9% (7) |
| over 80% | 0% (0) | 4% (3) |

## 3.2 Quality ratings of clusters

Experts were asked to rate the quality of a cluster, and although this is a rather subjective opinion, the correlation between this judgement and the number of words removed was calculated using Pearson's correlation coefficient. The trends are consistent with the analysis in the previous subsection; table 5 provides the breakdown of the quality ratings for clusters split between the two processes and the correlation of the quality to the percentage of words removed. The non-concatenative clusters generally have lower quality ratings when compared to the concatenative clusters. But both groups have a strong correlation between the percentage of words removed and the quality rating, clearly indicating that the perception of a cluster's quality is related to the percentage of words removed.

Table 5: Quality ratings of clusters, correlated to the percentage of words removed.

| Quality | NC | CON |
|---|---|---|
| Very Good | 17% (12) | 28% (22) |
| Good | 33% (24) | 36% (29) |
| Medium | 34% (25) | 18% (15) |
| Bad | 12% (9) | 14% (11) |
| Very Bad | 4% (3) | 4% (3) |
| Correlation: | 0.780 | 0.785 |

## 3.3 Hybridity in clustering

Clearly, there is a notable difference between the clustering of words from concatenative and non-concatenative morphological processes. Both have their strengths and pitfalls, but neither of the two processes excel or stand out over the other. One of the problems with non-concatenative clusters was that of size. The initial clusters were formed on the basis of the stems, and due to stem variation the non-concatenative clusters were rather small. Although the merging process catered for clusters to be put together and form larger clusters, the process was limited to a maximum of two merging operations. This might not have been sufficient for the small-sized non-concatenative clusters. In fact, only 10% of the NC clusters contained 30 or more words when compared to 22% of the concatenative clusters. Limiting merging in this fashion may have resulted in a few missed opportunities. This is because there's likely to be a lot of derived forms which are difficult to cluster initially due to stem allomorphy (arising due to the fact that root-based derivation involves infixation, and in Maltese, vowel melodies are unpredictable). So there are possibly many clusters, all related to the same root.

The problem of size with concatenative clusters was on the other side of the scale. Although the majority of clusters were of average size, large clusters tended to include many false positives. In order to explore this problem further, one possibility would be to check whether there is a correlation between the size of a cluster and the percentage of words removed from it. It is possible that the unsupervised technique does not perform well when producing larger clusters, and if such a correlation exists, it would be possible to set an empirically determined threshold for cluster size.

Given the results achieved, it is realistic to state that the unsupervised clustering technique could be further improved using the evaluated clusters as a development set to better determine the thresholds in the metrics proposed above. This improvement would impact both concatenative and non-concatenative clusters equally. In general, the clustering technique does work slightly better for the concatenative clusters, and this is surely due to the clustering of words on the basis of their stems. This is reflected by the result that 61% of the clusters had no words removed compared to 45% of the non-concatenative clusters. However, a larger number of concatenative clusters had a large percentage of words removed. Indeed, if the quality ratings were considered as an indicator of how the technique performs on the non-concatenative vs the concatenative clusters, the judgement would be medium to good for the non-concatenative and good for the concatenative clusters. Thus the performance is sufficiently close in terms of quality of the two groups to suggest that a single unsupervised technique can be applied to Maltese, without differentiating between the morphological sub-systems.

## 4 Classifying morphological properties

In our approach, morphological labelling is viewed as a classification problem with each morphological property seen as a feature which can be classified. Thus, the analysis of a given word can be seen as a sequence of classification problems, each assigning a label to the word which reflects one of its morphological properties. We refer to such a sequence of classifiers as a 'cascade'.

In this paper, we focus in particular on the verb category, which is morphologically one of the richest categories in Maltese. The main question is to identify whether there is a difference in the performance of the classification system when applied to lexemes formed through concatenative or non-concatenative processes. Our primary focus is on the classification of inflectional verb features. While these are affixed to the stem, the principal issue we are interested in is whether the co-training of the classifier sequence on an undifferentiated training set performs adequately on both lexemes derived via a templatic system and lexemes which have a 'whole', continuous stem.

### 4.1 The classification system

The classification system was trained and initially evaluated using part of the annotated data from the lexical resource Ġabra. The training data contained over 170,000 wordforms, and the test data, which was completely unseen, contained around 20,000 wordforms. A second dataset was also used which was taken from the Maltese national corpus (MLRS — Malta Language Resource Server[3]). This dataset consisted of 200 randomly selected words which were given morphological labels by two experts. The words were split half and half between Semitic (non-concatenative) and Romance/English (concatenative) origin. The verb category had 94 words, with 76 non-concatenative, and 18 concatenative. This is referred to as the *gold standard* dataset.

A series of classifiers were trained using annotated data from Ġabra, which contains detailed morphological information relevant to each word. These are **person, number, gender, direct object, indirect object, tense, aspect, mood** and **polarity**. In the case of *tense/aspect* and *mood*, these were joined into one single feature, abbreviated to **TAM** since they are mutually exclusive. These features are referred to as *second-tier* features, representing the morphological properties which the system must classify. The classification also relies on a set of *basic* features which are automatically extracted from a given word. These are **stems, prefixes, suffixes** and **composite suffixes**, when available[4], **consonant-vowel patterns** and **gemination**.

A separate classifier was trained for each of the second-tier features. In order to arrive at the ideal sequence of classifiers, multiple sequences were tested and the best sequence identified on the basis of performance on held-out data (for more detail see Borg (2016)). Once the optimal sequence was established, the classification system used these classifiers as a cascade, each producing the appropriate label for a particular morphological property and passing on the information learnt to the following classifier. The verb cascade consisted of the optimal sequence of classifiers in the following sequence: Polarity (Pol), Indirect Object (Ind), Direct Object (Dir), Tense/Aspect/Mood (TAM), Number (Num), Gender (Gen) and Person (Per).

The classifiers were trained using decision trees through the WEKA data mining software (Hall et al., 2009), available both through a graphical user interface and as an open-source java library. Other techniques, such as Random Forests, SVMs and Naïve Bayes, were also tested and produced very similar results. The classifiers were built using the training datasets. The first evaluation followed the traditional evaluation principles of machine learning, using the test dataset which contained unseen wordforms from Ġabra, amounting to just over 10% of the training data. This is referred to as the *traditional* evaluation.

However, there are two main aspects in our scenario that encouraged us to go beyond the traditional evaluation. First, Ġabra is made of automatically generated wordforms, several of which

---



[4]Composite suffixes occur when more than one suffix is concatenated to the stem, usually with enclitic object and indirect object pronouns, as in *qatil-hu-li* 'he killed him for me'.

are never attested (though they are possible) in the MLRS corpus. Second, the corpus contains several other words which are not present in *Ġabra*, especially concatenative word formations. Thus, we decided to carry out a gold standard (GS) evaluation to test the performance of the classification system on actual data from the MLRS corpus. The evaluation in this paper is restricted to the verb category.

## 4.2 Evaluation Results

We first compare the performance of the classification system on the test dataset collected from *Ġabra* to the manually annotated gold standard collated from the MLRS corpus. These results are shown in fig. 1. The first three features in the cascade — Polarity, Indirect Object and Direct Object — perform best in both the traditional and gold standard evaluations. In particular, the indirect object has practically the same performance in both evaluations. A closer look at the classification results of the words reveals that most words did not have this morphological property, and therefore no label was required. The classification system correctly classified these words with a *null* value. The polarity classifier on the other hand, was expected to perform better — in Maltese, negation is indicated with the suffix *-x* at the end of the word. The main problem here was that the classifier could apply the labels *positive*, *negative* or *null* to a word, resulting in the use of the null label more frequently than the two human experts.

The errors in the classification of the morphological property TAM were mainly found in the labelling of the values *perfective* and *imperative*, whilst the label *imperfective* performed slightly better. Similarly, the number and gender classifiers both had labels that performed better than others. Overall, this could indicate that the data representation for these particular labels is not adequate to facilitate the modelling of a classifier.

As expected, the performance of the classifiers on the gold standard is lower than that of a traditional evaluation setting. The test dataset used in the traditional evaluation, although completely unseen, was still from the same source as the training data (Ġabra) — the segmentation of words was known, the distribution of instances in the different classes (labels) was similar to that found in the training data. While consistency in training and test data sources clearly make for better results,

the outcomes also point to the possibility of overfitting, particularly as Ġabra contains a very high proportion of Semitic, compared to concatenative, stems. Thus, it is possible that the training data for the classifiers did not cover the necessary breadth for the verbs found in the MLRS corpus. To what extent this is impacting the results of the classifiers cannot be known unless the analysis separates the two processes. For this reason, the analysis of the verb category in the gold standard evaluation was separated into two, and the performance of each is compared to the overall gold standard performance. This allows us to identify those morphological properties which will require more representative datasets in order to improve their performance. Figure 2 shows this comparison.

The first three classifiers — polarity, indirect object and direct object — perform as expected, meaning that the concatenative lexemes perform worse than the non-concatenative. This confirms the suspicion that the coverage of Ġabra is not sufficiently representative of the morphological properties in the concatenative class of words. On the other hand, the TAM and Person classifiers perform better on the concatenative words. However, there is no specific distinction in the errors of these two classifiers.

One overall possible reason for the discrepancy in the performance between the traditional and gold standard evaluation, and possibly also between the concatenative and non-concatenative words, is how the words are segmented. The test data in the traditional evaluation setting was segmented correctly, using the same technique applied for the training data. The segmentation for the words in the MLRS corpus was performed automatically and heuristically, and the results were not checked for their correctness, so the classification system might have been given an incorrect segmentation of a word. This would impact the results as the classifiers rely upon the identification of prefixes and suffixes to label words.

## 5  Conclusions and Future Work

This paper analysed the results of the clustering of morphologically related words and the morphological labelling of words, with a particular emphasis on identifying the difference in performance of the techniques used on words of Semitic origin (non-concatenative) and Romance/English origin (concatenative).

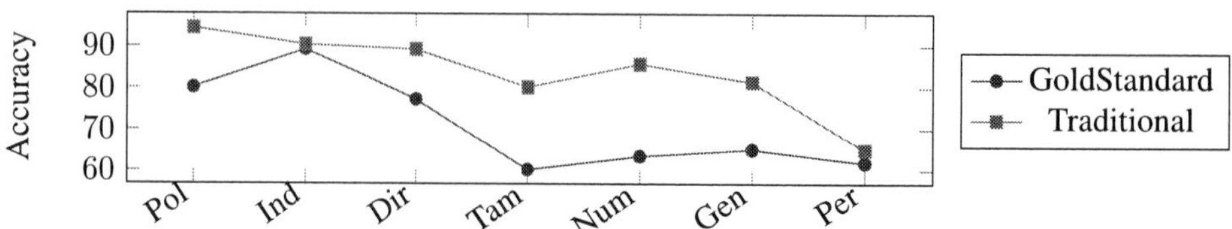

Figure 1: Comparison of the classification system using traditional evaluation settings and a gold standard evaluation.

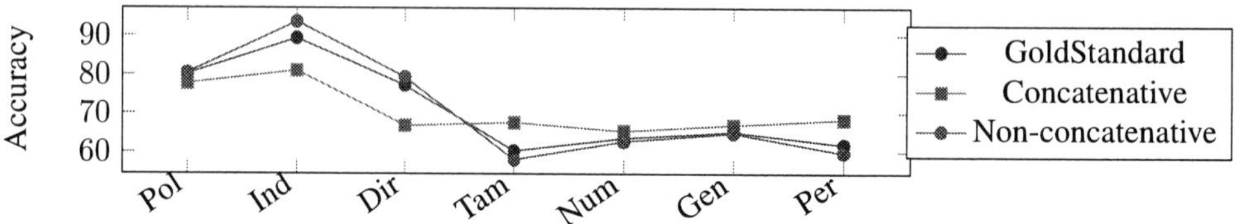

Figure 2: Comparison of the classifiers split between concatenative and non-concatenative words.

The datasets obtained from the clustering technique were split into concatenative and non-concatenative sets, and evaluated in terms of their quality and the number of words removed from each cluster. Although generally, the clustering techniques performed best on the concatenative set, scalability seemed to be an issue, with the bigger clusters performing badly. The non-concatenative set, on the other hand, had smaller clusters but the quality ratings were generally lower than those of the concatenative group. Overall, it seems that the techniques were geared more towards the concatenative set, but performed at an acceptable level for the non-concatenative set. Although the analysis shows that it is difficult to find a one-size-fits-all solution, the resulting clusters could be used as a development set to optimise the clustering process in future.

The research carried out in morphological labelling viewed it as a classification problem. Each morphological property is seen as a machine learning feature, and each feature is modelled as a classifier and placed in a cascade so as to provide the complete label to a given word. The research focussed on the verb category and two types of evaluations were carried out to test this classification system. The first was a traditional evaluation using unseen data from the same source as the training set. A second evaluation used randomly selected words from the MLRS corpus which were manually annotated with their morphological labels by two human experts. There is no complete morphological analyser available for Maltese, so

this was treated as a gold standard. Since the classifiers were trained using data which is predominantly non-concatenative, the performance of the classification system on the MLRS corpus was, as expected, worse than the traditional evaluation.

In comparing the two evaluations, it was possible to assess which morphological properties were not performing adequately. Moreover, the gold standard dataset was split into two, denoting concatenative and non-concatenative words, to further analyse whether a classification system that was trained predominantly on non-concatenative data could then be applied to concatenative data. The results were mixed, according to the different morphological properties, but overall, the evaluation was useful to determine where more representative data is needed.

Although the accuracy of the morphological classification system are not exceptionally high for some of the morphological properties, the system performs well overall, and the individual classifiers can be retrained and improved as more representative data becomes available. And although the gold standard data is small in size, it allows us to identify which properties require more data, and of which type. One of the possible routes forward is to extend the grammar used to generate the wordforms in Ġabra and thus obtain more coverage for the concatenative process. However, it is already clear from the analysis carried out that the current approach is viable for both morphological systems and can be well suited for a hybrid system such as Maltese.

# 6 Acknowledgements

The authors acknowledge the insight and expertise of Prof. Ray Fabri. The research work disclosed in this publication is partially funded by the Malta Government Scholarship Scheme grant.

# References

Malin Ahlberg, Markus Forsberg, and Mans Hulden. 2014. Semi-supervised learning of morphological paradigms and lexicons. In *Proceedings of the 14th Conference of the European Chapter of the Association for Computational Linguistics, Gothenburg, Sweden 26–30 April 2014*, pages 569–578.

Marco Baroni, Johannes Matiasek, and Harald Trost. 2002. Unsupervised discovery of morphologically related words based on orthographic and semantic similarity. In *Proceedings of the ACL-02 workshop on Morphological and phonological learning - Volume 6*, MPL '02, pages 48–57. Association for Computational Linguistics.

Kenneth R. Beesley. 1996. Arabic finite-state morphological analysis and generation. In *Proceedings of the 16th conference on Computational linguistics*, pages 89–94. Association for Computational Linguistics.

Albert Borg and Marie Azzopardi-Alexander. 1997. *Maltese: Lingua Descriptive Grammar*. Routledge, London and New York.

Claudia Borg and Albert Gatt. 2014. Crowd-sourcing evaluation of automatically acquired, morphologically related word groupings. In *Proceedings of the Ninth International Conference on Language Resources and Evaluation (LREC'14)*.

Claudia Borg. 2016. *Morphology in the Maltese language: A computational perspective*. Ph.D. thesis, University of Malta.

Joseph M. Brincat. 2011. *Maltese and other Languages*. Midsea Books, Malta.

John J. Camilleri. 2013. A computational grammar and lexicon for Maltese. Master's thesis, Chalmers University of Technology, Gothenburg, Sweden, September.

Burcu Can and Suresh Manandhar. 2012. Probabilistic hierarchical clustering of morphological paradigms. In *Proceedings of the 13th Conference of the European Chapter of the Association for Computational Linguistics*, pages 654–663. Association for Computational Linguistics.

Alexander Clark. 2002. Memory-based learning of morphology with stochastic transducers. In *Proceedings of the 40th Annual Meeting of the Association for Computational Linguistics (ACL)*, pages 513–520.

Alexander Clark. 2007. Supervised and Unsupervised Learning of Arabic Morphology. In Abdelhadi Soudi, Antal van den Bosch, Günter Neumann, and Nancy Ide, editors, *Arabic Computational Morphology*, volume 38 of *Text, Speech and Language Technology*, pages 181–200. Springer Netherlands.

Mathias Creutz and Krista Lagus. 2005. Inducing the morphological lexicon of a natural language from unannotated text. In *Proceedings of AKRR'05, International and Interdisciplinary Conference on Adaptive Knowledge Representation and Reasoning*, pages 106–113.

Mathias Creutz and Krista Lagus. 2007. Unsupervised models for morpheme segmentation and morphology learning. *ACM Trans. Speech Lang. Process.*, 4(1):1–34.

Sajib Dasgupta and Vincent Ng. 2007. High-performance, language-independent morphological segmentation. In *NAACL HLT 2007: Proceedings of the Main Conference*, pages 155–163.

Anne N. de Roeck and Waleed Al-Fares. 2000. A morphologically sensitive clustering algorithm for identifying Arabic roots. In *Proceedings of the 38th Annual Meeting on Association for Computational Linguistics*, ACL '00, pages 199–206. Association for Computational Linguistics.

Vera Demberg. 2007. A language-independent unsupervised model for morphological segmentation. In *Proceedings of the 45th Annual Meeting of the Association of Computational Linguistics*, pages 920–927.

Greg Durrett and John DeNero. 2013. Supervised learning of complete morphological paradigms. In *Proceedings of the North American Chapter of the Association for Computational Linguistics*, pages 1185–1195.

Ray Fabri, Michael Gasser, Nizar Habash, George Kiraz, and Shuly Wintner. 2014. Linguistic introduction: The orthography, morphology and syntax of semitic languages. In *Natural Language Processing of Semitic Languages*, Theory and Applications of Natural Language Processing, pages 3–41. Springer Berlin Heidelberg.

Ray Fabri. 2010. Maltese. In Christian Delcourt and Piet van Sterkenburg, editors, *The Languages of the New EU Member States*, volume 88, pages 791–816. Revue Belge de Philologie et d'Histoire.

Alex Farrugia. 2008. A computational analysis of the Maltese broken plural. Bachelor's Thesis, University of Malta.

M. L. Forcada, M. Ginestí-Rosell, J. Nordfalk, J. O'Regan, S. Ortiz-Rojas, J. A. Pérez-Ortiz, F. Sánchez-Martínez, G. Ramírez-Sánchez, and F. M. Tyers. 2011. Apertium: a free/open-source platform for rule-based machine translation. *Machine Translation*, 25(2):127–144.

John Goldsmith. 2001. Unsupervised learning of the morphology of a natural language. *Computational Linguistics*, 27:153–198.

Nizar Habash and Owen Rambow. 2005. Arabic tokenization, part-of-speech tagging and morphological disambiguation in one fell swoop. In *Proceedings of the 43rd Annual Meeting on Association for Computational Linguistics*, ACL '05, pages 573–580, Stroudsburg, PA, USA. Association for Computational Linguistics.

Nizar Habash, Owen Rambow, and George Kiraz. 2005. MAGEAD: A Morphological Analyzer and Generator for the Arabic Dialects. In *Proceedings of the ACL Workshop on Computational Approaches to Semitic Languages*, pages 17–24. The Association for Computer Linguistics.

Mark Hall, Eibe Frank, Geoffrey Holmes, Bernhard Pfahringer, Peter Reutemann, and Ian H. Witten. 2009. The weka data mining software: an update. *SIGKDD Explor. Newsl.*, 11(1):10–18.

Harald Hammarström and Lars Borin. 2011. Unsupervised learning of morphology. *Computational Linguistics*, 37:309–350.

Samarth Keshava and Emily Pitler. 2006. A simpler, intuitive approach to morpheme induction. In *PASCAL Challenge Workshop on Unsupervised Segmentation of Words into Morphemes*, pages 31–35.

Oskar Kohonen, Sami Virpioja, and Krista Lagus. 2010. Semi-supervised learning of concatenative morphology. In *Proceedings of the 11th Meeting of the ACL Special Interest Group on Computational Morphology and Phonology*, SIGMORPHON '10, pages 78–86, Stroudsburg, PA, USA. Association for Computational Linguistics.

Mikko Kurimo, Sami Virpioja, Ville Turunen, and Krista Lagus. 2010. Morpho Challenge competition 2005–2010: evaluations and results. In *Proceedings of the 11th Meeting of the ACL Special Interest Group on Computational Morphology and Phonology*, SIGMORPHON '10, pages 87–95. Association for Computational Linguistics.

Karthik Narasimhan, Regina Barzilay, and Tommi S. Jaakkola. 2015. An unsupervised method for uncovering morphological chains. *Transactions of the Association for Computational Linguistics (TACL)*, 3:157–167.

Hoifung Poon, Colin Cherry, and Kristina Toutanova. 2009. Unsupervised morphological segmentation with log-linear models. In *Proceedings of Human Language Technologies: The 2009 Annual Conference of the North American Chapter of the Association for Computational Linguistics*, NAACL '09, pages 209–217.

Aarne Ranta. 2011. *Grammatical framework: programming with multilingual grammars*. CSLI studies in computational linguistics. CSLI Publications,

Center for the Study of Language and Information, Stanford (Calif.).

Tamara Schembri. 2006. The Broken Plural in Maltese: An Analysis. Bachelor's Thesis, University of Malta.

Patrick Schone and Daniel Jurafsky. 2000. Knowledge-free induction of morphology using latent semantic analysis. In *Proceedings of the 2nd workshop on Learning language in logic and the 4th conference on Computational natural language learning - Volume 7*, ConLL '00, pages 67–72. Association for Computational Linguistics.

Patrick Schone and Daniel Jurafsky. 2001. Knowledge-free induction of inflectional morphologies. In *Proceedings of the second meeting of the North American Chapter of the Association for Computational Linguistics on Language technologies*, NAACL '01, pages 1–9. Association for Computational Linguistics.

Kairit Sirts and Sharon Goldwater. 2013. Minimally-supervised morphological segmentation using adaptor grammars. *Transactions of the Association for Computational Linguistics*, 1:255–266.

Benjamin Snyder and Regina Barzilay. 2008. Unsupervised multilingual learning for morphological segmentation. In *Proceedings of ACL-08: HLT*, pages 737–745, Columbus, Ohio. Association for Computational Linguistics.

Michael Spagnol. 2011. *A tale of two morphologies. Verb structure and argument alternations in Maltese*. Ph.D. thesis, University of Konstanz.

Antal Van den Bosch and Walter Daelemans. 1999. Memory-based morphological analysis. In *Proceedings of the 37th annual meeting of the Association for Computational Linguistics on Computational Linguistics*, pages 285–292.

David Yarowsky and Richard Wicentowski. 2000. Minimally supervised morphological analysis by multimodal alignment. In *Proceedings of the 38th Annual Meeting on Association for Computational Linguistics*, ACL '00, pages 207–216, Stroudsburg, PA, USA. Association for Computational Linguistics.

# A Morphological Analyzer for Gulf Arabic Verbs

**Salam Khalifa, Sara Hassan and Nizar Habash**
Computational Approaches to Modeling Language (CAMeL) Lab
New York University Abu Dhabi
{salamkhalifa,sah650,nizar.habash}@nyu.edu

## Abstract

We present CALIMA$_{GLF}$, a Gulf Arabic morphological analyzer currently covering over 2,600 verbal lemmas. We describe in detail the process of building the analyzer starting from phonetic dictionary entries to fully inflected orthographic paradigms and associated lexicon and orthographic variants. We evaluate the coverage of CALIMA$_{GLF}$ against Modern Standard Arabic and Egyptian Arabic analyzers on part of a Gulf Arabic novel. CALIMA$_{GLF}$ verb analysis token recall for identifying correct POS tag outperforms both the Modern Standard Arabic and Egyptian Arabic analyzers by over 27.4% and 16.9% absolute, respectively.

## 1 Introduction

Until recently, Dialectal Arabic (DA) was mainly spoken with little to no publicly available written content. Modern Standard Arabic (MSA) on the other hand is the official language in more than 20 countries, where most written documents from news articles, to educational materials and entertainment magazines, are written in MSA. Hence, most of the tools that are available for Natural Language Processing (NLP) tasks are focused on MSA. With the introduction of social media platforms online, dialectal written content is being produced abundantly. Using existing tools that were developed for MSA on DA proved to have limited performance (Habash and Rambow, 2006; Khalifa et al., 2016). Having resources specific to DA, such as morphological lexicons is important for Arabic NLP tasks, such as part-of-speech (POS) tagging and morphological disambiguation. Recently, dialects such as Egyptian (EGY) and Levantine (LEV) Arabic have been receiving increasing attention. Morphological analyzers for EGY and LEV proved to perform well when used for morphological tagging (Eskander et al., 2016). To our knowledge, there exist no full morphological analyzers for Gulf Arabic (GLF) that produce segmentation, POS analysis and lemmas. Although we note the work of Abuata and Al-Omari (2015) on developing a Gulf Arabic stemmer. In this paper, we present CALIMA$_{GLF}$,[1] a morphological analyzer for GLF. In the current work, we present the effort focusing on GLF verbs only. We utilize a combination of computational techniques in addition to explicit linguistic knowledge to create this resource. We also evaluate it against wide coverage tools for MSA and EGY. CALIMA$_{GLF}$ verb analysis token recall in terms of identifying correct POS tagging outperforms on both MSA and EGY by over 27.4% and 16.9% absolute, respectively. CALIMA$_{GLF}$ will be made publicly available to researchers working on Arabic and Arabic dialect NLP.[2]

The rest of this paper is organized as follows. In Section 2 we review related literature, then we briefly describe the main characteristics of GLF in Section 3. In Section 4 we describe the approach and the resources involved and evaluate in Section 5. We conclude and discuss future work in Section 6.

## 2 Related Work

### 2.1 Arabic Morphological Modeling

Much work has been done on Arabic morphological modeling, covering a wide range of different system designs. Earlier systems such as BAMA, SAMA and MAGEAD (Buckwalter, 2004; Graff

---

[1] In Arabic كلمة *kalimah* means 'Word'. We follow the naming convention from (Habash et al., 2012a) who developed CALIMA$_{EGY}$ since we are using the same format and analysis engine for the databases we create.

[2] CALIMA$_{GLF}$ can be obtained from http://camel.abudhabi.nyu.edu/resources/.

35

*Proceedings of The Third Arabic Natural Language Processing Workshop (WANLP)*, pages 35–45,
Valencia, Spain, April 3, 2017. ©2017 Association for Computational Linguistics

et al., 2009; Habash and Rambow, 2006) were entirely manually designed. Similarly, Habash et al. (2012a) developed CALIMA, a morphological analyzer for Egyptian Arabic (hence CALIMA$_{EGY}$). CALIMA$_{EGY}$ was developed based on a lexicon of morphologically annotated data using several methods and then manually verified. Furthermore, Salloum and Habash (2011) extended existing SAMA and CALIMA$_{EGY}$ resources using hand crafted rules which extended affixes and clitics based on matching on existing ones. Recently, Eskander et al. (2013) developed a technique that generates a morphological analyzer based on an annotated corpus. They describe a technique in which they define inflectional classes for lexemes that represents morphosyntactic features in addition to inflected stems. They automatically 'complete' these classes in a process called paradigm completion. They also show that using manually annotated iconic inflectional classes helps in the overall performance. Using the aforementioned paradigm completion technique, a Moroccan Arabic and a Sanaani Yemeni Arabic morphological analyzers were created (Al-Shargi et al., 2016). And very recently Eskander et al. (2016) presented a single pipeline to produce a morphological analyzer and tagger from a single annotation of a corpus; they produced resources for EGY and LEV. Other works that involve DA morphological modeling include the work of Abuata and Al-Omari (2015). Who developed a rule-based system to segment affixes and clitics in GLF text. They compare their results to other well known MSA stemmers.

In this paper, we create morphological paradigms similar to the iconic inflectional classes discussed by Eskander et al. (2013). Our paradigms map from morphological features to fully inflected orthographic forms. The paradigms abstract over templatic roots; and lexical entries are specified in a lexicon as root-paradigm pairs, in a manner similar to the work of Habash and Rambow (2006). We convert the paradigms to the database representation used in MADAMIRA (Pasha et al., 2014) and CALIMA$_{EGY}$ (Habash et al., 2012a).

## 2.2 Dialectal Orthography

Due to the lack of standardized orthography guidelines for DA, and given the major differences from MSA, dialects are usually written in ways that reflects the words' pronunciation or etymological relation to MSA cognates (Habash et al., 2012b), and even then with a lot of inconsistency. Furthermore, as with MSA, Arabic orthography ignores the spelling of short vowel diacritics, thus increasing the ambiguity of the written forms. As a result, it is rather challenging to computationally process *raw* DA text directly from the source, or even agree on a common normalization. Habash et al. (2012b) proposed a Conventional Orthography for Dialectal Arabic (CODA) as part of a solution allowing different researchers to agree on a set of DA orthographic conventions for computational purposes. CODA was first defined for EGY, but has been extended to Palestinian, Tunisian, Algerian, Maghrebi and Gulf Arabic (Jarrar et al., 2014; Zribi et al., 2014; Saadane and Habash, 2015; Turki et al., 2016; Khalifa et al., 2016). We follow the conventions defined by Khalifa et al. (2016) for CODA GLF.

## 2.3 Dialectal Arabic Resources

In addition to the above mentioned morphological analyzers, there exist other resources such as dictionaries and corpora for both DA and MSA. For annotated MSA corpora, several developed such as (Maamouri and Cieri, 2002; Maamouri et al., 2004; Smrž and Hajič, 2006; Habash and Roth, 2009; Zaghouani et al., 2014).

Many efforts targeted DA, notably, EGY (Gadalla et al., 1997; Kilany et al., 2002; Al-Sabbagh and Girju, 2012; Maamouri et al., 2012b; Maamouri et al., 2012a; Maamouri et al., 2014). As for LEV, there exist morphologically annotated corpora and a treebank (Jarrar et al., 2014; Jarrar et al., 2016; Maamouri et al., 2006). Newly developed corpora for other dialects include (Masmoudi et al., 2014; Smaïli et al., 2014; Al-Shargi et al., 2016; Khalifa et al., 2016) for Tunisian, Algerian, Moroccan, Yemeni and Gulf Arabic respectively. Other notable efforts targeted multiple dialects such as the COLABA project, and the Tharwa dictionary (Diab et al., 2010; Diab et al., 2014). Parallel dialectal corpora by Bouamor et al. (2014) and Meftouh et al. (2015), in addition to the highly dialectal online commentary corpus by Zaidan and Callison-Burch (2011).

Specifically for GLF, we use the Qafisheh Gulf Arabic Dictionary (Qafisheh, 1997) as well as the Gumar Corpus (Khalifa et al., 2016) in developing our analyzer.

# 3 Gulf Arabic

## 3.1 Background

From a linguistic point of view, Gulf Arabic refers to the linguistic varieties spoken on the western coast of the Arabian Gulf, that is Bahrain, Qatar, and the seven Emirates of the United Arab Emirates, as well as in Kuwait and the eastern region of Saudi Arabia (Holes, 1990; Qafisheh, 1977). We extend the use of the term 'Gulf Arabic' (GLF) to include any Arabic variety spoken by the indigenous populations residing the six countries of the Gulf Cooperation Council. In this paper, we focus specifically on Emirati Arabic.

## 3.2 Orthography

Similar to other dialects, GLF has no standard orthography (Habash et al., 2012b). As such, words may be written in a manner reflecting their pronunciation or their etymological relationship to MSA cognates. For example the word for 'dawn' /al-fayr/ may be written as الفير *Alfyr*[3] (reflecting pronunciation) or as الفجر *Alfjr* (reflecting its MSA cognate). In this work we follow the same CODA standards for GLF that were introduced by the authors in (Khalifa et al., 2016) extending the original CODA in (Habash et al., 2012b). We use CODA in developing the morphological databases; but we also add support for non-CODA variants and evaluate on raw non-CODA input. Another challenge caused by Arabic orthography in general (for MSA and other dialects including GLF) is that Arabic orthography does not require writing short vowel diacritics, which adds a lot of ambiguity.

## 3.3 Morphology

GLF shares many of the same morphological complexities of MSA and other Arabic dialects. Arabic rich morphology is represented templatically and affixationally with a number of attachable clitics. This representation in addition to the fact that short vowel diacritics are usually dropped in text add to the text's ambiguity. In comparison to MSA, EGY and LEV, GLF shares and differs in several aspects:

- Like MSA, but unlike EGY and LEV, GLF has no negation enclitic marker, namely the ش *iš* '[negation]' ending such as ما قلتش *mA qultiš* in EGY and LEV as opposed to ما قلت *mA qilt* in GLF 'I did not say'.

- Unlike MSA, but like EGY and LEV, GLF has an indirect object enclitic which is written separately in CODA (but not necessarily in raw form), e.g., قلتلك *qultlik* (CODA قلت لك *qult lik*) in LEV and قلتلج *qiltlij* (CODA قلت لج *qilt lij*) in GLF 'I told you[FS]'.

- GLF has different imperfect verb subject suffixes for second and third person plural and second person feminine singular from EGY and LEV, e.g. تقولوا *tquwlwA* in EGY and LEV and تقولون *tquwluwn* in GLF for 'you[P] say'; and تقولي *tquwliy* in EGY and LEV and تقولين *tquwliyn* in GLF for 'you[FS] say'. It is interesting to note that both forms exist in MSA where they indicate different moods.

- GLF shares with EGY and LEV the absence of the dual forms of the verb and imperfective moods, both of which are present in MSA.

- Unlike MSA, GLF shares with EGY and LEV the ambiguous forms of second masculine singular and first person perfective verbs, e.g., كتبت *katabt* 'I wrote or you wrote' in EGY, GLF and LEV; while MSA has *katabtu* 'I wrote' and *katabta* 'you wrote'.

- GLF has different second person singular direct object enclitics from EGY, LEV and MSA. The second masculine singular form in GLF ك *ik*, sounds like the second feminine singular form in EGY and LEV, and is differnt from MSA's ك *ka*; and the second feminine singular form in GLF ج *ij* (pronounced /itš/), is altogether different. For example, LEV شفتك *šuftik* maps to GLF شفتج *šiftij* 'I saw you[FS]'.

- The future verbal particle in GLF is ب *b* which is different from the MSA equivalent (س *sa*), and can be easily confused with the present progressive particle ب *b* in both EGY and LEV in. GLF does not have a progressive particle.

---

[3] All Arabic transliterations are provided in the Habash-Soudi-Buckwalter transliteration scheme (Habash et al., 2007).

## 4 Building CALIMA_GLF

### 4.1 General Approach

Our goal is to build a morphological analysis and generation model for GLF. We focus on verb forms in this paper, but plan to extend the work to other POS in the future. We employ two databases that capture the full morphological inflection space from lemmas and morphological features to fully inflected surface forms and in reverse. The two databases are (1) a collection of root-abstracted paradigms which map from features to root-abstracted stems, prefixes and suffixes; and (2) a lexicon specifying verbal entries in terms of roots and paradigm IDs. These two structures together define for any verb all the possible analyses allowed within GLF morphology. The two databases are then merged to create a full model. The merging can be done as a finite state machine. However, the implementation we chose is a variant based on the BAMA/SAMA databases following the representation used in MADAMIRA (Pasha et al., 2014) and CALIMA_EGY (Habash et al., 2012a).

Next we discuss step by step the process we took to build CALIMA_GLF, starting with a phonetic dictionary all the way to building a fully functional morphological analyzer that even models non-CODA spelling variants.

### 4.2 The Qafisheh Gulf Arabic Verb Lexicon

Our starting point is the Qafisheh Gulf Arabic Verb Lexicon (QGAVL), which is a portion of the Qafisheh (1997) dictionary. Each entry in the lexicon includes a root, perfective and imperfective verb inflections, Verb Form (as in form II or VII) and English gloss. See Table 1 for some example entries. The Arabic entries are in a phonetic representation and not in Arabic script. The verb forms are only in third person masculine singular inflection (PV3MS and IV3MS, for perfective and imperfective aspect, respectively); and no clitics are attached. In total, there are 2,648 verb entries.

### 4.3 Orthographic Mapping

The first step we took was to create the orthographic spelling of all the verb entries. This included mapping to the appropriate vowel spelling as well as following the CODA spelling rules for stem consonants and morphemes. This step was first done automatically and then checked manually for every entry. See Table 2 for an example of the result of mapping the entries in Table 1. We mapped the roots in two ways, one following CODA and one reflecting a phonological spelling. This information will be used later to make the analyzer robust to non-CODA spellings.

### 4.4 PV-IV Pattern Extraction

Next, we identified for each verb its orthographic inflected templatic pattern, i.e., the pattern that would directly produce the surface form once the root radicals are inserted. This approach to pattern definition is most like the work of Eskander et al. (2013) in it being a one shot application of root-template merging to generate surface orthography. The approach differs from the work of Habash and Rambow (2006), who use a large number of rewrite rules for phonology, morphology and orthography after inserting the roots into the templates.

The pattern extraction was done automatically and then manually checked. It was only done to the forms available in the lexicon so far (PV3MS and IV3MS). The PV-IV Pattern (perfective-imperfective pattern) uses digits (e.g., 1,2,3,4,5) to represent root radicals. In this pattern, all vowels and glottal stop (Hamza) forms are explicitly spelled because they tend to vary within single paradigms. For example, the first entry in Table 5 specifies the PV-IV Pattern 1A3-y1uw3, which when merged with the root radicals *qwl* generates the perfective and imperfective forms *qAl* and *yquwl*.

### 4.5 Basic Paradigm Construction

We identified 72 unique PV-IV patterns in the lexicon, which represent 72 different paradigms. Arabic Verb Forms (I, II, III, etc.) are too general to capture the different variations within the paradigms. That is due to the different root classes (i.e. hamzated, hollow, defective, geminate and sound); and other root-pattern interactions, such as the different forms of Form VIII (اقترب\افتعل, اضطرب\افطعل, ازدهر\افدعل, etc.). All of these phenomena can be handled with orthographic, phonological and morphological rules as was done by Habash and Rambow (2006). However, here we embedded the result of such rule application in the paradigm directly. See Table 3 for counts of PV-IV patterns per Verb Form.

| Root | Perfective 3MS | Imperfective 3MS | Form | English Gloss |
|---|---|---|---|---|
| gwl | gaal | yguul | I | to say, tell |
| syr | saar | ysiir | I | to leave, go |
| ṭrš | ṭarraš | yṭarriš | II | to send, forward s.th. |

Table 1: Example of a Qafisheh Gulf Arabic Verb Lexicon Entry.

| Phono Root | CODA Root | PV3MS | IV3MS | Form | English Gloss |
|---|---|---|---|---|---|
| گول Gwl | قول qwl | قال qAl | يقول yquwl | I | to say, tell |
| سير syr | سير syr | سار sAr | يسير ysiyr | I | to leave, go |
| طرش Trš | طرش Trš | طرّش Tar~aš | يطرّش yTar~iš | II | to send, forward s.th. |

Table 2: Orthographic mapping of the entries in Qafisheh Gulf Arabic Verb Lexicon. The Root is orthographically spelled in two ways reflecting phonology and etymology (CODA style); PV3MS and IV3MS refer to the perfective and imperfective third masculine singular verb forms.

| Verb Form | (وزن) | BP Count |
|---|---|---|
| I | (فَعَل) | 21 |
| II | (فَعَّل) | 6 |
| III | (فَاعَل) | 3 |
| IV | (أفعَل) | 3 |
| V | (تفَعَّل) | 5 |
| VI | (تفَاعَل) | 6 |
| VII | (انفَعَل) | 4 |
| VIII | (افتَعَل) | 10 |
| IX | (افعَلّ) | 1 |
| X | (اسْتَفعَل) | 7 |
| Q | (فَعلَل) | 3 |
| Qt | (تفَعلَل) | 3 |

Table 3: Basic Paradigm counts for every Verb Form Class (وزن *wazn*).

We use the PV-IV patterns as keys (indices) for the paradigms. We then proceed to build a database of Basic Paradigms (BP). A BP is defined as the complete set of possible morphological features (except for clitic features) along with the corresponding stem. The features included are Aspect (perfective **PV**, imperfective **IV**, command **CV**), Person (1, 2, 3), Gender (masculine **M**, feminine **F**, unspecified **U**), and Number (singular **S**, plural **P**). The total number of allowable feature combinations is 19. The BP is defined in a similar fashion to the iconic inflectional classes that was defined by Eskander et al. (2013). Each form of the BP is divided into prefix, stem template, and suffix. See Table 4 for examples of two BPs.

## 4.6 Affixational Orthographic Rules

While we covered most of the orthographic, phonological and morphological rules by embedding them in the BPs, there are still a small number of additional orthographic rules that apply to specific stem-suffix combinations. Specifically, suffixes beginning with ت *t* and ن *n* that attach to stems ending with the same letter are modified as a result of the orthographic gemination rule (الشّدّة Shadda). For example the verb نحت+ت *naHat+t* 'I sculpted' should be written as نحتّ *naHat~*; and the verb ضمن+نا *Daman+nA* 'we guaranteed' should be written as ضمنّا *Daman~A*. We automatically identified all root-paradigm pairs that cause the above rules to apply, and we created new paradigms from them. For example, the root نحت *nHt* is linked with the paradigm 1a2a3-yi12a3-**t** and the root ضمن *Dmn* is linked with the paradigm 1a2a3-yi12a3-**n**. This resulted in 32 additional paradigms, bringing the total to 104 paradigms.

## 4.7 Lexicon Construction

From the set of PV-IV patterns, which we used as paradigm keys, and the lexical entries converted from QGAVL, we constructed our lexicon automatically and then manually validated all the entries. The lexicon consists of 2,648 entries that are linked to the paradigms. See Table 5 for examples of the lexical entries in previous tables. Each entry specifies the root (in phonological spelling and CODA) as well as the paradigm key and gloss.

| Morph.Feat. | Paradigm 1A3-y1uw3 | | | | Paradigm 1a2~a3-y1a2~i3 | | | |
|---|---|---|---|---|---|---|---|---|
| | Prefix | Stem | Suffix | Example | Prefix | Stem | Suffix | Example |
| PV1US | | 1i3 | t | قلت | | 1a2~a3 | t | طرّشت |
| PV1UP | | 1i3 | nA | قلنا | | 1a2~a3 | nA | طرّشنا |
| PV2MS | | 1i3 | t | قلت | | 1a2~a3 | t | طرّشت |
| PV2FS | | 1i3 | tiy | قلتي | | 1a2~a3 | tiy | طرّشتي |
| PV2UP | | 1i3 | tawA | قلتوا | | 1a2~a3 | tawA | طرّشتوا |
| **PV3MS** | | **1A3** | | قال | | **1a2~a3** | | طرّش |
| PV3FS | | 1A3 | at | قالت | | 1a2~a3 | at | طرّشت |
| PV3UP | | 1A3 | awA | قالوا | | 1a2~a3 | awA | طرّشوا |
| IV1US | Aa | 1uw3 | | اقول | Aa | 1a2~i3 | | اطرّش |
| IV1UP | n | 1uw3 | | نقول | n | 1a2~i3 | | نطرّش |
| IV2MS | t | 1uw3 | | تقول | t | 1a2~i3 | | تطرّش |
| **IV3MS** | **y** | **1uw3** | | يقول | **y** | **1a2~i3** | | يطرّش |
| IV3FS | t | 1uw3 | | تقول | t | 1a2~i3 | | تطرّش |
| IV2FS | t | 1uw3 | iyn | تقولين | t | 1a2~3 | iyn | تطرّشين |
| IV2UP | t | 1uw3 | uwn | تقولون | t | 1a2~3 | uwn | تطرّشون |
| IV3UP | y | 1uw3 | uwn | يقولون | y | 1a2~3 | uwn | يطرّشون |
| CV2MS | | 1uw3 | | قول | | 1a2~i3 | | طرّش |
| CV2FS | | 1uw3 | iy | قولي | | 1a2~3 | iy | طرّشي |
| CV2UP | | 1uw3 | awA | قولوا | | 1a2~3 | awA | طرّشوا |

Table 4: Example of BP for a paradigm of Form I and another of Form II for the roots قول qwl and طرش Trš respectively. The verb قال qAl means 'he said' and the verb طرّش Tar~aš means 'he sent'.

| Phono Root | CODA Root | PV3MS | IV3MS | Paradigm Key | Form | English Gloss |
|---|---|---|---|---|---|---|
| گول Gwl | قول qwl | قال qAl | يقول yquwl | 1A3-y1uw3 | I | to say, tell |
| سير syr | سير syr | سار sAr | يسير ysiyr | 1A3-y1iy3 | I | to leave, go |
| طرش Trš | طرش Trš | طرّش Tar~aš | يطرّش yTar~iš | 1a2~a3-y1a2~i3 | II | to send, forward s.th. |

Table 5: Example of lexicon entries. For each entry there is: (a) a phonological root, which will be used to model possible non-CODA variations, (b) a CODA root, (c) two verbal forms (PV3MS and IV3MS), (d) the paradigm key, (e) Verb Form, and (f) English gloss.

## 4.8 Clitic Extension of the Basic Paradigms

At this point, we have a complete inflectional model of GLF verbs except that they do not include any of the numerous clitics written attached in Arabic. We define a set of rules for extending the paradigms to include the clitics. Our extensions include two types of resources.

**Clitic Locations and Forms** First is the list of clitics with their morpheme POS (a la Buckwalter tag) and their relative location around the basic inflected verb, and any conditions for their application. For example, the future particle proclitic ب b appears immediately before the basic verb form, but can only occur with imperfective verbs; the conjunction proclitics و wi 'and' and ف fa 'so' can appear as the first clitics in any series of clitics; and so on. All possible clitic combinations are then applied to each form in the paradigm along with the necessary spelling changes. The negative proclitic ما mA and the indirect pronominal enclitics introduced with the preposition ل are introduced as attached at this point (which is non-CODA compliant). With this information, we are able to model the verb ومابيكتبهالهم w+mA+b+y-ktb+hA+l+hm 'and+not+will+**he-write**+it+for+them' (the bolded substring is the only element from the BP).

We extended the paradigms with a total of 25 clitics, including five proclitics which are و wi 'and', ف fa 'so', the future particle ب b 'will' and the two negation particles ما mA and لا lA.

For the enclitics, we extended with all possible 10 direct object enclitics which are: ني *ny* 'me', نا *nA* 'us' , ج *ij* 'you[FS]', ك *ik* 'you[MS]' , ها *hA* 'she', هم *hum* 'them', هن *hun* 'them[FP]', كم *kum* 'you[P]', كن *kun* 'you[FP]' and their respective 10 indirect objects enclitics by adding the preposition ل *li* 'for'. With all of the additional clitics and their features, the total number of allowable feature combinations (or rows in the paradigms) increases from 19 to 24,321 per paradigm.

**Clitic Rewrite Rules** We apply a number of clitic rewrite rules which are mandated by CODA spelling conventions. One example is the change of the stem Alif Maqsura to Alif when it is not word final. For example the basic verb اشترى+ها *Aštrý+hA* 'he bought + it' is rewritten as اشتراها *AštrAhA* (ى *ý* → ا *A*). Another example is the drop of the Alif of the plural suffix pronouns وا *wA* when it is not word final. For example, اشتر0+ها *AštrwA+hA* 'they boaught + it' is rewritten as اشتروها *AštrwhA* (وا *wA* → و *w*).

### 4.9 Database Generation

To generate the database, we used the same toolkit used in (Al-Shargi et al., 2016; Eskander et al., 2016) which generates a morphological analyzer database in the representation used in MADAMIRA (Pasha et al., 2014) and CALIMA$_{EGY}$ (Habash et al., 2012a). The conversion was straightforward once we converted our paradigm and lexicon database to the forms expected by the database generation tool. This conversion included providing a POS tag for every prefix, stem and suffix. We use the Buckwalter POS tag style used by many other databases for Arabic morphology (Graff et al., 2009; Habash et al., 2012a).

### 4.10 Extending to Non-CODA Variants

The generated database at this point expects only CODA input, which is not realistic for dealing with *raw* dialectal text. We extended the database for the set of complex prefixes (pronoun prefixes and proclitics), complex suffixes (pronoun suffixes and enclitics) and stems. For the complex affixes we used the same extensions used in (Habash et al., 2012a) as we don't have enough annotated data to learn from. As for the stems, we inflected the phonological roots that correspond to the CODA roots in the lexicon to their respective stems, which are mapped to the CODA stems in the database. With these extensions we will be able to correctly model a non-CODA input like يابو *yAbw* 'they brought' as correct CODA form جابوا *jAbwA*.

## 5 Evaluation

### 5.1 Experimental Setup

**Dataset** We used a part of an Emirati novel in raw text from the Gumar corpus. We contextually annotated all the verbs appearing in first 4,000 words of the novel – a total of 620 verbs. The annotation includes identifying the CODA spelling, full Buckwalter tag and the morphemic segmentation. Table 6 shows an annotation example of one sentence from the data.

In this work we only use one dataset for the evaluation as we didn't use any feedback from the evaluation in the current state of work, i.e., this was a blind test.

**Metrics** We report token recall on verbs only. We report in terms of CODA spelling, segmentation and POS. We report in two modes of input: *raw* input and CODA compliant input of the same text. Token recall counts the percentage of the time one of the analyses returned by the morphological analyzer given a particular input word matches the gold analysis of the input word in the aspect evaluated (e.g., CODA, segmentation or POS). This is similar to the evaluation carried by Habash and Rambow (2006).

**Systems** We used six different analyzers for our experiments.

- SAMA analyzer for MSA (Graff et al., 2009).
- CALIMA$_{EGY}$ for EGY, which includes MSA (Habash et al., 2012a).
- CALIMA$_{GLF}$ for GLF.
- CALIMA$_{GLF\text{-}CODA}$ is CALIMA$_{GLF}$ without the extensions discussed in 4.10.
- CALIMA$_{GLF}$ extended with SAMA.
- CALIMA$_{GLF}$ extended with CALIMA$_{EGY}$.

### 5.2 Results

SAMA performs the least amongst all systems in all aspects which is consistent with results reported by Habash and Rambow (2006) and Khalifa et al. (2016). CALIMA$_{EGY}$ performs much

<table>
<tr><td colspan="5">Original Gulf Arabic</td></tr>
<tr><td colspan="5" dir="rtl">:: يوم الخميس :: على صوت اذان الفير [[كانت]] فطامي ناشه عليه ،، وعقب [[سارت]] [[تاخذ]]<br>شاور و [[وعت]] ابوها و مرت ابوها و عقب [[سارت]] [[اتصلي]] و [[تقرالها]]<br>كمن آيه ،، ويوم [[خلصت]] [[حضرت]] الريوق و [[دخنت]] البيت<br>و [[عدلته]] و [[نظفته]] ،، كل يوم على هالحاله ،، وهيه صابره ،،</td></tr>
<tr><td colspan="5">English literal translation<br>Thursday, upon the call for the dawn prayer, Fattami [[was]] awakened; then she [[went]] and [[took]]<br>a shower and [[woke]] her father and step mother up; and then she [[went]] to [[pray]] and [[read]]<br>few verses; and when she [[finished]], she [[prepared]] breakfast and [[scented]] the house with incense<br>and [[fixed]] it and [[cleaned]] it; every day is the same and she is always patient.</td></tr>
</table>

| Raw | CODA | Segmentation | Full POS tag | English Gloss |
|---|---|---|---|---|
| كانت kAnt | كانت kAnt | kAn+t | PV+PVSUFF_SUBJ:3FS | she was |
| سارت sArt | سارت sArt | sAr+t | PV+PVSUFF_SUBJ:3FS | she went |
| تاخذ tAx* | تاخذ tAx* | t+Ax* | IV3FS+IV | to take [3FS] |
| وعت wEt | وعت wEt | wE+t | PV+PVSUFF_SUBJ:3FS | she woke someone up |
| سارت sArt | سارت sArt | sAr+t | PV+PVSUFF_SUBJ:3FS | she went |
| اتصلي AtSly | تصلي tSly | t+Sly | IV3FS+IV | to pray [3FS] |
| تقرالها tqrAlhA | تقرا لها tqrAl hA | t+qrA+l+hA | IV3FS+IV+PREP+PRON_3FS | to read for herself |
| خلصت xlSt | خلصت xlSt | xlS+t | PV+PVSUFF_SUBJ:3FS | she finished |
| حضرت HDrt | حضرت HDrt | HDr+t | PV+PVSUFF_SUBJ:3FS | she prepared |
| دخنت dxnt | دخنت dxnt | dxn+t | PV+PVSUFF_SUBJ:3FS | she scented |
| عدلته Edlth | عدلته Edlth | Edl+t+h | PV+PVSUFF_SUBJ:3FS+PVSUFF_DO:3MS | she fixed it |
| نظفته nZfth | نظفته nZfth | nZf+t+h | PV+PVSUFF_SUBJ:3FS+PVSUFF_DO:3MS | she cleaned it |

Table 6: Annotation example. In this sentence, there are total of 12 verbs marked with [[ ]]. For each verb we provide the CODA spelling, morphemic segmentation and the full Buckwalter POS tag.

better than SAMA which is also consistent with previous results (Khalifa et al., 2016; Jarrar et al., 2014). CALIMA$_{GLF}$ outperforms both SAMA and CALIMA$_{EGY}$ on all measured conditions. The merged forms of CALIMA$_{GLF}$ (with SAMA and CALIMA$_{EGY}$) outperform CALIMA$_{GLF}$. The best system we have is the result of merging CALIMA$_{GLF}$ and CALIMA$_{EGY}$, which effectively includes GLF, EGY and MSA. The evaluation of CALIMA$_{GLF-CODA}$ highlights the added value of our non-CODA modeling, which contributed to over 11% absolute increase in recall (from CALIMA$_{GLF-CODA}$ to CALIMA$_{GLF}$) for raw input on all evaluated conditions.

## 5.3 Error Analysis

We conducted an error analysis on the analyzed verbs for CALIMA$_{GLF}$. We identified three main sources of errors. First are *typos* in the raw text which lead to no possible analysis. Examples include البس *Abls* instead of البس *Albs* 'I wear' and ادخلوو *Adxlww* instead of ادخلو *AdxlwA* 'come in'. These kinds of errors are around 19%. Second are non-CODA-compliant input words that lead to different segmentations

and POS, e.g., the word اتصلي *AtSly* (CODA تصلي *t+Sly* 'she prays') is analyzed as *AtSl+y* 'call! [FS]'. These make up around 18% of errors. Third are the out-of-vocabulary (OOV) cases, which for us include words with lemmas not in our lexicon, or words with affixes not modeled in our paradigms. For example, we encountered some EGY-like verbal constructions that we did not expect to see in GLF: تقوليلي *tqwlyly* 'you[FS] tell me' instead of تقولينلي *tqw-lynly*, تاخذولي 'you [P] take for me' instead of تاخذونلي *tAx*wnly*. These cases are about 63% of the errors. When we compare the performance of our best system (CALIMA$_{GLF}$+CALIMA$_{EGY}$) to CALIMA$_{GLF}$, we note that the errors of the first two types do not change, but there is a drop of 13% absolute in the OOV error cases.

## 6 Conclusion and Future Work

We presented CALIMA$_{GLF}$, a morphological analyzer for GLF currently covering over 2,600 verbal lemmas. CALIMA$_{GLF}$ verb analysis token recall with CODA input outperforms both SAMA and

| Analyzer | Raw Input | | | CODA Input | |
|---|---|---|---|---|---|
| | CODA | Segmentation | BW POS tag | Segmentation | BW POS tag |
| $CALIMA_{GLF}$ + $CALIMA_{EGY}$ | **90.7** | **85.5** | **87.3** | **92.7** | **92.3** |
| $CALIMA_{GLF}$ + SAMA | 89.7 | 83.9 | 84.4 | 91.1 | 90.7 |
| $CALIMA_{GLF}$ | **89.7** | **81.8** | **81.5** | **88.7** | **87.7** |
| $CALIMA_{GLF\text{-}CODA}$ | 78.4 | 70.5 | 68.7 | 88.7 | 86.0 |
| $CALIMA_{EGY}$ | 83.7 | 70.8 | 65.7 | 78.9 | 70.8 |
| SAMA | 71.6 | 52.7 | 51.8 | 64.4 | 60.3 |

Table 7: Token recall evaluation on CODA matching, Buckwalter POS tag and morphemic segmentation. Evaluation is on verbs only. The evaluated analyzers are (1) SAMA for MSA, (2) CALIMA$_{EGY}$ for EGY, which includes MSA, (3) CALIMA$_{GLF}$ for GLF, and (4) CALIMA$_{GLF\text{-}CODA}$, which is CALIMA$_{GLF}$ without the extension discussed in 4.10.

an CALIMA$_{EGY}$ by over 27.4% and 16.9% absolute, respectively, in terms of identifying correct POS tag. We plan to morphologically annotate a large portion of the Gumar corpus to learn different spelling variations and grow the coverage of lemmas. We also plan to extend CALIMA$_{GLF}$ beyond verbs using those annotations. We also plan to use a similar building process to create morphological analyzers and lexicons for other dialects given the availability of resources.

## Acknowledgments

We would like to thank Kevin Schluter and Meera Al Kaabi for helpful discussions and for providing us with transcribed entries of the Qafisheh dictionary used to build CALIMA$_{GLF}$. We also would like to thank Ramy Eskander for help in providing some of the tools we used to create the analyzer databases. We also are thankful to Maverick Alzate, who helped in the early stages of the conversion from the Qafisheh dictionary.

## References

Belal Abuata and Asma Al-Omari. 2015. A rule-based stemmer for Arabic Gulf Dialect. *Journal of King Saud University - Computer and Information Sciences*, 27(2):104 – 112.

Rania Al-Sabbagh and Roxana Girju. 2012. A supervised POS tagger for written Arabic social networking corpora. In Jeremy Jancsary, editor, *Proceedings of KONVENS 2012*, pages 39–52. ÖGAI, September. Main track: oral presentations.

Faisal Al-Shargi, Aidan Kaplan, Ramy Eskander, Nizar Habash, and Owen Rambow. 2016. A Morphologically Annotated Corpus and a Morphological Analyzer for Moroccan and Sanaani Yemeni Arabic. In *Proceedings of the International Conference on Language Resources and Evaluation (LREC)*, Portorož, Slovenia.

Houda Bouamor, Nizar Habash, and Kemal Oflazer. 2014. A multidialectal parallel corpus of arabic. In *Proceedings of the Ninth International Conference on Language Resources and Evaluation (LREC-2014)*. European Language Resources Association (ELRA).

Tim Buckwalter. 2004. Buckwalter Arabic Morphological Analyzer Version 2.0. LDC catalog number LDC2004L02, ISBN 1-58563-324-0.

Mona Diab, Nizar Habash, Owen Rambow, Mohamed AlTantawy, and Yassine Benajiba. 2010. Colaba: Arabic dialect annotation and processing. In *Proceedings of the LREC Workshop for Language Resources (LRs) and Human Language Technologies (HLT) for Semitic Languages: Status, Updates, and Prospects*.

Mona T Diab, Mohamed Al-Badrashiny, Maryam Aminian, Mohammed Attia, Heba Elfardy, Nizar Habash, Abdelati Hawwari, Wael Salloum, Pradeep Dasigi, and Ramy Eskander. 2014. Tharwa: A large scale dialectal arabic-standard arabic-english lexicon. In *LREC*, pages 3782–3789.

Ramy Eskander, Nizar Habash, and Owen Rambow. 2013. Automatic Extraction of Morphological Lexicons from Morphologically Annotated Corpora. In *Proceedings of tenth Conference on Empirical Methods in Natural Language Processing*.

Ramy Eskander, Nizar Habash, Owen Rambow, and Arfath Pasha. 2016. Creating resources for dialectal arabic from a single annotation: A case study on egyptian and levantine. In *Proceedings of COLING 2016, the 26th International Conference on Computational Linguistics: Technical Papers*, pages 3455–3465, Osaka, Japan, December.

Hassan Gadalla, Hanaa Kilany, Howaida Arram, Ashraf Yacoub, Alaa El-Habashi, Amr Shalaby, Krisjanis Karins, Everett Rowson, Robert MacIntyre, Paul Kingsbury, David Graff, and Cynthia McLemore. 1997. CALLHOME Egyptian Arabic Transcripts. In *Linguistic Data Consortium, Philadelphia*.

David Graff, Mohamed Maamouri, Basma Bouziri, Sondos Krouna, Seth Kulick, and Tim Buckwalter. 2009. Standard Arabic Morphological Analyzer (SAMA) Version 3.1. Linguistic Data Consortium LDC2009E73.

Nizar Habash and Owen Rambow. 2006. MAGEAD: A Morphological Analyzer and Generator for the Arabic Dialects. In *Proceedings of ACL*, pages 681–688, Sydney, Australia.

Nizar Habash and Ryan Roth. 2009. CATiB: The Columbia Arabic Treebank. In *Proceedings of the ACL-IJCNLP 2009 Conference Short Papers*, pages 221–224, Suntec, Singapore.

Nizar Habash, Abdelhadi Soudi, and Tim Buckwalter. 2007. On Arabic Transliteration. In A. van den Bosch and A. Soudi, editors, *Arabic Computational Morphology: Knowledge-based and Empirical Methods*. Springer.

N. Habash, R. Eskander, and A. Hawwari. 2012a. A Morphological Analyzer for Egyptian Arabic. In *NAACL-HLT 2012 Workshop on Computational Morphology and Phonology (SIGMORPHON2012)*, pages 1–9.

Nizar Habash, Mona T Diab, and Owen Rambow. 2012b. Conventional Orthography for Dialectal Arabic. In *LREC*, pages 711–718.

Clive Holes. 1990. *Gulf Arabic*. Croom Helm Descriptive Grammars. Routledge, London / New York.

Mustafa Jarrar, Nizar Habash, Diyam Akra, and Nasser Zalmout. 2014. Building a Corpus for Palestinian Arabic: a Preliminary Study. *ANLP 2014*, page 18.

Mustafa Jarrar, Nizar Habash, Faeq Alrimawi, Diyam Akra, and Nasser Zalmout. 2016. Curras: an annotated corpus for the Palestinian Arabic dialect. *Language Resources and Evaluation*, pages 1–31.

Salam Khalifa, Nizar Habash, Dana Abdulrahim, and Sara Hassan. 2016. A Large Scale Corpus of Gulf Arabic. In *Proceedings of the International Conference on Language Resources and Evaluation (LREC)*, Portorož, Slovenia.

H. Kilany, H. Gadalla, H. Arram, A. Yacoub, A. El-Habashi, and C. McLemore. 2002. Egyptian Colloquial Arabic Lexicon. LDC catalog number LDC99L22.

Mohamed Maamouri and Christopher Cieri. 2002. Resources for Arabic Natural Language Processing. In *International Symposium on Processing Arabic*, volume 1.

Mohamed Maamouri, Ann Bies, Tim Buckwalter, and Wigdan Mekki. 2004. The Penn Arabic Treebank: Building a Large-Scale Annotated Arabic Corpus. In *NEMLAR Conference on Arabic Language Resources and Tools*, pages 102–109, Cairo, Egypt.

Mohamed Maamouri, Ann Bies, Tim Buckwalter, Mona Diab, Nizar Habash, Owen Rambow, and Dalila Tabessi. 2006. Developing and Using a Pilot Dialectal Arabic Treebank. In *Proceedings of the Fifth International Conference on Language Resources and Evaluation, LREC06*.

Mohamed Maamouri, Ann Bies, Seth Kulick, Dalila Tabessi, and Sondos Krouna. 2012a. Egyptian Arabic Treebank DF Parts 1-8 V2.0 - LDC catalog numbers LDC2012E93, LDC2012E98, LDC2012E89, LDC2012E99, LDC2012E107, LDC2012E125, LDC2013E12, LDC2013E21.

Mohamed Maamouri, Sondos Krouna, Dalila Tabessi, Nadia Hamrouni, and Nizar Habash. 2012b. Egyptian Arabic Morphological Annotation Guidelines.

Mohamed Maamouri, Ann Bies, Seth Kulick, Michael Ciul, Nizar Habash, and Ramy Eskander. 2014. Developing an Egyptian Arabic Treebank: Impact of Dialectal Morphology on Annotation and Tool Development. In *Proceedings of the Ninth International Conference on Language Resources and Evaluation (LREC-2014)*. European Language Resources Association (ELRA).

Abir Masmoudi, Mariem Ellouze Khmekhem, Yannick Esteve, Lamia Hadrich Belguith, and Nizar Habash. 2014. A corpus and phonetic dictionary for tunisian arabic speech recognition. In *Proceedings of the Ninth International Conference on Language Resources and Evaluation (LREC-2014)*. European Language Resources Association (ELRA).

Karima Meftouh, Salima Harrat, Salma Jamoussi, Mourad Abbas, and Kamel Smaili. 2015. Machine translation experiments on padic: A parallel arabic dialect corpus. In *The 29th Pacific Asia conference on language, information and computation*.

Arfath Pasha, Mohamed Al-Badrashiny, Ahmed El Kholy, Ramy Eskander, Mona Diab, Nizar Habash, Manoj Pooleery, Owen Rambow, and Ryan Roth. 2014. MADAMIRA: A Fast, Comprehensive Tool for Morphological Analysis and Disambiguation of Arabic. In *In Proceedings of LREC*, Reykjavik, Iceland.

Hamdi A Qafisheh. 1977. A Short Reference Grammar of Gulf Arabic.

H.A. Qafisheh. 1997. *NTC's Gulf Arabic-English dictionary*. NTC Pub. Group.

Houda Saadane and Nizar Habash. 2015. A Conventional Orthography for Algerian Arabic. In *ANLP Workshop 2015*, page 69.

Wael Salloum and Nizar Habash. 2011. Dialectal to Standard Arabic Paraphrasing to Improve Arabic-English Statistical Machine Translation. In *Proceedings of the First Workshop on Algorithms and Resources for Modelling of Dialects and Language Varieties*, pages 10–21, Edinburgh, Scotland.

Kamel Smaïli, Mourad Abbas, Karima Meftouh, and Salima Harrat. 2014. Building resources for Algerian Arabic dialects. In *15th Annual Conference of the International Communication Association Interspeech*.

Otakar Smrž and Jan Hajič. 2006. The Other Arabic Treebank: Prague Dependencies and Functions. In Ali Farghaly, editor, *Arabic Computational Linguistics: Current Implementations*. CSLI Publications.

Houcemeddine Turki, Emad Adel, Tariq Daouda, and
Nassim Regragui. 2016. A Conventional Orthography for Maghrebi Arabic. In *Proceedings of the International Conference on Language Resources and Evaluation (LREC)*, Portorož, Slovenia.

Wajdi Zaghouani, Behrang Mohit, Nizar Habash, Ossama Obeid, Nadi Tomeh, Alla Rozovskaya, Noura Farra, Sarah Alkuhlani, and Kemal Oflazer. 2014. Large scale Arabic error annotation: Guidelines and framework. In *International Conference on Language Resources and Evaluation (LREC 2014)*.

Omar F Zaidan and Chris Callison-Burch. 2011. The Arabic online commentary dataset: an annotated dataset of informal arabic with high dialectal content. In *Proceedings of the 49th Annual Meeting of the Association for Computational Linguistics: Human Language Technologies: short papers-Volume 2*, pages 37–41. Association for Computational Linguistics.

Ines Zribi, Rahma Boujelbane, Abir Masmoudi, Mariem Ellouze, Lamia Belguith, and Nizar Habash. 2014. A Conventional Orthography for Tunisian Arabic. In *Proceedings of the Language Resources and Evaluation Conference (LREC), Reykjavik, Iceland*.

# A Neural Architecture for Dialectal Arabic Segmentation


**Younes Samih[1], Mohammed Attia[2], Mohamed Eldesouki[3], Hamdy Mubarak[3],
Ahmed Abdelali[3], Laura Kallmeyer[1] and Kareem Darwish[3]**

[1]Dept. of Computational Linguistics,University of Düsseldorf, Düsseldorf, Germany
[2]Google Inc., New York City, USA
[3]Qatar Computing Research Institute, HBKU, Doha, Qatar
[1]{samih,kallmeyer}@phil.hhu.de
[2]attia@google.com
[3]{mohamohamed,hmubarak,aabdelali,kdarwish}@hbku.edu.qa



## Abstract

The automated processing of Arabic dialects is
challenging due to the lack of spelling standards
and the scarcity of annotated data and resources
in general. Segmentation of words into their constituent tokens is an important processing step for
natural language processing. In this paper, we
show how a segmenter can be trained on only 350
annotated tweets using neural networks without
any normalization or reliance on lexical features
or linguistic resources. We deal with segmentation as a sequence labeling problem at the character level. We show experimentally that our model
can rival state-of-the-art methods that heavily depend on additional resources.


## 1 Introduction

The Arabic language has various dialects and variants that exist in a continuous spectrum. This variation is a result of multiple morpho-syntactic processes of simplification and mutation, as well as
coinage and borrowing of new words in addition
to semantic shifts of standard lexical items. Furthermore, there was a considerable effect of the
interweave between the standard Arabic language
that spread throughout the Middle East and North
Africa and the indigenous languages in different
countries as well as neighboring languages. With
the passage of time and the juxtaposition of cultures, dialects and variants of Arabic evolved and
diverged. Among the varieties of Arabic is so-
called Modern Standard Arabic (MSA) which is

the lingua franca of the Arab world, and is typically used in written and formal communications.
On the other hand, Arabic dialects, such as Egyptian, Moroccan and Levantine, are usually spoken
and used in informal communications.

The advent of the social networks and the spread
of smart phones, yielded the need for dialect-
aware smart systems and motivated the research
in Dialectal Arabic such as dialectal Arabic identification for both text (Eldesouki et al., 2016)
and speech (Khurana et al., 2016), morphological
analysis (Habash et al., 2013) and machine translation (Sennrich et al., 2016; Sajjad et al., 2013).

Due to the rich morphology in Arabic and its
dialects, *word segmentation* is one of the most important processing steps. Word segmentation is
considered an integral part for many higher Arabic
NLP tasks such as part-of-speech tagging, parsing
and machine translation. For example, the Egyptian word ومكتبهاش "wmktbhA\$" meaning: "and
he didn't write it") includes four clitics surrounding the the verb (stem) "ktb", and is rendered after
segmentation as "w+m+ktb+hA+\$". The clitics in
this word are the coordinate conjunction "w", the
negation prefix "m", the object pronoun "hA", and
the post negative suffix "\$".

In this paper, we present a dialectal Egyptian segmentater that utilizes Bidirectional Long-
Short-Term-Memory (BiLSTM) that is trained on
limited dialectal data. The approach was motivated by the scarcity of dialectal tools and resources. The main contribution of this paper is that
we build a segmenter of dialectal Egyptian using
limited data without the need for specialized lexi-




*Proceedings of The Third Arabic Natural Language Processing Workshop (WANLP)*, pages 46–54,
Valencia, Spain, April 3, 2017. ©2017 Association for Computational Linguistics

cal resources or deep linguistic knowledge that rivals state-of-the-art tools.

## Challenges of Dialectal Arabic

Dialectal Arabic (DA) shares many challenges with MSA, as DA inherits the same nature of being a Semitic language with complex templatic derivational morphology. As in MSA, most of the nouns and verbs in Arabic dialects are typically derived from a determined set of roots by applying templates to the roots to generate stems. Such templates may carry information that indicate morphological features of words such POS tag, gender, and number. Further, stems may accept prefixes and/or suffixes to form words which turn DA into highly inflected language. Prefixes include coordinating conjunctions, determiner, particles, and prepositions, and suffixes include attached pronouns and gender and number markers. This results in a large number of words (or surface forms) and in turn a high-level of sparseness and increased number of unseen words during testing.

In addition to the shared challenges, DA has its own peculiarities, which can be summarized as follows:

- Lack of standard orthography. Many of the words in DA do not follow a standard orthographic system (Habash et al., 2012).

- Many words do not overlap with MSA as result of language borrowing from other languages (Ibrahim, 2006), such as كافيه kAfiyh "cafe" and تاتو tAtuw "tattoo", or coinage, such as the negative particles مش mi$ "not" and بلاش balA$ "do not". Code switching is also very common in Arabic dialects (Samih et al., 2016).

- Merging multiple words together by concatenating and dropping letters such as the word مبيجلهاش mbyjlhA$ (he did not go to her), which is a concatenation of "mA byjy lhA$".

- Some affixes are altered in form from their MSA counterparts, such as the feminine second person pronoun ك k → كي ky and the second person plural pronoun تم tm → تو tw.

- Some morphological patterns that do not exist in MSA, such as the passive pattern Aitofa$Eal, such as اتكسر Aitokasar "it broke".

- Introduction of new particles, such is the progressive ب b meaning 'is doing' and the post negative suffix ش $, which behaves like the French "ne-pas" negation construct.

- Letter substitution and consonant mutation. For example, in dialectal Egyptian, the interdental sound of the letter ث v is often substituted by either ت t or س s as in كثير kvyr "much" → كتير ktyr and the glottal stop is reduced to a glide, such as جائز jA}iz "possible" → جايز jAyiz. Such features is deeply studied in phonology under lenition, softening of a consonant, or fortition, hardening of a consonant.

- Vowel elongation, such as راجل rAjil "man" from رجل rajul, and vowel shortening, such as ديما dayomA "always" from دايما dAyomA.

- The use of masculine plural or singular noun forms instead dual and feminine plural, dropping some articles and preposition in some syntactic constructs, and using only one form of noun and verb suffixes such as ين yn instead of ون wn and وا wA instead of ون wn respectively.

- In addition, there are the regular discourse features in informal texts, such as the use of emoticons and character repetition for emphasis, e.g. ادعووووولى AdEwwwwwwwliy "pray for me".

## 2 Related Work

Work on dialectal Arabic is fairly new compared to MSA. A number of research projects were devoted to dialect identification (Biadsy et al., 2009; Zbib et al., 2012; Zaidan and Callison-Burch, 2014). There are five major dialects including Egyptian, Gulf, Iraqi, Levantine and Maghribi. Few resources for these dialects are available such as the CALLHOME Egyptian Arabic Transcripts (LDC97T19), which was made available for research as early as 1997. Newly developed resources include the corpus developed by Bouamor et al. (2014), which contains 2,000 parallel sentences in multiple dialects and MSA as well as English translation.

For segmentation, Yao and Huang (2016) successfully used a bi-directional LSTM model for segmenting Chinese text. In this paper, we build on their work and extend it in two ways, namely combining bi-LSTM with CRF and applying on Arabic, which is an alphabetic language. Mohamed et al. (2012) built a segmenter based on memory-based learning. The segmenter has been trained on a small corpus of Egyptian Arabic comprising 320 comments containing 20,022 words from `www.masrawy.com` that were segmented and annotated by two native speakers. They reported a 91.90% accuracy on the task of segmentation. MADA-ARZ (Habash et al., 2013) is an Egyptian Arabic extension of the Morphological Analysis and Disambiguation of Arabic (MADA). They trained and evaluated their system on both Penn Arabic Treebank (PATB) (parts 1-3) and the Egyptian Arabic Treebank (parts 1-5) (Maamouri et al., 2014) and they reported 97.5% accuracy. MARAMIRA[1] (Pasha et al., 2014) is a new version of MADA and includes as well the functionality of MADA-ARZ which will be used in this paper for comparison. Monroe et al. (2014) used a single dialect-independent model for segmenting all Arabic dialects including MSA. They argue that their segmenter is better than other segmenters that use sophisticated linguistic analysis. They evaluated their model on three corpora, namely parts 1-3 of the Penn Arabic Treebank (PATB), Broadcast News Arabic Treebank (BN), and parts 1-8 of the BOLT Phase 1 Egyptian Arabic Treebank (ARZ) reporting an F1 score of 95.13%.

## 3 Arabic Segmentation Model

In this section, we will provide a brief description of LSTM, and introduce the different components of our Arabic segmentation model. For all our work, we used the Keras toolkit (Chollet, 2015). The architecture of our model, shown in Figure 2 is similar to Ma and Hovy (2016), Huang et al. (2015), and Collobert et al. (2011)

### 3.1 Long Short-term Memory

A recurrent neural network (RNN) belongs to a family of neural networks suited for modeling sequential data. Given an input sequence $x = (x_1, ..., x_n)$, an RNN computes the output vector $y_t$ of each word $x_t$ by iterating the following equations from $t = 1$ to $n$:



$$h_t = f(W_{xh}x_t + W_{hh}h_{t-1} + b_h)$$
$$y_t = W_{hy}h_t + b_y$$

where $h_t$ is the hidden states vector, $W$ denotes weight matrix, $b$ denotes bias vector and $f$ is the activation function of the hidden layer. Theoretically RNN can learn long distance dependencies, still in practice they fail due the vanishing/exploding gradient (Bengio et al., 1994). To solve this problem, Hochreiter and Schmidhuber (1997) introduced the long short-term memory RNN (LSTM). The idea consists in augmenting the RNN with memory cells to overcome difficulties with training and efficiently cope with long distance dependencies. The output of the LSTM hidden layer $h_t$ given input $x_t$ is computed via the following intermediate calculations: (Graves, 2013):

$$i_t = \sigma(W_{xi}x_t + W_{hi}h_{t-1} + W_{ci}c_{t-1} + b_i)$$
$$f_t = \sigma(W_{xf}x_t + W_{hf}h_{t-1} + W_{cf}c_{t-1} + b_f)$$
$$c_t = f_t c_{t-1} + i_t \tanh(W_{xc}x_t + W_{hc}h_{t-1} + b_c)$$
$$o_t = \sigma(W_{xo}x_t + W_{ho}h_{t-1} + W_{co}c_t + b_o)$$
$$h_t = o_t \tanh(c_t)$$

where $\sigma$ is the logistic sigmoid function, and $i$, $f$, $o$ and $c$ are respectively the input gate, forget gate, output gate and cell activation vectors. More interpretation about this architecture can be found in (Lipton et al., 2015). Figure 1 illustrates a single LSTM memory cell (Graves and Schmidhuber, 2005)

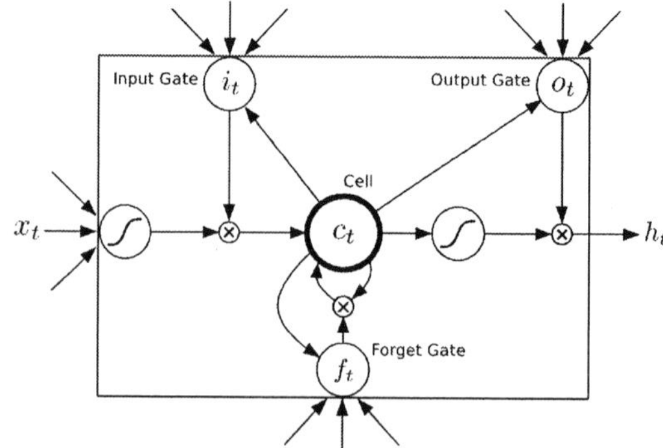


Figure 1: A Long Short-Term Memory Cell.

### 3.2 Bi-directional LSTM

Bi-LSTM networks (Schuster and Paliwal, 1997) are extensions to the single LSTM networks. They

---

[1]MADAMIRA release 20160516 2.1

are capable of learning long-term dependencies and maintain contextual features from the past states and future states. As shown in Figure 2, they comprise two separate hidden layers that feed forwards to the same output layer. A BiLSTM calculates the forward hidden sequence $\overrightarrow{h}$, the backward hidden sequence $\overleftarrow{h}$ and the output sequence $y$ by iterating over the following equations:

$$\overrightarrow{h_t} = \sigma(W_{x\overrightarrow{h}}x_t + W_{\overrightarrow{h}\overrightarrow{h}}\overrightarrow{h}_{t-1} + b_{\overrightarrow{h}})$$

$$\overleftarrow{h_t} = \sigma(W_{x\overleftarrow{h}}x_t + W_{\overleftarrow{h}\overleftarrow{h}}\overleftarrow{h}_{t-1} + b_{\overleftarrow{h}})$$

$$y_t = W_{\overrightarrow{h}y}\overrightarrow{h_t} + W_{\overleftarrow{h}y}\overleftarrow{h_t} + b_y$$

More interpretations about these formulas are found in Graves et al. (2013a).

### 3.3 Conditional Random Fields (CRF)

Over the last recent years, BiLSTMs have achieved many ground-breaking results in many NLP tasks because of their ability to cope with long distance dependencies and exploit contextual features from the past and future states. Still when they are used for some specific sequence classification tasks, (such as segmentation and named entity detection), where there is a strict dependence between the output labels, they fail to generalize perfectly. During the training phase of the BiLSTM networks, the resulting probability distribution of each time step is independent from each other. To overcome the independence assumptions imposed by the BiLSTM and exploit these kind of labeling constraints in our Arabic segmentation system, we model label sequence logic jointly using Conditional Random Fields (CRF) (Lafferty et al., 2001). CRF, a sequence labeling algorithm, predicts labels for a whole sequence rather than for the parts in isolation as shown in Equation 1. Here, $s_1$ to $s_m$ represent the labels of tokens $x_1$ to $x_m$ respectively, where $m$ is the number of tokens in a given sequence. After we have this probability value for every possible combination of labels, the actual sequence of labels for this set of tokens will be the one with the highest probability.

$$p(s_1...s_m | x_1...x_m) \tag{1}$$

$$p(\vec{s}|\vec{x};\vec{w}) = \frac{exp(\vec{w}.\vec{\Phi}(\vec{x},\vec{s}))}{\sum_{\vec{s'} \epsilon S^m} exp(\vec{w}.\vec{\Phi}(\vec{x},\vec{s'}))} \tag{2}$$

Equation 2 shows the formula for calculating the probability value from Equation 1. Here, $S$ is the set of labels. In our case $S =\{B, M, E, S, WB\}$, where $B$ is the beginning of a token, $M$ is the middle of a token, $E$ is the end of a token, $S$ is a single character token, and $WB$ is the word boundary. $\vec{w}$ is the weight vector for weighting the feature vector $\vec{\Phi}$. Training and decoding are performed by the Viterbi algorithm.

Note that replacing the softmax with CRF at the output layer in neural networks has proved to be very fruitful in many sequence labeling tasks (Ma and Hovy, 2016; Huang et al., 2015; Lample et al., 2016; Samih et al., 2016)

### 3.4 Pre-trained characters embeddings

A very important element of the recent success of many NLP applications, is the use of character-level representations in deep neural networks. This has shown to be effective for numerous NLP tasks (Collobert et al., 2011; dos Santos et al., 2015) as it can capture word morphology and reduce out-of-vocabulary. This approach has also been especially useful for handling languages with rich morphology and large character sets (Kim et al., 2016). We use pre-trained character embeddings to initialize our look-up table. Characters with no pre-trained embeddings are randomly initialized with uniformly sampled embeddings. To use these embeddings in our model, we simply replace the one hot encoding character representation with its corresponding 200-dimensional vector. Table 1 shows the statistics of data we used to train our character embeddings.

| Genre | Tokens |
|---|---|
| Facebook posts | 8,241,244 |
| Tweets | 2,813,016 |
| News comments | 95,241,480 |
| MSA news texts | 276,965,735 |
| **total** | **383,261,475** |

Table 1: character embeddings training data statistics

### 3.5 BiLSTM-CRF for Arabic Segmentation

In our model we consider Arabic segmentation as character-based sequence classification problem. Each character is labeled as one of the five labels $B, M, E, S, WB$ that designate the segmentation decision boundary. $B, M, E, WB$ represent Beginning, Middle, End of a multi-character segment, Single character segment, and Word Bound-

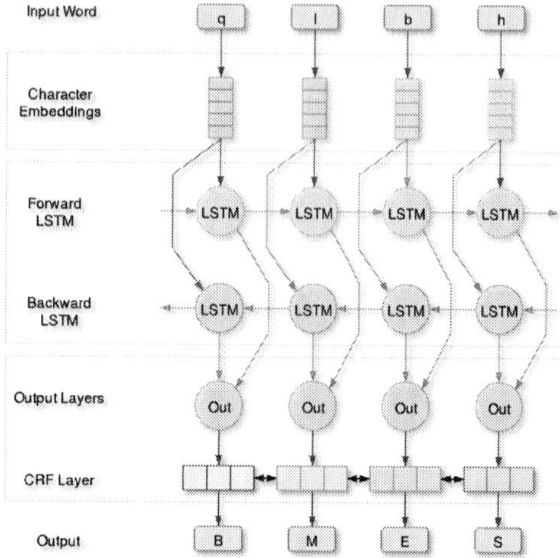


Figure 2: Architecture of our proposed neural network Arabic segmentation model applied to an example word. Here the model takes the word *qlbh*, "his heart" as its current input and predicts its correct segmentation. The first layer performs a look up of the characters embedding and stacks them to build a matrix. This latter is then used as the input to the Bi-directional LSTM. On the last layer, an affine transformation function followed by a CRF computes the probability distribution over all labels

ary respectively.

The architecture of our segmentation model, shown in Figure 2, is straightforward. It comprises the following three layers:

- Input layer: it contains character embeddings.

- Hidden layer: BiLSTM maps character representations to hidden sequences.

- Output layer: CRF computes the probability distribution over all labels.

At the input layer a look-up table is initialized by pre-trained embeddings mapping each character in the input to d-dimensional vector. At the hidden layer, the output from the character embeddings is used as the input to the BiLSTM layer to obtain fixed-dimensional representations for each character. At the output layer, a CRF is applied over the hidden representation of the BiLSTM to obtain the probability distribution over all the labels. Training is performed using stochastic gradient (SGD) descent with momentum 0.9 and batch size 50, optimizing the cross entropy objective function.

### 3.6 Regularization

**Dropout** Due to the relatively small size the training data set and development data set, overfitting poses a considerable challenge for our Dialectal Arabic segmentation system. To make sure that our model learns significant representations, we resort to dropout (Hinton et al., 2012) to mitigate overfitting. The basic idea of dropout consists in randomly omitting a certain percentage of the neurons in each hidden layer for each presentation of the samples during training. This encourages each neuron to depend less on other neurons to learn the right segmentation decision boundaries. We apply dropout masks to the character embedding layer before inputting to the BiLSTM and to its output vector. In our experiments we find that dropout with a rate fixed at 0.5 decreases overfitting and improves the overall performance of our system.

**Early Stopping** We also employ early stopping (Caruana et al., 2000; Graves et al., 2013b) to mitigate overfitting by monitoring the model's performance on development set.

## 4 Dataset

We used the dataset described in (Darwish et al., 2014). The data was used in a dialect identification task to distinguish between dialectal Egyptian and MSA. It contains 350 tweets with more than 8,000 words including 3,000 unique words written in Egyptian dialect. The tweets have much dialectal content covering most of dialectal Egyptian phonological, morphological, and syntactic phenomena. It also includes Twitter-specific aspects of the text, such as #hashtags, @mentions, emoticons and URLs.

We manually annotated each word in this corpus to provide: CODA-compliant writing (Habash et al., 2012), segmentation, stem, lemma, and POS, also the corresponding MSA word, MSA segmentation, and MSA POS. We make the dataset[2] available to researchers to reproduce the results and help in other tasks such as CODA'fication of dialectal text, dialectal POS tagging and dialect to MSA conversion. Table 2 shows an annotation ex-

---

[2]Dataset is available at `http://alt.qcri.org/resources/da_resources`

ample of the word بيقولك "byqwlk" (he is saying to you).

| Field | Annotation |
|---|---|
| Orig. word | بيقولك "byqwlk" |
| CODA | بيقول لك "byqwl lk" |
| Segmentation | ب+يقول ل+ك "b+yqwl l+k" |
| POS | PROG_PART+V PREP+PRON |
| Stem | يقول ل "yqwl l" |
| lemma | قال ل "qAl l" |
| MSA | يقول لك "yqwl lk" |
| MSA Segm. | يقول ل+ك "yqwl l+k" |
| MSA POS | V PREP+PRON |

Table 2: Annotation Example

For the purpose of this paper, we skip CODA'fication, and conduct segmentation on the original words to increase the robustness of the system. Therefore, the segmentation of the example in Table 2 is given as ب+يقو+ل+ك b+yqw+l+k. We need also to note that, by design, the perfective prefixes are not separated from verbs in the current work.

## 5 Experiments and Results

We split the data described in section 4 into 75 sentences for testing, 75 for development and the remaining 200 for training.

The concept We followed in LSTM sequence labeling is that segmentation is one-to-one mapping at the character level where each character is annotated as either beginning a segment (B), continues a previous segment (M), ends a segment (E), or is a segment by itself (S). After the labeling is complete we merge the characters and labels together, for example بيقولوا byqwlwA is labeled as "SBMMEBE", which means that the word is segmented as b+yqwl+wA. We compar results of our two LSTM models (BiLSTM and BiLSTM-CRF) with Farasa (Abdelali et al., 2016), an open source segementer for MSA[3], and MADAMIRA for Egyptian dialect. Table 3 shows accuracy for Farasa, MADAMIRA, and both of our models.

The results show that for this small test-set BiLSTM-CRF (92.65%) performs better than

[3]Available for download from: http://alt.qcri.org/tools/farasa/

| System | Accuracy |
|---|---|
| Farasa (Baseline[4]) | 88.34 % |
| MADAMIRA | 92.47 % |
| BiLSTM | 86.27 % |
| **BiLSTM-CRF** | **92.65 %** |

Table 3: $F_1$ and accuracy results on the test data. We consider Farasa our baseline. This table compares between Farasa, BiLSTM models with MADAMIRA

MADAMIRA (92.47%) by only 0.18% which is not statistically significant. The advantage of our system is that, unlike MADAMIRA which relies on a hand-crafted lexicon, our system generalizes well on unseen data. To illustrate this point, the test set has 1,449 words, and 586 of them (40%) are not seen in the training set. This shows how well the system is robust with OOV words.

## 6 Analysis

**MADAMIRA error analysis:**

When analyzing the errors (109 errors) in MADAMIRA, we found that they are most likely due to lexical coverage or the performance of morphological processing and variability.

- OOV words: e.g. الوايرلس AlwAyrls "the wireless", الهاشتاج AlHA$tAj "the hashtag".

- Spelling variation: e.g. الغطى AlgTY "the cover", لأهلى l>hly "to Ahly".

- Morphological inflection (imperative): e.g. شدي $dy "pull", فوقوا fwqwA "wake up".

- Segmentation ambiguity: e.g. ليه lyh meaning "why" or "to him", مالنا mAlnA meaning "our money" or "what we have".

- Combinations not known to MADAMIRA: e.g. متقفلوهاش mtqflwhA$ "don't close it", أوصفلكوا >wSflkwA "I describe to you".

- Different annotation convention: e.g. عشان E$An "because" and النهارده AlnhArdh "today" are one token in our gold data but analyzed as two tokens in MADAMIRA.

**BiLSTIM Error analysis:**

The errors in this system (199 errors) are broadly classified into three categories:

- Confusing prefixes and suffixes with stem's constituent letters: e.g. لطيفه lTyfh "nice", عالمي EAlmy "international".

- Not identifying segments: e.g. يارب yArb "O my Lord", قدامي qd Amy "in front of me".

- The majority of errors (108 instances) are bad sequences coming from invalid label combination, like having an E or M without a preceding B, or M without a following E. It seems that this label sequence logic is not yet fully absorbed by the system, maybe due to the small amount of training data.

**BiLSTIM-CRF Error analysis:**

This model successfully avoids the invalid sequence combinations found in BiLSTM. As pointed out by (Lample et al., 2016), BiLSTM makes independent classification decisions which does not work well when there are interdependence across labels (e.g., E or M must be preceded by B, and M must be followed by E). Segmentation is one such task, where independence assumption is wrong, and this is why CRF works better than the softmax in modeling tagging decisions jointly, correctly capturing the sequence logic.

The number of errors in BiLSTIM-CRF is reduced to 101 and the number of label sequences not found in the gold standard is reduced to just 14, yet with all of them obeying the valid sequence rules. The remaining errors are different from the errors generated by BiLSTM, but they are similar in that the mistokenization happens due to the system's inability to decide whether a substring (which out of context can be a valid token) is an independent token or part of a word, e.g. بخير bikhir "is well", ماشي mA$iy "OK".

## 7   Conclusion

Using BiLSTM-CRF, we show that we can build an effective segmenter using limited dialectal Egyptian Arabic labeled data without relying on lexicons, morphological analyzer or linguistic knowledge. The CRF optimizer for LSTM successfully captures label sequence logic and avoids invalid label combinations. The results obtained are comparable to a state-of-the-art system, namely MADAMIRA, or even better. Admittedly, the small test set used in this work might not allow us to generalize the claim, and we plan to run more expansive tests. Nonetheless, given that there are no standard dataset available for this task, objective comparison of different systems remains elusive. A number of improvements can possibly enhance the accuracy of our system further, including exploiting large resources available for MSA. Despite the differences dialects and MSA, there is significant lexical overlap between MSA and dialects. This is demonstrated by the accuracy of Farasa which was built to handle MSA exclusively, yet achieving 88.34% accuracy on the dialectal data. Thus, combining MSA and dialectal data in training or performing domain adaptation stands to enhance segmentation. Additionally, we plan to carry these achievements further to explore other dialects.

## References


Ahmed Abdelali, Kareem Darwish, Nadir Durrani, and Hamdy Mubarak. 2016. Farasa: A fast and furious segmenter for arabic. In *Proceedings of the 2016 Conference of the North American Chapter of the Association for Computational Linguistics: Demonstrations*, pages 11–16. Association for Computational Linguistics, San Diego, California.

Yoshua Bengio, Patrice Simard, and Paolo Frasconi. 1994. Learning long-term dependencies with gradient descent is difficult. *IEEE transactions on neural networks*, 5(2):157–166.

Fadi Biadsy, Julia Hirschberg, and Nizar Habash. 2009. Spoken arabic dialect identification using phonotactic modeling. In *Proceedings of the EACL 2009 Workshop on Computational Approaches to Semitic Languages*, Semitic '09, pages 53–61, Stroudsburg, PA, USA. Association for Computational Linguistics.

Houda Bouamor, Nizar Habash, and Kemal Oflazer. 2014. A multidialectal parallel corpus of arabic. In Nicoletta Calzolari (Conference Chair), Khalid Choukri, Thierry Declerck, Hrafn Loftsson, Bente Maegaard, Joseph Mariani, Asuncion Moreno, Jan Odijk, and Stelios Piperidis, editors, *Proceedings of the Ninth International Conference on Language Resources and Evaluation (LREC'14)*, Reykjavik, Iceland, may. European Language Resources Association (ELRA).

Rich Caruana, Steve Lawrence, and Lee Giles. 2000. Overfitting in neural nets: Backpropagation, conjugate gradient, and early stopping. In *NIPS*, pages 402–408.

François Chollet. 2015. keras. `https://github.com/fchollet/keras`.

Ronan Collobert, Jason Weston, Léon Bottou, Michael Karlen, Koray Kavukcuoglu, and Pavel Kuksa. 2011. Natural language processing (almost) from scratch. *Journal of Machine Learning Research*, 12:2493–2537.

Kareem Darwish, Hassan Sajjad, and Hamdy Mubarak. 2014. Verifiably effective arabic dialect identification. In *EMNLP*, pages 1465–1468.

Cicero dos Santos, Victor Guimaraes, RJ Niterói, and Rio de Janeiro. 2015. Boosting named entity recognition with neural character embeddings. In *Proceedings of NEWS 2015 The Fifth Named Entities Workshop*, page 25.

Mohamed Eldesouki, Fahim Dalvi, Hassan Sajjad, and Kareem Darwish. 2016. Qcri@ dsl 2016: Spoken arabic dialect identification using textual. *VarDial 3*, page 221.

Alex Graves and Jürgen Schmidhuber. 2005. Framewise phoneme classification with bidirectional lstm and other neural network architectures. *Neural Networks*, 18(5):602–610.

Alex Graves, Navdeep Jaitly, and Abdel-rahman Mohamed. 2013a. Hybrid speech recognition with deep bidirectional lstm. In *Automatic Speech Recognition and Understanding (ASRU), 2013 IEEE Workshop on*, pages 273–278. IEEE.

Alex Graves, Abdel-rahman Mohamed, and Geoffrey Hinton. 2013b. Speech recognition with deep recurrent neural networks. In *Acoustics, speech and signal processing (icassp), 2013 ieee international conference on*, pages 6645–6649. IEEE.

Alex Graves. 2013. Generating sequences with recurrent neural networks. *arXiv preprint arXiv:1308.0850*.

Nizar Habash, Mona T Diab, and Owen Rambow. 2012. Conventional orthography for dialectal arabic. In *LREC*, pages 711–718.

Nizar Habash, Ryan Roth, Owen Rambow, Ramy Eskander, and Nadi Tomeh. 2013. Morphological analysis and disambiguation for dialectal arabic. In *Hlt-Naacl*, pages 426–432.

Geoffrey E Hinton, Nitish Srivastava, Alex Krizhevsky, Ilya Sutskever, and Ruslan R Salakhutdinov. 2012. Improving neural networks by preventing co-adaptation of feature detectors. *arXiv preprint arXiv:1207.0580*.

Sepp Hochreiter and Jürgen Schmidhuber. 1997. Long short-term memory. *Neural computation*, 9(8):1735–1780.

Zhiheng Huang, Wei Xu, and Kai Yu. 2015. Bidirectional LSTM-CRF models for sequence tagging. *CoRR*, abs/1508.01991.

Zeinab Ibrahim. 2006. Borrowing in modern standard arabic. *Innovation and Continuity in Language and Communication of Different Language Cultures 9. Edited by Rudolf Muhr*, pages 235–260.

Sameer Khurana, Ahmed Ali, and Steve Renals. 2016. Multi-view dimensionality reduction for dialect identification of arabic broadcast speech. *arXiv preprint arXiv:1609.05650*.

Yoon Kim, Yacine Jernite, David Sontag, and Alexander M Rush. 2016. Character-aware neural language models. In *Thirtieth AAAI Conference on Artificial Intelligence*.

John D. Lafferty, Andrew McCallum, and Fernando C. N. Pereira. 2001. Conditional random fields: Probabilistic models for segmenting and labeling sequence data. In *Proc. ICML*.

Guillaume Lample, Miguel Ballesteros, Sandeep Subramanian, Kazuya Kawakami, and Chris Dyer. 2016. Neural architectures for named entity recognition. In *Proceedings of NAACL-HLT*, pages 260–270.

Zachary C Lipton, David C Kale, Charles Elkan, and Randall Wetzell. 2015. A critical review of recurrent neural networks for sequence learning. *CoRR*, abs/1506.00019.

Xuezhe Ma and Eduard Hovy. 2016. End-to-end sequence labeling via bi-directional lstm-cnns-crf. In *Proceedings of the 54th Annual Meeting of the Association for Computational Linguistics (Volume 1: Long Papers)*, pages 1064–1074, Berlin, Germany, August. Association for Computational Linguistics.

Mohamed Maamouri, Ann Bies, Seth Kulick, Michael Ciul, Nizar Habash, and Ramy Eskander. 2014. Developing an egyptian arabic treebank: Impact of dialectal morphology on annotation and tool development. In *LREC*, pages 2348–2354.

Emad Mohamed, Behrang Mohit, and Kemal Oflazer. 2012. Annotating and learning morphological segmentation of egyptian colloquial arabic. In *LREC*, pages 873–877.

Will Monroe, Spence Green, and Christopher D Manning. 2014. Word segmentation of informal arabic with domain adaptation. In *ACL (2)*, pages 206–211.

Arfath Pasha, Mohamed Al-Badrashiny, Mona Diab, Ahmed El Kholy, Ramy Eskander, Nizar Habash, Manoj Pooleery, Owen Rambow, and Ryan M Roth. 2014. Madamira: A fast, comprehensive tool for morphological analysis and disambiguation of Arabic. *Proc. LREC*.

Hassan Sajjad, Kareem Darwish, and Yonatan Belinkov. 2013. Translating dialectal Arabic to English. In *Proceedings of the 51st Annual Meeting of
the Association for Computational Linguistics (Volume 2: Short Papers)*, ACL '13, pages 1–6, Sofia,
Bulgaria.

Younes Samih, Suraj Maharjan, Mohammed Attia,
Laura Kallmeyer, and Thamar Solorio. 2016. Multi-
lingual code-switching identification via lstm recur-
rent neural networks. In *Proceedings of the Second
Workshop on Computational Approaches to Code
Switching,*, pages 50–59, Austin, TX.

Mike Schuster and Kuldip K Paliwal. 1997. Bidirectional recurrent neural networks. *IEEE Transactions
on Signal Processing*, 45(11):2673–2681.

Rico Sennrich, Barry Haddow, and Alexandra Birch.
2016. Neural machine translation of rare words with
subword units. In *Proceedings of the 54th Annual
Meeting of the Association for Computational Linguistics (Volume 1: Long Papers)*, pages 1715–1725,
Berlin, Germany, August. Association for Computational Linguistics.

Yushi Yao and Zheng Huang. 2016. Bi-directional
lstm recurrent neural network for chinese word segmentation. In *International Conference on Neural
Information Processing*, pages 345–353. Springer.

Omar F Zaidan and Chris Callison-Burch. 2014. Arabic dialect identification. *Computational Linguistics*, 40(1):171–202.

Rabih Zbib, Erika Malchiodi, Jacob Devlin, David
Stallard, Spyros Matsoukas, Richard Schwartz, John
Makhoul, Omar F. Zaidan, and Chris Callison-
Burch. 2012. Machine translation of arabic dialects.
In *Proceedings of the 2012 Conference of the North
American Chapter of the Association for Computa-
tional Linguistics: Human Language Technologies*,
NAACL HLT '12, pages 49–59, Stroudsburg, PA,
USA. Association for Computational Linguistics.

# Sentiment Analysis of Tunisian Dialect:
# Linguistic Resources and Experiments

†Salima Mdhaffar[1,2], †Fethi Bougares[1], †Yannick Estève[1] and ‡Lamia Hadrich-Belguith[2]

[1]LIUM Lab, University of Le Mans, France

[2]ANLP Research Group, MIRACL Lab, University of Sfax, Tunisia

†`firstname.lastname@univ-lemans.fr`

‡`firstname.lastname@fsegs.rnu.tn`

## Abstract

Dialectal Arabic (DA) is significantly different from the Arabic language taught in schools and used in written communication and formal speech (broadcast news, religion, politics, etc.). There are many existing researches in the field of Arabic language Sentiment Analysis (SA); however, they are generally restricted to Modern Standard Arabic (MSA) or some dialects of economic or political interest. In this paper we focus on SA of the Tunisian dialect. We use Machine Learning techniques to determine the polarity of comments written in Tunisian dialect. First, we evaluate the SA systems performances with models trained using freely available MSA and Multi-dialectal data sets. We then collect and annotate a Tunisian dialect corpus of 17.000 comments from Facebook. This corpus shows a significant improvement compared to the best model trained on other Arabic dialects or MSA data. We believe that this first freely available[1][2] corpus will be valuable to researchers working in the field of Tunisian Sentiment Analysis and similar areas.

## 1 Introduction

Sentiment Analysis (SA) involves building systems that recognize the human opinion from a text unit. SA and its applications have spread to many languages and almost every possible domain such as politics, marketing and commerce. With regard to the Arabic language, it is worth noting that the most Arabic social media texts are written in Arabic dialects and sometimes mixed with foreign languages (French or English for example).

Therefore dialectal Arabic is abundantly present in social media and micro blogging channels. In previous works, several SA systems were developed for MSA and some dialects (mainly Egyptian and middle east region dialects).

In this paper, we present an application of sentiment analysis to the Tunisian dialect. One of the primary problems is the lack of annotated data. To overcome this problem, we start by using and evaluating the performance using available resources from MSA and dialects, then we created and annotated our own data set. We have performed different experiments using several machine learning algorithms such as Multi-Layer Perceptron (MLP), Naive Bayes classifier, and SVM. The main contributions of this article are as follows: (1) we present a survey of the available resources for Arabic language SA (MSA and dialectal). (2) We create a freely available training corpus for Tunisian dialect SA. (3) We evaluate the performance of Tunisian dialect SA system under several configurations.

The remainder of this paper is organized as follows: Section 2 discusses some related works. Section 3 presents the Tunisian dialect features and its challenges. Section 4 details our Tunisian dialect corpus creation and annotation. In section 4 we report our experimental framework and the obtained results. Finally section 5 concludes this paper and gives some outlooks to future work.

## 2 Related work

The Sentiment Analysis task is becoming increasingly important due to the explosion of the number of social media users. The largest amount of SA research is carried for the English language, resulting in a high quality SA tools. For many other languages, especially the low resourced ones, an enormous amount of research is required to reach the same level of current applications dedicated

---

[1]This corpus is freely available for research purpose

[2]`https://github.com/fbougares/TSAC`



*Proceedings of The Third Arabic Natural Language Processing Workshop (WANLP)*, pages 55–61,
Valencia, Spain, April 3, 2017. ©2017 Association for Computational Linguistics

to English. Recently, there has been a considerable amount of work and effort to collect resources and develop SA systems for the Arabic language. However, the number of freely available Arabic datasets and Arabic lexicons for SA are still limited in number, size, availability and dialects coverage.

It is worth mentioning that the highest proportion of available resources and research publications in Arabic SA are devoted to MSA (Assiri et al., 2015). Regarding Arabic dialects, the Middle Eastern and Egyptian dialects received the lion's share of all research effort and funding. On the other hand, very small amounts of work are devoted to the dialects of Arabian Peninsula, Arab Maghreb and the West Asian Arab countries. Table 1 summarizes the list of all freely available SA corpora for Arabic and dialects that we were able to find. For more details about previous works on SA for MSA and its dialects, we refer the reader to the extensive surveys presented in (Assiri et al., 2015) and in (Biltawi et al., 2016).

From a technical point of view, the are two approaches to address the problem of sentiment classification: (1) machine learning based approaches and (2) lexicon-based approaches.

Machine learning approaches uses annotated data sets to train classifiers. The sentiment classifier is built by extracting discriminative features from annotated data and applying a Machine learning algorithm such as Support Vector Machines (SVM), Naïve Bayes (NB) and Logistic regression etc. Generally, the best performance is achieved by using n-grams feature, but also Part of speech (POS), term frequency (TF) and syntactic information can be used. (Shoukry and Rafea, 2012) examined two machine learning algorithms: SVM and NB. The dataset is collected from the Twitter social network using its API. Classifiers are trained using unigram and bigram features and the results show that SVM outperforms NB.

Another machine learning approach was used in (Rushdi-Saleh et al., 2011b) where they build the opinion corpus for Arabic (OCA) consisting of movie reviews written in Arabic. They also created an English version translated from Arabic and called *EVOCA* (Rushdi-Saleh et al., 2011b). Support Vector Machines (SVMs) and Naive Bayes (NB) classifiers are then used to create SA systems for both languages. The results showed that both classifiers gives better results on the Arabic version. For instance, SVM gives 90% F-measure on OCA compared to 86.9% on *EVOCA*.

(Abdul-Mageed et al., 2012), have presented SAMAR, a sentiment analysis system for Arabic social media, which requires identifying whether the text is objective or subjective before identifying its polarity. The proposed system uses the SVM-light toolkit for classification.

In lexicon-based approaches, opinion word lexicon are usually created. An opinion word lexicon is a list of words with annotated opinion polarities and through these polarities the application determine the polarity of blocks of text. (Bayoudhi et al., 2015) presented a lexicon based approach for MSA. First, a lexicon has been built following a semi automatic approach. Then, the lexicon entries were used to detect opinion words and assign to each one a sentiment class. This approach takes into account the advanced linguistic phenomena such as negation and intensification. The introduced method was evaluated using a large multi-domain annotated sentiment corpus segmented into discourse segments. Another work has been done in (Al-Ayyoub et al., 2015) where authors built a sentiment lexicon of about 120,000 Arabic words and created a SA system on top of it. They reported a 86.89% of classification accuracy.

## 3 Tunisian dialect and its challenges

The Arabic dialects vary widely in between regions and to a lesser extent from city to city in each region. The Tunisian dialect is a subset of the Arabic dialects of the Western group usually associated with the Arabic of the Maghreb and is commonly known, as the "Darija or Tounsi". It is used in oral communication of the daily life of Tunisians. In addition to the words from Modern Standard Arabic, Tunisian dialect is characterized by the presence of words borrowed from French, Berber, Italian, Turkish and Spanish. This phenomenon is due to many factors and historical events such as the Islamic invasions, French colonization and immigrations.

Nowadays, the Tunisian dialect is more often used in interviews, telephone conversations and public services. Moreover, Tunisian dialect is becoming very present in blogs, forums and online user comments. Therefore, it is important to consider this dialect in the context of Natural Lan-

| Corpus | Size | Language | Source | Reference |
|---|---|---|---|---|
| ASDT | 10000 com | MSA/dialects | Twitter | (Nabil et al., 2015) |
| OCA | 500 doc | MSA | Webpages/Films | (Rushdi-Saleh et al., 2011a) |
| BBN | 1200 com | Levant dialect | Social media | (Zbib et al., 2012) |
| LABR | 63000 com | MSA/dialects | goodreads | (Nabil et al., 2014) |
| ATT | 2154 com | MSA/dialects | TripAdvisor | (ElSahar and El-Beltagy, 2015) |
| HTL | 15572 com | MSA/dialects | TripAdvisor | (ElSahar and El-Beltagy, 2015) |
| MOV | 1524 com | MSA/dialects | elcinema | (ElSahar and El-Beltagy, 2015) |
| PROD | 4272 com | MSA/dialects | souq | (ElSahar and El-Beltagy, 2015) |
| RES | 10970 com | MSA/dialects | qaym | (ElSahar and El-Beltagy, 2015) |
| Twitter DataSet | 2000 com | MSA/Jordanian | Twitter | (Abdulla et al., 2013) |
| Syria Tweets | 2000 com | Syrian | Twitter | (Mohammad et al., 2015) |
| MASC | 8861 com | dialects | Jeeran/qaym/ Twitter/Facebook/ Google Play | (Al-Moslmi et al., 2017) |

Table 1: Publically available Arabic SA datasets. Sizes are presented by the number of documents (doc) and commentaries (com).

guage Processing (NLP). The development of SA system for Tunisian dialect faces many challenges due to: (1) the very limited number of previous research conducted in this dialect, (2) the lack of freely available resources for SA in this dialect, (3) and the absence of standard orthographies (Maamouri et al., 2014) (Zribi et al., 2014) and tools dedicated to this dialect.

Indeed, textual content of social networks is characterized by an intense orthographic heterogeneity which made its processing a serious challenge for NLP tools. This heterogeneity is augmented by the lack of normalization of dialectal writing system. Moreover, social networks communication is very impacted by the personal experience of each user. For instance, Tunisian users usually uses code-switching with English or French which depends of their second language.

Table 2 presents an example to highlight the orthographic heterogeneity issue in Tunisian dialect. The example presents the Tunisian dialect translation of the English expression ”how beautiful she is! ”. The translation is a single word which could be written using several spelling variants in Latin or Arabic script in the context of social networks.

## 4   Data set collection and annotation

Being aware of the challenges related to the tunisian dialect, we decided to create the first publicly available SA data set for this dialect. This

| Arabic script | Latin script |
|---|---|
| محلاها | Mahleha |
| ماحلاها | Ma7lahe |
| ما أحلاها | Ma7leha |
|  | Ma7laha |

Table 2: Example of Tunisian dialect spelling variants of an English expression.

data set is collected from Facebook users comments. Tunisian are among the most active Facebook Users in the Arab Region[3]. In fact, Tunisia is the 8th Arabic country in terms of penetration rates of Tunisian Facebook users, and almost tied as 2nd in the region alongside the UAE (United Arab Emirates) on the percentage of most active users out of total users (Salem, 2017).

This corpus is collected from comments written on official pages of Tunisian radios and TV channels namely *Mosaique FM*, *JawhraFM*, *Shemes FM*, *HiwarElttounsi TV* and *Nessma TV* during a period spanning January 2015 until June 2016.

The collected corpus, called **TSAC** (**T**unisian **S**entiment **A**nalysis **C**orpus), contains 17k user comments manually annotated to positive and negative polarities. Table 4 shows the basic statistics. In particular, we give the number of words, the number of unique words and the average length of

---

[3]http://www.arabsocialmediareport.com/ home/index.aspx

comments per polarity. We provide also the number of Arabic words and mixed comments.

|  | **Positive** | **Negative** |
|---|---|---|
| # Total Words | 63874 | 49322 |
| # Unique Words | 24508 | 17621 |
| AVG sentence length | 7.22 | 6.00 |
| # Arabic Words | 13896 | 8048 |
| # Mixed comments | 98 | 48 |
| # Comments | 8215 | 8845 |

Table 3: Statistics of the **TSAC** corpus.

The collected corpus is characterized by the use of informal and non-standard vocabulary such as repeated letters and non-standard abbreviations, the presence of onomatopoeia (e.g. pff, hhh, etc) and non linguistic content such as emoticons. Furthermore, the data set contains comments written in Arabic scripts, Latin scripts known as Arabizi (Darwish, 2014) and even a mixture of both. **TSAC** is a multi-domain corpus consisting of the text covering a maximum vocabulary from education, social and politics domain.

Given the nature of the raw collected data we did some cleaning before the annotation step. We manually : (1) removed the comments that are fully in other languages (French, English, etc.); (2) deleted the user names; (3) deleted URLs and (4) removed hash character from all Hashtags. Table 4, presents several examples for each polarity. We also added the Buckwalter transliteration and the English translation for the purpose of clarity.

## 5 Experiments and results

From machine learning perspective, the SA could be represented as text classification problem (binary classification in our case). In this section we present several experiments that we run in order to find out (1) the most desirable machine learning algorithms for our task and (2) the usefulness of training data from MSA and other dialects for the Tunisian dialect SA.

### 5.1 Training Data and features extraction

Table 5 presents the training and evalaution sets. For each corpus we report the dialect, the number of comments per polarity (positive /negative) and the vocabulary size ($|V|$). We used 3 different training corpus, OCA (**O**pinion **C**orpus for **A**rabic), LABR (**L**arge-scale **A**rabic **B**ook **R**eview) and **TSAC**. The OCA corpus contains

500 movie reviews in MSA, collected from forums and websites. It is divided into 250 positive and 250 negative reviews. In this work, we used a sentence level segmented version of OCA corpus described in (Bayoudhi et al., 2015)[4]. The LABR corpus is freely available[5] and contains over 63k book reviews written in MSA and different Arabic dialects. In our experiments we refer to this corpus as mixed dialect corpus (**D_Mix**). The evaluation corpus is a held-out portion, randomly extracted from the **TSAC** corpus to evaluate and compare different SA systems on Tunisian dialect.

In the literature, different linguistic features are generally extracted and successfully used for the SA task. Given the absence of linguistic tools (Part-of-Speech tagger, morphological analysers, lemmatizers, parsers, etc) for Tunisian dialect, we decided to run different classifiers using automatically learned features.

A fixed-length vector is learned in an unsupervised fashion using *Doc2vec* toolkit (Le and Mikolov, 2014) which has been shown to be useful for SA in English (Le and Mikolov, 2014). In this work, each sentence is considered as a document and represented, using *Doc2vec*, by a vector in a multi-dimensional space.

### 5.2 Classifiers

In SA literature, the most widely used machine learning methods are Support Vector Machines (SVM) and Naive Bayes (NB). On top of these methods, we investigated MLP classifier. All the experiments were conducted in Python using *Scikit* Learn[6] for classification and gensim[7] for learning vector representation. The input of the final sentiment classifier is the set of features vectors from *Doc2vec* toolkit. The output is the sentiment class $S \in \{Positive, Negative\}$.

### 5.3 SA experiments and evaluation

To evaluate the performance of SA on the Tunisian dialect validation set, we carried out several experiments using various configuration.

Seven experiments were carried out for each classifier depending on the training dataset: (1) using the Tunisian dialect training set, (2) using the

---

[4]Please contact *Bayoudhi et al.* to obtain a copy of the OCA sentence level segmented corpus

[5]http://www.mohamedaly.info/datasets/labr

[6]http://scikit-learn.org/

[7]https://radimrehurek.com/gensim/

| Label | Script | Example and Buckwalter transliteration | English translation |
|---|---|---|---|
| Negative | Arabic | mlA hmjyp / ملا همجية | What Savagery |
| Positive | Arabic | mslsl rwEp / مسلسل روعة | Wonderful series |
| Negative | Latin | Bsaraha Eni mati3jibnich | Really, I do not like |
| Positive | Latin | A7sen Moumethel ye3jebni barcha | The best actor, I like it very much |
| Negative | Mixed | ma8ir ta3li9... فضايح / fDAyH | Scandal...No comment |
| Positive | Mixed | Bravo صوت رائع / Swp rA}E | Well done great sound |

Table 4: **TSAC** annotation examples. Arabic words are given with their Buckwalter transliteration.

| | | Train set | | | Evaluation set | | |
|---|---|---|---|---|---|---|---|
| Corpus | Dialect | Positive | Negative | $\mid V \mid$ | Positive | Negative | $\mid V \mid$ |
| OCA | MSA | 4931 | 4931 | 32565 | n/a | n/a | n/a |
| LABR | D_Mix | 4880 | 4880 | 94789 | n/a | n/a | n/a |
| TSAC | TUN | 7145 | 6515 | 28480 | 1700 | 1700 | 10791 |

Table 5: Training corpus. All trained systems are evaluated using the **TSAC** evaluated set.

| Classifier | Training set | Positive | | Negative | | Error rate |
|---|---|---|---|---|---|---|
| | | P | R | P | R | |
| SVM | MSA | 0.44 | 0.15 | 0.49 | 0.80 | 0.52 |
| | D_Mix | 0.50 | 0.84 | 0.52 | 0.17 | 0.49 |
| | TUN | 0.77 | 0.77 | 0.77 | 0.76 | **0.23** |
| | MSA_D_Mix | 0.51 | 0.90 | 0.60 | 0.15 | 0.47 |
| | TUN_MSA | 0.74 | 0.83 | 0.80 | 0.71 | **0.23** |
| | TUN_D_Mix | 0.68 | 0.76 | 0.73 | 0.64 | 0.30 |
| | ALL | 0.71 | 0.81 | 0.78 | 0.66 | 0.26 |
| BNB | MSA | 0.43 | 0.28 | 0.46 | 0.62 | 0.55 |
| | D_Mix | 0.51 | 0.94 | 0.58 | 0.09 | 0.49 |
| | TUN | 0.56 | 0.70 | 0.60 | 0.46 | **0.42** |
| | MSA_D_Mix | 0.51 | 0.98 | 0.67 | 0.05 | 0.49 |
| | TUN_MSA | 0.55 | 0.77 | 0.62 | 0.37 | 0.43 |
| | TUN_D_Mix | 0.54 | 0.76 | 0.60 | 0.36 | 0.44 |
| | ALL | 0.54 | 0.82 | 0.62 | 0.30 | 0.44 |
| MLP | MSA | 0.52 | 0.40 | 0.51 | 0.64 | 0.48 |
| | D_Mix | 0.51 | 0.75 | 0.53 | 0.28 | 0.49 |
| | TUN | 0.78 | 0.78 | 0.78 | 0.78 | **0.22** |
| | MSA_D_Mix | 0.53 | 0.49 | 0.52 | 0.56 | 0.47 |
| | TUN_MSA | 0.76 | 0.78 | 0.77 | 0.76 | 0.23 |
| | TUN_D_Mix | 0.75 | 0.77 | 0.76 | 0.75 | 0.24 |
| | ALL | 0.74 | 0.77 | 0.76 | 0.73 | 0.25 |

Table 6: Results of Tunisian SA experiments using various classifiers with different training sets.

MSA training set, (3) using the mixed MSA and Arabic dialects training set and (4 to 7) using different combination of these datasets.

The performance of our different SA experiments are evaluated on the Tunisian dialect evaluation set and results are reported using precision and recall measures. Precision and recall are defined to express respectively the exactness and the sensitivity of the classifiers.

## 5.4 Results and Discussion

The results of the different classifiers with different experimental setups are presented in Table 6. As expected, the best classification performance of all the classifiers are obtained when the Tunisian dialect SA system is trained using (or including) the Tunisian dialect training set. We obtained an error rate of 0.23 with SVM, 0.22 with MLP and 0.42 with BNB.

As shown in table 6 SVM and MLP obtain similar results for all experimental setups. However, lower results are obtained with BNB classifier. We notice also no improvement when the SA systems are trained with additional training data from LABR and OCA. Overall, poorer results are obtained when SA systems are trained without the TSAC corpus. This is mainly due to :

- The OCA and LABR data sets are limited to one domain (movies and books respectively), while the evaluation set is multi-domain.

- The OCA and LABR data sets are written only in Arabic character, while the evaluation set contains Latin character.

- The lexical differences between Tunisian dialect, MSA and other dialects.For example, the English word *beautiful*, is written in Tunisian: مزيانة /mizoyaAnap, in Egyptian : حلوة / Hilowapo and in MSA : جميلة / jamiylapN)

Table 7 shows several outputs of our SA system with MLP classifier. We present examples for Positive and Negative classes and for both situation : when SA predict the correct polarity and when SA system fails.

## 6 Conclusions and feature work

In this paper we have presented the first freely available annotated sentiment analysis corpus for the Tunisian dialect. We have experimented and presented several SA experiments with different training configurations. Best results for Tunisian SA are obtained using the Tunisian training corpus. We believe that this corpus will help to boost research on SA of Tunisian dialect and to explore new techniques in this field. As future works we would like to perform a deep analysis of system outputs. We are planning also to work on the TSAC corpus normalization and to extend the corpus to include the neutral class.

## References


Muhammad Abdul-Mageed, Sandra Kübler, and Mona Diab. 2012. Samar: A system for subjectivity and sentiment analysis of arabic social media. In *Proceedings of the 3rd workshop in computational approaches to subjectivity and sentiment analysis*, pages 19–28. Association for Computational Linguistics.

Nawaf A Abdulla, Nizar A Ahmed, Mohammed A Shehab, and Mahmoud Al-Ayyoub. 2013. Arabic sentiment analysis: Lexicon-based and corpus-based. In *Applied Electrical Engineering and Computing Technologies (AEECT), 2013 IEEE Jordan Conference on*, pages 1–6. IEEE.

Mahmoud Al-Ayyoub, Safa Bani Essa, and Izzat Alsmadi. 2015. Lexicon-based sentiment analysis of arabic tweets. *International Journal of Social Network Mining*, 2(2):101–114.

Tareq Al-Moslmi, Mohammed Albared, Adel Al-Shabi, Nazlia Omar, and Salwani Abdullah. 2017. Arabic senti-lexicon: Constructing publicly available language resources for arabic sentiment analysis. *Journal of Information Science*, page 0165551516683908.

Adel Assiri, Ahmed Emam, and Hmood Aldossari. 2015. Arabic sentiment analysis: A survey. *International Journal of Advanced Computer Science and Applications*, 6(12).

Amine Bayoudhi, Hatem Ghorbel, Houssem Koubaa, and Lamia Hadrich Belguith. 2015. Sentiment classification at discourse segment level: Experiments on multi-domain arabic corpus. *Journal for Language Technology and Computational Linguistics*, page 1.

Mariam Biltawi, Wael Etaiwi, Sara Tedmori, and Amjad Hudaib andArafat Awajan. 2016. Sentimnt classification techniques for arabic language: A survey.

Kareem Darwish. 2014. Arabizi detection and conversion to arabic. *ANLP 2014*, page 217.

Hady ElSahar and Samhaa R El-Beltagy. 2015. Building large arabic multi-domain resources for sentiment analysis. In *International Conference on Intelligent Text Processing and Computational Linguistics*, pages 23–34. Springer.

| User comment | System output | Reference |
|---|---|---|
| ها الطفل قلولو يسكت امان ناقصين احنا مصاطة | POS | NEG |
| يا معلم راك ماسط !! تقعد مخيب راسك | POS | NEG |
| Alah la trabahkom la daniya w la a5ra | POS | NEG |
| Rajell w m3alem tounsi wakahou | POS | POS |
| أمنة فاخر أية من الجمال ولكي كل التحية من ليبيا | POS | POS |
| جعفور يامهبلهوم مشاء الله نشيخ عليك حتي ونتي ساكت | NEG | POS |
| ممتازة ومتمكنة في التمثيل لكن نريدوا الجديد | NEG | POS |
| Mitrobi bsaraha . | NEG | POS |
| 5iiiit ech nakraha | NEG | NEG |
| هذي هي حرية التعبير إلي تحكيو علاها؟؟؟ | NEG | NEG |

Table 7: Output examples of Tunisian SA system. For each example we present the predicted output and the reference.


Quoc V Le and Tomas Mikolov. 2014. Distributed representations of sentences and documents. In *ICML*, volume 14, pages 1188–1196.

Mohamed Maamouri, Ann Bies, Seth Kulick, Michael Ciul, Nizar Habash, and Ramy Eskander. 2014. Developing an egyptian arabic treebank: Impact of dialectal morphology on annotation and tool development. In *LREC*, pages 2348–2354.

Salameh Mohammad, M Mohammad Saif, and Svetlana Kiritchenko. 2015. Sentiment after translation: A case-study on arabic social media posts. In *Proceedings of the North American Chapter of the Association for Computational Linguistics (NAACL-2015)*.

Mahmoud Nabil, Mohamed A Aly, and Amir F Atiya. 2014. Labr: A large scale arabic book reviews dataset. *CoRR, abs/1411.6718*.

Mahmoud Nabil, Mohamed Aly, and Amir F Atiya. 2015. Astd: Arabic sentiment tweets dataset. In *Proceedings of the 2015 Conference on Empirical Methods in Natural Language Processing*, pages 2515–2519.

Mohammed Rushdi-Saleh, M Teresa Martín-Valdivia, L Alfonso Ureña-López, and José M Perea-Ortega. 2011a. Oca: Opinion corpus for arabic. *Journal of the American Society for Information Science and Technology*, 62(10):2045–2054.

Mohammed Rushdi-Saleh, Maria Teresa Martín-Valdivia, L Alfonso Ureña-López, and José M Perea-Ortega. 2011b. Bilingual experiments with an arabic-english corpus for opinion mining.

Fadi Salem. 2017. The arab social media report 2017: Social media and the internet of things: Towards data-driven policymaking in the arab world. *Dubai: MBR School of Government.*, 7.

Amira Shoukry and Ahmed Rafea. 2012. Sentence-level arabic sentiment analysis. In *Collaboration Technologies and Systems (CTS), 2012 International Conference on*, pages 546–550. IEEE.

Rabih Zbib, Erika Malchiodi, Jacob Devlin, David Stallard, Spyros Matsoukas, Richard Schwartz, John Makhoul, Omar F Zaidan, and Chris Callison-Burch. 2012. Machine translation of arabic dialects. In *Proceedings of the 2012 conference of the north american chapter of the association for computational linguistics: Human language technologies*, pages 49–59. Association for Computational Linguistics.

Inès Zribi, Rahma Boujelbane, Abir Masmoudi, Mariem Ellouze, Lamia Hadrich Belguith, and Nizar Habash. 2014. A conventional orthography for tunisian arabic. In *Proceedings of the Language Resources and Evaluation Conference (LREC), Reykjavik, Iceland*, pages 2355–2361.

# CAT: Credibility Analysis of Arabic Content on Twitter


**Rim El Ballouli,**[1] **Wassim El-Hajj,**[2] **Ahmad Ghandour,**[2] **Shady Elbassuoni,**[2]
**Hazem Hajj**[3] **and Khaled Shaban**[4]

[1] Department of Computer Science, University Joseph Fourier - Grenoble 1
[2] Department of Computer Science, American University of Beirut
[3] Department of Electrical and Computer Engineering, American University of Beirut
[4] Department of Computer Science, Qatar University

```
rim.el-ballouli@univ-grenoble-alpes.fr
{we07,arg06,se58,hh63}@aub.edu.lb, khaled.shaban@qu.edu.qa
```



## Abstract

Data generated on Twitter has become a rich source for various data mining tasks. Those data analysis tasks that are dependent on the tweet semantics, such as sentiment analysis, emotion mining, and rumor detection among others, suffer considerably if the tweet is not credible, not real, or spam. In this paper, we perform an extensive analysis on credibility of Arabic content on Twitter. We also build a classification model (CAT) to automatically predict the credibility of a given Arabic tweet. Of particular originality is the inclusion of features extracted directly or indirectly from the author's profile and timeline. To train and test CAT, we annotated for credibility a data set of $9,000$ Arabic tweets that are topic independent. CAT achieved consistent improvements in predicting the credibility of the tweets when compared to several baselines and when compared to the state-of-the-art approach with an improvement of $21\%$ in weighted average F-measure. We also conducted experiments to highlight the importance of the user-based features as opposed to the content-based features. We conclude our work with a feature reduction experiment that highlights the best indicative features of credibility.


## 1 Introduction

The Web has become a treasured source of opinions, news and information about current events. Twitter, Facebook, Instagram, and others play a vital role in publishing such information. This immense data has become a vital and rich source for tasks such as popularity index, elections, opinion mining, pro/con classification, emotion recognition, rumor detection, etc.

With the large scale of data generated on these outlets, it is inevitable that the credibility of the generated information would highly vary. This would in turn influence the opinions of the readers and the accuracy of the tasks performed on such data. A recent study by (Allcott and Gentzkow, 2017) indicated that fake news published on social media during and before the American presidential elections in November 2016, did have an effect on voters, but was not the reason behind the victory of Trump. Others suggest otherwise and confirm that fake news made Trump president. Take for instance an interview with the Washington Post, when fake news writer and promoter Paul Horner said that "I think Trump is in the White House because of me", hinting that his fake news were believed by the voters and even adopted and shared [1].

In this paper, we focus on tweets, being a main source of news and opinions, and propose a model, called CAT, that best classifies tweets as credible or not. We adopt the Merriam Webster definition of credibility that states: credibility is the quality of being believed or accepted as true, real or honest. CAT uses a binary classifier that classifies a given tweet as either credible or not. CAT is built on top of an exhaustive set of features which includes both content based and user-based features. Content-based features are features extracted from the tweet itself, for instance, sentiment, language, and text cues, whereas user-based features are extracted from the tweet author, for instance, exper-

---

[1] `https://goo.gl/3txvTd`




*Proceedings of The Third Arabic Natural Language Processing Workshop (WANLP)*, pages 62–71,
Valencia, Spain, April 3, 2017. ©2017 Association for Computational Linguistics

tise of the user generating the tweet, and the number of followers. In particular, we use 26 content-based features and 22 user-based features.

To train and test our classifier, we extracted over 9,000 Arabic tweets and annotated them with the help of six well-paid human judges using a custom crowd-sourcing platform. The 9,000 tweets were divided among the judges to obtain three annotations for each tweet. The judges annotated each tweet as either "credible", "non-credible" or "can't decide". To assist the annotators in accurately assessing the credibility of a given tweet, they were provided with useful cues such as the tweet itself and its author. While we based our experiments on Arabic content, our credibility model is general enough to predict the credibility of tweets in any language provided that the necessary resources for extracting some of the language dependent features such as sentiment are available.

Predicting the credibility of tweets has been previously studied to some extent. However, to the best of our knowledge, none of the previous work considered features from timeline or profile-picture face detection to assess the credibility of a given tweet. For example, (AlMansour, 2016) relies on some features including the presence of a profile picture to perform credibility assessment. However, in our approach, we do not only evaluate the presence of a profile picture, we also take this feature one step further by using Google cloud vision API to perform face detection and extract textual information that might be available in the picture. We compared CAT to several baselines and to a recent state of-the-art approach, namely, TweetCred (Gupta et al., 2014). CAT consistently surpassed the accuracy of the baseline approaches. It also outperformed TweetCred with an improvement of 16.7% in Weighted Average F-measure. While TweetCred relies in its classification on real-time features only, CAT utilizes the authors history for any clues that might be helpful in deciding on the credibility of the tweet.

Finally, most of the previous work on predicting the credibility of tweets have been based on annotated English tweets. In this paper, we propose a robust credibility classifier (CAT) that can work for tweets in any language and we test it on a relatively big data set of Arabic tweets. Our annotated data set of 9,000 Arabic tweets is made public to act as a valuable resource for future research in this area. Another credibility data set exists, but it is smaller and topic dependent (Al Zaatari et al., 2016).

## 2   Related Work

We broadly classified research on credibility into the work done on Arabic content and that done on English content. Credibility of Arabic content has not received profound attention from researchers and as such, this area has a lot of room for improvement. For English content, some researchers tackled the problem of judging the credibility of tweets. Others tackled the problem of judging the credibility of tweet clusters, and others built classifiers to judge the credibility of tweet authors instead of tweets. We overview each line of research next.

Credibility of Arabic tweets: In (Sultan et al., 2010), the authors propose a model to identify credible Arabic news on Twitter. Their model relies heavily on the similarity of the tweet content with collected news from reputable sources. They collected both tweets and news articles on trendy topics. After text processing, they represented both the tweet and the articles as TF-IDF vectors. They relied on the cosine similarity measure between the tweet and the articles to determine the tweet's credibility. The model is able to predict credibility of previously discussed topics on the web. Yet, it fails to assign credibility values for tweets discussing breaking events.

Credibility of English Tweets: In (Gupta et al., 2014), the authors developed the first real time credibility analyzer through a semi supervised ranking model (TweetCred). They extracted a total of 45 features, all of which can be extracted in real time. Their feature set did not include features related to a group of tweets. Neither did it include user-based features that are dependent on the previous tweet posts of a user. Next, the feature vectors for all the annotated tweets were given as input to SVM-Ranking algorithm as training data set. They used the trained model as a backend for their system. When a new Twitter feed comes in real-time, the rank of the tweet is predicted using the learned model and displayed to the user on a scale of 1 (low credibility) to 7 (high credibility). TweetCred relies in its classification on real-time features only, such as, count of re-tweets, and count of friends. CAT, however, utilizes the tweeter's history for any clues that might be helpful in deciding on the credibility of the tweet.

In (Landis and Koch, 1977), the authors tackled the same problem from another perspective where they proposed an automated ranking scheme to present the user with a ranked output of tweets according to credibility. They used SVM ranking scheme to rank the results according to the perceived credibility of the information contained in the tweet.

Credibility of tweet authors: In (Canini et al., 2011), the authors designed an automatic tool to rank social network users based on their credibility and relevance to the query. They defined information credibility of a source by expertise and topical relevance of the source discussion topic. Expertise is measured by calculating the proportion of ones followers who are likely to be in the search results. Relevance is measured using LDA topic modeling. This work though fails when determining the expertise of the author, since some authors with high social network status may be non-credible in general, or non-credible when discussing certain topics that they are not experts in, or biased with respect to the topic being discussed. Add to that and as will be concluded in our work, relying solely on the author is not sufficient to decide on credibility.

Credibility of tweet clusters: In (Castillo et al., 2011), the authors built an automatic tool to assess the level of credibility of news topics. Their credibility classifier relies on topic-based features i.e. features extracted from a group of tweets and not from individual tweets. In turn, the classifier classifies a cluster of tweets or a topic as credible or non credible While, this model is useful for detecting rumor topics, it cannot detect non-credible tweets within a credible topic. Next we discuss our approach.

## 3 Methodology

The process of creating CAT and testing it passed through multiple steps that include: data set collection, data set annotation, feature engineering, sentiment extraction, experimental evaluation, and finally feature analysis. The following sections explain the details of every step.

### 3.1 Data Set Collection

The data collection started by querying twitter API while specifying two conditions: the tweet should be written in Arabic, and it should include a hashtag. We collected around 17 million tweets in a period of two weeks. The next step was to per-form data cleaning on the 17 million tweets. The following data cleaning steps were performed: 1) all tweets composed *only* of religious quotations and versus were removed. To do this we used trigram matching with dictionaries we created to remove tweets that have words such as الله ، القرآن (*Alqr|n* - The holy book of Muslims, *Allh* - God) or words matching with Ahadeeth and Athkar found in المكتبة الشاملة - "Maktabah Alshamelah" [2]. 2) all tweets that are ads were removed, 3) all tweets that are composed of *only* emoticons or love/hate words were removed, and 4) all tweets that were sexual or composed of *only* badmouth words were removed. These data cleaning steps were mainly performed using regular expressions and also utilizing a self-created list of words and emoticons. We also removed all tweets that contain a hashtag without any text appended to it and all retweets to avoid duplication. Hence, a big portion of the collected tweets were retweets. After data cleaning, we grouped the tweets by the hashtags obtaining tweet clusters, each cluster containing related tweets. To ensure the topic independence of our data set, we randomly selected 10% of the tweets in every cluster and grouped them to obtain a data set of 9, 000 tweets that includes tweets addressing a wide variety of topics. Besides retrieving tweet text, metadata about the tweet and the tweet author were collected as well. We next describe the annotation process.

### 3.2 Annotation

To facilitate the annotation process we developed an in-house platform to collect annotations. While there exits other crowd-sourcing platforms such as Mechanical Turk and CrowdFlower, we relied on our own platform due to limitations imposed by existing platforms when dealing with Arabic data. For each tweet to be annotated, we provided the annotators with two URL links. The first link provided the annotator with the tweet text as displayed on Twitter. This option provided annotators with cues such as count of retweets, favorites that the tweet received, and the authors screen name. The second link provided the complete author profile as found on Twitter. The author profile is rich with cues that annotators can use to make their decisions. These cues include the follower count, previous tweet posts, author's profile image, and in some cases a brief description about

----

[2] http://shamela.ws/

the author. These two URLs (the tweet itself and the tweet's author profile) provided the annotators with rich information that can aid them in deciding whether a tweet is credible or not. Annotators were asked to either label a tweet as "credible" or "non-credible". They were also given the option to select "can't decide" when they felt confused or unsure. We also added the option of "deleted" since some authors delete their tweets after posting them or Twitter blocks the account in which case annotators will not be able to view the tweet. Each tweet received three annotations from three different annotators. Tweets that where labeled as "can't decide" by at least two annotators have been discarded. A majority vote was used to decide on the final labels of the tweets. In total, 60% of the 9,000 tweets were annotated as credible and 40% were annotated as non credible.

To ensure good annotation quality, seven annotators were exposed to a tutorial session discussing the annotation task before starting the annotation. Each was given a sample set to annotate before being recruited to complete the full annotation task. The sample set annotation was used to check the quality of the annotation task. The sample set included gold tweets which allowed us to test how annotators performed on this task. Two groups, each having three annotators were recruited to complete the full task and received monetary compensation for their annotations. During the full annotation task, we also injected gold tweets to assess the quality of annotations. Moreover, the full annotation task included repeated tweets, which were used as an additional way to assess the quality of annotations i.e. certain tweets are repeated twice in the data set and later we verified whether the annotator annotated the same tweet similarly. All annotators passed our gold tweets and were generally consistent with their annotation across repeated tweets. Each annotator had 10% of his assigned tweets as repeated tweets. These tweets were discarded form our data set to avoid confusion on the classifier's side.

To measure the inter-rater agreement per group, we computed Fleiss' kappa, which is used to measure agreement when there are more than two raters. The kappa score between the three annotators was 0.48. While there is no precise rule for interpreting kappa scores, the work in (Landis and Koch, 1977) suggests that such a kappa score translates to having a moderate agreement between the annotators. Substantial agreement is achieved with a kappa score greater than or equal 0.61. The achieved inter-rater agreement highlights the difficulty and subjectivity of this task. Take for example the sample tweets in Table 1. Example (a) is presenting the opinion of the tweet author and since the opinion has no bad words and is not very biased, the annotators considered it credible. Example (b) is also presenting the opinion of the tweet author, but the author said that he has a proof and did not present it; consequently, the annotators considered it as not credible. Example (c) presents the tweet author's point of view that is against the Syrian regime, which some annotators who were subjective agreed with and annotated it as credible, while others did not and annotated the tweet as not credible. It is certainly difficult to achieve higher agreement in tasks that are very subjective and are affected by the annotators background.

When grouping tweets by the day of creation, we found that on average 40% of the tweets generated per day were non-credible tweets. This highlights the importance of building a credibility model for tweets.

### 3.3 Credibility Features

In this section, we discuss the content-based and user-based features that were extracted from the tweets. Our feature-set is composed of 48 features broadly categorized into content-based and user-based features. Content-based features are features extracted from the tweet itself, whereas user-based features are extracted from the tweet author. Content-based features are composed of 26 features. These features are further grouped into four subcategories, which are sentiment, social, meta, and textual features. The sentiment category is composed of the tweet sentiment, whether positive, negative or neutral. Sentiment has been previously shown to be an indicator of credibility (Castillo et al., 2011; ODonovan et al., 2012; Kang et al., 2012) and hence included in the feature-set. The social category captures the social aspects of the tweet such as the count of user mentions, the number of retweets, etc. which can be all indicators of credibility. For instance, a tweet with many retweets might be more credible than ones with few or zero retweets. The meta category is composed of a single feature which is the day at which the tweet is posted, which might affect credibility

| | |
|---|---|
| (a) | وقوف العالم متفرجاً امام القضيه السوريه ماهو إلا خوف من ثورة شعوبهم ولكن تركوا سوريا على ماهي عليه لتكون درساً لشعوبهم التي تفكر بالثوره |
| | *wqwf AlEAlm mtfrjAF AmAm AlqDyh Alswryh mAhw <lA xwf mn vwrp \$Ewbhm wlkn trkwA swryA ElY mAhy Elyh ltkwn drsAF l\$Ewbhm Alty tfkr bAlvwrh* |
| | 'the world not reacting to the Syrian war is because leaders are afraid from an uprising but their people, but the leaders left Syria in its crisis so their people will think twice before doing an uprising themselves' |
| (b) | فعلاً الثورة السورية ثورة فتنة وعندي الدليل القاطع |
| | *fElAF Alvwrp Alswryp vwrp ftnp wEndy Aldlyl AlqATE* |
| | 'the Syrian revolution is surely a sedition and i have the proof' |
| (c) | نظام الاسد قوة نزعت منهم الرحمه و الأخلاق و الدين . يارب انصر أهلنا في سوريا |
| | *nZAm AlAsd qwp nzEt mnhm AlrHmh w Al>xlAq w Aldyn . yArb AnSr >hlnA fy swryA* |
| | 'The Syrian regime is deprived from ethics, mercy, and faith. May god bring victory to the Syrian people' |

Table 1: (a) a credible tweet, (b) a non-credible tweet, (c) confusing tweet that can be credible or non-credible

(weekday vs. weekend). Finally, the textual category includes features such as the count of exclamation marks and the count of unique characters.

Here is the list of all the content-based features: positive sentiment, negative sentiment, objectivity, count of mentions, has user mention, count of retweets, tweet is a retweet, tweet is a reply, retweeted, day of week, length of tweet in words, count chars and count words, count of urls, length of tweet in chars, count of hashtags, count of unique words, count of unique chars, has hashtag, has url, count of ?, count of !, has !, has ?, count of ellipses, has stock symbol, count of special symbols (\$ !), used url shortner.

User-based features are composed of 22 features. These features are further grouped into three subcategories, which are network, meta, and timeline. Network features include features that capture the connectivity between the tweet author and other twitter users. For instance, the counts of followers and friends, highlight the popularity of the tweet author. Meta features include registration age of the author, profile picture, whether she is a verified twitter user, etc. Timeline features are features that are extracted from the author's previous tweet posts, for instance, the rate of activity of the tweet author. Here is the list of all the user-based features: count of followers, count of friends, fo/fe, fe/fo, is verified, has description, length of description, has url, has default image, does the image hold a face, length of screen name, registration age, listed count, status count, favorites count, tweet time spacing, status retweet count, retweet fraction, average tweet length , average urls/mentions ratio in tweets, average number of hashtags, average tweet length, focus of user on topic.

We extract such an exhaustive set of features to study their actual impact on credibility assessment. The extraction of most features requires simple computations, with the exception of sentiment which is more complex (discussed next).

### 3.4 Sentiment Extraction

To extract the sentiment of a given tweet, we used ArSenL (Badaro et al., 2014) which is an Arabic sentiment lexicon. Four existing resources were used in the creation of ArSenL: English WordNet (EWN) (Miller et al., 1990), Arabic WordNet (AWN) (Black et al., 2006), English Senti-WordNet (ESWN) (Esuli and Sebastiani, 2006) and the Standard Arabic Morphological Analyzer (SAMA) (Maamouri et al., 2010). For each tweet, we removed all non-Arabic tokens such as URLs, user mentions, and hashtags. Next, a tweet was tokenized and fed into MADAMIRA (Pasha et al., 2014), a morphological analysis tool for Arabic text. Finally using the lemma for each word in the tweet, we extracted its corresponding positive, negative and objective scores from the ArSenL lexicon. To compute the positive score of the whole tweet we compute the average of all the words' positive sentiment in the tweet. The same method is used to obtain the whole tweet's negative and objective scores. Other more complex methods can be used to find the tweet sentiment

[(Hobeica et al., 2011), (Al Sallab et al., 2015), (Badaro et al., 2015), (Baly et al., 2016), (Al Sallab et al., in press 2017)], but we resorted to this method for simplicity.

## 4 Performance Evaluation

In this section, we present the credibility classifier (CAT) and evaluate it vs. multiple baselines and another well-known method. We used the annotated data and the extracted features to train a random forest decision tree classifier using scikit-learn python library [3]. A majority vote was used to decide on the labels of the tweets. We validate the applicability of our classifier (CAT) by doing two different experimental setups. First, we compare CAT to three baselines. Then, we compare CAT to a state-of-the-art tweet credibility classifier - TweetCred (Gupta et al., 2014).

### 4.1 CAT versus Baselines

In this experiment, we use the 9,000 annotated tweets to train and test CAT. We trained our classifier using multiple machine-learning algorithms such as NaÃŕve Bayes, SVM and Random Forest Decision Tree, however, we only report the results of the highest attaining algorithm in terms of Weighted Average F-measure (WAF-measure), namely the Random Forest Decision Tree. The Weighted Average F-measure is the sum of all F-measures, each weighted according to the number of instances with that particular class label. The Weighted Average F-measure allows a fair comparison whilst taking into consideration the classifier performance within both credible and non-credible classes. Using 10-fold cross validation, CAT achieved a WAF-measure of 75.8%.

We compared the performance of CAT to three common baselines. The first baseline is the stratified baseline, where the classifier makes random predication in accordance to the distribution of credible and non-credible tweets in the training set. Hence, if the training set includes 80% credible and 20% non-credible tweets, the stratified baseline randomly predicts 80% of the test set to be credible and 20% to be non-credible. The second baseline is one that makes uniform predictions such that both credible and non-credible classes are equally likely. The third baseline is the majority class baseline. Such a classifier predicts all tweets to belong to a single class and this class is

the majority class in the training set. Hence, if the training set is mostly composed of credible tweets then each instance in the test set will be labeled credible. Table 2 presents the Weighted average Precision, Recall, F-measure of our classifier CAT in comparison to the three baselincs. CAT consistently surpassed the WAF-measure of the baseline approaches indicating that the user-based and content-based features we used are worthy indicators of credibility. When considering the highest WAF-measure among the baselines, CAT achieves a percentage improvement of 47% over the best baseline (difference / original number).

| Classifier | Weighted Average Precision | Weighted Average Recall | Weighted Average F-measure |
|---|---|---|---|
| CAT | 76.1% | 76.3% | **75.8%** |
| Stratified | 51.5% | 51.3% | 51.4% |
| Uniform | 52.1% | 50.5% | 50.9% |
| Majority | 35.6% | 59.6% | 44.6% |

Table 2: CAT's against baseline classifiers

### 4.2 CAT versus TweetCred

We aim to compare CAT to a competitive approach existing in the literature, namely TweetCred (Gupta et al., 2014). We treated both TweetCred and CAT as black boxes, and obtained the credibility scores for each tweet in our data set using TweetCred's API and CAT's classifier . Consequently, we have two annotations for each tweet, the first annotation obtained from CAT and the second annotation obtained from TweetCred. Given these two labels we compare the performance of CAT to TweetCred. According to our knowledge, TweetCred is the best work available on credibility classification on Twitter.

TweetCred is a real-time web-based system for assessing credibility. It relies in its classification on features that can be extracted in real-time only; hence TweetCred may assess a new twitter feed in any language. Details of TweetCred were presented in the related work section. Since we could not receive TweetCred scores for some of the tweets, we removed those tweets from the experiment and re-evaluated CATs performance, in order to keep the comparison fair. The scores obtained from TweetCred API ranged from 1 to 7, where 1 indicates low credibility and 7 indicates high credibility. To fairly compare CAT to TweetCred we must project TweetCred's credibil-

---

[3]http://scikit-learn.org/stable/

ity scores to two values, namely credible or non-credible. To determine the cut-off threshold below which a tweet is non-credible using TweetCred, we used our annotations and TweetCred scores to train a decision tree. The cut-off threshold was determined to be 3. Hence, any tweet receiving a TweetCred score less than or equal to 3 is non-credible and is credible otherwise. Table 3 depicts the Weighted Average Precision, Recall, and the WAF-measure of both TweetCred and CAT. CAT outperforms TweetCred when classifying tweets by 16.7% in terms of the percentage increase in WAF-measure. Our intuition is that CAT outperformed TweetCred because TweetCred relies in its classification on real-time features only, such as, count of retweets and count of friends, while ignoring the tweet semantics and the author clues.

| Classifier | Weighted Average Precision | Weighted Average Recall | Weighted Average F-measure |
|---|---|---|---|
| CAT | 66.8% | 67.1% | **67.1%** |
| TweetCred | 58.6% | 56.9% | **57.5%** |

Table 3: CAT's against TweetCred Classifier

## 5 Feature Analysis

### 5.1 Content-based vs. User-based features

In this section, we present comparative analysis when training our classifier using content-based features versus user-based features. The main objective of this comparison is to know whether content based features only or user-based features only can be used as deciders for credibility. We trained our classifier using user-based features only and performed 10-fold cross validation. We repeated the same experiment but using content-based features only. As shown in table 4, a WAF-measure of 68.9% was achieved when using user-based features alone, which is 0.2% more than the WAF-measure achieved when content-based features were used alone. However, the best results are achieved when the features are combined. Consequently, we cannot solely rely on the tweet content alone or the author features alone to decide on tweet credibility; rather a combination of both cues is needed for a robust judgment.

### 5.2 Feature Reduction

In this section, we describe our feature reduction experiment that aimed at retaining worthy features and discarding features that might be misleading and harming the performance of our classifier. This process was composed of two steps. Step 1 involved picking a subset of features, and step 2 involved evaluating the efficiency of the selected subset. These two steps were repeated until the desired improvement was achieved.

| Features | Weighted Average Precision | Weighted Average Recall | Weighted Average F-measure |
|---|---|---|---|
| **user** | 69.7% | 70.1% | 68.9% |
| **content** | 69.1% | 68.5% | 68.7% |
| **CAT** | 76.1% | 76.3% | **75.8%** |

Table 4: CAT's evaluation using different feature sets

For Step 1 (picking a subset of the features), we used best-first search implementation available in WEKA - a well established data mining tool - to traverse the feature space (Hall et al., 2009). The feature space was represented as a graph and each node in the graph represented a possible combination of the available features. Hence, in total our feature space contained $2^{48}$ nodes. Edges connecting the graph nodes were determined by the content of each subset node. A node had an edge to another if the other node either added or removed a feature from the node's combination of features. Traversing the graph starting from an empty node (containing no features) and moving only along the edges that add a feature to the current combination is called forward traversal. On the other hand, starting from a full node (containing all 48 features) and moving along the edges that remove a feature from the current combination is called backward traversal. We performed feature reduction with both forward and backward traversal separately.

For Step 2 (evaluating the chosen subset), after deciding on the search direction and picking a starting node from the feature space graph, we evaluate the efficiency of the node's subset of features as follows. We build a classifier using the combination of features in the selected node and we perform 10-fold cross validation and keep track of the WAF-measure of the built classifier. Feature reduction is an optimization problem and we cannot predict how neighboring nodes will perform or whether a node will get us closer to our goal or not. Traversing the whole graph and evaluating every possible node in the feature space will give us the best feature subset, but this is not feasible. Consequently, we must determine a stale state, that is, a state after which the algorithm terminates graph traversal. The stale state for this experiment was set to 100. Consequently, the traversal algorithm terminated once it had expanded 100 nodes that did not improve on the best WAF-measure seen so far.

We evaluated around 1000-4000 subsets and the selected feature subsets were each less than half the original size, yet each outperformed the original feature set when it comes to WAF-measure. The best representative features were found to be as follows:

- User Features: Follower count, listed count, has description, has url, retweet fraction, average hashtags per tweet, average urls per tweet, tweet spacing (in minutes), expertise, average tweet length (in words), follower/friends ratio

- Content Features: count of url, negative sentiment score, count of exclamation, has url, count of unique chars, count of hashtag, count of ellipse

One of the features that was found to be highly crucial in determining the credibility of a given tweet is its sentiment, specifically the negative sentiment. Also, five of the effective features are related to URLs. For example, one of the features that was found to be very useful is the presence of a URL in the author's Twitter profile linking to her website. We found that 74% of the tweets whose authors provided a URL were credible, in contrast to only 47% of tweets whose authors' profiles were missing a URL. We conclude that tweets whose authors' profiles contain URLs are more likely to be credible than those that do not. We also noticed that the presence of a URL in a tweet is a very important feature. We found that 80% of tweets that had a URL in them were credible, whereas only 40% of tweets without a URL were credible. The above highlights the importance of the presence of a URL in both the tweet and in its author's profile. In addition, we also noticed that not only the presence of a URL is important, but also the count of URLs. For example, the average URLs count per tweet is another crucial feature. It is computed by looking at the previous tweet posts for the tweet author and computing the count of URLs she uses on average. We found that 88% of the tweets that were generated by authors who had an average of one URL per tweet in their history were credible. Moreover, we found that only 39% of tweets that did not have a URL linking to an external source were credible. On the other hand, 79% and 100% of tweets with 1 and 2 URLs, respectively, were annotated as credible.

All of the above are clear indicators of the importance of the presence and the count of URLs whether in the author profile, his/her past tweets or in the tweet itself. Next, we highlight relevant features extracted from the user timeline. Timeline features are user features extracted from the author's tweet history. The original feature set included 8 such features. To the best of our knowledge none of these features have been previously used for credibility classification. We found 5 features from the user timeline to be highly effective for credibility classification, namely retweet fraction, average URLs per tweet, tweet spacing (in minutes), average tweet length (in words), average hashtags per tweet. For instance, we observed that 85% of the tweets whose authors had on average 1.25 hashtags in their history were credible. We also noticed that authors who had a high retweet fraction had a higher probability of generating non-credible tweets.

Finally, while it is interesting and useful to know what are the most relevant features for credibility, we were also interested in finding the least important ones. To find such features we performed the same steps used to find the most important features for credibility classification however instead of using the reduced feature sets, we used their inverses. The inverse set of a reduced feature set will include all features in the feature space that have not been selected by feature reduction. One feature that was missing from all the reduced sets was the day of the week. This means that the day at which the tweet is generated has no correlation to its credibility and this is intuitive. Another irrelevant feature is the count and the presence of a user mention. Also the count of character and character to word ratio of the tweet were deemed irrelevant to credibility classification.

## 6 Conclusion

In this paper, we presented a novel credibility model for tweets called CAT. Our model is based on a machine-learning approach, and makes use of an exhaustive list of features, some of which are user based and some that are extracted from the text of the tweet itself. Our feature set includes many features extracted from the timeline of the tweet's author, which have never been looked at in the context of credibility. To test the validity of our model, we annotated a corpus of 9,000 Arabic tweets that are topic independent. The annotated corpus was used to train a binary classifier that consistently outperformed all baselines and a state-of-the-art approach in terms of Weighted Average F-measure. We also conducted a thorough analysis of the annotated corpus and carefully studied the effect of the various features on credibility prediction. For future work, we plan to incorporate Arabic specific features, for instance part of speech (POS) tags, and check their effect on classifying credibility. We also plan to try the exact method with the same set of features on tweets from other languages, and see if the proposed classifier continues to perform well on languages other than Arabic.

## References


Ahmad A Al Sallab, Ramy Baly, Gilbert Badaro, Hazem Hajj, Wassim El Hajj, and Khaled B Shaban. 2015. Deep learning models for sentiment analysis in arabic. In *ANLP Workshop 2015*, page 9.

Ahmad A Al Sallab, Ramy Baly, Gilbert Badaro, Hazem Hajj, Wassim El Hajj, and Khaled B Shaban. in press 2017. Aroma: A recursive deep learning model for opinion mining in arabic as a low resource language. *ACM Transactions on Asian and Low-Resource Language Information Processing*.

Ayman Al Zaatari, Reem El Ballouli, Shady ELbassouni, Wassim El-Hajj, Hazem Hajj, Khaled Bashir Shaban, and Nizar Habash. 2016. Arabic corpora for credibility analysis. *Proceedings of the Language Resources and Evaluation Conference (LREC)*, pages 4396–4401.

Hunt Allcott and Matthew Gentzkow. 2017. Social media and fake news in the 2016 election. Technical report, National Bureau of Economic Research.

Amal Abdullah AlMansour. 2016. *CREDIBILITY ASSESSMENT FOR ARABIC MICRO-BLOGS USING NOISY LABELS*. Ph.D. thesis, King's College London.

Gilbert Badaro, Ramy Baly, Hazem Hajj, Nizar Habash, and Wassim El-Hajj. 2014. A large scale arabic sentiment lexicon for arabic opinion mining. ANLP.

Gilbert Badaro, Ramy Baly, Rana Akel, Linda Fayad, Jeffrey Khairallah, Hazem Hajj, Wassim El-Hajj,

and Khaled Bashir Shaban. 2015. A light lexicon-based mobile application for sentiment mining of arabic tweets. In *ANLP Workshop 2015*, page 18.

Ramy Baly, Roula Hobeica, Hazem Hajj, Wassim El-Hajj, Khaled Bashir Shaban, and Ahmad Al-Sallab. 2016. A meta-framework for modeling the human reading process in sentiment analysis. *ACM Transactions on Information Systems (TOIS)*, 35(1).

W. Black, S. Elkateb, H. Rodriguez, M. Alkhalifa, P. Vossen, A. Pease, and C. Fellbaum. 2006. Introducing the arabic wordnet project. Proceedings of the 3rd International WordNet Conference (GWC-06), pp. 295-299.

Kevin Canini, Bongwon Suh, and Peter Pirolli. 2011. Finding credible information sources in social networks based on content and social structure. IEEE Third International Conference on Social Computing (Socialcom).

Carlos Castillo, Marcelo Mendoza, and Barbara Poblete. 2011. Information credibility on twitter. 20th International Conference on World Wide Web.

A. Esuli and F. Sebastiani. 2006. Sentiwordnet: A publicly available lexical resource for opinion mining. Proceedings of LREC pp. 417-422.

Aditi Gupta, Ponnurangam Kumaraguru, Carlos Castillo, and Patrick Meier. 2014. Tweetcred: A real-time web-based system for assessing credibility of content on twitter. arXiv Preprint arXiv:1405.5490.

Mark Hall, Eibe Frank, Geoffrey Holmes, Bernhard Pfahringer, Peter Reutemann, and Ian H Witten. 2009. The weka data mining software: an update. *ACM SIGKDD explorations newsletter*, 11(1):10–18.

Roula Hobeica, Hazem Hajj, and Wassim El Hajj. 2011. Machine reading for notion-based sentiment mining. In *Data Mining Workshops (ICDMW), 2011 IEEE 11th International Conference on*, pages 75–80. IEEE.

Byungkyu Kang, John O'Donovan, and Tobias HÃ¼llerer. 2012. Modeling topic specific credibility on twitter. ACM International Conference on Intelligent User Interfaces.

J Richard Landis and Gary G Koch. 1977. The measurement of observer agreement for categorical data. *biometrics*, pages 159–174.

M. Maamouri, D. Graff, B. Bouziri, S. Krouna, and S. Kulick. 2010. Ldc standard arabic morphological analyzer (sama) v. 3.1. LDC Catalog no.LDC2010L01.ISBN, pp. 1-58563, 2010.

G. A. Miller, R. Beckwith, C. Fellbaum, D. Gross, and K. J. Miller. 1990. Introduction to wordnet: An online lexical database. International Journal of Lexicography, vol. 3, pp. 235-244.

John ODonovan, Byungkyu Kang, Georg Meyer, Tobias Hollerer, and Sibel Adalii. 2012. Credibility in context: An analysis of feature distributions in twitter. Privacy, Security, Risk and Trust (PASSAT), International Conference on Social Computing (SocialCom).

A. Pasha, M. Al-Badrashiny, A. E. Kholy, R. Eskander, M. Diab, N. Habash, M. Pooleery, O. Rambow, and R. Roth. 2014. Madamira: A fast, comprehensive tool for morphological analysis and disambiguation of arabic. Proceedings of the 9th International Conference on Language Resources and Evaluation, Reykjavik, Iceland.

Mohammad Bin Sultan, Hend AlKhalifa, and Abdul-Malik AlSalman. 2010. Measuring the credibility of arabic text content in twitter. Digital Information Management (ICDIM).

# A New Error Annotation for Dyslexic texts in Arabic


**Maha M Alamri**
School of Computer Science
Bangor University
Bangor, UK
maha.alamri@bangor.ac.uk

**William J Teahan**
School of Computer Science
Bangor University
Bangor, UK
w.j.teahan@bangor.ac.uk



## Abstract

This paper aims to develop a new classification of errors made in Arabic by those suffering from dyslexia to be used in the annotation of the Arabic dyslexia corpus (BDAC). The dyslexic error classification for Arabic texts (DECA) comprises a list of spelling errors extracted from previous studies and a collection of texts written by people with dyslexia that can provide a framework to help analyse specific errors committed by dyslexic writers. The classification comprises 37 types of errors, grouped into nine categories. The paper also discusses building a corpus of dyslexic Arabic texts that uses the error annotation scheme and provides an analysis of the errors that were found in the texts.


## 1 Introduction

Gallagher and Kirk (1989) divided learning disabilities into two types: developmental learning disabilities and academic learning disabilities. Developmental learning disabilities include attention, memory, perceptual, perceptual-motor, thinking and language disorders; while academic learning disabilities include reading, spelling, handwriting, arithmetic and writing expression disorders. This paper focuses on spelling disabilities, with a focus on the spelling difficulties encountered by people suffering from dyslexia. The word dyslexia originates from the Greek and signifies "difficulty with words" (Ghazaleh, 2011). Dyslexia International (2014) has reported that dyslexia affects around one in ten individuals.

Dyslexia has become a topic of debate in different fields, including education, psychology, neuropsychology, linguistics and other sciences.

Some studies have attempted to analyse and explain textual errors committed by writers with this condition, though to date there is no standard error classification specifically for dyslexia errors.

Most of the studies carried out in this field did not categorise the errors but focused only on listing them. This study addresses this gap by developing a new dyslexia error classification system based on the results of a number of dyslexia error analysis studies as described in the next section.

This paper is organised as follows. Section 2 covers studies that discuss the errors caused by dyslexia. Section 3 describes the classifications used to annotate Arabic dyslexia errors. Section 4 contains an evaluation of these classifications. Section 5 discusses building the Arabic dyslexia corpus, followed by section 6 which explains the annotation process. Section 7 shows the analysis of dyslexic errors. Lastly, some suggestions for further work and conclusions are presented in Section 8.

## 2 Basis of dyslexic error classification for Arabic texts (DECA)

The DECA developed for this study relies on the findings of the studies mentioned below that discuss dyslexia errors from different aspects. For instance, Burhan et al. (2014), discuss the errors using a survey of teachers on which errors they believe are most common.

According to Ali (2011), spelling disabilities often cause letter reversals, also known as mirror writing and writing from left to right. As Arabic is written from right to left, writing from left to right can result in a correctly written sentence; mirror writing causes the sentence to be reversed. Ali (2011) also highlights other common errors including omission, addition, substitution and transposition. Dyslexic students also have difficulties




*Proceedings of The Third Arabic Natural Language Processing Workshop (WANLP)*, pages 72–78,
Valencia, Spain, April 3, 2017. ©2017 Association for Computational Linguistics

differentiating between letters with similar forms and different sounds.

Abu-Rabia and Taha (2004) examined the spelling mistakes made by speakers and writers of Arabic. They compared dyslexia with two groups of participants, namely, participants with, a young readers' group, matched with the dyslexic participants by reading level and an age-matched group. The study revealed seven types of errors: phonetic errors, semi-phonetic errors, dysphonetic errors, visual letter confusion, errors relating to irregular spelling rules, word omission and functional word omission. Other errors included students spelling an Arabic word according to how it is pronounced in the local spoken dialect of Arabic that they use in their day-to-day life, rather than using the correct Arabic spelling for it.

In order to examine the errors of female students with dyslexia Alamri and Teahan (2013) created a corpus of 1,067 words in a pilot project. During analysis, they identified a number of common spelling errors, including but not limited to: inability to specify the correct form of the Hamza; difficulty in short and long vowels; Tanween and exchanging ظ with ض , ض with ظ , ت with ة or

ه and ة or ه with ت .

Burhan et al. (2014) also studied common errors made by students with learning disabilities; however, they used the viewpoints of teachers to identify the degree of common errors of 28 different kinds of errors.

Abunayyan (2003) created a document called "Error Analysis in Spelling - تحليل الأخطاء في مادة الإملاء", which is used in Saudi Arabia to analyse the spelling errors of dyslexic students in primary schools, it contains 23 different error types.

The following are three studies that give a brief overview of further studies, which examined dyslexic errors, corpora or lists of errors in other languages. These studies are relevant as they are examples of error annotations language resources that have been developed in other languages (although as stated nothing similar has been done for Arabic until now).

Pedler (2007) created a spelling correction programme that focuses on errors in words committed by individuals with dyslexia. This version comprises approximately 12,000 English words and 833 marked-up errors. The corpus used in this study comprised different resources, such as homework, online typing texts, texts created by dyslexic students studying for the IT NVQ and texts created by students on the dyslexia mailing list. Pedler (2007) created an English confused words list defined as "a small group of words that are likely to be confused with one another", such as 'form' and 'from'. The list included 833 sets of words which are regularly confused that were extracted from the corpus of texts written by people with dyslexia.

Rello (2014) compiled a Spanish corpus (Dyscorpus) comprising texts written by dyslexic children aged 6-15 years. The corpus comprised 83 texts: 54 taken from school essays and homework exercises and 29 from parents of dyslexic children, totalling 1,171 errors. Dyscorpus is annotated and provides a list of unique errors.

Rauschenberger et al. (2016) collected texts written in German from homework exercises, dictations and school essays. The corpus comprised 47 texts written by 8 to 17 year old students. The texts contained a list of 1,021 unique errors. The researchers created a new resource of German errors and annotated errors with a combination of linguistic characteristics.

## 3 Dyslexic error classification for Arabic texts (DECA)

There seems to be a consensus among researchers on some types of errors made by people suffering from dyslexia, such as 'omission'. However, some types of errors are only reported in single studies, for instance the 'functional words omission' error reported by Abu-Rabia and Taha (2004). These errors were excluded from this study because the prospect of their appearance is limited.

Most of the types in the classification deal with unique specificities of the Arabic language. The system of Arabic writing contains characteristics such as diacritics which does not exist in other languages. However, there are some types in the classification that occur in other languages, such as omission, substitution and addition. A classification of annotated errors was created for the Arabic corpus of this study which can help researchers of dyslexia in Arabic understand and identify error types more easily.

The DECA classification comprises a list of errors grouped into types and categories. The category is more general than the type: it specifies whether the error occurs in the Hamza, in the Al-madd, and so forth. Each error category is further subdivided into a variable error type. The nine error categories are "Hamza, Almadd, Confusion, Diacritics, Form, Common error, Differences, Writing method, Letters written but not pronounced (or Vice Versa)". A category called "Other" was also created to handle any error that does not yet have a "tag". The first version of the classification contained 35 error types. In each category, an error type called "Other" is added if the errors are not listed in the category. Alfaifi et al. (2013) suggests the use of two characters to represent the tag: the first specifying the category and the second specifying the error type; for example, in الهمزة على الألف (Alif Hamza Above), the tag would be <HA>with the (H) indicating the category الهمزات (Hamza), and the (A) indicating the error type (Above)على الألف.

To illustrate further, if the erroneous word is ثيمر and the correct word is ثمار; thus, the writer would write ي instead of the diacritical ثِ and deleted the letter ا. The erroneous word has one wrong letter added in one location and another correct letter missing in another location. Therefore, to indicate the two different types of errors, (_) can be used between the tags as follows: <DY_AA>.

## 4 Evaluating the DECA

Pustejovsky and Stubbs (2012) suggest that on the first round of annotations, it is best to select a sample of corpus to annotate in order to find out how well the annotation task works in practice. This will also help to evaluate the comprehensiveness, appropriateness and clarity of the classification and to determine if it serves the purpose of the error analysis.

Following Pustejovsky and Stubbs (2012) approach, 5000 words were chosen as a sample. The annotators used the classification Version 1 to annotate all errors completely manually, using the original handwritten text before transcribing it into an electronic form. They then provided a list of the types of errors encountered that matched with the classification and indicated if there were any new types not listed in the classification. The findings showed that all errors in the samples were annotated using the classification, except for two new

types, which are "تكرار الحروف - Repeated letters" and " عدم القدرة على التفريق بين شكل الحرف إذا كان في بداية الكلمة أو وسطه أو نهايته - Form of the letter in the Beginning, Middle or End". Version 1 was edited to include these two errors. Therefore, Version 2 of the classification contained 9 categories and 37 errors types, as shown in Table 1.

Following this exercise, questionnaires were sent to two evaluators who had agreed to participate in this study. The evaluators were primary school teachers who teach children with learning disabilities. They were given the DECA Version 2 and were asked to read through the list of error categories and give feedback on whether they felt it comprised all the errors committed by dyslexic students and if the categories were appropriate. They were also asked to read through the sample text and tag it with the appropriate error tag.

Both evaluators found the correct tag for all sentences, except for one sentence containing the error word "Which - اللتي" where one chose the <FR>tag rather than <LT>. Both found the tags to be appropriately named. When asked how easily they found the right tag, their answers ranged from easy to difficult according to the sentence. Moreover, they found that the table presented all the types of dyslexic errors and that it was comprehensive.

## 5 Building the Arabic corpus (BDAC)

The size of the BDAC corpus is 27,136 words and 8000 errors in texts collected from Saudi Arabian primary schools, online forms and texts provided by parents. All participants were diagnosed with dyslexia by professionals. The texts written by dyslexics aged between 8 to 12 year olds, with some texts written by youths aged 13. The BDAC corpus contains texts written by both male and female students.

As some texts were handwritten, further work is needed for transcription into an electronic form. In addition, since some teachers or parents did not transcribe the correct text that the dyslexic wrote, further work is also required either by trying to find the correct text or by choosing the word in accordance with the written text as much as possible.

An example of a handwritten text written by 10 year-old girl with dyslexia shown in Figure 1.

| TAG | Error Type - نوع الخطأ | Category - فئة |
|---|---|---|
| <HH> | الهمزة على السطر - Hamza on Line | الهمزات<br>Hamza |
| <HA> | الهمزة على الألف - Alif Hamza Above | |
| <HB> | الهمزة تحت الألف - Alif Hamza Below | |
| <HY> | الهمزة على الياء - Ya Hamza Above | |
| <HW> | الهمزة على الواو - Waw Hamza Above | |
| <OH> | لم تذكر في الهمزات - Other | |
| <AA> | مد الألف - Alif Madd | المدود<br>Almadd |
| <AW> | مد الواو - Waw Madd | |
| <AY> | مد الياء - Ya Madd | |
| <OM> | لم تذكر في المدود - Other | |
| <CT> | بين التاء المفتوحة والتاء المربوطة أو الهاء - Confusion in Tah and Tah Marbuta/Hah | الخلط<br>Confusion |
| <CH> | بين الهاء والتاء المربوطة - Confusion in Hah and Tah Marbuta | |
| <CA> | بين الألف الممدودة والألف المقصورة - Confusion in Alif and Alif Maksura | |
| <CD> | بين الظاء والضاد - Confusion in Dha and Tha | |
| <CV> | الخلط بين حروف متشابهة - Confusion in Similar Letters | |
| <OC> | لم تذكر في الخلط - Other | |
| <DN> | نون مكان التنوين - N in Tanwin | الحركات<br>Diacritics |
| <DW> | واو مكان الضمة - W in Damma | |
| <DY> | ياء مكان الكسرة - Y in Kasra | |
| <OD> | لم تذكر في الحركات - Other | |
| <FW> | وصل ملحقه الفصل من الحروف أو فصل ملحقه الوصل من الحروف - Word Boundary Errors | شكل الكلمة<br>Form |
| <FR> | تكرار الحروف - Repeated Letters | |
| <FM> | أخطاء متعددة - Multi Errors | |
| <OP> | لم تذكر في الشكل - Other | |
| <MO> | حذف - Omission | الأخطاء الشائعة<br>Common errors |
| <MA> | إضافة - Addition | |
| <MS> | تبديل - Substitution | |
| <MT> | تحويل - Transposition | |
| <DD> | عدم القدرة على تفريق بين حروف متشابهة لفظا المختلفة شكلا - Different Forms, Same Phonetics | الاختلافات<br>Differences |
| <DF> | عدم القدرة على التفريق بين شكل الحرف إذا كان في بداية الكلمة أو وسطه أو نهايته - Form of the Letter in the Beginning, Middle or End | |
| <DI> | الكتابة بناء على اللهجة المحلية - Local Language | |
| <DS> | كتابة كلمة مشابهة للمعنى - Writing a Word that is Similar to the Meaning | |
| <OI> | لم تذكر في الاختلافات - Other | |
| <WM> | مرآة - Mirror | طريقة الكتابة<br>Writing method |
| <WL> | الكتابة من اليسار لليمين - Left to Right | |
| <OW> | لم تذكر في الكتابة - Other | |
| <LS> | لام الشمسية - Sun Letters | حروف تكتب ولا تنطق أو العكس<br>Letter written but not pronounced or vice versa |
| <LM> | دخول اللام على ماقبله (ال) - Adding letter (L) to words start with letters (AL) | |
| <LA> | ألف بعد واو الجماعة - Alif Fariqa | |
| <LL> | (لاكن - لاكنها ...) - (Lakn ...) | |
| <LH> | (هذا - هذه - هذان) - (Hada ...) | |
| <LT> | (اللتي) - (Allty) | |
| <LD> | (اللذي) - (Alldhy) | |
| <LK> | (ذلك - بذلك ...) - (Dahlk ...) | |
| <OL> | لم تذكر في حروف - Other | |
| <OT> | لم تذكر في أي مجموعة - Other | أخرى - Other |

Table 1: Dyslexic error classification for Arabic texts (DECA).

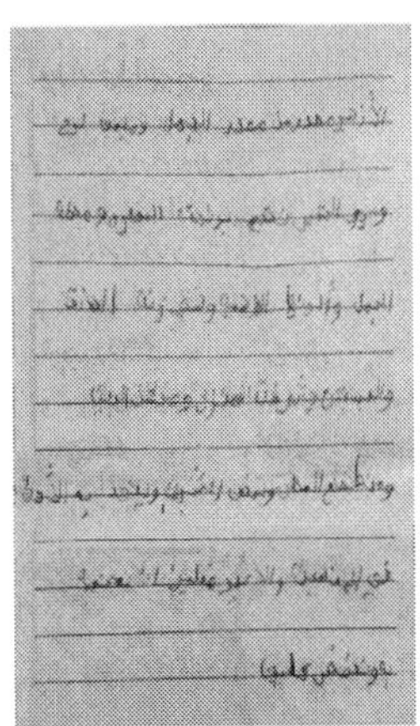





Figure 1: Text written by 10-year-old girl with dyslexia.

In comparison with other languages, three studies carried out on different languages — English (12,000 words), Spanish (1,171 words) and German (1,021 words) (Pedler, 2007; Rello, 2014; Rauschenberger et al., 2016) — provide strong evidence that a small corpus of around 1,000 errors can yield useful results.

## 6 Annotating the BDAC corpus

As Granger (2003) points out, error annotation is a very tedious task that needs to be undertaken with care, but it has an immensely significant outcome as it makes it possible for the researcher to gain quick access to particular error statistics.

In order to illustrate the annotation process, Figure 2 shows a screenshot of a Java program that was created in order to speed up the annotation process. A Java program was developed to convert (tokenise) the text into tokens. Each token is located in a separate line, and the erroneous words are manually annotated with each type of error based on the classification and the correct spelling of the erroneous word.

As shown in Figure 2, the text includes 43 tokens. In the example below, the first error is located in token 2. Thus, the annotator chose token 2, as it is an error word, by double-clicking on the error (token 2) in the text area labelled "Raw Text ـ النص الاصلي", then chose the correct word from the text area labelled "Correct Text ـ النص الصحيح", again by double-clicking. Next, the appropriate tag was selected from the list. After that, "Apply - تنفيذ" is clicked, and it appears in the "Raw Text ـ النص الاصلي" area as shown in Figure 2. The procedure is repeated with each error found in the text. In the case of a word that contains more than one type of error, as denoted by token 6, the annotator can add another tag via the "+" button, and choose another tag which is separated by (_). As a result, the annotation for token 6 is:

```
Tn="6" CorrectForm="أقتبس" Tag="HA_MA" ErrorForm="اسقتبس"
```

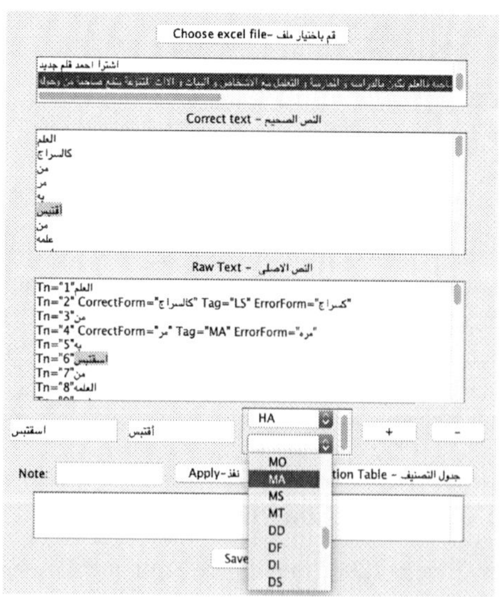

Figure 2: Screenshot of Java program to aid manual annotation process.

Each error token requires two annotations: one for the correct word and the second for the error type, as follows:

```
Tn="1" CorrectForm="الشمس" Tag="LS" ErrorForm="اشمس"
```

where:

- **Tn** = Token number (position of the word within the sentence).

- **CorrectForm** = The correct spelling of the word.

- **Tag** = Contains abbreviation of the error type.

- **ErrorForm** = The error word.

The BDAC corpus (27,136 words) has been fully annotated using DECA Version 2. The combined information was ultimately converted to an XML file as shown in Figure 3 below:

```
<Record_info>
    <Participant_info>
        <Age>10</Age>
        <Gender>Female - انثى</Gender>
    </Participant_info>
    <Text_info>
        <TextSource>HW - الواجب</TextSource>
        <Text n="1">
            <Category>word - كلمة</Category>
            <RawText>البن</RawText>
            <CorrectText>اللبن</CorrectText>
            <Error_analysis>
                <Token Tn="1" CorrectForm="اللبن" Tag="LM">البن</Token>
            </Error_analysis>
        </Text>
    </Text_info>
</Record_info>
```

Figure 3: A sample of the XML format used for the BDAC.

## 7   Analysis of Dyslexic Errors

Annotating the corpus has a significant advantage in terms of being able to search for particular error types or groups of errors in exactly the same way as individual words are searched (Nicholls, 2003). Once the annotation is carried out, corpus analysis becomes the simple procedure of extracting the tags or error and their corresponding target word. Some errors occur more than others in the corpus. Table 2 below shows the frequency of errors for the top five errors.

| Error word | Number of Occurrences |
|---|---|
| On - علا | 64 |
| Which - التي | 59 |
| Which - الذي | 47 |
| To - الى | 35 |
| That - ذالك | 31 |

Table 2: Frequency of errors.

The correct form for the first error (علا) is (على). The error type is (CA), which falls under the "Confusion – الخلط" category. The second, third and fifth errors fall under the "Letter written but not pronounced or vice versa – حروف تكتب ولا تنطق أو العكس" category, for which the correct forms are (التي) (الذي) (ذلك), respectively. Finally, the fourth error falls under the "Hamza – الهمزات" category, where the correct form is (إلى) and the error type is (HB).

The highest number of errors for specific category was for the "Common errors – الأخطاء الشائعة" category with 2,717 error words; followed by 1,621 errors in the "Hamza – الهمزات" category and 1,553 errors in the "Confusion – الخلط" category. The lowest two types of errors fell within the "Differences – الاختلافات" and "Form – شكل الكلمة" categories.

The Alif Madd (مد الألف) error was the most frequent type of error making up 13.43% of total number of errors. This is in contrast with Burhan et al. (2014) finding that (كلمات مبدوءة بـ (أل) إذا سبقتها اللام المكسورة) are the most frequent type of errors made by Arabic dyslexic students from the teachers' viewpoint.

The most common errors in made by dyslexic persons are addition (13.4%), omission (10.98%), substitution (6.36%) and transposition (3.23%). This contrasts with Alamri and Teahan's (2013) study which found that the highest number of errors were errors of omission rather than addition.

Dyslexic people are popularly known to confuse Tah and Tah Marbuta/Hah (بين التاء المفتوحة والتاء المربوطة أو الهاء), with

6.55% of the errors falling under this type of error. This is consistent with Burhan et al. (2014) who found that this type of error is noticeably more apparent in the writing of people who suffer from dyslexia.

## 8 Conclusion and recommendations for further work

The DECA was introduced in response to the lack of a standard classification for dyslexia errors in Arabic. It was developed on the basis of prior error classification studies. Two people assessed the DECA classification for Arabic dyslexic errors and found it to be reliable and effective. The last version of the DECA includes 37 types of errors classified under nine categories.

The findings could be helpful for the field of pedagogy in general and for researchers of dyslexia in particular. This classification is valuable and can serve as a springboard to provide improved aid to this target group and also make the annotators' task less stressful.

Further work is required to improve the DECA in collaboration with special education needs and corpus linguistics specialists. Since the BDAC was collated from writings of residents of only one country (Saudi Arabia), one way to improve the classification is by collecting further texts from various countries. This may yield different types of errors, which could then be added to the classification developed in this study as a standard error classification which could be applied to other Arabic dyslexia corpora.

## Acknowledgments

We deeply thank teachers, parents and all children for providing Arabic texts written by dyslexics.

## References

Salim Abu-Rabia and Haitham Taha. 2004. Reading and spelling error analysis of native. *Reading and Writing*, 17(7-8):651–690.

Ibrahim S. Abunayyan. 2003. Error analysis in spelling (form 5 /M3).

Maha M. Alamri and William J. Teahan. 2013. Investigating dyslexic Arabic text. Master's thesis, School of Computer Science, Bangor.

Abdullah Alfaifi, Eric Atwell, and Ghazi Abuhakema. 2013. Error annotation of the arabic learner corpus. In *Language Processing and Knowledge in the Web*, pages 14–22. Springer.

Mohammed A. M. Ali. 2011. *Learning difficulties between skills and disorders*. Dar Safa Publishing - Distribution, Amman.

Hamadneh Burhan, Mohammad M. Al-Salahat, Maher T. Al-Shradgeh, and Wael A. Alali. 2014. Degree of common misspellings of students with learning disabilities. *The International Interdisciplinary Journal of Education (IIJOE)*, 3(6).

Dyslexia International. 2014. DI-Duke report, April.

James J. Gallagher and Samuel A. Kirk. 1989. *Educating exceptional children*. Boston: Houghton Mifflin Company.

Esfandiari B. Ghazaleh. 2011. A study of developmental dyslexia in middle school foreign language learners in iran. *Argumentum*, 7:159–169.

Sylviane Granger. 2003. Error-tagged learner corpora and call: A promising synergy. *CALICO journal*, pages 465–480.

Diane Nicholls. 2003. The cambridge learner corpus: Error coding and analysis for lexicography and elt. In *Proceedings of the Corpus Linguistics 2003 conference*, volume 16, pages 572–581.

Jennifer Pedler. 2007. *Computer correction of real-word spelling errors in dyslexic text*. Ph.D. thesis, Birkbeck, University of London.

James Pustejovsky and Amber Stubbs. 2012. *Natural language annotation for machine learning*. O'Reilly Media, Inc.

Maria Rauschenberger, Luz Rello, Silke Fchsel, and Jrg Thomaschewski. 2016. A language resource of German errors written by children with dyslexia. In *Proceedings of the Tenth International Conference on Language Resources and Evaluation (LREC 2016)*, Paris, France, may. European Language Resources Association (ELRA).

Luz Rello. 2014. *A Text Accessibility Model for People with Dyslexia*. Ph.D. thesis, Department of Information and Communication Technologies, University Pompeu Fabra.

# An Unsupervised Speaker Clustering Technique based on SOM and I-vectors for Speech Recognition Systems


**Hany Ahmed, Mohamed S. Elaraby, Abdullah M. Moussa**
**Mustafa Abdallah, Sherif M. Abdou, Mohsen Rashwan**
RDI, Cairo Egypt
Cairo University, Cairo Egypt
`hanyahmed@rdi-eg.com, mhmd.sl.elhady@gmail.com,`
`a.m.moussa@ieee.org, m.a.elhosiny@eng.cu.edu.eg`
`{sherif.abdou,mrashwan}@rdi-eg.com`


## Abstract


In this paper, we introduce an enhancement for speech recognition systems using an unsupervised speaker clustering technique. The proposed technique is mainly based on I-vectors and Self-Organizing Map Neural Network (SOM). The input to the proposed algorithm is a set of speech utterances. For each utterance, we extract 100-dimensional I-vector and then SOM is used to group the utterances to different speakers. In our experiments, we compared our technique with Normalized Cross Likelihood ratio Clustering (NCLR). Results show that the proposed technique reduces the speaker error rate in comparison with NCLR. Finally, we have experimented the effect of speaker clustering on Speaker Adaptive Training (SAT) in a speech recognition system implemented to test the performance of the proposed technique. It was noted that the proposed technique reduced the WER over clustering speakers with NCLR.


## 1 Introduction

Arabic Automatic Speech Recognition (ASR) is a challenging task, because of the dominance of non-diacritized text material, the several dialects, and the morphological complexity. Another factor that has a negative impact on the advance of Arabic ASR research is the lack of open resources to develop state of the art systems. During recent years, it has been shown that, in large vocabulary speech recognition systems, performance were significantly improved using speaker adaptation. Nowadays, speaker adaptation techniques are crucial in all the advanced speech recognition systems. Speaker adaptation uses data from specific speaker to move the parameters of a speaker-independent system towards a speaker dependent one.

Speaker clustering which is defined as; an unsupervised classification of voiced speech segments based on speaker characteristics (Margarita et al., 2008) is used to boost Speaker Adaptive training in ASR systems. The target of clustering is assigning a unique label to all speech segments uttered by the same speaker.

In recent years, several speaker clustering methods have been proposed, ranging from hierarchical ones, such as the bottom-up methods and the top-down ones, to optimization methods, such as the K-means algorithm and the self-organizing maps. Self-Organizing Map (SOM) is considered as a powerful tool for speaker clustering (Moattar and Homayounpour, 2012).

In this paper, we introduce a fast automatic speaker clustering technique based on SOM and I-Vectors (Dehak et al., 2011) as input features. Our proposed SOM has a feed-forward structure with a single computational layer arranged in 2 dimensions (rows and columns). Assigning correct speaker identification for each utterance can boost the adaptation performance in ASR systems. We have compared our technique with the well-known algorithm Normalized Cross Likelihood Ratio (NCLR). Speaker Clustering using SOM has notably reduced the word error rate of ASR results over both clustering using NCLR and the baseline system (were no speaker clustering performed).

The rest of the paper is organized as follows: Section 2 provides a description of the system used and explains the proposed fast automatic clustering algorithm; Section 3 describes the experimental results. The final conclusions are included in section 4.

79


*Proceedings of The Third Arabic Natural Language Processing Workshop (WANLP)*, pages 79–83,
Valencia, Spain, April 3, 2017. ©2017 Association for Computational Linguistics

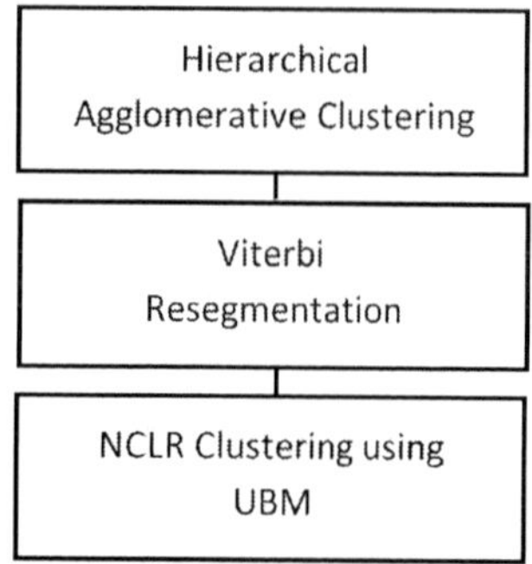

Figure 1: NCLR Block Diagram

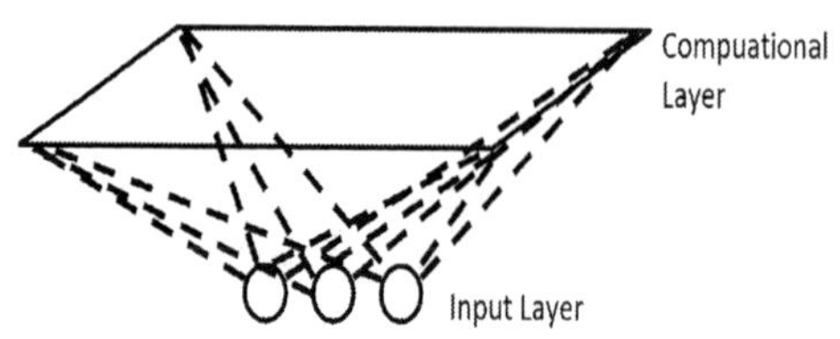


Figure 2: SOM Architecture

## 2 Speaker Clustering Experiments

### 2.1 NCLR Speaker Clustering

In order to perform speaker clustering we utilized the technique proposed in (Rouvier et al., 2013). The mentioned system uses the Normalized Cross Likelihood Ratio (NCLR) which is described in (Le et al., 2007) as: $NCLR(M_i, M_j) = \frac{1}{N_j}log(\frac{L(X_i|M_i)}{L(X_i|M_j)}) + \frac{1}{N_j}log(\frac{L(X_j|M_j)}{L(X_j|M_i)})$ The term $\frac{L(X_j|M_j)}{L(X_j|M_i)}$ measures how well speaker model $M_i$ scores with speaker data $X_j$ relative to how well speaker model $M_j$ scores with its own data $X_j$.

Figure 1 shows the block diagram that describes the clustering system mentioned above which we used in our experiments.

**Hierarchical Agglomerative Clustering (HAC):** Pre-segmented wave files are fed into HAC system which uses the BIC (Bayesian Information Criterion) measure (Chen and Gopalakrishnan, 1998).

**Viterbi Resegmentation:** the Viterbi uses GMM trained by Expectation Maximization (EM) to refine speaker boundaries.

**NCLR Clustering:** speaker models are adapted by a 512 diagonal GMM-UBM system. Afterwards NCLR is used to recombine adapted speaker models.

### 2.2 SPEAKER CLUSTERING USING SOM

A self-organizing map (SOM) is a type of Neural Networks. It is trained using unsupervised learning algorithm to produce map which is discrete representation of the input training samples. SOMs operate in two main modes: training and mapping. Training builds the map using input training samples, this process is called vector quantization, while mapping classifies a new input vector.

**I-vector Extraction:** In recent years, many approaches have been proposed to enhance speaker recognition system performance. The most popular are those based on generative models, like Gaussian Mixture Models based on Universal Background Model (GMM-UBM). Other generative models such as Eigen-voices, and the most powerful one, the Joint Factor Analysis (JFA) (Kenny et al., 2008), have been built on the success of the GMM-UBM approach.

Unlike JFA, the idea consists in finding a low dimensional subspace of the GMM super vector space, named the total variability space that represents both speaker and channel variability. The vectors in the low dimensional space are called I-vectors. In 2008 NIST speaker recognition evaluation (Wooters and Huijbregts, 2008), I-vector features were used for the first time. The I-vectors are smaller in size to reduce the execution time of the recognition task while maintaining recognition performance similar to that obtained with JFA.

**SOM Clustering:** Assigning correct speaker identification for each utterance can boost the SAT adaptation performance in ASR systems. For the offline decoding task, we introduce a fast automatic speaker clustering technique based on SOM and I-Vectors as input features. Our used SOM has a feed-forward structure with a single computational layer arranged in 2 dimensions (rows and columns). Each neuron is fully connected to all the source nodes in the input layer, as shown in Figure 2.

In our experiments, we construct a SOM map in which the number of rows is variable while the number of columns is forced to be 1 column.

For each utterance, a 100 dimension I-vector is calculated and considered as a spatially con-

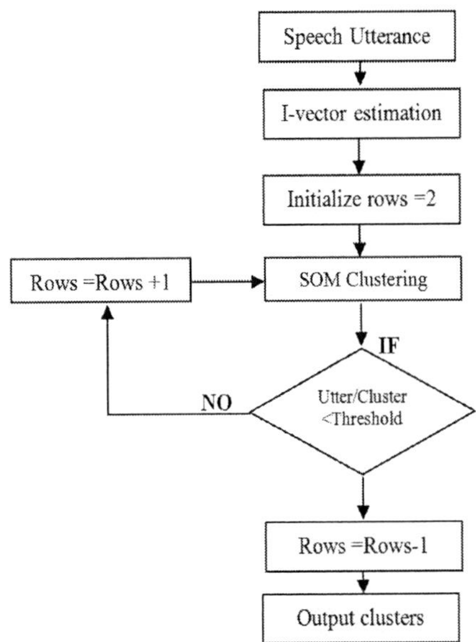

Figure 3: SOM Clustering Flow Chart

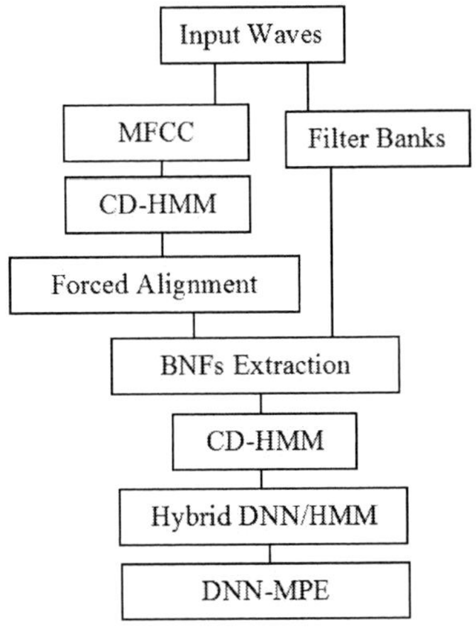

Figure 4: ASR Block Diagram

tinuous feature vector to our clustering technique. Figure 3 describes the flow chart of our proposed method.

## 2.3 Clustering Results

We have run our experiments on the Development data of the Multi Genre Broadcast MGB-2 challenge described in (Ali et al., 2016). The data consists of 10 hours of Aljazeera TV Broadcast. Table 1 illustrates the results of the NCLR clustering algorithm verses the proposed SOM technique. The metric used to measure the systems' performance is the Speaker Error Rate (SER) defined in (Anguera, 2006) as:

$$SER = \frac{\Sigma_{s=1}^{S}(max(N_{ref(s)}, N_{hyp(s)}) - N_{correct(s)})}{\Sigma_{s=1}^{S} dur(s).N_{ref}}$$

where $S$ is the total number of segments where both reference and hypothesis segment agree on same speaker and $N_{ref}$ is the number of speakers in segment s.

Table 1 shows SER of the proposed SOM technique verses the NCLR technique.

| Metric | SOM | NCLR |
|--------|------|-------|
| SER | 4.96% | 5.42% |

Table 1: SER of SOM clustering vs SER of NCLR

## 3 Automatic Speech Recognition (ASR) System

We integrate the results of both Clustering techniques we experimented with Automatic Speech Recognition System (ASR).

### 3.1 ASR System Components

Figure 4 describes the block diagram of the ASR system.

**MFCCs HMM System:** Context Dependent HMM CD-HMM is trained over 500 hours of the MGB Challenge training data. The model obtained is used to force align training data.

**Bottleneck Features (BNFs) :** DNNs have proved to be effective in Acoustic modeling (Hinton et al., 2012). DNNs can be used either as the main classifier for acoustic modeling or as a prior step to extract acoustic features then train the main classifier. We used both mentioned techniques. After aligning all the given waves, a Deep Neural Network consists of five 1500-neuron hidden layers, with a 40 neuron Bottleneck layer, was trained on top of filter banks. 40 dimensional BNFs were extracted from the BNF layer and used to train SAT/HMM-DNN system.

**Hybrid DNN-HMM and DNN-MPE:** Finally the 40 BNFs are extracted to train a hybrid DNN-HMM followed by the discriminative training for DNN (Vesel et al., 2013).

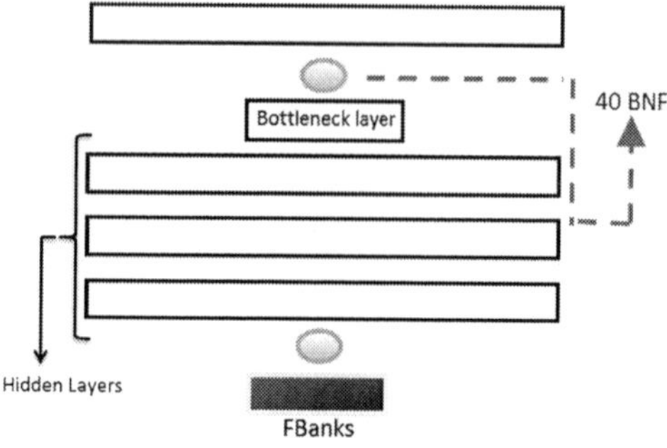



Figure 5: Bottleneck Features Extraction

In our experiments we have used the Kaldi toolkit (Povey et al., 2011) for acoustic modelling.

## 3.2 Impact of clustering on ASR

In our experiments, it has been proven that using SOM improves the system performance by reducing WER.

Using the SOM to specify new speaker labels for development data and replicating the decoding process on different ASR system, the following enhancements have been verified; First, for the SI-tandem ASR system trained on top of BNFs + fMLLR features, the SOM clustering has given a relative reduction in WER by 3.05% over the tandem BNFs +fMLLR (SI) where all speaker segments per episode were given the same label. Moreover, the mentioned system has given an absolute reduction of 1.16% over the tandem BNFs +fMLLR (SI) integrated with NCLR (SI-NCLR) clustering technique.

Table 2 shows the Speaker Independent (SI) results of the GMM-HMM tandem system trained over BNFs and fMLLR features.

| Experiment | WER |
|---|---|
| Tandem (BNFs + fMLLR) (SI) | 37.91 |
| Tandem (BNFs + fMLLR) (SI-NCLR) | 37.41 |
| **Tandem (BNFs + fMLLR) (SI-SOM)** | **36.75** |

Table 2: Tandem GMM-HMM Speaker-Independent results

Second, for the SD-tandem ASR system trained on top of BNFs + fMLLR features, the SOM clustering has given a relative reduction in WER by 4.22% over the tandem BNFs +fMLLR (SD). In addition, the mentioned system has given an absolute reduction of 1.52% over the tandem BNFs +fMLLR (SD) (SD-NCLR).

Table 3 shows the Speaker Dependent (SD) results of the GMM-HMM tandem system over BNFs and fMLLR features.

| Experiment | WER |
|---|---|
| Tandem (BNFs + fMLLR) (SD) | 36.00 |
| Tandem (BNFs + fMLLR) (SD-NCLR) | 34.96 |
| **Tandem (BNFs + fMLLR) (SD-SOM)** | **34.48** |

Table 3: Tandem GMM-HMM Speaker-Dependent results

Third, for the hybrid DNN/HMM system trained on top of fMLLR +BNFs with Sequence Discriminative training criterion (DNN/HMM-MPE), the SOM clustering gave a relative reduction of 3.84% in WER of the hybrid system that used no clustering technique. In comparison with the hybrid system where NCLR clustering was applied, the SOM gave a relative reduction in WER of 1.87%.

Table 4 shows the final results of the hybrid DNN-HMM trained with Minimum phoneme error rate criterion (MPE).

| Clustering Technique | WER |
|---|---|
| Tandem DNN/HMM-MPE (SD) | 27.8 |
| Tandem DNN/HMM-MPE (SD-NCLR) | 27.24 |
| **Tandem DNN/HMM-MPE (SD-SOM)** | **26.73** |

Table 4: Hybrid DNN/HMM-MPE results

It is noticeable that the performance of the hybrid system improved after using the proposed clustering technique.

## 4 Conclusion

In this paper, we have proposed an algorithm for automatic speaker clustering based on Self-Organizing Map. The performance of the new algorithm has been compared with a well-known technique of speaker clustering (Normalized Cross Likelihood Ratio). The experimental results on Multi Genre Broadcast data have shown noticeable reduction in Speaker Error Rate. The clustering algorithm has been integrated with state of art Automatic Speech Recognition techniques to boost Speaker adaptive training performance. It is experimentally verified that the proposed technique achieved notable reduction in word error rate compared to the traditional tandem system. In addition, the proposed algorithm attained a reduction in word error rate in comparison with the reduction attained by NCLR clustering technique.

## Acknowledgments

The authors would like to show their gratitude to Professor Hassanin M. Al-Barhamtoshy of King Abdulaziz University (KAU) for his support in the project. This research was done by the computational power support provided by King Abdulaziz University.

## References

A. Ali, P. Bell, J. Glass, Y. Messaoui, H. Mubarak, S. Renals, and Y. Zhang. 2016. The mgb-2 challenge: Arabic multi-dialect broadcast media recognition. *Proc. Spoken Language Technology Workshop (SLT)*.

X. Anguera. 2006. *Robust speaker diarization for meetings*. Ph.D. thesis, Universitat Politcnica de Catalunya.

S. Chen and P. Gopalakrishnan. 1998. Speaker, environment and channel change detection and clustering via the bayesian information criterion. *Proc. of DARPA Broadcast News Transcription and Understanding Workshop, Lansdowne, Virginia, USA, February,pp. 127132*.

N. Dehak, P. Kenny, R. Dehak, and P. Ouellet. 2011. Front-end factor analysis for speaker verification. *IEEE Transactions on Audio Speech and Language Processing 19(4):788 - 798*.

G. Hinton, D. Yu L. Deng, G. E Dahl, A. Mohamed, N. Jaitly, A. Senior, V. Vanhoucke, P. Nguyen, T. N Sainath, and B. Kingsbury. 2012. Deep neural networks for acoustic modeling in speech recognition: The shared views of four research groups. *IEEE Signal Processing Magazine 29, 8297*.

P. Kenny, P. Ouellet, N. Dehak, V. Gupta, and P. Dumouchel. 2008. A study of inter-speaker variability in speaker verification. *IEEE Transactions on Audio, Speech and Language Processing 16(5):980 - 988*.

V. Le, O. Mella, and D. Fohr. 2007. Speaker diarization using normalized cross likelihood ratio. *Interspeech (Vol. 7, pp. 1869-1872)*.

K. Margarita, V. Moschou, and C. Kotropoulos. 2008. Speaker segmentation and clustering. *Signal processing 88(5), 1091-1124*.

M. H. Moattar and M. M. Homayounpour. 2012. A review on speaker diarization systems and approaches. *Speech Commun. 54, 10651103*.

D. Povey, A. Ghoshal, G. Boulianne, L. Burget, O. Glembek, N. Goel, M. Hannemann, P. Motlicek, Y. Qian, and P. Schwarz. 2011. The kaldi speech recognition toolkit. *IEEE 2011 workshop on automatic speech recognition and understanding IEEE Signal Processing Society,*.

M. Rouvier, G. Dupuy, E. Khoury P. Gay, T. Merlin, and S. Meignier. 2013. An open-source state-of-the-art toolbox for broadcast news diarization. *Interspeech, Lyon (France), 25-29 Aug*.

K. Vesel, A. Ghoshal, L. Burget, and D. Povey. 2013. Sequence-discriminative training of deep neural networks. *Interspeech (pp. 2345-2349)*.

C. Wooters and M. Huijbregts. 2008. The icsi rt07s speaker diarization system. *Multimodal Technologies for Perception of Humans: International Evaluation Workshops CLEAR 2007 and RT 2007*.

# SHAKKIL: An Automatic Diacritization System for Modern Standard Arabic Texts


**Amany Fashwan**
Phonetics and Linguistics Department,
Faculty of Arts, Alexandria University,
Alexandria, Egypt
a.fashwan@gmail.com

**Sameh Alansary**
Phonetics and Linguistics Department,
Faculty of Arts, Alexandria University,
Alexandria, Egypt
sameh.alansary@bibalex.org



## Abstract

This paper sheds light on a system that would be able to diacritize Arabic texts automatically (SHAKKIL). In this system, the diacritization problem will be handled through two levels; morphological and syntactic processing levels. The adopted morphological disambiguation algorithm depends on four layers; Uni-morphological form layer, rule-based morphological disambiguation layer, statistical-based disambiguation layer and Out Of Vocabulary (OOV) layer. The adopted syntactic disambiguation algorithms is concerned with detecting the case ending diacritics depending on a rule based approach simulating the shallow parsing technique. This will be achieved using an annotated corpus for extracting the Arabic linguistic rules, building the language models and testing the system output. This system is considered as a good trial of the interaction between rule-based approach and statistical approach, where the rules can help the statistics in detecting the right diacritization and vice versa. At this point, the morphological Word Error Rate (WER) is 4.56% while the morphological Diacritic Error Rate (DER) is 1.88% and the syntactic WER is 9.36%. The best WER is 14.78% compared to the best-published results, of (Abandah et al., 2015); 11.68%, (Rashwan et al., 2015); 12.90% and (Habash et al., 2009); 13.60%.


## 1 Introduction

Modern Standard Arabic (MAS) is currently the sixth most widely spoken language in the world with estimated 422 million native speakers. It is usually written without diacritics which makes it difficult for performing Arabic text processing. In addition, this often leads to considerable ambiguity since several words that have different diacritic patterns may appear identical in a diacritic-less setting. In fact, a text without diacritics may bring difficulties for Arabic readers. It is also problematic for Arabic processing applications where the lack of diacritics adds another layer of ambiguity when processing the input data (Shaalan et al., 2009).

Diacritics restoration is the problem of inserting diacritics into a text where they are missing. Predicting the correct diacritization of the Arabic words elaborates the meaning of the words and leads to better understanding of the text, which in turn is much useful in several real life applications such as Information Retrieval (IR), Machine Translation (MT), Text-to-speech (TTS), Part-Of-Speech (POS) tagging and others.

For full diacritization of an Arabic words, two basic components are needed:

**1) Morphology-dependent** that selects the best internal diacritized form of the same spelling; e.g. the word علم "Elm" has different diacritized forms; عِلْم "Eilom" "science", عَلَم "Ealam" "flag", عَلَّم "Eal~ama" "taught" and عَلِم "Ealima" "knew".

**2) Syntax-dependent** that detects the best syntactic case of the word within a given sentence; i.e. its role in the parsing tree of that sentence. For example; دَرَسْتُ عِلْمَ الرِّيَاضِيَّاتِ "darasotu Eiloma Alr~iyADiy~Ati" "I studied Mathematics" implies the syntactic diacritic of the target word - which is an "object" in the parsing tree - is "Fatha", while يُفِيدُ عِلْمُ الرِّيَاضِيَّاتِ جَمِيعَ الْعُلُومِ "yufiydu Eilomu Alr~iyADiy~Ati jamiyEa AloEuluwmi" "Mathematics benefits all sciences" implies the syntactic diacritic of the target word which is a "subject"




*Proceedings of The Third Arabic Natural Language Processing Workshop (WANLP)*, pages 84–93,
Valencia, Spain, April 3, 2017. ©2017 Association for Computational Linguistics

in the parsing tree - is "Damma" (Rashwan et al., 2009).

## 2 Related Work

Diacritic restoration has been receiving increasing attention and has been the focus of several studies. Different methods such as rule-based, example-based, hierarchical, morphological and contextual-based as well as methods with Hidden Markov Models (HMM) and weighted finite state machines have been applied for the diacritization of Arabic text.

Among these trials, that are most prominent, (Habash and Rambow, 2005; 2007a), (Zitouni et al., 2006), (Diab et al., 2007), (Roth et al., 2008), (Shaalan et al., 2008; 2009), (Habash et al., 2009), (Rashwan et al., 2009;2011; 2014; 2015), (Metwally et al., 2016), (Abandah et al., 2015), (Chennoufi and Mazroui, 2016a; 2016b), and (Alansary, 2016a).

In addition, some software companies have developed commercial products for the automatic diacritization of Arabic; Sakhr Arabic Automatic Diacritizer[1], Xerox's Arabic Morphological Processor[2] and RDI's Automatic Arabic Phonetic Transcriptor (Diacritizer/Vowelizer)[3]. Moreover, there are also other free online available systems; Meshkal Arabic Diacritizer[4], Harakat Arabic Diacritizer[5], Al-Du'aly[6], Farasa[7] and Google Tashkeel which is no longer working where the tool is not available now.

It has been noticed that most of the previous systems use different statistical approaches in their diacritization systems and few trials use the rule-based approach. The difference between the current proposed system and the others is the interaction between the rule-based approach and statistical approach using different machine learning techniques, where the rule-based can help the statistical-based in detecting the right diacritization and vice versa. In addition, extracting and implementing some syntactic rules for case ending restoration where, to our knowledge, none of the previous systems make use of syntax with the

exception of (Shahrour et al., 2015), (Chennoufi and Mazroui, 2016b) and (Alansary, 2016a) who have integrated syntactic rules.

## 3 System Data Sets

The used data in the current system was selected from a Morphologically Annotated Gold Standard Arabic Resource (**MASAR**) for MSA (Alansary, 2016b). The texts were selected from different sources; Newspapers, Net Articles and Books. Moreover, these selected texts covered more than one genre. Each word is tagged with features, namely, Lemma, Gloss, prefixes, Stem, Tag, suffixes, Gender, Number, Definiteness, Root, Stem Pattern, Case Ending, Name Entity and finally Vocalization. In the current proposed system, the data is subdivided into three kinds of data sets: **a) "Training Data"** about 450,000 words. **b) "Development Data"** about 55,000 words, and **c) "Testing Data"** about 55,000 words.

### 3.1 Extracting Arabic Linguistic Rules

It must be noted that extracting Arabic linguistic rules is not an easy task where these rules must be represented in a generalized format in a way that simulates the concerned component of the language. So these rules need to be constrained in a certain order to avoid overlapping among them. In this stage a number of rules related to morphology, definiteness and case ending are extracted from the training data set in a formalized and generalized format and implemented in the system.

As concerning to morphological rules, we are concerned with extracting some rules that help in detecting the POS of a certain words depending on the preceding or succeeding POS tags or word forms. In addition to the previous kind of rules, other rules have been extracted to detect the whole morphological analysis and hence the full internal diacritization depending on the preceding or succeeding POS tags or word forms. These rules get only the correct solution for the words context and consequently eliminate all wrong solutions. In addition, they may get only one morphological/diacritized form or get more than one correct morphological analysis after eliminating the wrong solutions. The extracted morphological rules are of 11 categories; Prepositional Phrases, Subjunctive Particles, Jussive Particles, Accusative Particles, Interrogative Particles, Pronouns, Verb Particles, Amendment Particle "l'kin", Time and Place Adverbs, Verbs and

---


[1]http://aramedia.com/nlp2.htm [Acc. 12-2-2015].

[2]http://aramedia.com/diacritizer.htm [Acc. 12-2-2015].

[3]http://www.rdi-eg.com/technologies/arabic_nlp.htm [Acc. 12-2-2015].

[4]http://tahadz.com/mishkal [Acc. 4-4-2015].

[5]http://harakat.ae/ [Acc. 4-4-2015].

[6]http://faraheedy.mukhtar.me/du2alee/tashkeel [Acc. 20-8-2016]

[7]http://qatsdemo.cloudapp.net/farasa/ [Acc. 28-12-2016]

Some Word Forms. In each category, a number of sub rules are extracted and implemented.

One of these rules states that the accusative particles ">an~a/PART", "li>an~a/PART" and "ka >an~a/PART" that have empty suffix may be followed by NOUN, PRON, PREP and some particles. Consequently, no ADJ, ADV, IV or PV (except 'layos/PV') follows these stems as Rule (1) shows:

**Rule (1)**

(Stem [Previous] % ">an~a/PART" & Suf [Previous] = "")

{ [Current]: @ Tag %"NOUN"

@ Tag = "PRON"

@ Tag = "PREP"

@ Stem = "layos/PV"

@ Stem = "lA/PART"

@ Stem = "mA/PART"

@ Stem = "lam/PART"

}

Ex. (1) shows that if the word form to be analyzed is "أفضل" ">fDl", in this case the Rule (1) will be applied and it will eliminate the PV, IV and ADJ forms of this word; "أَفْضَلَ" ">afoDala" "bestow", "أُفَضِّل" ">ufaD~il" "prefer", "أُفَضَّل" ">ufaD~al" "be prefered", and "أَفْضَل" ">afoDal" "better/best" and the nominal form of this word; "أَفْضَل" ">afoDal" "better/best" will be selected and assigned to this word.

**Ex. (1)** فهو يرى أن أفضل المقترحات هو المقترح الفيدرالي

fahuwa yaraY >an~a >afoDal AlomuqotaraHAt huwa AlomuqotraH AlofiydorAliy

He believes that the best proposals is the federal proposal

The realization of nominal case in Arabic is complicated by its orthography, which uses optional diacritics to indicate short vowel case morphemes, and by its morphology, which does not always distinguish between all cases. Additionally, case realization in Arabic interacts heavily with the realization of definiteness, leading to different realizations depending on whether the nominal is indefinite, i.e., receiving nunation (تنوين), definite through the determiner Al+ (ال+) or definite through being the governor of an EDAFAH possessive construction (إضافة) (Habash et al., 2007b). In addition, case ending realization in Arabic interacts in some cases with other information: **1. Word Patterns:** the diptote word patterns (الممنوع من الصرف) refer to a category of nouns and adjectives that have special case ending when they are indefinite since they do not take tanween. It must be noticed that when these words are definite, they take regular case ending diacritics.

**2. Verb Transitivity:** the transitivity of the verbs helps sometimes in detecting the subject (which receives nominative case ending) and object (which receives the subjunctive case ending).

**3. Feminine Plural Word Forms:** in Arabic, the object receives the case ending for the genitive case instead of the subjunctive case; this is in the case of those words end with "ات" "At/NSUFF" "جمع المؤنث السالم" (Fashwan, 2016). In order to detect the case ending diacritics, a prior step is done where some Arabic linguistic rules have been extracted and implemented to detect the definiteness of each word depending on its context or its selected morphological analysis. In addition, the stem pattern of each stem has been detected depending on its root, stem and lemma. Moreover, the transitivity of each verb has been detected depending on its lemma.

After that, some Arabic linguistic rules have been extracted and implemented to detect the case ending depending on a window of -/+ 3 words around the focused word taking into consideration the context, the selected morphological analysis, definiteness feature, stem pattern and verb's transitivity. The extracted case ending rules are of 4 categories; rules for Detecting Case Ending (MOOD) of the Imperfect Verbs, rules for detecting the case ending of Noun Phrases, rules for detecting the case ending of Adverb phrases and rules for detecting the case ending of adjectival phrases. One of these rules states that if there is a noun phrase preceded by "أَمَّا" ">am~A" "as for/concerning" or "لَوْلَا" "lawolA" "if not" then the noun must be in nominative case taking into consideration the definiteness feature; if the noun is "INDEF" then the noun must receive nunation (Tanween Damma ''), but if the noun is "DEF" or "EDAFAH" then the noun must receive Damma '' as Rule (2) shows:

**Rule (2)**

((Stem [Previous] = ">am~A/CONJ" (or) Stem [Previous] = "lawolA/CONJ") & NP/Tag [Current] %"NOUN")

(NP/Definiteness [Current] = "INDEF")

{ [Current]: @ Case Ending/Syntactic Diacritic = "N"

}

(NP/Definiteness [Current] = "DEF" (or) NP/Definiteness [Current] = "EDAFAH")

{ [Current]: @ Case Ending/Syntactic Diacritic = "u"

}

In Ex. (2), the first condition of Rule (2) is applied and the case ending diacritic of the word "صَدِيقٌ" "SadiyqN" "friend" is Tanween Damma '"' 'N'. In Ex. (3), the second condition of Rule (2) is applied and the case ending diacritic of the word "صَدِيقُ" "Sadiysqu" "friend" is Damma '"' "u".

**Ex. (2)** لَوْلَا صَدِيقٌ لِي أَخْبَرَنِي بِالْأَمْرِ

lawolA SadiyqN liy >axobaraniy biAlo>amori
Except for a friend told me about this matter

**Ex. (3)** أَمَّا صَدِيقُ طُفُولَتِي فَلَهُ مِنِّي كُلُّ الْحُبِّ
>am~A Sadiyqu Tufuwlatiy falahu min~iy kul~u AloHub~i
As for my childhood friend, all the love from me

Table 1 shows the number of the extracted linguistic rules for being used for both morphological and syntactic processing levels. For more details about these extracted rules, see (Fashwan, 2016).

| Rules Type | Rules No. |
|---|---|
| Morphological Rules | 178 |
| Syntactic Rules | 473 |
| Definiteness Rules | 46 |
| **Total No. of Rules** | **697** |

Table 1: Extracted Rules Number.

### 3.1.1 Building the Language Models

To reach the best morphological/diacritized form of the words to be analyzed statistically, there are three processes have been used (sub-section 4.1.3). According to these processes a number of Language Models (LM)s are built using the training data set:

- **POS LM:** a quad gram LM of Prefixes_Tags_Sufixes sequences used to detect the best POS if there are more than one tag for the word to be analyzed in relation to preceding and succeeding (if found) POS(s). It is used in building four smoothed language models using Good-Turing Discounting, Kneser-Ney Smooting,

Witten-Bell Discounting and Katz Back-Off Smoothing (Manning and Schütze, 1999) to select the best technique.

- **Word Form, Lemma, Tag and Stem LM:** a bi-gram LM of Word_Lemma_Stem_Tag sequences used to detect the best lemma, tag or stem of the word to be disambiguated taking into consideration the word form itself.

- **Word Form, Suffix Stem and Tag LM**: a bi-gram LM of Word_Suffix_Stem_Tag sequences used to detect the best suffix of the word to be disambiguated in relation to preceding and succeeding (if found) suffixes taking into consideration the word form itself.

## 4 SHAKKIL Diacritization System

In this system, the diacritization problem will be handled through two levels; morphological processing level (for detecting the internal diacritics) and syntactic processing level (for detecting the case ending diacritics).

The morphological processing level depends on four layers. The first three layers are similar to BASMA's (Alansary, 2015). The first layer is direct matching between the words that have only one morphological analysis and their diacritized forms, the second is disambiguating the input by depending on contextual morphological rules, and the third is disambiguating the input statistically by using machine learning techniques. However, the three layers in this algorithm are applied sequentially for the whole input, unlike BASMA's system that applies the layers word by word. In each of these layers, a step towards the morphological diacritization of the input text is performed as figure 1 shows. Moreover, this algorithm makes use of the relations between the words and their contexts, whether the preceding or the succeeding words, but BASMA depends only on the morphological disambiguation of the preceding words. In addition to these three layers, another layer is used; the Out Of Vocabulary (OOV) layer.

The adopted syntactic algorithm is a rule based approach that detects the main constituents of the morphological analysis output and applies the suitable syntactic rules to detect the case ending.

### 4.1 Morphological Processing Level

### 4.1.1 Uni-Morphological Form Layer

This layer is only concerned with words that have only one diacritized form as well as one POS tag. For example, the word "الْاِحْتِلَال" "AliHotilAl" "occupation" has only one diacritized form with

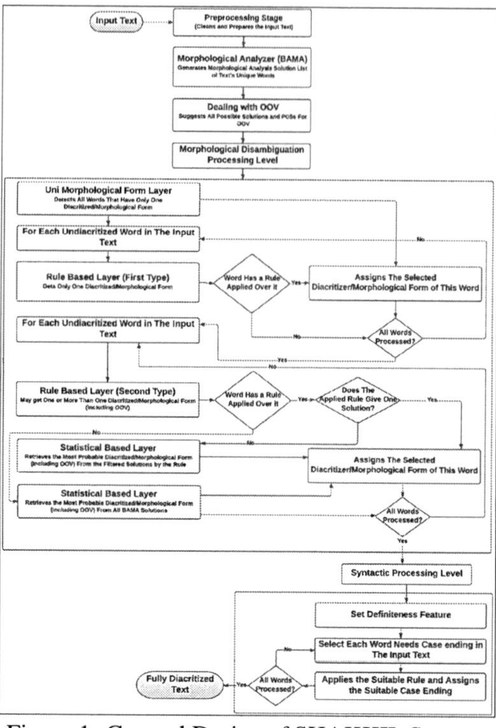

Figure 1: General Design of SHAKKIL System.

only one POS tag; NOUN

In this layer, the adopted morphological disambiguation algorithm does not disambiguate the words according to its word order in the text; however, it begins with matching directly all the words that have uni-morphological/diacritized form and assigns this analysis to the word. This layer is considered as the key for disambiguating other words in the other layers whether they are the preceding or the succeeding words. It may help in: **1)** disambiguating the other words in the rule-based layer if they are governed by a rule that provides one morphological/diacritized form, **2)** disambiguating the other words in the statistical-based layer or **3)** disambiguating the other words by the help of both the rule-based layer and the statistical-based layer if they are governed by a rule that provides more than one morphological/diacritized form.

### 4.1.2   Rule Based Morphological Disambiguation Layer

The main goal of implementing the morphological rules is to help in eliminating the wrong solution and making the searching problem easier while selecting the best POS or a complete morphological analysis of the non-disambiguated words and hence detecting the internal diacritization. The extracted and implemented rules in this layer are of

two types:

**1.**   Rules always help in providing only one morphological/diacritized form for some non-disambiguated words without the need to use the statistical-based layer and word text orders. Most of the rules of this type are concerned with the relation between some non-disambiguated word forms and the preceding or succeeding words.

**2.** Rules may provide one or more than one solution depending on the word form solutions' variation. If the rule provides only one analysis solution, then this analysis is assigned to the word directly and there will be no need for applying the statistical-based layer. However, if the applied rule provides more than one solution (morphological/diacritized form) the statistical-based layer will be applied in order to get the best solution, depending on the solutions provided by the rules. In the case of having more than one solution for a certain word after applying the rule, following the text word order is a must. The system will depend on a window of -/+ 3 analyzed words around this word to obtain the best solution through the statistical-based layer, as sub-section 4.1.3 shows. The disambiguated words in this layer by rules only may help the statistical-based layer in disambiguating the succeeding word, if it is not analyzed yet. In addition, the disambiguated words through the statistical-based layer may be governed by a rule that helps in disambiguating the succeeding word if it is not analyzed yet.

### 4.1.3   Statistical Based Morphological Disambiguation Layer

As mentioned before, to reach the best morphological/diacritized form of the words to be analyzed statistically, there are three processes have been used. It must be noted that these processes are not used in all cases while disambiguating the word to be analyzed.

The first one is for getting the best POS score from analysis solutions of the word to be analyzed in relation to the preceding and succeeding (if found) POS depending on some smoothing techniques. The second one is for getting the best stem, tag or lemma score with relation to the word form itself. It is used in two cases:

**1)** When the POS of the word's analyses are the same. **2)** When the POS model detects best POS and it is found that this POS has more than one lemma or diacritized form.

The third one is for getting the best suffix score

from analysis solutions for the word to be analyzed. It is used when the word to be disambiguated has more than one suffix. The top scoring solution of the word is then selected.

### 4.1.4 Dealing with OOV Words

For predicting the OOV words, a prior step is taken; preprocessing the stems of the training data. The stems of the training data are used to get a list of unique 4307 diacritized patterns with their templates and frequencies. The patterns are prepared by converting the consonants in the stem to placeholder while keeping the vowels, hamazat hamazat ("آ" ">", "إ" "<", "ؤ" "&", "ئ" "}", ... etc.) and weak letters "حروف العلة" "واي" "wAy". In addition, POS of patterns are taken into consideration as figure 2 shows.

```
- <OOV_Pattern>
     <OOV_Patterns>{}---</OOV_Patterns>
     <Diac_Patterns>{i}o-a-a-</Diac_Patterns>
     <Tags>PV</Tags>
     <Count>1</Count>
  </OOV_Pattern>
- <OOV_Pattern>
     <OOV_Patterns>{}--A-</OOV_Patterns>
     <Diac_Patterns>{i}o-i-A-</Diac_Patterns>
     <Tags>NOUN</Tags>
     <Count>17</Count>
  </OOV_Pattern>
- <OOV_Pattern>
     <OOV_Patterns>{}--A-y</OOV_Patterns>
     <Diac_Patterns>{i}o-i-A-iy~</Diac_Patterns>
     <Tags>ADJ</Tags>
     <Count>8</Count>
  </OOV_Pattern>
- <OOV_Pattern>
     <OOV_Patterns>{--</OOV_Patterns>
     <Diac_Patterns>{i-~a-</Diac_Patterns>
     <Tags>PV</Tags>
     <Count>1</Count>
  </OOV_Pattern>
- <OOV_Pattern>
     <OOV_Patterns>{---</OOV_Patterns>
     <Diac_Patterns>{i-~a-a-</Diac_Patterns>
     <Tags>PV</Tags>
     <Count>164</Count>
  </OOV_Pattern>
- <OOV_Pattern>
     <OOV_Patterns>{-->
</OOV_Patterns>
     <Diac_Patterns>{i-~a-a></Diac_Patterns>
     <Tags>PV</Tags>
     <Count>1</Count>
  </OOV_Pattern>
- <OOV_Pattern>
     <OOV_Patterns>{--Y</OOV_Patterns>
     <Diac_Patterns>{i-~a-aY</Diac_Patterns>
     <Tags>PV</Tags>
     <Count>1</Count>
  </OOV_Pattern>
```

Figure 2: Patterns List with their Diacritized Patterns and Tags.

The POS helps, in some cases, in limiting the scope of the search of the matched pattern, where, for example, if the OOV word has been detected as having "ال" "Al" at the beginning of it, this means the system should search for the detected pattern in the patterns of nouns or adjectives.

While detecting the input text analysis solutions, each word is checked by the system to determine whether it has analyses solutions from BAMA or it is OOV. When the word form is checked as OOV, the system switches to the OOV module. In this module, the system tries to get all word's possible morphological constituents (a combination of prefixes, stem and suffixes). Then, it uses the list of detected stems and gets their counterpart diacritized patterns.

The selected pattern is used to retrieve the suitable diacritic for the stem. Moreover, the system chooses the POS tag of the diacritized pattern and assign it to the diacritized stem where each selected solution is added to text's solutions. While working in the morphological disambiguation processing level, if the OOV word has more than one matched POS tag, the system detects the best one depending on step one and two of subsection (4.1.3).

It must be noted that there are no out of vocabulary (OOV) words in MASAR data since they are analyzed manually as if they are analyzed by BAMA and then added in BAMA's dictionaries so that they would be analyzed correctly the next time they are used.

### 4.2 Syntactic Processing Level

The task of the syntactic processing level is to predict the syntactic case of a sequence of morphologically diacritized words given their POS tags, definiteness, stem pattern and/or transitivity and hence assigning the suitable case ending diacritics. Some limitations violate the rules for setting the case ending of syntactic diacritic, since the rules are limited to use a window of -/+3 words before the focused word.

Before diacritizing the word syntactically, its POS tag is checked first. Using the POS tag of the word, it is decided how the syntactic diacritization of this word should be handled. As mentioned before, the extracted rules in this level simulates one of the language processing approaches that computes a basic analysis of sentence structure rather than attempting full syntactic analysis; shallow syntactic parsing. It is an analysis of a sentence which identifies the constituents (noun groups, verb groups, prepositional groups adjectival groups, adverbial groups), but does not specify their internal structure, nor their role in the main sentence.

The extracted rules for detecting the imperfect verb case ending, the case ending of noun, the case ending of adjectives, the case ending of adverbs and the case ending of some proper nouns (sub-section 3.1) have been implemented in the current proposed system, taking into consideration the phrases in which each of the previous categories occur.

## 5 Evaluation

A blind data set that is not part of the development of the system is then used to evaluate the system versus the gold annotated data. Two error rates are calculated: diacritic error rate (**DER**) which indicates how many letters have been incorrectly restored with their diacritics, and word error rate (**WER**) which indicates how many words have at least one diacritic error. Table 2 shows the total error rate of the system as a whole and WER and DER for each layer in morphological processing level and the percentage of words that has been detected by the help of each layer using different machine learning techniques.

The comparison between the different smoothing techniques shows that Witten-Bell discounting and Kneser-Ney smoothing techniques results are close; however, Kneser-Ney smoothing technique is the best one in detecting the best morphological analysis (internal diacritic) and case ending diacritics in the current proposed system. Consequently, the Kneser-Ney smoothing technique is used while comparing the results of the current systems with other state of the art systems.

| System | Diacritized | Good-Turing & Katz Back-off | | Witten-Bell | | Kneser-Ney | |
|---|---|---|---|---|---|---|---|
| | Words% | DER | WER | DER | WER | DER | WER |
| 1$^{st}$ Layer | 55.86% | 0.01% | 0.02% | 0.01% | 0.02% | 0.01% | 0.02% |
| 2$^{nd}$ Layer | 9.53% | 0.06% | 0.15% | 0.06% | 0.15% | 0.06% | 0.15% |
| 3$^{rd}$ Layer | 28.75% | 1.59% | 3.85% | 1.26% | 3.09% | 1.20% | 2.86% |
| 2$^{nd}$ & 3$^{rd}$ Layers | 5.86% | 0.53% | 1.32% | 0.50% | 1.37% | 0.61% | 1.53% |
| Morphological Level | 100% | 2.19% | 5.34% | 1.83% | 4.63% | 1.88% | 4.56% |
| Case Ending | --- | --- | 10.25% | --- | 9.93% | --- | 9.36% |
| Overall Results | --- | --- | 15.59% | --- | 14.56% | --- | 13.92% |

Table 2: System Evaluation Results.

### 5.1 Error Analysis

When checking the results, we find that the first two layers of the proposed system have the lowest WER and DER, then, the third layer. The statistical based layer only gives the highest WER and DER. In what follows, some error analysis in each layer is reviewed:

- **In the uni-morphological layer,** it has been found that the error rate is a result of some possessive nouns or present verbs that have affixed possessive. In such words, the case ending diacritic is assigned within the word, not at its end. For example, the word "يُمَارِسهَا" "yumArishA" "he + practice/pursue/exercise", has three moods with three different cases ("´" "u", "`" "a", " ˚ " "o") within the word form. When the system fails to

detect the suitable case ending diacritic according to the context, the blind testing process counts this wrong diacritic as a morphological (internal error) not a syntactic error. If the testing process has been done for the internal diacritics and syntactic case separately, the results are expected to be enhanced.

- **In the rule-based layer,** the errors in this layer happen for some reasons; the first is when the word that is governed by a rule that makes the succeeding or preceding word to be diacritized wrongly. In EX. (4), the word "أن" ">n" is diacritized wrongly as "أَنَّ" ">an~a" not "أنْ" ">ano" according to this context. This leads to diacritize the word "ظَلَّ" "Zal~a" as "ظِلَّ" "Zil~a" affected by the rule mentioning that only nouns occurs after "أَنَّ". The same problem appeared in the uni-morphological form layer appears in this layer. In addition, when the applied rule gives more than one available solution and the statistical based layer is used to select the best solution, the statistical based layer may choose a wrong one.

**Ex. (4)** بَعْدَ أَنَّ ظِلَّ قُرُونًا عَدِيدَةً

baEoda >an~a Zil~a quruwnAF EadiydapF
After that shadow many centuries

- **In the statistical-based layer,** although it can predict the correct diacritized form in most of cases even if the same word appears in the same sentence with two different POS and diacritics, it cannot, in other cases, predict the suitable diacritic form. In Ex. (5) the same word "طالب" "TAlb" have been diacritized with two different diacritics according to the context, where the first word is a verb while the second one is a noun.

**Ex. (5)** طَالَبَ وَزِير التَّرِبِيَة وَالتَّعْلِيم بِالْإِهْتِمَام بِكُلّ طَالِب عَلَى حَدّ سَوَاء

TAlaba waziyr Alt arobiyap waAlt aEoliym biAl{ihotimAm bikul TAlib EalaY Had sawA'
The Minister of Education demanded with the interest for each student alike

In some other cases, the statistical-based layer can predict the correct POS but it fails in detecting the best lemma that helps to differentiate among the different word forms diacritization. In Ex. (6), the system fails to detect the correct diacritized form of the word "المحافظة" "AlmhAfZp" where it should be "الْمُحَافِظَة" "AlmuHAfiZap" "the + governess".

Ex. (6) وَقَامَتُ الْمُحَافَظَة بِإِضْدَار قَرَار بِتَعْيِين نَائِب لَهَا

wa qAmato AlomuHAfaZap bi<iSodAr qarAr
bitaEoyiyn nA}ib lahA
The issuance of the province's decision to appoint
a deputy for her

Moreover, the statistical based layer may fail to
detect both correct POS and the correct diacritized
form of the word to be analyzed. In Ex. (7), the
input word "علي" "Ely" wrongly diacritized with
wrong POS where the system edited it to "عَلَى"
"EalaY/PREP" while it should be in this sentence
as "عَلِيّ" "Ealiy~/NOUN_PROP". This wrong POS
and diacritization leads to have wrong case ending
for both this word and the succeeding one.

Ex. (7) عَلَى طِفْلٍ صَغِيرٍ يَبْلُغُ مِنْ الْعُمْرِ عَشَرَةَ أَعْوَامٍ
EalaY TifolK SagiyrK yabolug mino AloEumori
Ea$arapa >aEowAmK
A small child at the age of ten years

The problem of detecting the proper nouns is
similar to the previous problem where there are a
lot of words in Arabic that may be used as proper
nouns and nouns or adjectives. Predicting these
words wrongly leads to have wrong case ending
for both the word and the succeeding one.
- **In the syntactic processing level,** Assigning a
wrong POS, transitivity or definiteness to a word,
may lead to wrong syntactic case. In Ex. (8), the
word "هدف" "hadaf" "goal/target" has assigned
definiteness as "EDAFAH" as a result of considering "وحيد" "waHiyd" "alone" as "NOUN_PROP".
This problem leads to set the case ending as ' ' "i"
not ' ' "K".

Ex. (8) بَعْدَ عَدِمِ النَّجَاحِ فِي إِحْرَازِ هَدَفٍ وَحِيدٍ
baEoda Eadami Aln~ajaHi fiy <iHorAzi Hadafi
waHiydo
After the lack of success in achieving Waheed's
goal

## 5.2 Comparing the System with Other State of the Art Systems

In order to have an objective evaluation of the system, the same testing data (LDC's Arabic Treebank) that was used in the other systems was used
to compare the results. It is a part of Arabic Tree
Bank part 3 (ATB3) from "An-Nahar" Lebanese
News Agency. It consists of 91 articles (about
52.000 word) covering the period from October
15, 2002 to December 15, 2002. In the testing process, 51.63% of the words are diacritized in the
first layer, 5.56% of the words are diacritized by
rule-based layer only, 8.26% of the words are diacritized by both rule-based and statistical-based
layers, 32.99% of the words are diacritized by
statistical-based layer only, and finally 1.56% of
the word are diacritized in OOV layer. In OOV
layer, the system could predict the words with
WER of 11.2% and DER of 6.7%. Table 4 summarizes the results of the current proposed system

| Systems | Total WER | | Ignoring Last | |
| --- | --- | --- | --- | --- |
| | WER | DER | WER | DER |
| (Zitouni et al., 2006) | 17.30% | 5.10% | 7.90% | 2.50% |
| (Habash et al., 2009) | 13.60% | NA | 5.20% | NA |
| (Rashwan et al., 2015) | 12.90% | NA | NA | NA |
| (Abandah et al., 2015) | 11.68% | NA | 3.54% | 1.28% |
| (Metwally et al., 2016) | 13.70% | NA | 4.3% | NA |
| (Chennoufi and Mazroui, 2016b) | NA | NA | 1.86% | 0.71% |
| Current System | 14.78% | 4.11% | 4.81% | 1.93% |

Table 3: Summary of the Comparison between the State-Of-The-Art Systems.

The comparison indicates that (Abandah et al.,
2015), (Rashwan et al., 2015) and (Habash et
al., 2009) outperform the current system's results.
However, the results are still close to (Metwally et
al., 2016).

## 6 Conclusion

In this work, we depend on Arabic morphological
rules as well as different machine learning techniques for detecting the morphological diacritics
(internal diacritics). In addition, we adopt a rule-
based approach that depends on POS morphological sequences, definiteness classifier, stem pattern
and verb transitivity for detecting the case ending
diacritics. Evaluation of the proposed system is
made in comparison with other best state of the art
systems. The best WER of the morphological diacritization achieved by the system is 4.81% and
the best syntactic diacritization achieved is 9.97%
compared to the best-published results. Since this
work is in progress, these results are expected to
be enhanced by extracting more Arabic linguistic rules (morphological and syntactic), adding
more semantic features, using different machine
learning techniques for morphological and syntactic processing levels and implementing the improvements by working on larger amounts of data.
For enhancing the OOV results more patterns with
more features need to be handled.

# References


Gheith A. Abandah, Alex Graves, Balkees Al-Shagoor, Alaa Arabiyat, Fuad Jamour, and Majid Al-Taee. 2015. Automatic diacritization of arabic text using recurrent neural networks. *International Journal on Document Analysis and Recognition (IJDAR)*, 18(2):183–197.

Mohamed Attia Mohamed Elaraby Ahmed. 2000. A large-scale computational processor of the arabic morphology, and applications. Master's thesis, Faculty of Engineering, Cairo University Giza, Egypt.

Sameh Alansary. 2015. Basma: Bibalex standard arabic morphological analyzer. In *15th International Conference on Language Engineering*. The Egyptian Society of Language Engineering (ESOLE).

Sameh Alansary. 2016a. Alserag: An automatic diacritization system for arabic. In *16th International Conference on Language Engineering*. The Egyptian Society of Language Engineering (ESOLE).

Sameh Alansary. 2016b. Masar: A morphologically annotated gold standard arabic resource. In *16th International Conference on Language Engineering*. The Egyptian Society of Language Engineering (ESOLE).

Tim Buckwalter. 2004. Buckwalter arabic morphological analyzer version 2.0. linguistic data consortium, university of pennsylvania, 2002. ldc cat alog no.: Ldc2004l02. Technical report, ISBN 1-58563-324-0.

Amine Chennoufi and Azzeddine Mazroui. 2016a. Impact of morphological analysis and a large training corpus on the performances of arabic diacritization. *International Journal of Speech Technology*, 19(2):269–280.

Amine Chennoufi and Azzeddine Mazroui. 2016b. Morphological, syntactic and diacritics rules for automatic diacritization of arabic sentences. *Journal of King Saud University-Computer and Information Sciences*.

Mona Diab, Mahmoud Ghoneim, and Nizar Habash. 2007. Arabic diacritization in the context of statistical machine translation. In *Proceedings of MT-Summit*.

Amany Fashwan and Sameh Alansary. 2016. A rule based method for adding case ending diacritics for modern standard arabic texts. In *16th International Conference on Language Engineering*. The Egyptian Society of Language Engineering (ESOLE).

Amany Fashwan. 2016. Automatic diacritization of modern standard arabic texts: A corpus based approach. Master's thesis, Faculty of Arts, University of Alexanderia, Egypt.

Nizar Habash and Owen Rambow. 2005. Arabic tokenization, part-of-speech tagging and morphological disambiguation in one fell swoop. In *Proceedings of the 43rd Annual Meeting on Association for Computational Linguistics*, pages 573–580. Association for Computational Linguistics.

Nizar Habash and Owen Rambow. 2007a. Arabic diacritization through full morphological tagging. In *Human Language Technologies 2007: The Conference of the North American Chapter of the Association for Computational Linguistics; Companion Volume, Short Papers*, pages 53–56. Association for Computational Linguistics.

Nizar Habash, Ryan Gabbard, Owen Rambow, Seth Kulick, and Mitchell P. Marcus. 2007b. Determining case in arabic: Learning complex linguistic behavior requires complex linguistic features. In *EMNLP-CoNLL*, pages 1084–1092.

Nizar Habash, Owen Rambow, and Ryan Roth. 2009. Mada+ tokan: A toolkit for arabic tokenization, diacritization, morphological disambiguation, pos tagging, stemming and lemmatization. In *Proceedings of the 2nd international conference on Arabic language resources and tools (MEDAR), Cairo, Egypt*, volume 41, page 62.

Christopher D. Manning and Hinrich Schütze. 1999. *Foundations of statistical natural language processing*, volume 999. MIT Press.

Aya S. Metwally, Mohsen A. Rashwan, and Amir F. Atiya. 2016. A multi-layered approach for arabic text diacritization. In *Cloud Computing and Big Data Analysis (ICCCBDA), 2016 IEEE International Conference on*, pages 389–393. IEEE.

Mohsen A. Rashwan, Mohammad Al-Badrashiny, Mohamed Attia, and Sherif Abdou. 2009. A hybrid system for automatic arabic diacritization. In *The 2nd International Conference on Arabic Language Resources and Tools*.

Mohsen A. Rashwan, Al-Badrashiny Mohamad, Mohamed Attia, Sherif Abdou, and Ahmed Rafea. 2011. A stochastic arabic diacritizer based on a hybrid of factorized and unfactorized textual features. *IEEE Transactions on Audio, Speech, and Language Processing*, 19(1):166–175.

Mohsen A. Rashwan, Ahmad A. Al Sallab, Hazem M. Raafat, and Ahmed Rafea. 2014. Automatic arabic diacritics restoration based on deep nets. *ANLP 2014*, page 65.

Mohsen A. Rashwan, Ahmad A. Al Sallab, Hazem M. Raafat, and Ahmed Rafea. 2015. Deep learning framework with confused sub-set resolution architecture for automatic arabic diacritization. *IEEE Transactions on Audio, Speech, and Language Processing*, 23(3):505–516.

Ryan Roth, Owen Rambow, Nizar Habash, Mona Diab, and Cynthia Rudin. 2008. Arabic morphological tagging, diacritization, and lemmatization using lexeme models and feature ranking. In *Proceedings of* the 46th Annual Meeting of the Association for Computational Linguistics on Human Language Technologies: Short Papers*, pages 117–120. Association for Computational Linguistics.

Khaled Shaalan, Hitham M. Abo Bakr, and Ibrahim Ziedan. 2008. A statistical method for adding case ending diacritics for arabic text. In *Proceedings of Language Engineering Conference*, pages 225–234.

Khaled Shaalan, Hitham M. Abo Bakr, and Ibrahim Ziedan. 2009. A hybrid approach for building arabic diacritizer. In *Proceedings of the EACL 2009 workshop on computational approaches to semitic languages*, pages 27–35. Association for Computational Linguistics.

Anas Shahrour, Salam Khalifa, and Nizar Habash. 2015. Improving arabic diacritization through syntactic analysis. In *EMNLP*, pages 1309–1315.

Imed Zitouni, Jeffrey S. Sorensen, and Ruhi Sarikaya. 2006. Maximum entropy based restoration of arabic diacritics. In *Proceedings of the 21st International Conference on Computational Linguistics and the 44th annual meeting of the Association for Computational Linguistics*, pages 577–584. Association for Computational Linguistics.

# Arabic Tweets Treebanking and Parsing: A Bootstrapping Approach


**Fahad Albogamy**
School of Computer Science,
University of Manchester,
Manchester, M13 9PL, UK
albogamf@cs.man.ac.uk

**Allan Ramsay**
School of Computer Science,
University of Manchester,
Manchester, M13 9PL, UK
allan.ramsay@cs.man.ac.uk

**Hanady Ahmed**
CAS, Arabic department,
Qatar University,
2713, Al Hala St, Doha, Qatar
hanadyma@qu.edu.qa



## Abstract

In this paper, we propose using a "boot-strapping" method for constructing a dependency treebank of Arabic tweets. This method uses a rule-based parser to create a small treebank of one thousand Arabic tweets and a data-driven parser to create a larger treebank by using the small treebank as a seed training set. We are able to create a dependency treebank from unlabelled tweets without any manual intervention. Experiments results show that this method can improve the speed of training the parser and the accuracy of the resulting parsers.


## 1 Introduction

Rule-based parsers have been developed and used for decades in the NLP community. In such parsers, linguistic rules are written to represent knowledge about the syntactic structure of a language. The parser produces the resulting parse trees by applying these rules to input sentences. It uses a dictionary or lexicon to store information about each word in input text before applying the linguistic rules. Although this kind of parser is widely-used in a variety of NLP systems to provide deep linguistic analyses, they have disadvantages: they are slow and it is time-consuming, expensive and tedious to construct dictionaries and to write the rules by expert linguists and hard to maintain them.

In recent years, data-driven parsers have been widely used due to the availability of annotated data such as the Penn Treebank (PTB) (Marcus et al., 1993) and the Penn Arabic Treebak (PATB) (Maamouri et al., 2004). These parsers are robust and produce state-of-the-art results compared to rule-based ones. However, the reliance on anno-

tated data is one of the significant disadvantages of using data-driven parsers because a large amount of rich annotated data is not always available for many languages and domains due to various factors (Ramasamy and Žabokrtský, 2011).

In the domain of Arabic tweets, we decided to use a data-driven approach, but for that a suitable collection of training data (treebank) should be available for training, and to our knowledge no such dataset has yet been created. For this reason, we have developed a bootstrapping technique for constructing a dependency treebank of the Arabic tweets by using a rule-based parser (RBP) and a data-driven parser (MaltParser). We are able to create a dependency treebank from unlabelled tweets without any manual intervention. Experiments results show that using MaltParser and RBP to construct a large training set (treebank) is better in terms of speed of training and accuracy of parsing than constructing it by using RBP only.

The rest of this paper is organised as follows: In Section 2, we give an overview of the related work, followed by a description of our bootstrapping approach in Section 3. In Section 4, we discuss the evaluation, results and their analysis. In Section 5, we reflect on the work described in the main paper.

## 2 Related Work

Although data-driven parsers have achieved state-of-the-art results on well-formed texts, they have not performed well on user-generated text because the nature of the texts found in user-contributed online forums rarely complies with the standard rules of the underlying language, which makes them challenging for traditional NLP tools, including data-driven approaches, even if domain adaptation techniques have been used (Seddah et al., 2012).

The nature of the text content of Arabic tweets




*Proceedings of The Third Arabic Natural Language Processing Workshop (WANLP)*, pages 94–99,
Valencia, Spain, April 3, 2017. ©2017 Association for Computational Linguistics

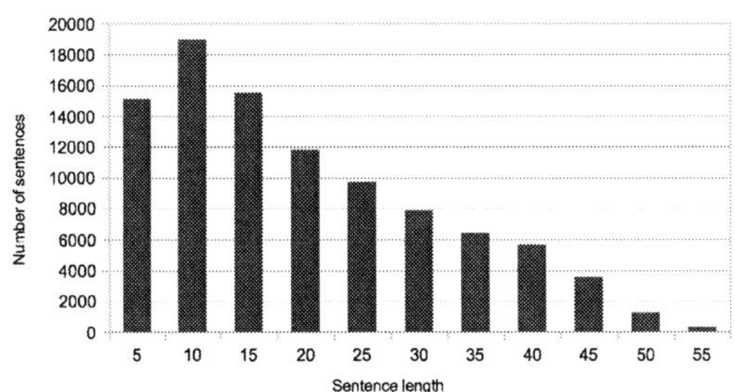

Figure 1: Length of tweets

is very mixed. It includes quite long sentences (20% of sentences are 25 or more words. See Figure 1) that are reasonably well-written (these can be considerably longer than sentences in English tweets because of the fact that Arabic is very economical with characters), very informal material with large numbers of errors and neologisms, and material which is just complete nonsense. Therefore, annotated data for well-edited genres such as PTB and PATB is not suited to the domain of tweets (Kong et al., 2014). As a result, there is an increasing interest in the development of treebanks of user-generated text. These are usually small manually annotated corpora: English Web Treebank (16K sentences) (Bies et al., 2012), Tweebank Treebank (929 sentences) (Kong et al., 2014), Spanish Web Treebank (2846 sentences) (Taulé et al., 2015) and French Social Media Bank (FSMB) (1700 sentences) (Seddah et al., 2012).

Our work is, to best of our knowledge, the first step towards developing a dependency treebank for Arabic tweets which can benefit a wide range of downstream NLP applications such as information extraction, machine translation and sentiment analysis. We explore the idea that producing a small treebank using a rule-based parser will suffice to train an initial MALT-style parser, which we can then use, in conjunction with the rule-based parser, to produce a much larger treebank which can be used to improve the performance of the base parser.

We used RBP to produce a dependency treebank partly to save effort instead of annotating it manually but also to remove the nonsense from the training data. If a tweet is just complete nonsense (and very many are!), then even if we ascribed a structure to them we would not want to use this to train our data-driven parser, since this structure

will not be replicated in unseen tweets. Given that the RBP will fail to provide an analysis of such material, it acts as an automatic filter to remove it. RBP is, however, quite slow and to construct a large treebank using it is very time-consuming and difficult to make a big treebank. Therefore, we just use it to produce a small treebank as a seed training for MaltParser and using a bootstrapping technique to make a larger treebank out of it.

## 3  The Bootstrapping Method

Bootstrapping is used to create labelled training data from large amounts of unlabelled data (Cucerzan and Yarowsky, 2002).

We use a rule-based chart parser (RBP) similar to the one described in (Ramsay, 1999). This parser stops if it finds a complete analysis of a tweet: if does not find a complete analysis after a predetermined number of edges have been created, it stops and returns the largest non-overlapping potential fragments. We have no lexicon because of the rapidly changing nature of tweets and the presence of misspellings, both accidental and deliberate – tweets make use of a very open lexicon, to the point that even after you have looked at over a million tweets you will still find that one in ten words is unknown (Albogamy and Ramsay, 2015). Instead we use a tagger with a coarse-grain tagset, simply labelling all nouns as NN, all verbs as VB and so on. It is striking that even without fine-grained subcategorisation labels (e.g. between intransitive, transitive and sentential complement verbs) RBP produces good quality analyses when it produces anything at all.

Because RBP looks for maximal fragments it can also analyse tweets which actually consist of more than one sentence with no punctuation between them. The following tweet for instance consists of three separate sentences:

@alabbas75@DrA_Farouk235

هذا حق بمحمد الله و نحب الله ورسوله محمد وكل

نبياء والرسل ولعن الله خوارج العصر

The RBP returns three sub trees (largest fragments) that represent these sentences as we can see in Figure 2.

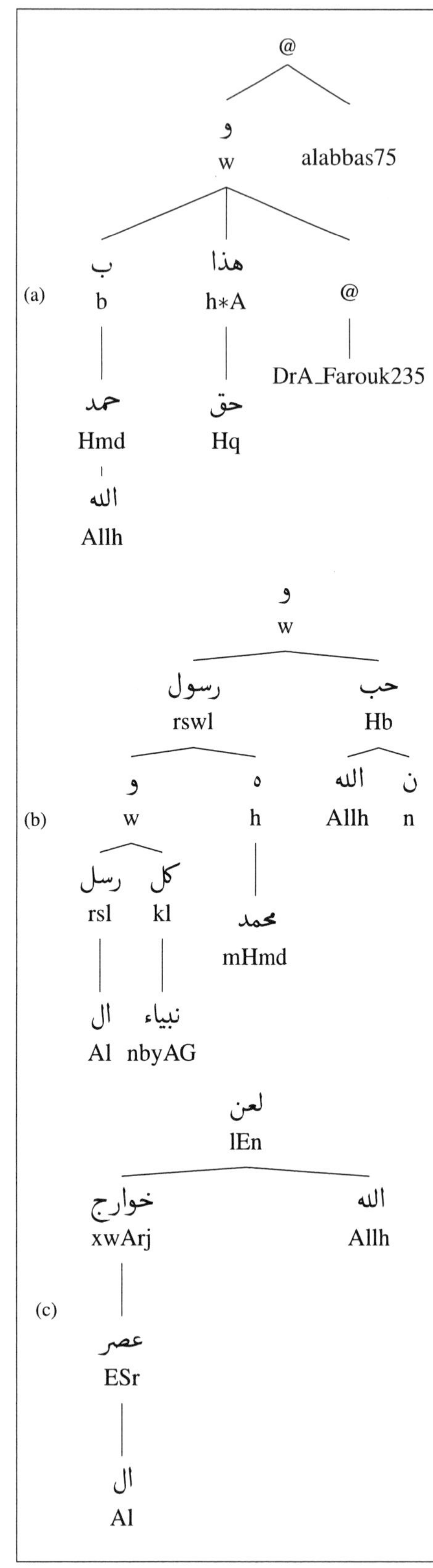

Figure 2: RBP segments a tweet to three fragments

We also use a data-driven parser (version of MaltParser) with three basic data structures a queue of unexamined words, a stack of words that have been considered but which have not been assigned heads, and a collection of `<head, relation, daughter>` triples; and with three basic actions, namely shift (move an item from the queue to the stack), `leftArc` (make the top item on the stack a daughter of the head of the queue and remove it from the stack), `rightArc` (make the head of the queue a daughter of the top item of the stack, remove the head of the queue and move the top item of the stack back to the queue) (Nivre et al., 2006).

The bootstrapping method (Figure 3) begins by using RBP to parse an existing POS-tagged corpus to create a small treebank of one thousand Arabic tweets. Then, MaltParser is trained on the small treebank which was created by RBP and used to parse a much larger set of POS-tagged Arabic tweets. During parsing, the RBP is used as a filter. To use it as a filter, we run the RBP but only allow hypothesises that correspond to links that were suggested by MaltParser so it produces a tree if and only if that tree was produced by MaltParser. As a result, all dependency analyses which do not conform to the defined language rules are omitted. All the resulting legal dependency trees are moved to the training pool to create a larger treebank. In Figure 4, MaltParser returns the whole tree for a tweets, but RBP agrees only upon the sub tree in the box. Finally, MaltParser is retrained on the large treebank. One potential drawback of the

*1. Create dependency trees for a seed set of 1K Arabic tweets by using the rule-driven parser (an initial treebank).*
*2. Train MaltParser (a baseline model) on the initial treebank.*
*3. Parse 10K Arabic tweets with the baseline model and filter out all analyses which do not conform to the language rules by using RBP m1.*
*4. Train a new model on m1.*
*5. Test the new model on the reserved 1K test set.*

Figure 3: Bootstrapping approach

bootstrapping technique is that the parser can reinforce its own bad behaviour. However, we control this by parsing a large amount of data and then by using the largest legal fragments according to the grammar for which a well-formed parse is obtained and added to the training pool. By this way, we make sure that the parser will not learn from bad data.

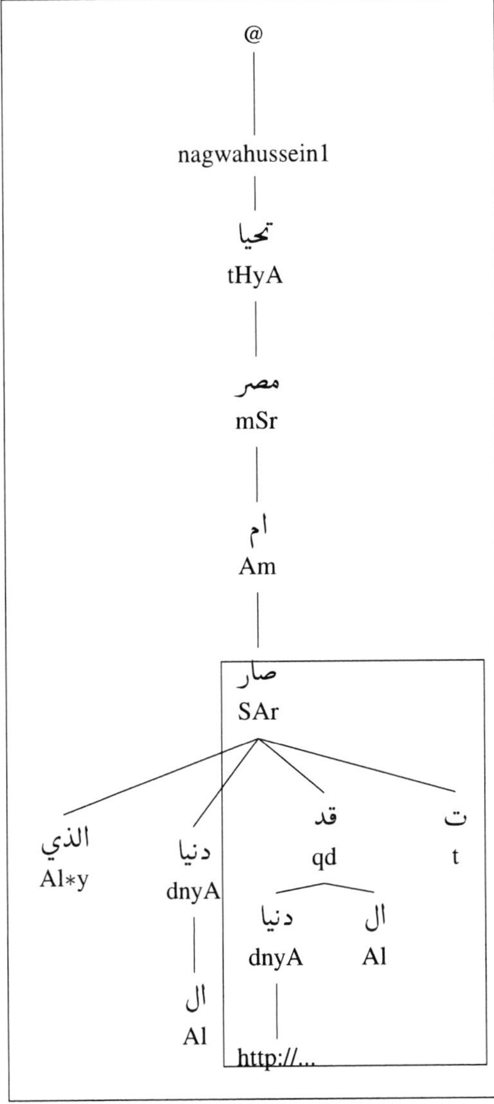


Figure 4: Using RBP as a Filter

## 4 Evaluation

The speed is a crucial factor to take into account when parsing Arabic tweets since there are millions of tweets that need to be parsed. Therefore, rule-based parsers are not suitable in this domain because they are slow (as mentioned in the literature and proved by the first experiment below). To parse Arabic tweets, we decided to use a data-driven parser, namely MaltParser. However, this kind of approaches needs training data (treebank). Therefore, we did two experiments to construct a treebank with a reasonable size. In the first experiment we used RBP only whereas in the second experiment we used RBP and MaltParser as described in Section 3.

### 4.1 Experimental Setup

The corpus from which we extract our dataset is an existing POS-tagged corpus taken from Twitter. Twitter Stream API was used to retrieve tweets from the Arabian Peninsula by using latitude and longitude coordinates of these regions since Arabic dialects in these regions share similar characteristics and they are the closest Arabic dialects to MSA. The corpus was tagged by the Arabic tweets tagger described in (Albogamy and Ramsay, 2016). We sampled 10K tagged tweets from the corpus to experiment on them.

### 4.2 Results

In our experiments, we used two different strategies to create a dependency treebank: using RBP only and using RBP and MaltParser in a bootstrapping technique. We do the evaluation on tweets that RBP gives analyses for. The accuracy of other tweets which do not have sensible analyses cannot be tested because it is impossible to say what the right answer would be. As we mentioned earlier, one of the reasons of using RBP is to eliminate nonsense tweets then it is reasonable to test only on filtered tweets because the vast majority of other tweets are nonsense and do not have sensible parsed trees.

In the first experiment, we used RBP to create a treebank from 10K tagged tweets. Then, we trained MaltParser on it. It took 20K seconds to construct the treebank and the accuracy of MaltParser after trained on the treebank is 68% (see Table 1). In the second experiment, we ran RBP on 1K tagged tweets to create a small treebank. It took 1K seconds to construct the small treebank and the accuracy of MaltParser after training on the small treebank (which we are using as a baseline model) is 64%. Then, the baseline model ran on 10K Arabic tweets and RBP is used to filter out all analyses which do not conform to the language rules and it took 4K seconds to construct larger treebank and the accuracy of MaltParser after training on the larger treebank is 71%. The

97

| Size (words) | Strategy | Accuracy | Training time(sec) |
| --- | --- | --- | --- |
| 162K | RBP | 68% | 20K |

Table 1: Constructing treebank by using RBP

| Size (words) | Strategy | Accuracy | Training time(sec) |
| --- | --- | --- | --- |
| 15K | RBP | 64% | 1K |
| 162K | Bootstrapping MALT+RBP | **71%** | 4K |

Table 2: Constructing treebank by bootstrapping

whole bootstrapping method took 5k seconds to create a reasonable size treebank.

In both experiments, we are able to create a dependency treebank from unlabelled tweets without any manual intervention. Experiments results show that using MaltParser and RBP in a bootstrapping approach to construct a large training set is better than constructing it by using RBP only in terms of the speed of training and the constructing the treebank (20K seconds to construct a 162K treebank just using RBP, 5K seconds to construct a treebank of the same size using RBP to analyse 15K words and MaltParser filtered by RBP to analyse the remaining 147K) and the accuracy of parsing (see Table 2). We tested on a reserved testset of 1K tweets, using 5-fold cross validation.

The results of the tests on our parsing approach yield an accuracy of 71%. We have compared our parsing accuracy and the size of treebank with similar work for English tweets (Kong et al., 2014) and French social media data (Seddah et al., 2012). Those two parsers yield accuracies 80% and 67.8% respectively and the size of our treebank is much larger than their treebanks. Our results show improvements over the performance of French parsing for social media data and it is not far behind English parsing for tweets. Moreover, we did not use any manual intervention for creating our treebank whereas they used human annotated data.

## 5 Conclusion

We have described a bootstrapping technique, which uses a rule-based parser to construct a small treebank of Arabic tweets based on an existing POS-tagged corpus, which then trains a data-driven parser on this treebank to parse a much larger pool of unlabeled Arabic tweets to create a large treebank. The results reported from the evaluation of this approach show that it can make a reasonable size dependency treebank that conforms to the rules of the rule-based parser and improve the speed of training and the accuracy of the parsing. This method does not require annotated data or human-supervised training.

## Acknowledgments

The authors would like to thank the anonymous reviewers for their encouraging feedback and insights. Fahad would also like to thank King Saud University for their financial support. Hanady Ahmed and Allan Ramsay's contribution to this publication was made possible by the NPRP award [NPRP 7-1334-6-039 PR3] from the Qatar National Research Fund (a member of The Qatar Foundation). The statements made herein are solely the responsibility of the authors.

## References

Alfred V. Aho and Jeffrey D. Ullman. 1972. *The Theory of Parsing, Translation and Compiling*, volume 1. Prentice-Hall, Englewood Cliffs, NJ.

Fahad Albogamy and Allan Ramsay. 2015. POS tagging for Arabic tweets. *Recent Advances in Natural Language Processing*, page 1.

Fahad Albogamy and Allan Ramsay. 2016. Fast and robust POS tagger for Arabic tweets using agreement-based bootstrapping. *LREC*.

American Psychological Association. 1983. *Publications Manual*. American Psychological Association, Washington, DC.

Ann Bies, Justin Mott, Colin Warner, and Seth Kulick. 2012. English web treebank. *Linguistic Data Consortium, Philadelphia, PA*.

Ashok K. Chandra, Dexter C. Kozen, and Larry J. Stockmeyer. 1981. Alternation. *Journal of the Association for Computing Machinery*, 28(1):114–133.

Silviu Cucerzan and David Yarowsky. 2002. Bootstrapping a multilingual part-of-speech tagger in one person-day. In *proceedings of the 6th conference on Natural language learning-Volume 20*, pages 1–7. Association for Computational Linguistics.

Dan Gusfield. 1997. *Algorithms on Strings, Trees and Sequences*. Cambridge University Press, Cambridge, UK.

Lingpeng Kong, Nathan Schneider, Swabha Swayamdipta, Archna Bhatia, Chris Dyer, and Noah A Smith. 2014. A dependency parser for tweets.

Mohamed Maamouri, Ann Bies, Tim Buckwalter, and Wigdan Mekki. 2004. The Penn Arabic Treebank: Building a large-scale annotated Arabic corpus. In *NEMLAR conference on Arabic language resources and tools*, volume 27, pages 466–467.

Mitchell P Marcus, Mary Ann Marcinkiewicz, and Beatrice Santorini. 1993. Building a large annotated corpus of English: The Penn Treebank. *Computational linguistics*, 19(2):313–330.

Joakim Nivre, Johan Hall, and Jens Nilsson. 2006. Maltparser: A data-driven parser-generator for dependency parsing. In *Language Resources and Evaluation*.

Loganathan Ramasamy and Zdeněk Žabokrtský. 2011. Tamil dependency parsing: results using rule based and corpus based approaches. In *International Conference on Intelligent Text Processing and Computational Linguistics*, pages 82–95. Springer.

Allan Ramsay. 1999. Parsing with discontinuous phrases. *Natural Language Engineering*, 5(03):271–300.

Djamé Seddah, Benoit Sagot, Marie Candito, Virginie Mouilleron, and Vanessa Combet. 2012. The French social media bank: a treebank of noisy user generated content. In *COLING 2012-24th International Conference on Computational Linguistics*.

Mariona Taulé, M Antonia Martí, Ann Bies, Montserrat Nofre, Aina Garí, Zhiyi Song, Stephanie Strassel, and Joe Ellis. 2015. Spanish treebank annotation of informal non-standard web text. In *International Conference on Web Engineering*, pages 15–27. Springer.

# Identifying Effective Translations
# for Cross-lingual Arabic-to-English User-generated Speech Search

**Ahmad Khwileh**[1]**, Haithem Afli**[2]**, Gareth J. F. Jones**[2] **and Andy Way**[2]
ADAPT Centre, School of Computing
Dublin City University
Dublin 9, Ireland
(1) `ahmad.khwileh2@mail.dcu.ie`
(2) `{hafli, gjones, away}@computing.dcu.ie`

## Abstract

Cross Language Information Retrieval (CLIR) systems are a valuable tool to enable speakers of one language to search for content of interest expressed in a different language. A group for whom this is of particular interest is bilingual Arabic speakers who wish to search for English language content using information needs expressed in Arabic queries. A key challenge in CLIR is crossing the language barrier between the query and the documents. The most common approach to bridging this gap is automated query translation, which can be unreliable for vague or short queries. In this work, we examine the potential for improving CLIR effectiveness by predicting the translation effectiveness using Query Performance Prediction (QPP) techniques. We propose a novel QPP method to estimate the quality of translation for an Arabic-Engish Cross-lingual User-generated Speech Search (CLUGS) task. We present an empirical evaluation that demonstrates the quality of our method on alternative translation outputs extracted from an Arabic-to-English Machine Translation system developed for this task. Finally, we show how this framework can be integrated in CLUGS to find relevant translations for improved retrieval performance.

## 1 Introduction

The growing archives of online digital content are increasingly diverse in style, media and the language used. Within this content the balance between use of languages is very uneven. An important case of this effect is Arabic multimedia content where the amount of content available is proportionally very small. This results in a significant demand from bilingual Arabic speakers to access information in other languages, most notably English. Cross Language Information Retrieval (CLIR) is an effective tool to bridge the language barrier between user search queries in one language and the target documents in another language (Oard and Diekema, 1998; Khwileh et al., 2016). The simplest and most commonly adopted approach in CLIR is to use machine translation (MT) to translate the user's query. In most cases, MT is used as a black box as an input stage to an otherwise unchanged monolingual search system Many different MT systems have been studied in CLIR research for different tasks, e.g. (Oard and Hackett, 1998; Magdy and Jones, 2014). However, no single MT system has been reported to be effective for all CLIR tasks.

The effectiveness of an MT system for CLIR is primarily evaluated by examining the retrieval quality associated with the translated queries. We follow this practice in this paper, by considering translation quality in terms of measured IR performance on an experimental test collection. We investigation concentrates on a cross-lingual user-generated speech search (CLUGS) task (Khwileh et al., 2015). In this work, we propose a prediction framework that utilises Query Performance Prediction (QPP) methods to estimate expected IR performance for specific query translation based both on the translated query itself and the output of the translation process. As part of our investigation we explore the use of QPP to select from an N-best list of alternative translations for q query generated by an statistical MT systems.

In the next section we give some background and describe the motivation behind our CLUGS task. Section 3 gives an overview of the QPP approaches that we study in this investigation. Section 4 introduces our proposed prediction framework for CLUGS. Section 5 outlines our experimental settings. Section 6 evaluates the proposed framework and section 7 shows this approach can indeed be utilised for finding relevant translations in CLUGS. Section 8 concludes, together with some avenues for future work.



*Proceedings of The Third Arabic Natural Language Processing Workshop (WANLP)*, pages 100–109,
Valencia, Spain, April 3, 2017. ©2017 Association for Computational Linguistics

## 2 Cross-lingual Arabic-to-English Search for User-generated Speech

The current explosive growth in internet-based social media networks content is creating massive volumes of online multimedia content. This includes User-Generated Speech (UGS) content which is being uploaded to social media sites websites such as YouTube and Facebook. These increasing quantities of UGS data, together with its complex and inconsistent structure, are creating the need for sophisticated Spoken Content Retrieval (SCR) systems to locate relevant material. This presents new challenges and exciting opportunities for IR research. SCR technologies require the combination of speech processing technologies with IR methods. SCR typically utilises Automatic Speech Recognition (ASR) to generate text transcripts of spoken audio. At a simple level, SCR can be considered as the application of IR techniques to ASR transcripts. However, errors in ASR transcripts and the nature of spoken content present significant challenges for SCR (Larson and Jones, 2012).

Figure 1: Example of the content variation issue across languages: Video search results for Arabic and English queries.

Beyond these challenges in SCR, further challenges are raised in a multilingual search setting. As noted earlier, one of the scenarios for multilingual search is CLIR where a searcher uses a query in one language to find relevant content in another one, where relevant content in the query language is either sparse or not available.

This is a particularly notable issue for Arabic which is spoken by an estimated 420M speakers in different countries, making it one of the most-spoken languages in the world. Arabic has been the language with the largest growth in Internet users in the last decade with an estimated 2500% growth. In 2016, there were an estimated 168M Internet users with 45% Internet penetration (Internetworldstats.com, 2016). However, the Arabic content available online is still minimal, estimated as being less than 0.1% of the Internet content. The massive gap between available content and speakers of the language means that bilingual Arabic speakers will often seek relevant content in another language. To illustrate this situation consider the example in Figure 1. This shows the search engine with a simple Arabic query محاضرة في نظم استرجاع المعلومات and the equivalent English query *Information retrieval system lecture*

The *Google* video search engine[1] located more than 29,000 matching results in English with all top-ranked results being relevant with high-quality metadata. However, for Arabic, only 203 matching results were located with only one of the top-10 results indicated as relevant.

### 2.1 Related Work

Addressing CLIR for Arabic speakers provides a real-world use case where research into improved CLIR is important due to its linguistic challenges and political importance (Darwish et al., 2014).

Relevant linguistic features include the complexity of morphological and syntactic structures that require special processing. Indeed, MT for Arabic to English is considered one of the most difficult challenges in CLIR, and effective techniques working with special characteristics of the Arabic language are required (Alqudsi et al., 2014). Previous CLIR work on Arabic has been limited to standard text-based TREC 2001/2002 CLEF[2] tracks (Oard and Gey, 2002; Besançon et al., 2009; Darwish et al., 2014). The data collections used in these tasks were standard Text Arabic news collection collected from AFP. Another larger AFP newswire Arabic collection was released by the INFILE Track in CLEF 2008/2009 (Besançon et al., 2009), but unfortunately received no participation. To date most work on Arabic CLIR has actually focused on the other side of the story, i.e. the retrieval of Arabic documents based on English queries (English-to-Arabic CLIR). Which enabling access to information from Arabic sources, does not address the needs to Arabic speakers. In this work, we study a CLIR task that enables Arabic users to search for the relevant spoken content from the English web. In previous work we investigated the use of Google Translate [3] as a black box off-the-self MT system for this task (2015) We found that the main challenges of this task arise due to noise in the search index for the user-generated data, and how Arabic translation errors can significantly harm retrieval effectiveness.

Despite the problems in translation problems for CLIR encountered when using off-the-shelf

---

[1] Retrieved from www.google.com/video on 2016-12-01
[2] http://clef2016.clef-initiative.eu/
[3] https://cloud.google.com/translate/

MT systems such as Google and Bing Translate[4], have been observed to outperform open-box MT systems developed by CLIR researchers for many language pairs (Zhou et al., 2012). For instance, during the CLEF 2009 workshop (Leveling et al., 2009a; Leveling et al., 2009b), the best performing non-off-the-shelf MT achieved just 70% of the performance achieved by Google Translate. However, in our earlier work we found that the use of black-box MT for Arabic is still ineffective compared to other languages pairs (such as French-to-English CLIR) (2015).

From examination of the behaviour of MT systems, it is clear that while the "best" translation produced by the MT does not always produce the most effective translation for optimal CLIR performance, better translations are often produced with lower translation confidence by the MT system. In this investigation, we seek to use Query Performance Prediction (QPP) methods developed in the IR community, to improve CLEF effectiveness for Arabic-English search using an open-box MT system. We then study the effectiveness of this approach against standard online black-box MT for a CLUGS search task. In the next sections we describe these QPP techniques and how we utilize them in our CLUGS task.

## 3   Query Performance Prediction

The motivation behind QPP methods in IR is to estimate the performance of the query at retrieving relevant documents. This inference can be used to tune the retrieval settings to maximize the overall system effectiveness. QPP is divided into pre- and post-retrieval methods. In pre-retrieval QPP, prediction is based on analysing the query difficulty (Hauff et al., 2008; He and Ounis, 2004; He and Ounis, 2006). The estimated query difficulty defines that, given a certain query, whether relevant content is hard (low retrieval performance) or easy (high retrieval performance) to find. Thus, difficulty can be used as an indication of the retrieval performance of the current query. In post-retrieval QPP, the retrieval results of the query are analysed to estimate its performance (Kurland et al., 2011; Shtok et al., 2012). Pre-retrieval methods are more efficient than post-retrieval, causing less overhead to the retrieval system since no retrieval is required for the prediction. In this work we study the application of both pre- and post- methods QPP to predict the translation

quality of queries in CLIR. In the next sections we describe the QPP approaches we use in this task.

### 3.1   Pre-retrieval QPP

Existing approaches to pre-retrieval QPP are based on measuring the statistics/characteristics of the query terms calculated over the index collection. The most widely used and effective techniques rely on the Inverse Document Frequency (IDF) of query terms, called IDF-based QPP. IDF-based QPP approaches are implemented by taking an aggregation of the IDF values across the query terms such as AvIDF (Average of IDF values), the SUMIDF (the sum of all values) or MAXIDF (the maximum value) (Cronen-Townsend et al., 2002). The IDF value for a term in this work has generally been calculated using the INQUERY formula explained in (Allan et al., 1995) and (He and Ounis, 2006). Another common IDF-based QPP is the Averaged Inverse Collection Term Frequency (avICTF) of the query terms (Plachouras et al., 2004; He and Ounis, 2006). The formula for this predictor is explained in detail in (He and Ounis, 2006). IDF-based predictors have shown positive correlation with query performance over multiple standard IR tasks (Plachouras et al., 2004; He and Ounis, 2004; Hauff et al., 2008; Hauff, 2010).

Other pre-retrieval QPP methods are based on analysing the linguistic features of the query terms such as the the query length (AvQL) which is based on the average number of content words (non stop-words) in a query (He and Ounis, 2004; Mothe and Tanguy, 2005; He and Ounis, 2006), and Query Scope (QS) which makes use of the document frequencies (DF) of the terms (He and Ounis, 2004; He and Ounis, 2006). A higher DF of the query terms indicates that they are very common, and so probably not helpful for finding relevant documents, as they would result in a lower effectiveness of the query.

A more complex technique proposed by Zhao et al. (2008), is the Summed Collection Query similarity (SCQ). SCQ approaches utilise both Term Frequency (TF) and IDF to predict the query performance. Similar to the IDF-based QPP, there are also three different aggregation methods of SQC across the query terms. AvSQC, takes the average across the query terms; SumSQC, which takes the sum of all resultant similarities; and MaxSQC which takes the maximum value among them. SQC is explained in detail in (Zhao et al., 2008; Hauff, 2010). Zhao et al. (2008) also proposed another QPP method that is computationally more expensive called VarTFIDF. which is based on

---



[4]https://www.microsoft.com/en-us/translator/translatorapi.aspx

the distribution of the TF.IDF weights (Zobel and Moffat, 2006) across the query terms. Similar to SQC and IDF QPP approaches, VarTFIDF QPP has a three different versions (SUM,MAX,Avg) based on the used aggregation across the query terms.

In this work, we argue that IDF is not a good predictor for this task. This argument is also supported by our initial investigation of the problem and the following hypothesis. By definition, IDF gives a higher weight to unique terms across the search collection. While this might be useful for a retrieval model to rank documents, using IDF is not reliable for QPP since it also gives high values for translation candidates which are *misleading* terms. We define misleaders as terms that are rare across the collection (hence having high IDF values), but not relevant to the topic of the current query. These misleaders can result in query topic drift (Mitra et al., 1998) and thus negatively impact on retrieval effectiveness. Another source of misleader terms is words which are Out-of-Vocabulary (OOV) with respect to the MT. In this situation the MT system produces incorrect translations of terms which the MT system cannot by definition translate correctly.

To deal with misleaders arising from IDF issues, we propose a new simple prediction technique which we refer to as the Average Term Fluency (AvgFL). Term fluency estimates whether a query contains the same terms that appear in relevant documents. Higher fluency is assumed to lead to better query-document matching, and hence improved QPP effectiveness. We rely on the collection frequency (cf) of each term to indicate its fluency on the given collection $D$. The $cf$ is normalized by the DF to penalize non-helpful terms which appear in all documents in collection. The proposed AvgFL is calculated as shown in Equation (1); where $k$ is the number of $t$ terms in query $Q$, $cf_t$ is the cf which is the number of times $t$ appears in the collection $D$. $df_t$ indicates the DF which is the number of documents contains the term $t$.

$$AvgFL(Q) = \frac{1}{k}\sum_{t \epsilon Q}^{k}(log(cf_t+1)/(log(df_t+1)+1)) \tag{1}$$

### 3.2 Post-Retrieval QPP

State-of-the-art post-retrieval QPP techniques use information induced from analyzing the retrieval scores $Score(d)$ of the results set $D_q^{[res]}$ produced by retrieval method $M$, where $D_q^{[res]}$ represents the list of document ids retrieved for a query together with their ranks $\mathcal{R}i$ and scores $Score(d)$ sorted according to their relevancy to a query $q$.

In probabilistic terms, the resultant score $Score(d)$ of a document $d$ represents the estimated relevance probability $r$ of a document $d$ with respect to $q$ $Score(d) \equiv \mathcal{P}(d|q,r)$. These QPP methods are based on analyzing the performance of the top $k$ ranked documents, which includes all documents that have rank $\mathcal{R}i$ that is less than $k$ ($\forall d \epsilon D_q^{[res]} d_{\mathcal{R}i}$ where $0 \leqslant ri \leqslant k$) (Zhou and Croft, 2007; Shtok et al., 2012).

WIG is a well-established QPP technique based on the weighted entropy of the top $k$ ranked documents (Zhou and Croft, 2007). This technique works by comparing the scores of the top-k documents $\forall d \epsilon D_q^{[k]} Score(d)$ to that obtained by the corpus $Score(D)$. WIG is defined in equation (2).

$$WIG(q,M) = \frac{1}{k}\sum_{d \epsilon D_k}\frac{1}{\sqrt{|q|}}(Score(d)-Score(D)) \tag{2}$$

Another similar post-retrieval QPP technique is the Normalised Query Commitment (NQC) (Shtok et al., 2012). This technique is based on estimating the potential amount of query drift in the list of top $k$ documents by measuring the standard deviation of their obtained retrieval scores. A high standard deviation indicates reduced topic drift and hence probable improved retrieval effectiveness. NQC is defined in equation (3) where $\overline{\mu} = \frac{1}{k}\sum_{d \epsilon D_q^{[k]}} Score(d)$.

$$NQC(q,M) = \frac{1}{Score(D)}\sqrt{\sum_{d \epsilon D_q^{[k]}}\frac{1}{k}(Score(d)-Score(\overline{\mu})} \tag{3}$$

Both WIG and NQC are tuned to have a strong linear relationship with the performance of the query in which the only variable that needs to be decided is the top-$k$ documents.

For our task, we introduce a modified version of the WIG called Weighted Relevancy Gain (WRG) that focuses on the scores of the top-ranked assumed *relevant* documents vs other top-ranked but assumed *non-relevant* documents. Unlike previous predictors, this approach assumes that the set top-$k$ documents $D_q^{[k]}$ for each query is composed of two subsets $D_q^{[rel]}$ and $D_q^{[nrel]}$ defined as follows: $D_q^{[rel]}$ is the set of $rel$ relevant documents that are assumed relevant for query $q$ where $\forall d \epsilon D_q^{[res]}$ ($d_{\mathcal{R}i}$ where $0 \leqslant \mathcal{R}i \leqslant rel < k$), and $D_q^{[nrel]}$ is the set of documents that are assumed non-relevant and ineffective for Relevancy. These documents are ranked among the top-$k$ documents and right after the $rel$ documents ($rel < nrel < k$) as in $\forall d \epsilon D_q^{[res]}$ ($d_{\mathcal{R}i}$ where $rel < \mathcal{R}i \leqslant nrel$).

The WRG predictor aims to analyze the quality of the $rel$ documents by measuring the likelihood that they contain significant variation. This is estimated by measuring the weighted entropy of the assumed $rel$ documents against the

top-ranked yet non-relevant $nrel$ set of documents. Unlike WIG, which uses the *centroid* of *all* non-relevant documents ($Score(D)$), WRG uses the *centroid* of the $nrel$ documents scores :
$Cnrel \equiv Cent(Score(D_q{}^{[nrel]})) \equiv \frac{1}{nrel} \sum_{d \in D_q{}^{[nrel]}} Score(d)$
as a reference point for estimating of the effectiveness as shown in equation (4).

$$WRG(q,D_{rel}) = \frac{1}{rel} \sum_{d \in D_{rel}} \frac{1}{\sqrt{|q|}} \left( \frac{Cnrel}{Score(d)} \right)$$

(4)

WRG requires 2 parameters: the number of $rel$ documents and the number of $nrel$ documents to perform the actual estimation.

## 4  Using QPP for CLUGS

We propose to utilize QPP for CLUGS as follows. Assume $T_q$ is an MT translated version of $q$ and $T_q{}^{[n]}$ is the list of n-best translations generated by an MT translation system $T$. Assuming $\mathcal{Q}$ is the event of being an effective translation of $q$ for getting relevant content in CLUGS, the goal of this prediction task is to estimate $\mathcal{P}(T_q|q, \mathcal{Q})$ (the likelihood of the translation $T_q$ given that a relevance event happens for $q$), which seeks to answer the following question :

*What is the probability $\mathcal{P}(.)$ for each translation candidate $T_q$ from the top n-list generated by translation system $T$ being an effective translation $\mathcal{Q}$ of a query q for CLUGS?*

Our proposed framework relies on QPP to rank the best translations $T_q{}^{[n]}$ generated by MT system $T$ based on the probability function $\mathcal{P}(T_q|q,\mathcal{Q})$. We use the previously explained QPP methods in section 3 to predict the retrieval effectiveness of each translation candidate $T_q$. For example, we assume that AvICTF can be taken as prediction function $\mathcal{F}$ to indicate the effectiveness of translations candidates $T_q$ as $\mathcal{P}(T_q|q,\mathcal{Q}) \equiv \mathcal{F}(T_q) \equiv AvICTF(T_q)$.

## 5  Experimental Setup

In order to evaluate QPP for our CLUGS task we configured three modules as follows. A CLIR system, an MT system to generate the N-best translations, and a QPP system to parse each query candidate of the n-best list and assign a prediction value to it.

The CLUGS task is similar to the one described in (Khwileh et al., 2015). The task is based on the blip1000 collection which contains 14,838 transcripts automatically extracted using an ASR system from videos which were uploaded to a video-sharing website by 2,237 different uploaders, covering a 25 different topics (Schmiedeke et al., 2013).

For the query topic set, we use a modified monolingual *adhoc* version of the 60 different original English topics developed within the MediaEval 2012 Search and Hyperlinking task[5] which was developed by Khwileh et al. (2016).

To setup the CLIR system, similar to the procedure adopted in our earlier investigation (2015), we used two native Arabic (AR) speakers who are also fluent on English (EN) to write their equivalent versions of the queries in Arabic for each of these EN topics.

We configured and trained an AR-to-EN MT system to translate each AR query to EN. Our MT system is a phrase-based (Koehn et al., 2003), that is developed using the Moses Statistical Machine Translation (SMT) toolkit (Koehn et al., 2007). Word alignments in both directions were calculated using a multi-threaded version of the GIZA++ [6] tool (Gao and Vogel, 2008). The parameters of our MT system were tuned on a development corpus using Minimum Error Rate Training (Och, 2003). The AR-to-En MT system was trained using the bilingual training corpora listed in Table 1 from LDC for MSA (Modern Standard Arabic) training. The size of the tuning set is 111.8K and 138.2K of Arabic and English tokens. All AR data are tokenised using MADA-ARZ version 0.4 (Habash et al., 2013).

| Corpus | AR genre | AR tokens | EN tokens |
|---|---|---|---|
| bolt |  | 1.70M | 2.05M |
| thy | Egyptian | 282k | 362k |
| bbnturk |  | 1.52M | 1.58M |
| bbnegy |  | 514k | 588k |
| gale |  | 4.28M | 5.01 M |
| fouo | MSA | 717 k | 791k |
| ummah |  | 3.61M | 3.72M |
| iraqi | Iraqi | 1M | 1.14M |
| bbnlev | Levantine | 1.59M | 1.81M |
| Total |  | 15.2M | 17M |

Table 1: The sizes and the genres of bilingual training corpora.

We extracted the top 100 translations list for each query generated by the MT system. The overall number of query candidates generated by was 5,863 with an average of over 90 different translations per query. These queries were used in searching the EN ASR transcripts extracted from the blip1000 collection.

The Terrier retrieval platform[7] was used as the IR component of our experimental setup. Stop

---

[5]http://www.multimediaeval.org/mediaeval2012/
[6]Available at http://www.cs.cmu.edu/~qing/
[7]http://terrier.org/

words were removed based on the standard Terrier list, and stemming performed using the Terrier implementation of Porter stemming. Retrieval was carried out using the PL2 retrieval model using the settings recommended for this CLUGS task in Khwileh et al. (Khwileh et al., 2016), with the empirically-determined hyper-parameters that $c = 1$.

## 5.1 Parameters
### Tuning for the Post-retrieval QPP

As explained in section 3.2, post-retrieval QPP methods require some parameters to be tuned. For the experiments reported in this work, we used the following approach to tune NQC, WIG and WRG. We used the *optimal paradigm*, proposed in (Shtok et al., 2012), that is based on using values of free parameters that yield optimal prediction performance for each predictor on set of queries. We used the 60 monolingual EN queries as test set to obtain these optimal parameters for each predictor. Parameters $k$ (in WIG and NQC), $rel$ and $nrel$ (in WRG) were tuned through manual data sweeping within the range of [5, 100] with an interval of 5, and through the range of [100,500] with an interval of 50. The optimal $k$ parameters obtained for WIG was 10, while for NQC it was 150, these are indeed similar to those recommended in (Shtok et al., 2012). For the WRG, we found that 30 is the optimal parameter for $rel$ and 60 for $nrel$.

## 6 Evaluating Prediction Quality

The effectiveness of QPP methods is usually evaluated by measuring correlation between values assigned by the QPP method and the actual performance, in terms of average precision (AP), of each query. The quality of each predictor is evaluated in our CLUGS task by measuring the Pearson linear correlation coefficient $\rho$ between both the AP, which is measured using human relevant assessment for each candidate translation for extracted 100-best and the values assigned to these queries by each prediction method. For each predictor, we follow the implementation reported in the citation shown in the first column of Table 2. For the SQC and VarTFIDF, we report only the best result obtained out of the three aggregations (Max, Avg and Sum) due to space limitations. In addition to Pearson's correlation, we also tested Kendalls tau and Spearman correlations to report the nonlinear relationship between these predictors and the retrieval performance. The prediction quality for each of these predictors on our CLUGS task is shown in Table 2.

## 6.1 Pre-retrieval Quality

As can be seen from the results shown in Table 2, IDF-based predictors are found to have the least robustness across other predictors. The reliability issue regarding misleading terms (as discussed in section 3.1) significantly impacts the prediction quality of these predictors. To further illustrate this issue, consider the example query
سوفتويرات لتصميم و برمجة مواقع الويب.
This query has two candidates EN translations (T1 and T2) as follows:
T1 : " سوفتويرات
*for the development and web design"* and
T2 : " سوفتويرات *for the development and design internet".*

The main difference between these translations is "web" vs "internet". While the word "internet" is more unique term with a higher IDF value, it is considered as a misleader to this query since it shifts the original topic of the query "web design". Thus, this has resulted in a query topic-drift, and hence a false prediction of its performance.

In contrast, prediction quality is improved for all QPP methods which are less focused on the uniqueness of the terms and do not rely *solely* on the IDF in its calculation (i.e. Qs, SQC). AvgFL is shown to have the highest quality over all tested QPP methods, showing a consistent statistically significant prediction across different correlation measures. This arises as result of its robustness in utilising the fluency measure to discriminate between different translations, penalising these which are OOV or very unique words in the collection.

## 6.2 Post-retrieval Quality

The post-retrieval QPP methods are more robust and perform better than the pre-retrieval methods overall. This is due to the fact that post-retrieval methods are based on the actual scores of the translations in which at least one retrieval run was used for the prediction. Unlike, pre-retrieval methods, post-retrieval requires exhaustive parameter tuning, as explained in section 5.1. Both parameter tuning and the time required to generate the post-retrieval QPP was a major efficiency issue by comparison to pre-retrieval QPR (average time to generate the pre-retrieval QPPs was around 10% to that of the post-retrieval QPPs). WRG has the highest prediction quality across all predictors. The robustness of WRG is due to the fact that it relies on stronger evidence; which is the score of the relevant documents. While NQC/WIG rely only on one parameter, i.e. the top $k$ ranked doc-

| | Pearson | Kendall's tau | Spearman's |
|---|---|---|---|
| VarTFIDF (Zhou and Croft, 2007) | -0.20 | -0.165 | -0.194 |
| SCQ (Zhou and Croft, 2007) | 0.248 | 0.137 | 0.201 |
| Qs (He and Ounis, 2004) | **-0.319** | -0.221 | **-0.29** |
| AvQL (Mothe and Tanguy, 2005) | -0.193 | -0.126 | -0.208 |
| SumIDF (Cronen-Townsend et al., 2002) | 0.069 | 0.110 | 0.163 |
| AvgIDF (Cronen-Townsend et al., 2002) | 0.030 | 0.086 | 0.128 |
| MaxIDF (Scholer et al., 2004) | -0.044 | 0.019 | 0.035 |
| AvICTF (He and Ounis, 2006) | 0.118 | 0.162 | 0.210 |
| AvgFL (Equation 1) | **0.446** | **0.313** | **0.395** |
| WRG (Equation 4 ) | **0.463** | **0.321** | **0.384** |
| WIG (Equation 2 ) | **0.405** | 0.260 | **0.333** |
| NQC (Equation 3 ) | **0.385** | 0.22 | **0.321** |

Table 2: Correlation Coefficients vs AP for each query translation from Ar-to-En vs each QPP. Correlation that are significant at the 0.05 confidence level are marked in **bold**.

uments, WRG relies on further tuning of the top $k$ parameter into both the $rel$ and $nrel$ documents to provide better estimation. This, on one hand, helps WRG to identify relevant translations that can in fact distinguish the relevant document from the non relevant ones, but on the other hand, raises efficiency concerns about WRG, since it takes almost twice the time required for WIG/NQC tuning.

## 7 Finding Relevant Translations in CLUGS

In this section, we investigate the potential for these QPP techniques to be used in an adaptive CLIR algorithm that is able to automatically identify the most relevant translations. The main idea is to use the translation candidate that is predicted to have the highest retrieval effectiveness for each query. Using the same settings explained in section 5, we implement the adaptive CLIR algorithm as follows.

1. For each query, the MT system is used to generate up to the 100-best possible translations which form a selection pool.
2. QPP is used to score each translation candidate from the selection pool based on its estimated retrieval performance.
3. Retrieval is then performed using the translation that is predicted to be most effective.

We investigate using all QPP methods [8] shown in Table 2 to evaluate this adaptive CLIR algorithm.

We compare these adaptive CLIR techniques to three baselines as follows:
Google translate as example of an off-shelf black-box MT tool, similar to our work in (Khwileh et al., 2015); SingleBest, which is the 1-best translation output generated by Moses MT;
100BestAP, which uses the ground-truth data to get the best performing translation in terms of AP from the 100-best translations generated by Moses MT.

---

[8]We used the same parameters learned for post-retrieval QPP in 5.1

The adaptive and baseline retrieval performance results for the CLIR experiments are shown in Table 3 in terms of the Mean Average Precision (MAP) obtained. For clarity, we also report the percentage of improvement over each of these baselines as an additional columns (i.e. the *over SingleBest* column indicates the improvement in MAP over the SingleBest baseline).

The *Baseline CLIR* results from Table 3 show that black-box Google MT out-performed the SingleBest output from the open-box Moses by 11.8% which confirms the previously reported results in (Leveling et al., 2009b) that using black-box MT can be easier and more effective than just using the Singlebest. On the other hand, the result from the open-box with ideal AP (100BestAP) confirms that the open-box MT can indeed be improved by looking at other translations candidates that are more **relevant** for CLIR.

The *Adaptive CLIR using Pre-Retrieval* block of Table 3 shows how pre-retrieval QPP can be used to find the best translation from the 100-best extracted. This confirms the conclusion obtained from Table 2 where the proposed method is the most effective in getting the single best translation for CLIR with effectiveness comparable to that of the black box MT system and obtained 11% performance improvement over the SingleBest baseline. The *Adaptive CLIR using Post-Retrieval* block of Table 3 shows how the post-retrieval QPP methods are the most effective for finding the most effective translation in CLIR. This confirms previously reported conclusions on comparing pre-retrieval and post-retrieval, i.e. that post-retrieval QPP is always more effective (Hauff, 2010). The WRG predictor is the most effective with significant improvement 28% over the SingleBest and 14% over the black-box. This also confirms that the correlation results reported in Table 2 where WRG has the highest correlation to AP when it comes to predicting the translation quality.

| | MAP | over blackbox MT | over SingleBest | Over 100BestAP |
|---|---|---|---|---|
| Baseline CLIR | | | | |
| Off-shelf black-box | 0.2535 | - | 11.8% | -28.9% * |
| 100BestAP | 0.3566 | 28.9%* | 57.3%* | - |
| SingleBest | 0.2267 | -11.8% | - | -57.3%* |
| Adaptive CLIR using Post-Retrieval | | | | |
| **WRG** | **0.2899** | **14.4%** | **27.9%*** | **-18.7%** |
| NQC | 0.2379 | -6.2% | 4.9% | -33.3%* |
| WIG | 0.2423 | -4.4% | 6.9% | -32.1%* |
| Adaptive CLIR using Pre-Retrieval | | | | |
| MAXIDF | 0.2082 | -17.9% | -8.2% | -41.6%* |
| QL | 0.1827 | -27.9%* | -19.4%* | -48.8%* |
| SumSQC | 0.1995 | -21.3%* | -12.0% | -44.1%* |
| **AvgFL** | **0.2507** | **-1.1%** | **10.6%** | **-29.7%*** |
| avgICTF | 0.2219 | -12.5% | -2.1% | -37.8%* |
| SumVarTFIDF | 0.1619 | -36.1%* | -28.6%* | -54.6%* |
| Qs | 0.2103 | -17.0% | -7.2% | -41.0%* |

Table 3: Baseline and adaptive CLIR results using both pre-retrieval and post-retrieval QPP. Percentages % with * indicate *statistically significant* different change at 0.05 confidence level

Overall, results from Table 3 indicate that QPP techniques can indeed help re-ranking the translation candidates of open-box MT, and hence improve its translation quality for CLIR purposes. Both AvgFL and WRG predictors, which were designed specifically for this task, served as an adequate reference to find the most effective translations and improve over the SingleBest output that is suggested originally by the MT system. However, none of the reported adaptive CLIR results were able to match or even come close to the ideal performance baseline (100BestAP). This suggests that there is still scope for further improvement. By contrast, these QPP methods are a stand-alone IR metric that is completely unsupervised and works on a query-by-query basis. Training a machine-learning algorithm that combines several QPPs together with other MT-based signals may achieve more robust/accurate prediction for this task. We leave this investigation for future work.

## 8 Conclusions

This paper has presented a framework for predicting translation quality for a CLUGS task. We proposed a novel unsupervised approach to estimate the effectiveness of a translation when there is no human evaluation of retrieval available. Our experimental investigation reveals that IDF-based prediction is not effective for this task because of the misleading very unique terms which can result in unreliable prediction. We proposed a new Pre-retrieval QPP technique for this task called AvgFL that is designed to detect misleading very unique and OOV words.

For post-retrieval QPP, we also proposed WRG (Weighted Relevancy Gain) that is modified version of the well-established WIG predictor (Zhou and Croft, 2007) and tuned to focus on the information entropy of the relevant documents. Our experimental investigation reports the robustness of these proposed approaches in predicting the translation effectiveness for an Ar-to-En CLUGS task over other state-of-art QPP methods. We found that post-retrieval QPP can be more accurate than pre-retrieval QPP for this task, although it suffers from efficiency issues. Finally, our experiments demonstrated how these predictors could be utilised by a CLIR model that is adaptively able to find the most-relevant translations for IR.

For future work, we plan to experiment with combining different QPP techniques together with other MT-based signals for improved prediction quality. We also plan to use the proposed framework to develop a new CLIR model to estimate the translation quality from different MT systems with different translation outputs.

## Acknowledgments

This research was partially supported by Science Foundation Ireland in the ADAPT Centre (Grant 13/RC/2106) (www.adaptcentre.ie) at Dublin City University.

## References

James Allan, Lisa Ballesteros, James P. Callan, W. Bruce Croft, and Zhihong Lu. 1995. Recent experiments with INQUERY. In *Proceedings of The Fourth Text REtrieval Conference, TREC 1995, Gaithersburg, Maryland, USA, November 1-3, 1995*.

Arwa Alqudsi, Nazlia Omar, and Khalid Shaker. 2014. Arabic machine translation: a survey. *Artificial Intelligence Review*, 42(4):549–572.

Romaric Besançon, Stéphane Chaudiron, Djamel Mostefa, Ismaïl Timimi, Khalid Choukri, and Meriama Laïb. 2009. Overview of CLEF 2009 INFILE track. In *Working Notes for CLEF 2009 Workshop co-located with the 13th European Conference on Digital Libraries (ECDL 2009) , Corfù, Greece, September 30 - October 2, 2009*.

Stephen Cronen-Townsend, Yun Zhou, and W. Bruce Croft. 2002. Predicting query performance. In *SIGIR 2002: Proceedings of the 25th Annual International ACM SIGIR Conference on Research and Development in Information Retrieval, August 11-15, 2002, Tampere, Finland*, pages 299–306.

Kareem Darwish, Walid Magdy. 2014. Arabic information retrieval. *Foundations and Trends® in Information Retrieval*, 7(4):239–342.

Q. Gao and S. Vogel. 2008. Parallel implementations of word alignment tool. In *Software Engineering, Testing, and Quality Assurance for Natural Language Processing*, SETQA-NLP '08, pages 49–57, in Columbus, Ohio, USA.

Nizar Habash, Ryan Roth, Owen Rambow, Ramy Eskander, and Nadi Tomeh. 2013. Morphological analysis and disambiguation for dialectal arabic. In *Human Language Technologies: Conference of the North American Chapter of the Association of Computational Linguistics, Proceedings, June 9-14, 2013, Westin Peachtree Plaza Hotel, Atlanta, Georgia, USA*, pages 426–432.

Claudia Hauff, Djoerd Hiemstra, and Franciska de Jong. 2008. A survey of pre-retrieval query performance predictors. In *Proceedings of the 17th ACM Conference on Information and Knowledge Management, CIKM 2008, Napa Valley, California, USA, October 26-30, 2008*, pages 1419–1420.

Claudia Hauff. 2010. *Predicting the effectiveness of queries and retrieval systems*. Ph.D. thesis, Centre for Telematics and Information Technology University of Twente.

Ben He and Iadh Ounis. 2004. Inferring query performance using pre-retrieval predictors. In *String Processing and Information Retrieval, 11th International Conference, SPIRE 2004, Padova, Italy, October 5-8, 2004, Proceedings*, pages 43–54.

Ben He and Iadh Ounis. 2006. Query performance prediction. *Information Systems*, 31(7):585–594.

Internetworldstats.com. 2016. Internet world users by language top 10 languages. http://www.internetworldstats.com/stats7.htm. Retrieved: 2017-01-04.

Ahmad Khwileh and Gareth J. F. Jones. 2016. Investigating segment-based query expansion for user-generated spoken content retrieval. In *14th International Workshop on Content-Based Multimedia Indexing, CBMI 2016, Bucharest, Romania, June 15-17, 2016*, pages 1–6.

Ahmad Khwileh, Debasis Ganguly, and Gareth J. F. Jones. 2015. An investigation of cross-language information retrieval for user-generated internet video. In *Experimental IR Meets Multilinguality, Multimodality, and Interaction - 6th International Conference of the CLEF Association, CLEF 2015, Toulouse, France, September 8-11, 2015, Proceedings*, pages 117–129. Springer.

Ahmad Khwileh, Debasis Ganguly, and Gareth J. F. Jones. 2016. Utilisation of metadata fields and query expansion in cross-lingual search of user-generated internet video. *Journal of Artificial Intelligence Research*, 55:249–281.

P. Koehn, Franz J. Och, and D. Marcu. 2003. Statistical phrase-based translation. In *Proceedings of the 2003 Conference of the North American Chapter of the Association for Computational Linguistics on Human Language Technology*, volume 1, pages 48–54, Edmonton, Canada.

P. Koehn, H. Hoang, A. Birch, C. Callison-Burch, M. Federico, N. Bertoldi, B. Cowan, W. Shen, C. Moran, R. Zens, C. Dyer, O. Bojar, A. Constantin, and E. Herbst. 2007. Moses: open source toolkit for statistical machine translation. In *Proceedings of the 45th Annual Meeting of the ACL on Interactive Poster and Demonstration Sessions*, pages 177–180, Prague, Czech Republic.

Oren Kurland, Anna Shtok, David Carmel, and Shay Hummel. 2011. A unified framework for post-retrieval query-performance prediction. In *Conference on the Theory of Information Retrieval*, pages 15–26. Springer.

Martha Larson and Gareth J. F. Jones. 2012. Spoken content retrieval: A survey of techniques and technologies. *Foundations and Trends in Information Retrieval*, 5(45):235–422.

Johannes Leveling, Dong Zhou, Gareth J. F. Jones, and Vincent Wade. 2009a. Tcd-dcu at tel@ clef 2009: Document expansion, query translation and language modeling. In *Working Notes for CLEF 2009 Work-shop co-located with the 13th European Conference on Digital Libraries (ECDL 2009) , Corfù, Greece, September 30 - October 2, 2009.*, volume 30.

Johannes Leveling, Dong Zhou, Gareth J. F. Jones, and Vincent Wade. 2009b. Document expansion, query translation and language modeling for ad-hoc IR. In *Multilingual Information Access Evaluation I. Text Retrieval Experiments, 10th Workshop of the Cross-Language Evaluation Forum, CLEF 2009, Corfu, Greece, September 30 - October 2, 2009, Revised Selected Papers*, pages 58–61.

Walid Magdy and Gareth J. F. Jones. 2014. Studying machine translation technologies for large-data clir tasks: a patent prior-art search case study. *Information Retrieval*, 17(5-6):492–519.

Mandar Mitra, Amit Singhal, and Chris Buckley. 1998. Improving automatic query expansion. In *SIGIR '98: Proceedings of the 21st Annual International ACM SIGIR Conference on Research and Development in Information Retrieval, August 24-28 1998, Melbourne, Australia*, pages 206–214.

Josiane Mothe and Ludovic Tanguy. 2005. Linguistic features to predict query difficulty. In *ACM Conference on research and Development in Information Retrieval, SIGIR, Predicting query difficulty-methods and applications workshop*, pages 7–10.

Douglas W. Oard and Anne R. Diekema. 1998. Cross-language information retrieval. *Annual review of information science and technology*, 33:223–256.

Douglas W. Oard and Fredric C. Gey. 2002. The trec 2002 arabic/english clir track. In *TREC,In The Eleventh Text REtrieval Conference: TREC 2002 (Gaithersburg, MD, Nov. 2002)*, pages 17–26. E.M.Voorhees et al. eds. NIST Special Publication 500-251.

Douglas W. Oard and Paul G. Hackett. 1998. Document translation for cross-language text retrieval at the university of maryland. In *Information Technology: The Sixth Text REtrieval Conference (TREC-6)*, pages 687–696. US Dept. of Commerce, Technology Administration, National Institute of Standards and Technology.

Franz J. Och. 2003. Minimum error rate training in statistical machine translation. In *Proceedings of the 41st Annual Meeting on Association for Computational Linguistics*, volume 1, pages 160–167, Sapporo, Japan.

Vassilis Plachouras, Ben He, and Iadh Ounis. 2004. University of glasgow at TREC 2004: Experiments in web, robust, and terabyte tracks with terrier. In *Proceedings of the Thirteenth Text REtrieval Conference, TREC 2004, Gaithersburg, Maryland, USA, November 16-19, 2004*.

Sebastian Schmiedeke, Peng Xu, Isabelle Ferrané, Maria Eskevich, Christoph Kofler, Martha A Larson, Yannick Estève, Lori Lamel, Gareth J. F. Jones, and Thomas Sikora. 2013. Blip10000: a social video dataset containing spug content for tagging and retrieval. In *Proceedings of the 4th ACM Multimedia Systems Conference*, pages 96–101. ACM.

Falk Scholer, Hugh E. Williams, and Andrew Turpin. 2004. Query association surrogates for web search. *Journal of the American Society for Information Science and Technology*, 55(7):637–650.

Anna Shtok, Oren Kurland, David Carmel, Fiana Raiber, and Gad Markovits. 2012. Predicting query performance by query-drift estimation. *ACM Transactions on Information Systems (TOIS)*, 30(2):11.

Ying Zhao, Falk Scholer, and Yohannes Tsegay. 2008. Effective pre-retrieval query performance prediction using similarity and variability evidence. In *Advances in Information Retrieval, 30th European Conference on IR Research, ECIR 2008, Glasgow, UK, March 30-April 3, 2008. Proceedings*, pages 52–64.

Yun Zhou and W. Bruce Croft. 2007. Query performance prediction in web search environments. In *SIGIR 2007: Proceedings of the 30th Annual International ACM SIGIR Conference on Research and Development in Information Retrieval, Amsterdam, The Netherlands, July 23-27, 2007*, pages 543–550.

Dong Zhou, Mark Truran, Tim Brailsford, Vincent Wade, and Helen Ashman. 2012. Translation techniques in cross-language information retrieval. *ACM Computing Surveys (CSUR)*, 45(1):1.

Justin Zobel and Alistair Moffat. 2006. Inverted files for text search engines. *ACM computing surveys (CSUR)*, 38(2):6.

# A Characterization Study of Arabic Twitter Data with a Benchmarking for State-of-the-Art Opinion Mining Models

Ramy Baly,[1] Gilbert Badaro,[1] Georges El-Khoury,[1] Rawan Moukalled,[1] Rita Aoun,[1]
Hazem Hajj,[1] Wassim El-Hajj,[2] Nizar Habash,[3] Khaled Bashir Shaban[4]

[1] Department of Electrical and Computer Engineering, American University of Beirut
[2] Department of Computer Science, American University of Beirut
[3] Computational Approaches to Modeling Language Lab, New York University Abu Dhabi
[4] Department of Computer Science, Qatar University
{rgb15,ggb05,gbe03,rrm32,rra47}@mail.aub.edu
{hh63,we07}@aub.edu.lb, nizar.habash@nyu.edu
khaled.shaban@qu.edu.qa

## Abstract

Opinion mining in Arabic is a challenging task given the rich morphology of the language. The task becomes more challenging when it is applied to Twitter data, which contains additional sources of noise, such as the use of unstandardized dialectal variations, the non-conformation to grammatical rules, the use of Arabizi and code-switching, and the use of non-text objects such as images and URLs to express opinion. In this paper, we perform an analytical study to observe how such linguistic phenomena vary across different Arab regions. This study of Arabic Twitter characterization aims at providing better understanding of Arabic Tweets, and fostering advanced research on the topic. Furthermore, we explore the performance of the two schools of machine learning on Arabic Twitter, namely the feature engineering approach and the deep learning approach. We consider models that have achieved state-of-the-art performance for opinion mining in English. Results highlight the advantages of using deep learning-based models, and confirm the importance of using morphological abstractions to address Arabic's complex morphology.

## 1 Introduction

Opinion mining, or sentiment analysis, aims at automatically extract subjectivity information from text (Turney, 2002) whether at sentence or document level (Farra et al., 2010). This task has attracted a lot of researchers in the last decade due to the wide range of real world applications that are interested in harvesting public opinion in different domains such as politics, stock markets and marketing.

Huge amounts of opinion data are generated, on a daily basis, in many forums, personal blogs and social networking websites. In particular, Twitter is one of the most used social media platforms, where users generally express their opinions on everything from music to movies to politics and all sort of trending topics (Sareah, 2015). Furthermore, Arabic language is the $5^{th}$ most-spoken language worldwide (UNESCO, 2014), and has recently become a key source of the Internet content with a 6,600% growth in number of users compared to the year 2000 (Stats, 2016). Therefore, developing accurate opinion mining models for Arabic tweets is a timely and intriguing problem that is worth investigating.

However, applying Natural Language Processing (NLP) and learning opinion models for Arabic Twitter data is not straightforward due to several reasons. Tweets contain large variations of unstandardized dialectal Arabic (DA), in addition to significant amounts of misspellings and grammatical errors, mainly due to their length restriction. They also contain "Arabizi", where Arabic words are written using Latin characters. Due to the cultural diversity across the Arab world, an opinion model that is developed for tweets in one region may not be applicable to extract opinions from tweets in another region. Finally, tweets usually contain special tokens such as hashtags, mentions, multimedia objects and URLs that need to be han-



*Proceedings of The Third Arabic Natural Language Processing Workshop (WANLP)*, pages 110–118,
Valencia, Spain, April 3, 2017. ©2017 Association for Computational Linguistics

dled appropriately, in order to make use of the subjective information they may implicitly carry.

In this paper, we present a characterization study of Twitter data collected from different Arab regions, namely Egypt, the Levant and the Arab Gulf. This study illustrates how the discussed topics, the writing style and other linguistic phenomena, vary significantly from one region to another, reflecting different usages of Twitter around the Arab world. We also evaluate the model that ranked first at SemEval-2016 Task 4 (Nakov et al., 2016) on "Sentiment Analysis in Twitter". This model is developed for opinion mining in English, and uses feature engineering to extract surface, syntactic, semantic and Twitter-specific features. Therefore, we extract an equivalent feature set for Arabic to train a model for opinion mining in Arabic tweets. We compare this model to another class of models that are based on deep learning techniques. In particular, we use recursive deep models that achieved high performances (Socher et al., 2013; Tai et al., 2015). Experimental results show the advantage of deep learning at learning subjectivity in Arabic tweets without the need for artificial features that describe the properties and characteristics of Twitter data.

The rest of this paper is organized as follows. Section 2 describes previous work on opinion mining with particular focus on application to Twitter data. Section 3 presents the characterization study and highlights distinctive characteristics of tweets collected from different Arab regions. Section 4 describes the opinion models that we evaluate in this paper, and experimental results are presented in Section 5. Conclusion is provided in Section 6.

## 2 Related Work

Opinion Mining models for Arabic are generally developed by training machine learning classifiers using different types of features. The most common features are the word *n*grams features that were used to train Support Vector Machines (SVM) (Rushdi-Saleh et al., 2011; Aly and Atiya, ; Shoukry and Rafea, 2012), Naïve Bayes (Mountassir et al., 2012; Elawady et al., 2014) and ensemble classifiers (Omar et al., 2013). Word *n*grams were also used along with syntactic features (root and part-of-speech *n*-grams) and stylistic (letter and digit *n*grams, word length, etc.). These features performed well after reduction via the Entropy-Weighted Genetic Algorithm

(EWGA) (Abbasi et al., 2008). Sentiment lexicons also provided an additional source of features that proved useful for the task (Abdul-Mageed et al., 2011; Badaro et al., 2014; Badaro et al., 2015).

Many efforts have been made to develop opinion models for Arabic Twitter data and creating annotated Twitter corpora (Al Zaatari et al., 2016). A framework was developed to handle tweets containing Modern Standard Arabic (MSA), Jordanian dialects, Arabizi and emoticons, by training different classifiers under different features settings of such linguistic phenomena (Duwairi et al., 2014). A distant-based approach showed improvement over existing fully-supervised models for subjectivity classification (Refaee and Rieser, 2014a). A subjectivity and sentiment analysis (SSA) system for Arabic tweets used a feature set that includes different forms of the word (lexemes and lemmas), POS tags, presence of polar adjectives, writing style (MSA or DA), and genre-specific features including the user's gender and ID (Abdul-Mageed et al., 2014). Machine translation was used to apply existing state-of-the-art models for English to translations of Arabic tweets. Despite slight accuracy drop caused by translation errors, these models are still considered efficient and effective, especially for low-resource languages (Refaee and Rieser, 2014b; Salameh et al., 2015).

A new class of machine learning models based on deep learning have recently emerged. These models achieved high performances in both Arabic and English, such as the Recursive Auto Encoders (RAE) (Socher et al., 2011; Al Sallab et al., 2015), the Recursive Neural Tensor Networks (RNTN) (Socher et al., 2013) and Generalized Regression Neural Networks (GRNN) (Hobeica et al., 2011; Baly et al., 2016).

Finally, we describe models that won SemEval-2016 on "Sentiment Analysis in Tweets" in English (Nakov et al., 2016). For three-way classification, the winner model is based on training two Convolutional Neural Networks, and combining their outputs (Deriu et al., 2016). These networks share similar architectures but differ in the choice of some parameters, such as the embeddings and the number of convolution filters. As for five-way classification, the winner model uses feature engineering. It extracts a collection of surface, syntactic, semantic and genre-specific features to train a SVM classifier.

## 3   Arabic Tweets Characterization

Developing opinion mining models requires understanding the different characteristics of the texts that they will be applied to. For instance, dealing with reviews requires different features and methods compared to comments or tweets, as each of these types have their own characteristics. Furthermore, when dealing with Arabic data, it is important to appreciate the rich cultural and linguistic diversity across the Arab region, which may translate into different challenges that need to be addressed during model development. First, we describe the general features of Twitter data, and then we present an analysis of three sets of tweets collected from main Arab regions: Egypt, the Arab Gulf and the Levant.

Twitter is a micro-blogging website where people share messages that have a maximum length of 140 characters. Despite their small size, the tweets' contents are quite diverse and can be made up of text, emoticons, URLs, pictures and videos that are internally mapped into automatically shortened URLs, as in Table 1, example (a). Users tend to use informal styles of writing to reduce the length of the text while it can still be interpreted by others. Consequently, Twitter data become noisy as they contain significant amounts of misspellings, and do not necessarily follow the grammatical structure of the language, as shown in Table 1, example (b). Arabizi and code-switching are frequently used and observed in tweets, as shown in Table 1, example (c). Hashtags are very common and are used to highlight keywords, to track trending topics or events, to promote products and services, and for other personal purposes including fun and sarcasm. Also, "user mentions" are quite common and have different usages including tagging users in tweets to start a conversation, replying to someone's tweet and giving credit for some media or source. Table 1, example (d) shows how hashtags and mentions are used in Tweets. Finally, users can react to a tweet in three different ways, either using (1) "Like" by pressing the heart button, (2) "Reply" by mentioning the author and typing their comment in a new tweet, or (3) "Re-Tweet" by sharing it to their own followers.

We manually analyzed three sets of tweets that were retrieved from Egypt, the Arab Gulf and the Levant, using the Twitter4J API (Yamamoto, 2014). We refer to these sets of tweets as "EGY", "GULF" and "LEV", respectively, where each set contains 610 tweets. Examples of tweets written in each of the region's dialect are shown in Table 1, examples (e,f and g). We did not use a specific query as a keyword, in order to retrieve tweets covering the different topics being discussed in each region. We also did not use the API's language filter, in order to retrieve tweets that may be written in Arabizi. For each set, one of the authors analyzed the used languages, the discussed topics and the presence of emoticons, sarcasm, hashtags, mentions and elongation.

Table 2 shows the distribution of the different topics in each set. Table 3 shows the different writing styles and languages that are used in each set. Table 4 illustrates, for each set, the percentage of tweets that contain special Twitter tokens.

|  | EGY | LEV | GULF |
|---|---|---|---|
| Religion | 20.0% | 22.3% | 32.1% |
| Personal | 35.1% | 58.9% | 50.5% |
| Politics | 3.6% | 5.3% | 4.4% |
| Sports | 0.3% | 6.9% | 1.3% |
| Other news | 2.9% | 1.6% | 1.9% |
| Spam | 8.5% | 3.4% | 5.6% |
| Foreign | 29.5% | 1.6% | 4.1% |

Table 2: Topics discussed in each set.

|  | LEV | EGY | GULF |
|---|---|---|---|
| MSA | 28.5% | 40.7% | 55.7% |
| Local dialect | 18.4% | 31.5% | 28.5% |
| Arabizi | 0.7% | 1.9% | 0.0% |
| English | 13.4% | 7.2% | 4.1% |
| Foreign | 31.8% | 1.6% | 4.4% |
| N/A | 7.2% | 7.1% | 7.2% |

Table 3: Languages and writing styles in each set.

| Special tokens | EGY | LEV | GULF |
|---|---|---|---|
| User mentions | 17.1% | 31.6% | 34.6% |
| Hashtags | 7.5% | 13.4% | 13.7% |
| Emoticons | 20.3% | 30.9% | 25.6% |
| Elongation | 2.6% | 8.2% | 3.3% |

Table 4: Use of special Twitter tokens in each set.

It can be observed that most of the tweets in "GULF" are written in MSA, and to a less extent using the local dialect. Compared to the other

| (a) | ☺ ☺ ☺ https://t.co/aszVLSZIpx |
|---|---|

| (b) | توصيات سينمائية اللّي ماتابع هذا المسلسل فاته دراما واكشن موطبيعي التقيّم 9.0/10 |
|---|---|
| | *twSyAt synmA}yp Ally mA tAbE h∗A Almslsl fAth drAmA wAk$n mwTbyEy Altqyym 9.0/10* |
| | 'cinematic recommendations who did not follow this series has missed unreal drama and action assessment 9.0/10' |

| (c) | *mat2lysh alkalm dah 5lyna saktin* (example of Egyptian dialect Arabizi) |
|---|---|
| | 'don't say such a thing let's keep quiet' |

| (d) | @drkh189 @nogah015 @Almogaz #كفى بالوكالة حروب حوالينا اللّي كل |
|---|---|
| | *@drkh189 @nogah015 @Almogaz kl Ally HwAlynA Hrwb bAlwkAlp #kfY* |
| | '@drkh189 @nogah015 @Almogaz all what's happening around us are proxy wars #enough' |

| (e) | هو في حد لسه بيجيب فاكهة و حاجات كتير بالآسعار دي؟ (example of tweet in Egyptian Arabic) |
|---|---|
| | *hw fy Hd lsh byjyb fAkhp w HAjAt ktyr bAl>sEAr dy?* |
| | 'is there still anybody who brings fruits and many other stuff with these prices?' |

| (f) | @Mnallhfc علمي علمش بس شكله معروف بس انا وياش الّي ما نعرفه (example of tweet in Arab Gulf dialect) |
|---|---|
| | *Elmy Elm$ bs $klh mErwf bs AnA wyA$ Al∼y mA nErfh* |
| | 'I know the same as you know, but it seems he is known but we don't know him' |

| (g) | ومش مخلّين تويت مش عاملين في منشن عن القضية (example of tweet in Levantine) |
|---|---|
| | *wm$ mxl∼yn twyt m$ EAmlyn mn$n En AlqDyp* |
| | 'and they haven't left a tweet without a mention of the case' |

Table 1: Samples of tweets, with their English translations and transliterations[2], highlighting the different linguistic phenomena that can be observed in Twitter data.

sets, a significant amount of these tweets discuss religious topics. It can also be observed that Arabizi and code switching do not appear, and that tweets written in English are rare. Regarding the "EGY" set, MSA is less common compared to "GULF", and a significant number of tweets are written using Egyptian Arabic. Most of the tweets discuss personal matters (nearly 59%). Also, Arabizi and code switching are rarely used. Finally, emoticons and user mentions are more frequently used compared to the other sets. As for the "LEV" set, it can be observed that both MSA and DA are used less than the other sets. Most of these tweets discuss personal matter, while religious topics are less discussed. A significant portion of the tweets are written in English, and many are written in foreign languages that pertain to neighboring countries (e.g., Cyprus and Turkey). Finally, it can be observed that elongation (letter repetition) is not common in the collected sets of tweets, and that Arabizi and code switching are infrequent as well.

This analysis confirms that Twitter is used differently (different characteristics, features and topics), across the Arab world. This implies that different opinion models are needed to account for the peculiarities of each region's tweets.

## 4 Opinion Mining Models

In this section, we describe two models that achieved state-of-the-art performances in opinion mining. The first model won the SemEval-2016 Task 4 on "Sentiment Analysis in Twitter" (English), and uses feature engineering to train an opinion classifier (Balikas and Amini, 2016). The second model is based on modeling compositionality using deep learning techniques (Socher et al., 2013). In this paper, we evaluate these models for opinion mining in Arabic tweets.

### 4.1 Opinion Mining with Feature Engineering

According to (Nakov et al., 2016; Balikas and Amini, 2016), training a SVM with a collection of surface, syntactic, semantic features achieved state-of-the-art results on opinion mining in English tweets. Below, we describe the equivalent set of features that we extracted to train a similar model for opinion mining in Arabic tweets.

- Character $n$-grams; $n \in [3, 5]$.

- Word $n$-grams; $n \in [1, 4]$. To account for the complexity and sparsity of Arabic language, we extract lemma $n$-grams since lemmas have better generalization capabilities than raw words (Habash, 2010).

- Counts of exclamation marks, question marks, and both exclamation and question marks.

- Count of elongated words.

- Count of negated contexts, defined by phrases that occur between a negation particle and the next punctuation.

- Counts of positive emoticons and negative emoticons, in addition to a binary feature indicating if emoticons exist in a given tweet.

- Counts of each part-of-speech (POS) tag in the tweet.

- Counts of positive and negative words based on ArSenL (Badaro et al., 2014), AraSenti (Al-Twairesh et al., 2016) and ADHL (Mohammad et al., 2016) lexicons.

We also add to this set the two binary features indicating the presence of user mentions and URL or media content. Many of these features align with the factors that we single out in the characterization study presented in Section 3.

### 4.2 Opinion Mining with Recursive Neural Networks

Most deep learning models for opinion mining are based on the concept of compositionality, where the meaning of a text can be described as a function of the meanings of its parts and the rules by which they are combined (Mitchell and Lapata, 2010). In particular, the Recursive Neural Tensor Networks (RNTN) model has proven successful for opinion mining in English (Socher et al., 2013). Figure 1 illustrates the application of a RNTN to predict the sentiment of a three-word sentence $\{C_1, C_2, C_3\}$, where words are represented with vectors that capture distributional syntactic and semantic properties (Bengio et al., 2003; Collobert and Weston, 2008; Mikolov et al.,

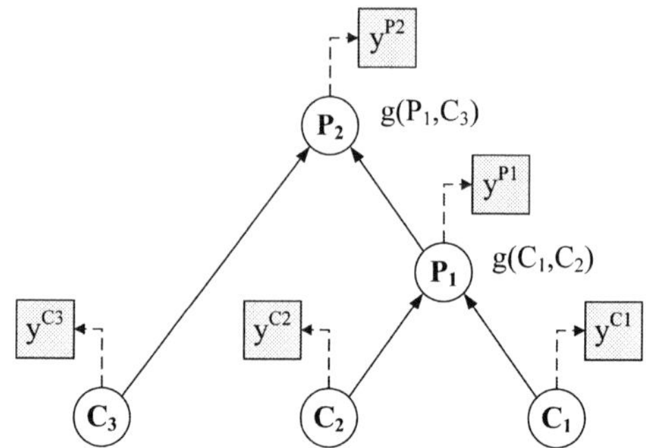



Figure 1: The application of RNTN for opinion prediction in a three-word sentence.

2013). Each sentence is represented in the form of a binary parse tree. Then, at each node of the tree, a tensor-based composition function combines the child nodes' vectors (e.g., $C_1, C_2$) and produces the parent node's vector (e.g., $P_1$). This process repeats recursively until it derives a vector for each node $C_i$ in the tree, including the root node that corresponds to the whole sentence. These vectors are then used to train a softmax classifier to predict the opinion distribution $y^{C_i} \in \mathbb{R}^K$ for the text represented by the $i^{th}$ node, where $K$ is the number of opinion classes. Further details are available in (Socher et al., 2013).

Training a RNTN model requires a sentiment treebank; a collection of parse trees with sentiment annotations at all levels of constituency. For English, the Stanford sentiment treebank was developed to train the RNTN (Socher et al., 2013). For Arabic, we developed the Arabic Sentiment Treebank (ArSenTB) by annotating $\sim$123K constituents pertaining to 1,177 comments extracted from the Qatar Arabic Language Bank (QALB) (Zaghouani et al., 2014).

## 5 Experiments and Results

In this section, we evaluate the performance of the feature engineering and deep learning-based models for opinion mining in Arabic tweets. We focus on the task of three-way opinion classification, where each tweet should be classified as positive, negative or neutral.

### 5.1 Dataset and Preprocessing

For our experiments, we use the Arabic Sentiment Twitter Data (ASTD) (Nabil et al., 2015) that consists of 10,006 tweets belonging to Egyptian Twitter accounts. These tweets are annotated with four labels: positive (799), negative (1,684), neutral (832) and objective (6,691). Due to the highly skewed distribution of the classes, and since our focus is to perform opinion classification rather than subjectivity classification, we excluded the objective tweets, reducing the size of the data to 3,315 tweets with reasonable class distribution: 24% (positive), 51% (negative) and 25% (neutral). This data is split into a train set (70%), a development set (10%) and a test set (20%).

Each tweet is preprocessed by (1) replacing user mentions and URLs with special "global" tokens, (2) extracting emoticons and emojis using the "emoji" java library (Vdurmont, 2016) and replacing them with special tokens (for this we used the emojis sentiment lexicon from (Novak et al., 2015), and prepared our own emoticons lexicon), (3) normalizing hashtags by removing the "#" symbol and the underscores that are used to separate words in composite hashtags, and (4) normalizing word elongations (letter repetitions).

To extract features for the SVM classifier, we performed lemmatization and POS tagging using MADAMIRA v2.1, the state-of-the-art morphological analyzer and disambiguator in Arabic (Pasha et al., 2014), that uses the Standard Arabic Morphological Analyzer (SAMA) (Maamouri et al., 2010). Since the evaluation corpus is in Egyptian Arabic, we used MADAMIRA in the Egyptian mode. It is worth noting that some recent efforts have added Levantine to MADAMIRA, but it is not public yet (Eskander et al., 2016).

### 5.2 Experimental Setting

We only included $n$-grams that occurred more than a pre-defined threshold $t$, where $t \in [3, 5]$. Preliminary experiments showed that using the radial basis function (RBF) kernel is better than using the linear kernel. We used the development set to tune the model's parameters, namely the cost of misclassification and $\gamma$ the width of the kernel, Then, the model with the parameters that achieved the best results is applied to the unseen test set.

As for the RNTN model, we generated word embeddings of size 25 by training the skip-gram embedding model (Mikolov et al., 2013) on the QALB corpus, which contains nearly 500K sentences. We train RNTN using ArSenTB, and then apply the trained model to perform opinion classification in tweets. We alleviate the impact of

sparsity by training RNTN using lemmas, which is similar to our choice of training SVM using lemma $n$-grams.

Finally, the different models are evaluated using accuracy and the F1-score averaged across the different classes.

### 5.3 Results

Table 5 illustrates the performances achieved with the state-of-the-art models in feature engineering (SVM$_{all,lemmas}$) and deep learning (RNTN$_{lemmas}$). We compare to the following baselines: (1) the majority baseline that automatically assigns the most frequent class in the train set, and (2) the SVM trained with word $n$-grams (SVM$_{baseline}$), which has been a common approach in the Arabic opinion mining literature. To emphasize the impact of lemmatization, we include the results of SVM trained with features from (Balikas and Amini, 2016) and using word instead of lemma $n$-grams (SVM$_{all,words}$). We also include the results of RNTN trained with raw words (RNTN$_{words}$).

|  | Accuracy | Average F1 |
| --- | --- | --- |
| Majority | 51.0% | 22.5% |
| SVM$_{baseline}$ | 55.7% | 29.0% |
| SVM$_{all,words}$ | 49.5% | 41.6% |
| SVM$_{all,lemmas}$ | 51.7% | 43.4% |
| RNTN$_{words}$ | 56.2% | 51.1% |
| RNTN$_{lemmas}$ | 58.5% | 53.6% |

Table 5: Performance of the different models for opinion mining, evaluated on the ASTD dataset.

Results in Table 5 show that augmenting SVM with the different features from (Balikas and Amini, 2016) achieved significant performance improvement compared to the baseline SVM. It can also be observed that using the lemma feature to represent raw words contributes to this high performance, and confirms the importance of lemmas at reducing the lexical sparsity of Arabic language. Finally, the RNTN achieves best performance although it was trained on a dataset that is different from the tweets that are used for testing. We expect the performance of RNTN to further increase when it is trained on Twitter data. These results confirm the advantage of recursive deep learning that model semantic compositionality, over models that rely on feature engineering.

## 6  Conclusion

In this paper, we described the main challenges of processing Arabic language in Twitter data. We presented a characterization study that analyzes tweets collected from different Arab regions including Egypt, the Arab Gulf and the Levant. We showed that Twitter have different usages across these regions.

We report the performance of two state-of-the-art models for opinion mining. Experimental results indicate the advantage of using deep learning models over feature engineering models, as the RNTN achieved better performances although it was trained using a non-Twitter corpus. Results also indicate the importance of lemmatization at handling the complexity and lexical sparsity of Arabic language.

Future work will include evaluating opinion mining models on tweets from different Arab regions and covering different topics. Also, we intend to apply an automatic approach for analyzing tweet characteristics instead of the manual approach. We will exploit existing tools and resources for automatic identification of dialects in tweets.

We aim to perform cross-region evaluations to confirm whether different opinion models are needed for different regions and dialects, or a general model can work for any tweet regardless of its origins. This effort involves the collection and annotation of Twitter corpora for the different regions analyzed above.

## Acknowledgments

This work was made possible by NPRP 6-716-1-138 grant from the Qatar National Research Fund (a member of Qatar Foundation). The statements made herein are solely the responsibility of the authors.

## References

Ahmed Abbasi, Hsinchun Chen, and Arab Salem. 2008. Sentiment analysis in multiple languages: Feature selection for opinion classification in web forums. *ACM Transactions on Information Systems (TOIS)*, 26(3):12.

Muhammad Abdul-Mageed, Mona T. Diab, and Mohammed Korayem. 2011. Subjectivity and sentiment analysis of modern standard arabic. In *Proceedings of the 49th Annual Meeting of the Association for Computational Linguistics: Human Language Technologies: short papers-Volume 2*, pages 587–591. Association for Computational Linguistics.

Muhammad Abdul-Mageed, Mona Diab, and Sandra Kübler. 2014. Samar: Subjectivity and sentiment analysis for arabic social media. *Computer Speech & Language*, 28(1):20–37.

Ahmad A. Al Sallab, Ramy Baly, Gilbert Badaro, Hazem Hajj, Wassim El Hajj, and Khaled B. Shaban. 2015. Deep learning models for sentiment analysis in arabic. In *ANLP Workshop 2015*, page 9.

Nora Al-Twairesh, Hend Al-Khalifa, and AbdulMalik Al-Salman. 2016. Arasenti: Large-scale twitter-specific arabic sentiment lexicons. *Proceedings of the 54th Annual Meeting of the Association for Computational Linguistics*, pages 697–705.

Ayman Al Zaatari, Reem El Ballouli, Shady ELbassouni, Wassim El-Hajj, Hazem Hajj, Khaled Bashir Shaban, and Nizar Habash. 2016. Arabic corpora for credibility analysis. *Proceedings of the Language Resources and Evaluation Conference (LREC)*, pages 4396–4401.

Mohamed A. Aly and Amir F Atiya. Labr: A large scale arabic book reviews dataset.

Gilbert Badaro, Ramy Baly, Hazem Hajj, Nizar Habash, and Wassim El-Hajj. 2014. A large scale arabic sentiment lexicon for arabic opinion mining. *ANLP 2014*, 165.

Gilbert Badaro, Ramy Baly, Rana Akel, Linda Fayad, Jeffrey Khairallah, Hazem Hajj, Wassim El-Hajj, and Khaled Bashir Shaban. 2015. A light lexicon-based mobile application for sentiment mining of arabic tweets. In *ANLP Workshop 2015*, page 18.

Georgios Balikas and Massih-Reza Amini. 2016. Twise at semeval-2016 task 4: Twitter sentiment classification. *arXiv preprint arXiv:1606.04351*.

Ramy Baly, Roula Hobeica, Hazem Hajj, Wassim El-Hajj, Khaled Bashir Shaban, and Ahmad Al-Sallab. 2016. A meta-framework for modeling the human reading process in sentiment analysis. *ACM Transactions on Information Systems (TOIS)*, 35(1):7.

Yoshua Bengio, Réjean Ducharme, Pascal Vincent, and Christian Jauvin. 2003. A neural probabilistic language model. *Journal of machine learning research*, 3(Feb):1137–1155.

Ronan Collobert and Jason Weston. 2008. A unified architecture for natural language processing: Deep neural networks with multitask learning. In *Proceedings of the 25th international conference on Machine learning*, pages 160–167. ACM.

Jan Deriu, Maurice Gonzenbach, Fatih Uzdilli, Aurelien Lucchi, Valeria De Luca, and Martin Jaggi.

2016. Swisscheese at semeval-2016 task 4: Sentiment classification using an ensemble of convolutional neural networks with distant supervision. *Proceedings of SemEval*, pages 1124–1128.

RM Duwairi, Raed Marji, Narmeen Sha'ban, and Sally Rushaidat. 2014. Sentiment analysis in arabic tweets. In *Information and communication systems (icics), 2014 5th international conference on*, pages 1–6. IEEE.

Rasheed M. Elawady, Sherif Barakat, and Nora M. Elrashidy. 2014. Different feature selection for sentiment classification. *International Journal of Information Science and Intelligent System*, 3(1):137–150.

Ramy Eskander, Nizar Habash, Owen Rambow, and Arfath Pasha. 2016. Creating resources for dialectal arabic from a single annotation: A case study on egyptian and levantine. In *Proceedings of COLING 2016, the 26th International Conference on Computational Linguistics: Technical Papers*, pages 3455–3465, Osaka, Japan, December. The COLING 2016 Organizing Committee.

Noura Farra, Elie Challita, Rawad Abou Assi, and Hazem Hajj. 2010. Sentence-level and document-level sentiment mining for arabic texts. In *2010 IEEE International Conference on Data Mining Workshops*, pages 1114–1119. IEEE.

Nizar Y. Habash. 2010. Introduction to arabic natural language processing. *Synthesis Lectures on Human Language Technologies*, 3(1):1–187.

Roula Hobeica, Hazem Hajj, and Wassim El Hajj. 2011. Machine reading for notion-based sentiment mining. In *Data Mining Workshops (ICDMW), 2011 IEEE 11th International Conference on*, pages 75–80. IEEE.

Mohamed Maamouri, Dave Graff, Basma Bouziri, Sondos Krouna, Ann Bies, and Seth Kulick. 2010. Standard arabic morphological analyzer (sama) version 3.1. *Linguistic Data Consortium, Catalog No.: LDC2010L01*.

Tomas Mikolov, Ilya Sutskever, Kai Chen, Greg S. Corrado, and Jeff Dean. 2013. Distributed representations of words and phrases and their compositionality. In *Advances in neural information processing systems*, pages 3111–3119.

Jeff Mitchell and Mirella Lapata. 2010. Composition in distributional models of semantics. *Cognitive science*, 34(8):1388–1429.

Saif M. Mohammad, Mohammad Salameh, and Svetlana Kiritchenko. 2016. How translation alters sentiment. *J. Artif. Intell. Res.(JAIR)*, 55:95–130.

Asmaa Mountassir, Houda Benbrahim, and Ilham Berrada. 2012. An empirical study to address the problem of unbalanced data sets in sentiment classification. In *Systems, Man, and Cybernetics (SMC), 2012 IEEE International Conference on*, pages 3298–3303. IEEE.

Mahmoud Nabil, Mohamed A. Aly, and Amir F. Atiya. 2015. Astd: Arabic sentiment tweets dataset. In *EMNLP*, pages 2515–2519.

Preslav Nakov, Alan Ritter, Sara Rosenthal, Fabrizio Sebastiani, and Veselin Stoyanov. 2016. Semeval-2016 task 4: Sentiment analysis in twitter. *Proceedings of SemEval*, pages 1–18.

Petra Kralj Novak, Jasmina Smailović, Borut Sluban, and Igor Mozetič. 2015. Sentiment of emojis. *PloS one*, 10(12):e0144296.

Nazlia Omar, Mohammed Albared, Adel Qasem Al-Shabi, and Tareq Al-Moslmi. 2013. Ensemble of classification algorithms for subjectivity and sentiment analysis of arabic customers' reviews. *International Journal of Advancements in Computing Technology*, 5(14):77.

Arfath Pasha, Mohamed Al-Badrashiny, Mona T. Diab, Ahmed El Kholy, Ramy Eskander, Nizar Habash, Manoj Pooleery, Owen Rambow, and Ryan Roth. 2014. Madamira: A fast, comprehensive tool for morphological analysis and disambiguation of arabic. In *LREC*, volume 14, pages 1094–1101.

Eshrag Refaee and Verena Rieser. 2014a. Can we read emotions from a smiley face? emoticon-based distant supervision for subjectivity and sentiment analysis of arabic twitter feeds. In *5th International Workshop on Emotion, Social Signals, Sentiment and Linked Open Data, LREC*.

Eshrag Refaee and Verena Rieser. 2014b. Subjectivity and sentiment analysis of arabic twitter feeds with limited resources. In *Workshop on Free/Open-Source Arabic Corpora and Corpora Processing Tools Workshop Programme*, page 16.

Mohammed Rushdi-Saleh, M. Teresa Martín-Valdivia, L. Alfonso Ureña-López, and José M. Perea-Ortega. 2011. Oca: Opinion corpus for arabic. *Journal of the American Society for Information Science and Technology*, 62(10):2045–2054.

Mohammad Salameh, Saif Mohammad, and Svetlana Kiritchenko. 2015. Sentiment after translation: A case-study on arabic social media posts. In *HLT-NAACL*, pages 767–777.

Faiza Sareah. 2015. Interesting statistics for the top 10 social media sites. *Small Business Trends*.

Amira Shoukry and Ahmed Rafea. 2012. Sentence-level arabic sentiment analysis. In *Collaboration Technologies and Systems (CTS), 2012 International Conference on*, pages 546–550. IEEE.

Richard Socher, Jeffrey Pennington, Eric H. Huang, Andrew Y. Ng, and Christopher D. Manning. 2011. Semi-supervised recursive autoencoders for predicting sentiment distributions. In *Proceedings of the conference on empirical methods in natural language processing*, pages 151–161. Association for Computational Linguistics.

Richard Socher, Alex Perelygin, Jean Wu, Jason Chuang, Christopher D. Manning, Andrew Ng, and Christopher Potts. 2013. Recursive deep models for semantic compositionality over a sentiment treebank. In *Proceedings of the 2013 Conference on Empirical Methods in Natural Language Processing*, pages 1631–1642, Seattle, Washington, USA, October. Association for Computational Linguistics.

Internet World Stats. 2016. Internet world users by language. http://www.internetworldstats.com/stats7.htm.

Kai Sheng Tai, Richard Socher, and Christopher D. Manning. 2015. Improved semantic representations from tree-structured long short-term memory networks. *arXiv preprint arXiv:1503.00075*.

Peter D. Turney. 2002. Thumbs up or thumbs down?: semantic orientation applied to unsupervised classification of reviews. In *Proceedings of the 40th annual meeting on association for computational linguistics*, pages 417–424. Association for Computational Linguistics.

UNESCO. 2014. World arabic language day. http://bit.ly/2lwRFYt.

Vdurmont. 2016. The missing emoji library for java. https://github.com/vdurmont/emoji-java.

Yusuke Yamamoto. 2014. Twitter4j-a java library for the twitter api.

Wajdi Zaghouani, Behrang Mohit, Nizar Habash, Ossama Obeid, Nadi Tomeh, Alla Rozovskaya, Noura Farra, Sarah Alkuhlani, and Kemal Oflazer. 2014. Large scale arabic error annotation: Guidelines and framework. In *LREC*, pages 2362–2369.

# Robust Dictionary Lookup in Multiple Noisy Orthographies

**Lingliang Zhang, Nizar Habash and Godfried Toussaint**
New York University Abu Dhabi
Abu Dhabi, UAE
`{lingliang.zhang,nizar.habash,gt42}@nyu.edu`

## Abstract

We present the MultiScript Phonetic Search algorithm to address the problem of language learners looking up unfamiliar words that they heard. We apply it to Arabic dictionary lookup with noisy queries done using both the Arabic and Roman scripts. Our algorithm is based on a computational phonetic distance metric that can be optionally machine learned. To benchmark our performance, we created the ArabScribe dataset, containing 10,000 noisy transcriptions of random Arabic dictionary words. Our algorithm outperforms Google Translate's "did you mean" feature, as well as the Yamli smart Arabic keyboard.

## 1 Introduction

The research effort reported here was motivated by the experience of second-language learners of Arabic who, upon hearing an unfamiliar word, would repeatedly guess different spelling variations until they either give up or find a word that made sense in the context. In the data we collected, subjects were only able to spell an Arabic word correctly 35% of the time. This difficulty arises because many Arabic phones are distinguished from each other only by phonetic features that often do not exist in the learner's native language, such as pharyngealization. Furthermore, for a variety of reasons, both learners and native speakers often write Arabic words imprecisely using a variety of Roman-script conventions, such as Arabizi (Darwish, 2014), and this presents a difficult problem for disambiguating the intended word.

We address this problem with a novel algorithm MultiScript Search for phonetic searching across

| Target word: تضخيم (tDxym) | | | |
|---|---|---|---|
| طبخين (Tbxyn) | طبحيم (TbHym) | تبخيم (tbxym) | تبخين (tbxyn) |
| thabheem | Tat7iim | tohpriim | tawbheem |
| ta'95eem | topk'chim | takreem | tabheem |

Table 1: Example of the Arabic dictionary lookup task for both Arabic and Roman script.

multiple orthographies, and apply it to performing dictionary lookup of Arabic words from noisy user inputs in both the Arabic and Roman scripts. The task of dictionary lookup here is defined as a user hearing a single word and typing their best guess of how it sounds in a system that will look the word up in a dictionary. An example of how users searched for the word تضخيم (tDxym)[1] 'magnification' is given in Table 1.

Our phonetic search algorithm can be generally applied to any language-script pair and does not require training data. But, we also present a machine learning method to boost the performance of our algorithm if training data is available. The algorithm first performs mapping from user input to phones, and then it searches in the dictionary for words that have a low phonetic distance from the query. We investigate a number of algorithms for both the grapheme-to-phoneme mapping, and also for calculating phonetic distance.

To benchmark our lookup accuracy, we created the ArabScribe dataset, which is comprised of almost 10,000 transcriptions from 103 participants with different degrees of knowledge of Arabic. The participants heard random Arabic dictionary words and transcribed them using either the English or Arabic keyboards (i.e., in Roman script

---

[1] Arabic transliteration is presented in the Habash-Soudi-Buckwalter scheme (Habash et al., 2007).



*Proceedings of The Third Arabic Natural Language Processing Workshop (WANLP)*, pages 119–129,
Valencia, Spain, April 3, 2017. ©2017 Association for Computational Linguistics

or in Arabic script). We benchmarked our system against two widely used tools to look up unfamiliar Arabic words, Google Translate and the Yamli Smart Arabic Keyboard. We show that we exceed the performance of both tools.

The paper will proceed as follows. In Section 2 we discuss the related literature in transliteration, spell correction and phonetic distance mapping. In Section 3 we describe our high level algorithm and the variations we tested. In Section 4 we describe the ArabScribe dataset. Section 5 presents our search recall results and our benchmark against the Google and Yamli systems. In Section 6, we summarize our findings and present a discussion on potential future work.

## 2   Related Work

The principal contribution and distinction of our work against previous work in the related areas of transliteration and spelling correction is that we are concerned with recovering from hearing errors rather than errors arising from spelling or ambiguous orthography. To our knowledge, there has not been any empirical research into the accuracy of the task of phonetic dictionary lookup of spoken words.

**Spelling Correction**   Within a single orthography, a closely related problem is spellchecking. Commonly used algorithms employ statistical and edit-distance models over letters, phones or metaphone (Whitelaw et al., 2009; Kukich, 1992; Damerau, 1964; Oflazer, 1996; Atkinson, 2005; Philips, 1990; Toutanova and Moore, 2002). Our algorithm is distinguished from these, in that we are not only addressing the case where the user doesn't know how to spell the word, but the much more challenging case where they have not heard the sound correctly.

Whitelaw et al. (2009) describe the Google spell check system which takes a statistical approach using massive unannotated web corpora. Their dictionary of canonical terms contains the most common tokens appearing online, and they match misspelled words to their canonical form using a combination of a language context and Levenshtein edit distance. Then, they build a statistical model of how substrings change. Spelling suggestions are scored as a function of the probability of the substring substitutions combined with a language model. This statistical approach has the advantage that it requires no formal language

definition, instead requiring a large amount of linguistic data and computational resources. While it is a very effective spell checker, it does not perform well on noisy user input of guessed spellings of unfamiliar words as it is trained on web corpora which are written by people who have a generally stronger command of the language and therefore errors are often due to typos rather than not knowing how to spell the word. There is unfortunately no published material about the exact method used by Google's transliteration or Yamli smart keyboard to map Roman-script input into Arabic words.

In the context of spelling correction for Arabic, there has been a large number of efforts and resources (Shaalan et al., 2010; Alkanhal et al., 2012; Eskander et al., 2013; Mohit et al., 2014; Zaghouani et al., 2014) (among others).[2] All of these efforts focus on contextual spelling correction or conventionalization. In this work we contribute a new data set, ArabScribe, that may be of use in that area of research.

**Transliteration**   Transliteration systems invariably use either a direct mapping between substrings in the two scripts (Al-Onaizan and Knight, 2002; AbdulJaleel and Larkey, 2003; El-Kahky et al., 2011; Al-Badrashiny et al., 2014), or use an intermediate script such as the International Phonetic Alphabet (IPA) (Brawer et al., 2010) or Double Metaphones (Philips, 2000).

AbdulJaleel and Larkey (2003) proposed a statistical method for transliteration between Arabic and English. It does statistical alignment of a corpus of transliterated proper names, and produces the probability of transliterations of short n-grams between the two scripts. Then, input terms are segmented into the available n-grams, and all possible transliterations are produced and scored based on their joint probabilities. Habash (2009) used an ambiguous mapping that utilized the sounds-like indexing system Double Metaphones (Philips, 2000) combined with the direct mapping scores defined by Freeman et al. (2006) to handle out-of-vocabulary words in the context of Arabic-English machine translation. Freeman et al. (2006) extended Levenshtein Edit Distance to allow for improved matching of Arabic and English versions of the same proper names. El-Kahky et al. (2011) use graph reinforcement models to learn mapping

---

[2]For more information on Arabic natural language processing, see Habash (2010).

between characters in different scripts in the context of transliteration mining.

Al-Badrashiny et al. (2014) present a similar system where words are transcribed using a finite state transducer constructed from an aligned parallel Arabizi-Arabic corpus. The disadvantage of this and other learned methods (Ristad and Yianilos, 1998; Lin and Chen, 2002; Mangu and Brill, 1997; Jiampojamarn et al., 2009) is that they require aligned parallel corpora whereas our approach performs well without any data. We note that training data for attempted dictionary lookup of heard words is extremely scarce. Brawer et al. (2010) present an automatic transliteration system used to internationalize place names for Google Maps. Their approach relies on hand crafting rule sets, that map between orthographies and the IPA. Their approach does not require any training data; however, it requires expert knowledge of the writing system of different languages and is difficult for languages like English, which do not have a simple orthographic to phonetic mapping. However, it is advantageous because adding rules for a single orthographic system allows transliteration between all language pairs. As with the AbdulJaleel system, this approach does not address noisy information retrieval, where the target term may be incorrectly heard or spelled.

**Phonetic Similarity Models**  Several phonetic similarity models have been discussed in the literature. In general, algorithms either directly compare phonetic pairs, or make use of phonetic feature vectors. Our approach in this paper uses phonetic features vectors to compute phonetic similarity.

Kuo et al. (2007) proposed a similarity model between English and Mandarin Chinese using phonetic confusion matrices. These are NxM matrices, giving the similarity two phone sets of size N and M. These similarities are generated statistically, either through aligned transliterations that have been converted to phones, or from errors produced in automatic speech recognition systems. However, the size of these matrices grow quadratically with the size of the phone set, so can require large amounts of training data.

Kondrak (2003) introduces an algorithm for calculating phonetic distance using separate phonetic feature vectors for vowels and consonants, with heuristic weights ascribed to each feature, and then calculating the best alignment using the Wagner-Fischer edit distance dynamic programming algorithm (Wagner and Fischer, 1974). There is a fixed cost for skipping a specific phone, and otherwise a cost for substitutions of phones proportionate to the difference in their weighted feature vectors.

Sriram et al. (2004) present a generic method for cross-linguistic search that shares the two stage approach in this paper, with a grapheme-to-phoneme model followed by matching in phonetic space with a distance metric. However, they only describe a rule based grapheme-to-phoneme system in abstract and do not present any sort of performance evaluation for their algorithm. Their search algorithm also requires the alignment and calculation of phonetic distance of the query against the entire database of search terms, which can be prohibitively expensive for large query sets.

## 3  MultiScript Search Algorithm

Our algorithm operates in two stages. First, the query term is converted from Arabic or Roman script into several possible phone sequences using several grapheme to phone conversion techniques. Then we use a phonetic distance algorithm to do search state enumeration based on a trie built from a phonetic Arabic dictionary.

We test different variations of grapheme to phone conversation techniques and phonetic distance metrics. For grapheme to phone conversion, we investigate using a simple manually created finite state transducer, and using deep bi-directional long short term recurrent neural networks. For the phonetic distance metric, we investigate using simple Levenshtein edit distance, unweighted phone feature vectors, and unweighted consonant and vowel feature vectors. We also show a method to train the system to produce weighted distance costs for performance increase.

### 3.1  Grapheme to Phone Model

#### 3.1.1  Finite State Transducer

We can define a very simple finite state transducer, which maps an orthographic input into a set of one or more IPA string outputs. This FST is compiled from a simple hand written list of rules of many-to-many mapping between orthographic substrings and single IPA phones. Creating such a list only requires basic knowledge of the orthographic system of the script.

The Arabic script FST is relatively simple, with

Figure 1: Overview of Phonetic Similarity Search algorithm

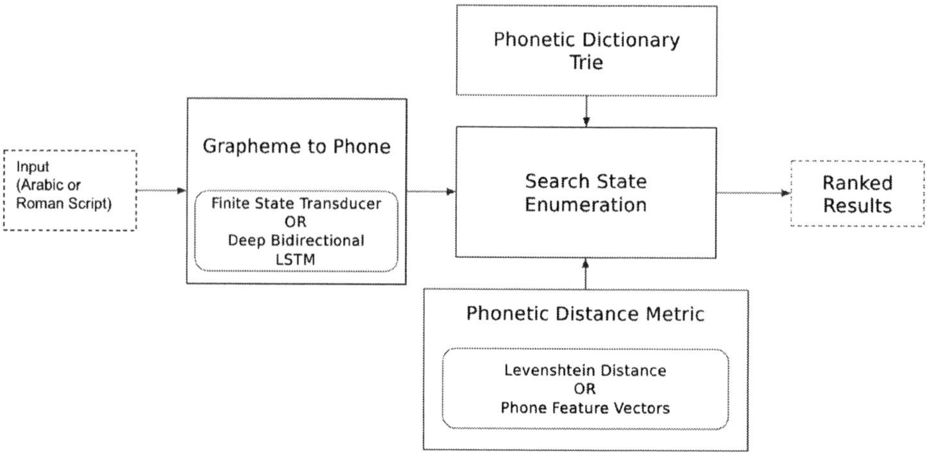

most consonants just mapping to a single IPA output, but with one-to-many mappings for some characters such as the long vowels. Our Arabic FST contains all the rules described in Biadsy et al. (2009).

The Roman script FST contains Arabizi-specific heuristic mappings from one- or two-character Roman-script strings into IPA found in the Arabic language, e.g. *gh* mapping to /ʁ/. It also includes digits, such as 5 mapping to /x/ خ and 7 mapping to /ħ/ ح. We also introduce the constraint that IPA phones that are repeated in the output string are collapsed into a single phone, to deal with doubled characters (i.e., كتّاب *ktAb* /kutta:b/ 'authors' is mapped to /kuta:b/).

### 3.1.2 BiLSTM Recurrent Neural Network

A common strategy for grapheme to phone mapping is to use recurrent neural networks trained on parallel orthography to phonetic corpora. We train a deep bidirectional long-short term memory cells (LSTM), loosely based on the grapheme-to-phoneme model presented by Rao et al. (2015). Our RNN has two hidden layers, each containing 512 LSTM cells in both the forwards and backwards directions. We use the connectionist temporal classification cost (CTC) function to train the network (Graves et al., 2006). The use of the CTC cost function helps us avoid doing phone alignments between our parallel corpora. We decode the neural net outputs using a beam search with width 100, taking only the top 1 result.

We train on two different parallel corpora. The first is the CMU pronouncing dictionary, a pho-

netic dictionary for English.[3] We also train on a hybrid corpus, which contains data from both CMU dictionary and ArabScribe. We do not train LSTM for Arabic orthography because there is not enough variation in the mapping between the script and the phonetic output to justify their use.

### 3.2 Search State Enumeration

Our goal is to find the words in the phonetic dictionary with the lowest phonetic distance from our query input encoded as phones. A naive approach would be to use the Wagner-Fischer dynamic programming algorithm to calculate the optimal alignment of insertions, deletions and substitutions, of our query against all terms in the dictionary. However, the cost of this would be prohibitive. Instead, we dynamically search for the most phonetically similar words by maintaining a set of search states against a phonetic trie containing our dictionary. An overview of the approach is in Figure 1.

We first build a trie containing the phonetic representation of all words in the Arabic dictionary. We use the IPA as our phone set. For our dictionary, we use fully diacritized lemmas from the Buckwalter Morphological Analyzer (Buckwalter, 2004). We convert the fully diacritized Arabic into phones using the simple rule based method proposed in Biadsy et al. (2009). We store all these terms in a trie data structure, where each node optionally contains a set of words for which it is the terminating node.

<hr>

[3]http://www.speech.cs.cmu.edu/cgi-bin/cmudict

Given a user input, we convert it into one or more phone strings, using one of our grapheme to phone algorithms. For each of these phone strings, we initialize a 4-tuple search state $(queryString, queryIndex, trieNode, cost)$ which represent the IPA encoded query, the index of the current phone in that string that is being consumed, the current node in the trie and the accumulated cost. For the initial search on "qamuus" (Arabic for 'dictionary'), one such four-tuple might be: $(kamus, 0, root, 0)$.

We then do search state enumeration until we discover $N$ final search states which are our results for a $TopN$ search. The search state enumeration process is illustrated in Figure 2. We define a function $Transition$, that takes our search state $s$, and returns a set $S'$ of zero or more search states. $Transition$ allows the search state to accept a single *insertion*, *deletion*, or *substitution* edit as in the Wagner-Fischer algorithm (Wagner and Fischer, 1974). The exact cost increase of each new search state $s$ depends on the phonetic distance algorithm that we select.

$$Transition(s) = S'$$
$$S' = Ins(s) \cup Del(s) \cup Sub(s)$$
$$s'.cost \geq s.cost \quad \forall s' \in S'$$

$$Ins(s) = \{\, s' \mid s'.tNode \in s.tNode.children \,\}$$
$$Del(s) = \{\, s' \mid s'.qIndex = s.qIndex + 1 \quad \}$$
$$Sub(s) = \{\, s' \mid s'.qIndex = s.qIndex + 1 \quad \wedge$$
$$s'.tNode \in s.tNode.children \,\}$$

We are looking for the words with the lowest phonetic distance overall, or equivalently, the lowest cost paths to final search states. A search state is considered final if we have consumed all characters in our query, and our resulting trie node is the end of a dictionary word. These conditions can be expressed as:

$$isFinal(s) = (s.qIndex == len(s.qString)$$
$$\wedge\ s.tNode.word \neq NULL)$$

An optimization we use to prevent enumerating the entire tree is using a min-heap, containing all the search states we have seen. We always pop the minimum search state, and therefore are guaranteed to traverse the global set of search states in cost order. For searching a query that fully matches a dictionary word, the number of transitions to discover the first word is equal exactly to the number of characters in the phonetic representation of that word.

If we use a Fibonacci heap as our min-heap, the worst case complexity of this algorithm is $O(ldq\log(dl))$, where $d$ is the length of the longest phonetic string in our dictionary, and $l$ is the number of phones in our alphabet, and $q$ is the length of the query, considering a complete Trie. However, as this algorithm discovers search states in cost order, in practice it is quite fast and does not need to enumerate many states before termination. It is also practical to implement a cost ceiling, after which transitions no longer need occur as you are too phonetically distant to have meaningful results. In this case, the phonetic search can be guaranteed to always terminate in a reasonable time.

## 3.3 Phonetic Distance Metric

We present below three strategies for defining the cost of insertion, deletion and substitution edits.

### 3.3.1 Levenshtein Distance

We investigate a naive approach where the cost of all insertion, deletion and substitution operations has a cost of 1. Thus, we find results that have low edit distance to our query. This approach is widely used in applications such as conventional spell correction, transliteration similarity and music information retrieval (Freeman et al., 2006; Toussaint and Oh, 2016).

### 3.3.2 Phone Binary Feature Vector

Again we define the cost of insertion and deletion edits to be 1. We represent phones using a 21-valued binary feature vector based on the Panphon package (Mortensen, 2016). Each feature is assigned either a value of + positive, - negative, or 0 as not relevant. The cost of substitution is then simply the distance between the two phones, which is calculated by sum the weights of the relevant non-zero features divided by the total weight of all features that are relevant in at least one of the two phones. For the untrained version, the weight of all features is equal to 1.

Figure 2: Search State Enumeration

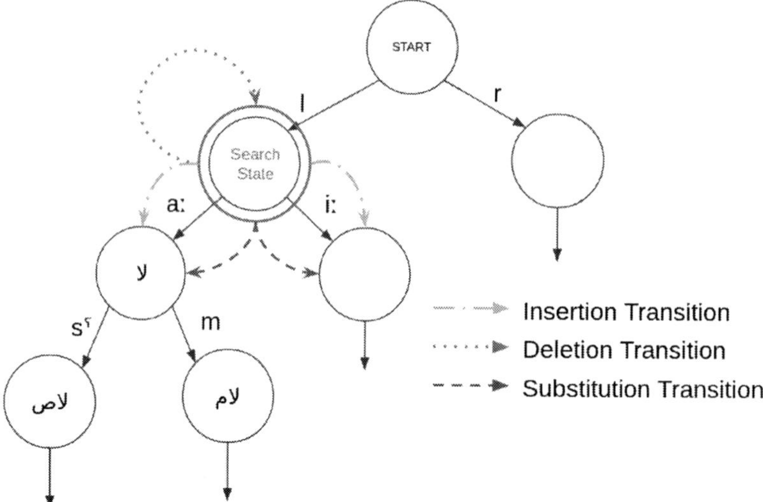



$$D(p, q) = \frac{\sum_i W_i I(p_i, q_i) R(p_i, q_i)}{\sum_i W_i R(p_i, q_i)}$$

$$I(x, y) = \begin{cases} 1, & if\, x == y \\ 0, & otherwise \end{cases}$$

$$R(x, y) = \begin{cases} 1, & if\, (x! = 0 \vee y! = 0) \\ 0, & otherwise \end{cases}$$

Because we divide by the sum of all relevant weights, the output of our distance function is always in the range of $[0, 1]$, with $D(x, x) = 0$. To improve performance, we introduce two language specific rules. For Roman-script inputs, substitutions between consonants and vowels are disallowed; and for Arabic-script inputs, vowel insertions are free, as Arabic is usually written without short vowel diacritics.

### 3.3.3 Machine Learned Weights

A machine learning method is introduced to improve the accuracy of phonetic search by fine tuning the weights associated with inserting, deleting and substituting phones on a corpus of transcriptions. Each discrete phone $p$ is given insertion and deletion costs in the range $[0, 10]$, while substitutions are given the range $[0, 1]$. The higher range for insertions and deletions is to allow insertion and deletion errors to take a higher cost than sub-

stitutions; this prevents our algorithm from enumerating over many unlikely insertion and deletions. A weight $W_i$ is also assigned to each phone feature, but our distance function $D(p, q)$ still produces costs in the range $[0, 1]$. The weights are trained such that the phonetic distance between a given transcription and the actual word is minimized relative to the phonetic distances between the transcription and all other words in the training set.

We define an edit vector $\vec{E}_{t,w}$ between a transcription $t$ and a word $w$ as the sum of all edits required in the shortest path between the phonetic representations of $t$ and $w$ as calculated by the Wagner-Fischer algorithm (Wagner and Fischer, 1974). We define an arbitrary but fixed ordering on our set of phones $P$ and on our phone features $F$. Thus the first $2|P|$ indices of $\vec{E}$ represent the number of inserts and deletions on specific phones, and the last $|F|$ indices represent the number of times a specific feature was different between two phones.

We construct an edit matrix for each transcription $\mathbf{M_t}$, where the first row $M_t^0$ is the edit vector between the transcription and the target word, followed by the edit vectors between the transcription and all other words in our training set. For Arab-Scribe, we use 41 phones and 21 phone features so the dimension of $\vec{E}$ is $2(41) + 21 = 103$. Our training set contains 400 words, so our edit matrix has dimensions $(400, 103)$.

To train, we initialize three weight variable vectors for insertion $\vec{W}_i$, deletion $\vec{W}_d$ and substitution $\vec{W}_s$ of length $|P|$, $|P|$ and $|F|$, respectively. We make a concatenated projected weight vector as follows:

$$\vec{W}_{\mathrm{proj}} = concatenate(10 \cdot sigmoid(W_i),$$
$$10 \cdot sigmoid(W_d),$$
$$\frac{W_s^2}{\sum_i W_s^{i2}})$$

This makes $\vec{W}_{\mathrm{proj}}$ align with $\vec{E}$ element-wise. We do the *sigmoid* and division by squared sum operations in order to force the cost of edits into the ranges we specified above. Finally we define the cost function for a given transcription $t$ as:

$$C_t = exp(D \cdot \frac{\vec{E}_{t,w} \cdot \vec{W}_{\mathrm{proj}}}{\mathbf{M}_t \vec{W}_{\mathrm{proj}}}) - 1$$

Where $D$ is a scaling factor hyper-parameter that punishes higher costs much more than lower costs, therefore forcing the training to improve the more difficult cases rather than over-optimizing the easy cases. The optimal value is dependent on the data size but we found $D = 500$ worked well for the ArabScribe training set. Note $C_t = 0$ when $t$ is a perfect transcription.

We do batch gradient descent with early stop at the point test performance drops. In our case, the entire ArabScribe training set could fit in memory, but for larger training sets stochastic gradient descent is recommended.

## 4   The ArabScribe Dataset

In order to benchmark the performance of our algorithms, and to provide training data for the bidirectional LSTM and trained weight vectors, we created the ArabScribe dataset of Arabic transcriptions. This dataset is freely available for research purposes.[4]

We randomly selected 500 MSA lemmas (the words) from the list of lemmas in our dictionary, the Buckwalter Arabic Morphological Analyzer (BAMA) (Buckwalter, 2004). BAMA contains 36,918 lemmas total. Five native speakers were recorded slowly and clearly speaking 100 words each, covering all 500 entries. Then, 103 participants listened to up to 100 words each. Each

[4]ArabScribe can be downloaded from `http://camel.abudhabi.nyu.edu/resources/`.

| | |
|---|---|
| No Experience | 26 |
| 0-1 years of Arabic education | 45 |
| 1-2 years of Arabic education | 14 |
| 2+ years of Arabic education | 6 |
| Heritage speaker | 3 |
| Native speaker | 9 |
| **Total** | **103** |

Table 2: ArabScribe participant skill levels

| | **Arabic Script** | **Roman Script** |
|---|---|---|
| **Train** | 654 | 1342 |
| **Test** | 2,580 | 5,357 |
| **Total** | 3,234 | 6,699 |

Table 3: ArabScribe transcription types

participant was assigned either the "English keyboard" (with digits and common punctuation) or sometimes the "Arabic keyboard" (without diacritics) if they reported that they could type Arabic. They were required to transcribe each word they heard in a way that was most natural to them. We collected 3,234 transcriptions with the Arabic keyboard (Arabic script) and 6,699 transcriptions with the English keyboard (Roman Script).

We collected native language and Arabic skill level of each participant were also collected. The skill levels are:

1. No Arabic experience

2. 0-1 years of Arabic education

3. 1-2 years of Arabic education

4. 2+ years of Arabic education

5. Heritage speaker (some Arabic exposure from family background but not fluent)

6. Native speaker

We tried to balance the dataset for having all words transcribed by an equal number of participants at all skill levels with both the Arabic and English keyboards. The transcriptions were also divided into a 20% testing set comprised of 100 words, and a 80% training set comprised of the other 400 words. Table 2 gives the the breakdown of the range of Arabic skill levels of the participants in our experiment; and Table 3 gives the breakdown of the number of samples in the train and test sets.

| Script | Grapheme-to-Phone | Distance Metric | Top 1 | Top 10 |
|---|---|---|---|---|
| Roman | EngLSTM | Levenshtein | 19.6% | 21.3% |
| Roman | HybridLSTM | Levenshtein | 20.5% | 22.3% |
| Roman | EngLSTM | MultiScript Untrained | 19.9% | 37.1% |
| Roman | HybridLSTM | MultiScript Untrained | 21.4% | 36.8% |
| Roman | FST | Levenshtein | 43.6% | 49.1% |
| Roman | FST | MultiScript Untrained | 36.8% | 53.3% |
| **Roman** | **FST** | **MultiScript Trained** | **46.0%** | **60.7%** |
| Arabic | - | Exact Match | 34.9% | - |
| Arabic | FST | Levenshtein | 54.7% | 57.3% |
| Arabic | FST | MultiScript Untrained | 54.4% | 65.4% |
| **Arabic** | **FST** | **MultiScript Trained** | **55.0%** | **69.0%** |

Table 4: Recall rates for different methods in TopN dictionary lookup

## 5  Experimental Results

To benchmark our phonetic search algorithm, we search against each transcription from our test set against the Arabic dictionary of all terms from BAMA. We then look for the correct word in the top 1 and top 10 results returned. We varied the grapheme-to-phone technique and distance metric, and performed the test on both the Roman and Arabic script data. For grapheme-to-phone techniques, we used the finite state transducers (FST) for Arabic and Roman scripts. We also trained a BiLSTM for Roman script only on either the English dictionary (EngLSTM) or a mix of the English dictionary and the ArabScribe training set (HybridLSTM). For the distance metrics, we used the Levenshtein distance metric, and the untrained and trained varieties of the MultiScript algorithm. The full results are listed in Table 4. Our Baseline techniques are exact matching for Arabic Script and searching using the FST with a Levenshtein edit distance (Damerau, 1964) for Roman Script. In general the LSTM based techniques performed poorly compared to the FST techniques. MultiScript without training was similar in performance to the Levenshtein distance metric. However, using a FST with trained MultiScript Search was the best performer for both Roman and Arabic Script. The top performing algorithms identified the target word within the top 10 results for 69.0% of cases with Arabic script, and 60.7% of cases with Roman script.

FSTs likely outperformed BiLSTMs because the English LSTM is not capable of producing any phones in the Arabic phone set, and it also cannot recognize Arabizi special symbols such as punctuation and digits. Training with some samples from ArabScribe slightly boosted the LSTM performance, but we hypothesize that the very small size of this training set made it ineffective. However, a disadvantage of the FST approach, is that it was tailored for the English-Arabic mapping, and would not generalize well to searching against other language pairs.

We found that for both Arabic and Roman script inputs, the accuracy of the algorithm is much higher for participants with more experience. This is likely because they can hear the sounds more accurately and also because they recognize more of the words in the test set. Our recall rate for advanced learners (2+ years of Arabic education) was 87% for Arabic script input and 78.5% for Roman script input. This search accuracy is in fact slightly higher than what native speakers scored which was 85.4% and 77.8% for Arabic and Roman script, respectively. Users with Arabic experience found their desired word in the top 10 significantly more often than beginner learners (0-1 years experience), whose recall rates were only 56.1% for Arabic script and 55.7% for Roman script. The full recall rates of FST+MultiScript search can be found in Table 5.

The instances in which MultiScript failed to match were often because the user thoroughly misheard the sound, or that there were too many real Arabic words similar to the target word which all were matched with low phonetic distance scores. Some errors also arose due to our FST not being complex enough to account for all the different ways people write the sounds they hear.

| Arabic Experience | Roman | Arabic |
|---|---|---|
| Native Speaker | 68.1% | 84.4% |
| Heritage Speaker | 63.3% | No Data |
| Advanced (2+ years) | 70.8% | 87.2% |
| Intermediate (1-2 years) | 53.3% | 69.0% |
| Beginner (0-1 years) | 55.7% | 56.1% |
| No Experience | 44.9% | N/A |

Table 5: Top 10 recall rates at different skill levels for FST + MultiScript trained search.

| Method | Recall |
|---|---|
| Google Translate Roman Top 1 | 21.5% |
| **MultiScript Roman Top 1** | **46.0%** |
| Yamli Roman Top 10+ | 44.5% |
| **MultiScript Roman Top 10** | **60.7%** |
| Google Translate Arabic Top 1 | 9.4% |
| **MultiScript Arabic Top 1** | **31.0%** |

Table 6: Benchmarking against Google Translate and Yamli on **non-exact** dictionary matches.

**Benchmarking against Google and Yamli**
Two popular tools that are commonly used by students of Arabic to look up unfamiliar words are Google Translate[5], through the "did you mean feature", and the Yamli Smart Arabic Keyboard[6]. We recognize that this comparison is not entirely fair as these tools target a much larger problem domain. However, we do this comparison as these are the tools most commonly used by students to address this unfamiliar word lookup problem.

Google Translate sometimes offers a single correction for non-dictionary word inputs, so we compare it to MultiScript top 1. For Arabic script inputs, 35% of the inputs were spelled exactly correctly, so we only measure rates of recovery from spelling errors rather than the rate of finding the correct word. The Yamli smart keyboard is a transliteration system where users can type Arabic using Roman letters, and it can return more than 10 suggestions per typed word, so we benchmark it against MultiScript top 10.

The results of this comparative benchmark are presented in Table 6. We significantly outperformed both Google Translate and Yamli in this specific dictionary lookup task for both Arabic and Roman scripts.

## 6 Conclusion and Future Work

We have demonstrated a novel algorithm for performing an efficient phonetic search against a large Arabic dictionary using both the Roman and Arabic scripts. We have also introduced the ArabScribe dataset containing around 10,000 transcription attempts of Arabic words in Roman and Arabic scripts. A comparative benchmark shows that our best setup significantly improves on the widely used Google Translate "did you mean" feature, as well as the Yamli Arabic smart keyboard.

Though our work was done for Arabic only, the only language specific methods involved were the finite state transducer rules and the system could easily be extended to other languages and orthographies. Other extensions of this work would be to apply these phonetic search algorithms in targeted information retrieval for one or more orthographies. For example, it could be applied in searching for names of people on Wikipedia, or names of places in a mapping application. It would also be interesting to see how the performance of the system improves with much larger scales of training data, and if using multivalued phone features would improve the distance metric.

## Acknowledgments

The creation of ArabScribe data set was support by a New York University Abu Dhabi Capstone Project Fund.

## References

Nasreen AbdulJaleel and Leah S. Larkey. 2003. Statistical transliteration for English-Arabic cross language information retrieval. In *Proceedings of the twelfth international conference on Information and knowledge management*, pages 139–146. ACM.

Mohamed Al-Badrashiny, Ramy Eskander, Nizar Habash, and Owen Rambow. 2014. Automatic Transliteration of Romanized Dialectal Arabic. *CoNLL-2014*, page 30.

Yaser Al-Onaizan and Kevin Knight. 2002. Machine transliteration of names in Arabic text. In *Proceedings of the ACL-02 workshop on Computational approaches to semitic languages*, pages 1–13. Association for Computational Linguistics.

Mohamed I. Alkanhal, Mohammed A. Al-Badrashiny, Mansour M. Alghamdi, and Abdulaziz O. Al-Qabbany. 2012. Automatic Stochastic Arabic Spelling Correction With Emphasis on Space Insertions and Deletions. *IEEE Transactions on Audio, Speech & Language Processing*, 20:2111–2122.

---

[5]https://translate.google.com/
[6]http://www.yamli.com/arabic-keyboard/

Kevin Atkinson. 2005. GNU Aspell. *Dostupno na: http://aspell. net/[01.10. 2013]*.

Fadi Biadsy, Nizar Habash, and Julia Hirschberg. 2009. Improving the Arabic pronunciation dictionary for phone and word recognition with linguistically-based pronunciation rules. In *Proceedings of Human Language Technologies: The 2009 Annual Conference of the North American Chapter of the Association for Computational Linguistics*, pages 397–405. Association for Computational Linguistics.

Sascha Brawer, Martin Jansche, Hiroshi Takenaka, and Yui Terashima. 2010. Proper name transcription/transliteration with ICU transforms. In *34th Internationalization and Unicode Conference*.

Tim Buckwalter. 2004. Buckwalter Arabic morphological analyzer version 2.0. Linguistic Data Consortium, University of Pennsylvania, 2002. LDC catalog no.: LDC2004l02. Technical report, ISBN 1-58563-324-0.

Fred J. Damerau. 1964. A technique for computer detection and correction of spelling errors. *Communications of the ACM*, 7(3):171–176.

Kareem Darwish. 2014. Arabizi detection and conversion to Arabic. *ANLP 2014*, page 217.

Ali El-Kahky, Kareem Darwish, Ahmed Saad Aldein, Mohamed Abd El-Wahab, Ahmed Hefny, and Waleed Ammar. 2011. Improved transliteration mining using graph reinforcement. In *Proceedings of the Conference on Empirical Methods in Natural Language Processing*, pages 1384–1393. Association for Computational Linguistics.

Ramy Eskander, Nizar Habash, Owen Rambow, and Nadi Tomeh. 2013. Processing Spontaneous Orthography. In *Proceedings of the 2013 Conference of the North American Chapter of the Association for Computational Linguistics: Human Language Technologies (NAACL-HLT)*, Atlanta, GA.

Andrew Freeman, Sherri Condon, and Christopher Ackerman. 2006. Cross linguistic name matching in English and Arabic. In *Proceedings of the Human Language Technology Conference of the NAACL, Main Conference*, pages 471–478, New York City, USA.

Alex Graves, Santiago Fernández, Faustino Gomez, and Jürgen Schmidhuber. 2006. Connectionist temporal classification: labelling unsegmented sequence data with recurrent neural networks. In *Proceedings of the 23rd international conference on Machine learning*, pages 369–376. ACM.

Nizar Habash, Abdelhadi Soudi, and Tim Buckwalter. 2007. On Arabic Transliteration. In A. van den Bosch and A. Soudi, editors, *Arabic Computational Morphology: Knowledge-based and Empirical Methods*. Springer.

Nizar Habash. 2009. Remoov: A tool for online handling of out-of-vocabulary words in machine translation. In *Proceedings of the 2nd International Conference on Arabic Language Resources and Tools (MEDAR)*, Cairo, Egypt.

Nizar Habash. 2010. *Introduction to Arabic Natural Language Processing*. Morgan & Claypool Publishers.

Sittichai Jiampojamarn, Aditya Bhargava, Qing Dou, Kenneth Dwyer, and Grzegorz Kondrak. 2009. Directl: a language-independent approach to transliteration. In *Proceedings of the 2009 Named Entities Workshop: Shared task on transliteration*, pages 28–31. Association for Computational Linguistics.

Grzegorz Kondrak. 2003. Phonetic alignment and similarity. *Computers and the Humanities*, 37(3):273–291.

Karen Kukich. 1992. Techniques for automatically correcting words in text. *ACM Computing Surveys (CSUR)*, 24(4):377–439.

Jin-Shea Kuo, Haizhou Li, and Ying-Kuei Yang. 2007. A phonetic similarity model for automatic extraction of transliteration pairs. *ACM Transactions on Asian Language Information Processing (TALIP)*, 6(2):6.

Wei-Hao Lin and Hsin-Hsi Chen. 2002. Backward machine transliteration by learning phonetic similarity. In *proceedings of the 6th conference on Natural language learning-Volume 20*, pages 1–7. Association for Computational Linguistics.

Lidia Mangu and Eric Brill. 1997. Automatic rule acquisition for spelling correction. In *ICML*, volume 97, pages 187–194.

Behrang Mohit, Alla Rozovskaya, Nizar Habash, Wajdi Zaghouani, and Ossama Obeid. 2014. The first qalb shared task on automatic text correction for arabic. In *Proceedings of the EMNLP 2014 Workshop on Arabic Natural Language Processing (ANLP)*, pages 39–47.

David Mortensen. 2016. Panphon. `https://github.com/dmort27/panphon`.

Kemal Oflazer. 1996. Error-tolerant finite-state recognition with applications to morphological analysis and spelling correction. *Computational Linguistics*, 22(1):73–89.

Lawrence Philips. 1990. Hanging on the metaphone. *Computer Language*, 7(12 (December)).

Lawrence Philips. 2000. The double metaphone search algorithm. *C/C++ Users Journal*, June.

Kanishka Rao, Fuchun Peng, Haşim Sak, and Françoise Beaufays. 2015. Grapheme-to-phoneme conversion using long short-term memory recurrent neural networks. In *2015 IEEE International Conference on Acoustics, Speech and Signal Processing (ICASSP)*, pages 4225–4229. IEEE.

Eric Sven Ristad and Peter N. Yianilos. 1998. Learning string-edit distance. *IEEE Transactions on Pattern Analysis and Machine Intelligence*, 20(5):522–532.

K. Shaalan, R. Aref, and A. Fahmy. 2010. An approach for analyzing and correcting spelling errors for non-native Arabic learners. *Proceedings of Informatics and Systems (INFOS)*.

S. Sriram, P. P. Talukdar, S. Badaskar, K. Bali, and A. G. Ramakrishnan. 2004. Phonetic distance based crosslingual search. In *Proc. of the Intl. Conf. on Natural Language Processing*.

Godfried T. Toussaint and Seung Man Oh. 2016. Measuring musical rhythm similarity: Edit distance versus minimum-weight many-to-many matchings. In *Proceedings of the 16th International Conference on Artificial Intelligence*, pages 186–189, Las Vegas, USA, July 25–28.

Kristina Toutanova and Robert C. Moore. 2002. Pronunciation modeling for improved spelling correction. In *Proceedings of the 40th Annual Meeting on Association for Computational Linguistics*, pages 144–151. Association for Computational Linguistics.

Robert A. Wagner and Michael J. Fischer. 1974. The string-to-string correction problem. *Journal of the ACM (JACM)*, 21(1):168–173.

Casey Whitelaw, Ben Hutchinson, Grace Y. Chung, and Gerard Ellis. 2009. Using the web for language independent spellchecking and autocorrection. In *Proceedings of the 2009 Conference on Empirical Methods in Natural Language Processing: Volume 2-Volume 2*, pages 890–899. Association for Computational Linguistics.

Wajdi Zaghouani, Behrang Mohit, Nizar Habash, Ossama Obeid, Nadi Tomeh, Alla Rozovskaya, Noura Farra, Sarah Alkuhlani, and Kemal Oflazer. 2014. Large scale Arabic error annotation: Guidelines and framework. In *LREC*, pages 2362–2369.

# Arabic POS Tagging: Don't Abandon Feature Engineering Just Yet


**Kareem Darwish**  **Hamdy Mubarak**  **Ahmed Abdelali**  **Mohamed Eldesouki**

Qatar Computing Research Institute (QCRI)

HBKU, Doha, Qatar

{kdarwish,hmubarak,aabdelali,mohamohamed}@hbku.edu.qa



## Abstract

This paper focuses on comparing between using Support Vector Machine based ranking (SVM$^{Rank}$) and Bidirectional Long-Short-Term-Memory (bi-LSTM) neural-network based sequence labeling in building a state-of-the-art Arabic part-of-speech tagging system. Using SVM$^{Rank}$ leads to state-of-the-art results, but with a fair amount of feature engineering. Using bi-LSTM, particularly when combined with word embeddings, may lead to competitive POS-tagging results by automatically deducing latent linguistic features. However, we show that augmenting bi-LSTM sequence labeling with some of the features that we used for the SVM$^{Rank}$-based tagger yields to further improvements. We also show that gains realized using embeddings may not be additive with the gains achieved due to features. We are open-sourcing both the SVM$^{Rank}$ and the bi-LSTM based systems for the research community.


## 1 Introduction

Part-of-speech (POS) tagging is an important building blocking in many natural language processing applications such as parsing and named entity recognition. An Arabic word is composed of one or more segments (or clitics), which are typically a stem to which prefixes and suffixes may be attached. Arabic POS tagging involves assigning appropriate in-context POS tags to each clitic. Tagging can be done for each clitic in sequence or for all clitics in a word simultaneously. Much work has been done on Arabic POS tagging and many morphological and surface-level features have been shown to improve tagging. Re-

cent work on sequence labeling using deep neural networks, particularly using bidirectional Long-Short-Term-Memory (bi-LSTM) and word embeddings, has been shown to be effective for POS tagging in different languages, without the need for explicit feature engineering. In essence, deep neural networks may be able to capture latent linguistic features automatically. In the context of this work, we compare using a discriminative classification technique, namely Support Vector Machine based Ranking (SVM$^{Rank}$), that requires significant feature engineering with bi-LSTM neural network with and without feature engineering and word embeddings. We experiment with tagging each clitic in context and with tagging all clitics in a word collectively. We also compare both systems with MADAMIRA, which is a state-of-the-art Arabic POS tagging system. We show that adding explicit features to the bi-LSTM neural network and employing word embeddings separately improve POS tagging results. However, combining both explicit features and embeddings together leads sub-optimal results. For testing, we employ the so-called "WikiNews" test set which is composed of freely available recent news articles in multiple genre (Abdelali et al., 2016). We are making all resultant systems available as open-source systems.

The contributions of this paper are as follows:

- We compare using SVM$^{Rank}$ to using bi-LSTM with and without feature engineering and word embeddigns in Arabic POS tagging. We show that feature engineering improves POS tagging significantly.

- We explore the effectiveness of many features including morphological and contextual features for tagging each clitic or each word in-context.




*Proceedings of The Third Arabic Natural Language Processing Workshop (WANLP)*, pages 130–137,
Valencia, Spain, April 3, 2017. ©2017 Association for Computational Linguistics

- We open-source both Arabic POS taggers, both of which are written entirely in Java. The SVM$^{Rank}$-based system has a load time of 5 seconds and can process about 2,000 word/second on an laptop with Intel i7 processor with 16 GB of RAM.

## 2 Background

### 2.1 Challenges of Arabic Language

Arabic language is a Semitic language with complex templatic derivational morphology. The Arabic nouns, adjectives, adverbs, and verbs are typically derived from a closed set of approximately 10,000 roots of length 3, 4, or rarely 5 letters. Arabic nouns and verbs are derived from these roots by applying templates to the roots to generate stems. Such templates may carry information that indicate morphological features of words such POS tag, gender, and number. For example, given a 3-letter root with 3 consonants CCC, a valid template may be CwACC , where the infix "wA" is inserted. This template is typically an Arabic broken, or irregular, plural template for a noun of template CACC or CACCp for masculine or feminine respectively. Further, stems may accept prefixes and/or suffixes to form words. Prefixes include coordinating conjunctions, determiner, and prepositions, and suffixes include attached pronouns and gender and number markers. English POS tagging techniques face a problem when dealing with agglutinative and highly inflected languages such as Arabic. This results in a large number of words (or surface forms) and in turn a high-level of sparseness and a large number of previously unseen words. Further, Arabic words embed morphological information such as gender and number and syntactic information such as case and gender and number agreement.

Traditional Arab linguists divide Arabic words into three classes, namely: nouns, verbs, and particles. Such coarse categorization is not suitable for many higher NLP tasks such as parsing. Therefore, more comprehensive tagsets have been created to capture the morphological and syntactic aspects of the words in Arabic. For most, the number of Arabic clitic-level POS tags is small, while the number of valid composite word-level tags is typically large. The proposed clitic-level tagsets range from simplified tagsets such as the *CATiB* tagset (Habash and Roth, 2009; Habash et al., 2009a) which has only six POS tags to more complex tagsets such as that of the *Penn Arabic Treebank* (ATB), which has 70 tags (Maamouri et al., 2004). In our work, we elected to use the tagest proposed by Darwish et al. (2014) which is a simplified version of ATB tagset and uses 18 tags only.

### 2.2 Arabic POS Tagging

Most recent work on Arabic POS tagging has used statistical methods. Diab (2009) used an SVM classifier to ascertain the optimal POS tags. The classifier was trained on the ATB data. Essentially, they treated the problem as a sequence-labeling problem. Another popular system for Arabic POS tagging is MADAMIRA, which uses an underlying morphological analyzer and is also trained on the ATB (Habash et al., 2009b; Pasha et al., 2014). We use MADAMIRA to compare to our work. Darwish et al. (2014) introduced the use of stem templates to improve POS tagging and to help ascertain the gender and the number of nouns and adjectives. They reported an accuracy of 98.1% on ATB data when using gold segmentation and employing different features such as word surface forms, list matching, and stem-templates.

In recent developments, deep neural networks were used to develop taggers that achieve good POS tagging accuracy. Plank et al. (2016) used bi-LSTM neural network to build taggers for 22 languages. The models achieved significant results for morphologically complex languages including Arabic. The models were built using the Universal Dependencies project v1.2 (Nivre et al., 2015) data. Ling et al. (2015) used bi-LSTM (Hochreiter and Schmidhuber, 1997) combining words and characters vector representations to achieve comparable results to state-of-the-art English POS tagging. Wang et al. (2015) used only word-embeddings on a bi-LSTM neural network to train a POS tagger; their approach achieved 97.26% accuracy on WSJ testset. The highest accuracy reported on this testset was 97.25% by Huang et al. (2012) .

## 3 Our Part-of-Speech Taggers

Our Arabic part-of-speech (POS) tagging uses the simplified ATB tag set proposed by (Darwish et al., 2014) and shown in Table 1. The POS tagger attempts to find the optimal tag for each word in a sentence. We present here two different approaches for POS tagging. The first uses SVM$^{Rank}$ to guess POS tags at the level of cli-

| POS | Description | POS | Description |
| --- | --- | --- | --- |
| ADV | adverb | ADJ | adjective |
| CONJ | conjunction | DET | determiner |
| NOUN | noun | NSUFF | noun suffix |
| NUM | number | PART | particles |
| PREP | preposition | PRON | pronoun |
| PUNC | punctuation | V | verb |
| ABBREV | abbreviation | CASE | alef of tanween fatha |
| JUS | jussification attached to verbs | VSUFF | verb suffix |
| FOREIGN | non-Arabic as well as non-MSA words | FUT_PART | future particle "s" prefix and "swf" |

Table 1: Part-of-speech tag set of Farasa.

tics or words using clitic and word level features as well as context-level features. The second uses Bi-LSTM recurrent-neural-network with clitic level features to guess POS tags at clitic level.

## 3.1 SVM$^{Rank}$-based POS Tagger

The POS tagger uses SVM$^{rank}$ (Joachims, 2006) with a linear kernel to determine the best POS tag for each word. It was trained on parts 1 (v. 4.1), 2 (v. 3.1), and 3 (v. 2) of the ATB (Maamouri et al., 2004). Instead of testing the POS tagger on a subset of the ATB, which may lead to artificially-high results due to its limited lexical diversity, we tested our system on the WikiNews test set, which includes 70 WikiNews articles from 2013 and 2014 and composed of $18,300$ words that are manually-segmented and POS tagged (Darwish and Mubarak, 2016). The WikiNews test set covers a variety of topics, namely: politics, economics, health, science and technology, sports, arts, and culture. We followed two paths for POS tagging, namely:

- (Clitic) we guess the POS tag for each clitic in a word, and then we combine the tags of the clitics of a word.

- (Word) we guess the compound POS tag for the whole word.

In both paths, we constructed a feature vector for each possible POS tag for each clitic or word. We supplied these vectors to SVM$^{Rank}$ indicating which vector should rank highest given feature values. We then use SVM$^{Rank}$ (Joachims, 2006) to learn feature weights. We use a linear kernel with a trade-off factor between training errors and margin equal to 100 (parameters tuned on

offline experiments carried out over a development set that was set aside from ATB). All possible POS tags for a clitic or a word are scored using the classifier, and the POS with the highest score is picked.

### 3.1.1 Tagging Clitics

Given a sentence composed of the clitics $c_{-n} \cdots c_0 \cdots c_m$, where $c_0$ is the current clitic and its proposed POS tag, we train the classifier using the following features, which are computed using the maximum-likelihood estimate on our training corpus:

- $p(POS|c_0)$ and $p(c_0|POS)$.

- $p(POS|c_{-i}..c_{-1})$ and $p(POS|c_1..c_j)$; $i, j \in [1, 4]$.

- $p(POS|c_{-i_{POS}}..c_{-1_{POS}})$ and $p(POS|c_{1_{POS}}..c_{j_{POS}})$; $i, j \in [1, 4]$. Since we don't know the POS tags of these clitics *a priori*, we estimate the conditional probability as:

$$\sum p(POS|c_{-1_{possible\_POS}}..c_{-i_{possible\_POS}}) .$$

For example, if the previous clitic could be a NOUN or ADJ, then $p(POS|c_{-1}) = p(POS|NOUN) + p(POS|ADJ)$.

If the clitic is a stem, we also compute the following features:

- $p(POS|stem\_template)$. Arabic words are typically derived from a closed set of roots that are placed in so-called stem templates to generate stems. For example, the root `ktb` can be fit in the template `CCAC` to generate the stem `ktAb` (book). Stem templates may conclusively have one POS tag (e.g., yCCC is always a V) or favor one tag over another (e.g., CCAC is more likely a NOUN than an ADJ). We used Farasa to determine the stem template (Abdelali et al., 2016).

- $p(POS|prefix)$ and $p(POS|suffix)$. Some prefixes and suffixes restrict the possible POS tags for a stem. For example, a stem preceded by DET is either a NOUN or an ADJ.

- $p(POS|prefix, prev\_word\_prefix)$, $p(POS|prev\_word\_suffix)$ and $p(POS|prev\_word\_POS)$. Arabic has agreement rules for noun phrases and idafa constructs that cover definiteness, gender, and number. Both these features help capture agreement indicators.

- $p(POS|MetaType)$. We assign each clitic a "meta types". The meta types can help the classifier identify different POS tags. The meta types are:

  - *NUM*: If a clitic is a sequence of numerals or matches a gazetteer of numbers spelled out in words.
  - *FOREIGN*: If all characters are Latin.
  - *PUNCT*: If it is composed of non-letters.
  - *ARAB*: If composed of Arabic letters only.
  - *PREFIX*: If it ends with "+" after segmentation (ex. "Al+").
  - *SUFFIX*: If it starts with "+" after segmentation (ex. "+h").

### 3.1.2 Tagging Words

In this setup, we attempt to tag the entire word at once instead of tagging each clitic separately. Similar to the tagging of clitics in subsection 3.1.1, we train $\text{SVM}^{Rank}$ using word-level features. Given a word sequence $w_{-n}...w_0...w_m$, we used the following features:

- $p(w_0|POS)$ and $p(POS|w_0)$

- $p(POS|w_{0\,word\_template})$ – The word-template here is the stem-template plus the prefixes and suffixes. For example, the stem of the "Al+ktAb" (the book) is "ktAb" with the stem-template "fEAl", and the word-template is "Al-fEAl".

- $p(POS|MetaType)$ – This is the meta type defined earlier with clitics, except that "PREFIX" and "SUFFIX" meta types are excluded.

- $p(POS|w_{0\,prefixes})$ – The prefixes are just the prefixes that are attached to the word.

- $p(POS|w_{0\,suffixes})$ – The suffixes are just the suffixes that are attached to the word.

- $p(POS|w_{0\,prefixes}, w_{-1\,prefixes})$ – This helps in capturing gender and number agreement.

- $p(POS|w_{0\,prefixes}, w_{-1\,prefixes}, w_{-1\,POS})$ – This also helps in capturing gender and number agreement.

- $p(POS|w_{-1\,suffixes})$

- $p(POS|w_{-1\,POS})$ – Since we don't know the POS tags of words *a priori*, we estimate the conditional probability using the same method we employed for clitics.

- $p(POS|w_{-2\,POS}, w_{-1\,POS})$

- $p(POS|w_{1\,POS}, w_{2\,POS})$

- $p(POS|w_{1\,POS}, w_{2\,POS}, w_{3\,POS})$

- $p(POS|VerbOrNot)$ – For this feature, we automatically analyzed all the unique words in ten years worth of Aljazeera.net articles using Al-Khalil morphological analyzer (Boudchiche et al., 2016). The articles contains 95.4 million tokens including 613k unique tokens. Given the different analyses of Al-Khalil, if it analyzed a word as a verb only, this feature is set to "V". If it appears as possibly a verb or some other POS, this feature becomes "possible-V". Otherwise, the feature is "not-V". Al-Khalil attempts to provide all the possible analysis of a word, but does not provide any ranking of the solutions. Since this is a word-level feature and not a clitic-level feature, we only used it in this setup.

- $P(POS|NounOrNot)$ – As with VerbOrNot, this feature is also based on the Al-Khalil analyzer, where the feature assumes the values "Noun", "possible-Noun", or "not-Noun".

- Word context features: $p(POS|w_{-1})$, $p(POS|w_1)$, $p(POS|w_{-2}, w_{-1})$, $p(POS|w_{-3}, w_{-2}, w_{-1})$, and $p(POS|w_{-4}, w_{-3}, w_{-2}, w_{-1})$

### 3.1.3 OOVs and pre-Filtering

For both clitic and word tagging, In case we could not compute a feature value during training (e.g., a clitic was never observed with a given POS tag), the feature value is assigned a small $\epsilon$ value equal to $10^{-10}$. If the clitic is a prefix or a suffix, then stem-specific features are assigned the same $\epsilon$ value.

In order to improve efficiency and reduce the choices the classifier needs to pick from, we employ some heuristics that restrict the possible POS tags to be considered by the classifier: (*i*) If a word is composed of one clitic, and the clitic is a number, restrict to "NUM". We check if the clitic is composed of digits or matches a gazetteer of numbers spelled out in words.
(*ii*) If a word is composed of Latin letters, restrict to "FOREIGN".
(*iii*) If punctuation, restrict to "PUNCT".
(*iv*) If a clitic is a stem and we can figure out the stem-template, restrict POS tags to those that have been seen for that stem-template during training. Similarly, if we can figure out the word-template, we restrict POS tags to those that have been seen for the word-template during training.
(*v*) If a clitic is a stem, restrict to POS tags that have been seen during training given the prefixes and suffixes of the word.

### 3.2 bi-LSTM Part-of-Speech Tagger

Bi-LSTM neural networks has been shown to be very effective for tagging sequential data, e.g. language modeling, speech utterances (Zen and Sak, 2015), handwritten text (Messina and Louradour, 2015), and scene text recognition (Hassanien, 2016). Further, word embeddings have demonstrated their potential for capturing statistical properties of natural language (Sutskever et al., 2011; Wang et al., 2015; Palangi et al., 2016). Along these directions, we modeled POS tagging as a sequence to sequence learning problem. We used a bi-LSTM neural-network model (Ling et al., 2015) to learn the expected tagset given an input for the model as a sequence of features $f_1, ..., f_n$ that could include word representations –embeddings– as well. The expected output of the network feed-forward states $S_i^f$ contains the tag

sets information for the parts 0 to $i$, while the back-forward state $S_i^b$ contains the information for the part $i + 1$ to $n$. The forward and backward states are combined, for each output $i$ as follows:
$$l_i = tanh(L^f S_i^f + L^b S_i^b + b_l)$$
where $L^f$, $L^b$ and $b_l$ denote the parameters for combining the forward and backward states.

We experimented with a number of settings where the clitic sequence was augmented with a subset of features that includes character sequences, word meta type, stem template (Darwish et al., 2014), and also combined with 200 dimension word embeddings learned over the aforementioned collection of text containing 10 years of Al-Jazeera articles[1]. To create the embeddings, we used word2vec with continuous skip-gram learning algorithm with an 8 gram window (Mikolov et al., 2013)[2]. For the bi-LSTM experiments, we used the Java Neural Network Library[3], which is tuned for POS tagging(Ling et al., 2015). We extended the library to produce the additional aforementioned features.

## 4 Evaluation and Discussion

### 4.1 SVM Approach

We trained the POS tagger using the aforementioned sections of the ATB (Maamouri et al., 2004). Testing was performed on the WikiNews dataset (Darwish and Mubarak, 2016). Table 2 reports on the accuracy of our POS tagger on the WikiNews dataset and compares it to MADAMIRA. The word-level SVM-based system beats the clitic-level system by 0.4% accuracy and achieves nearly identical results to MADAMIRA (with less than 0.005% difference). Using the word-level system has the advantage of being able to capture more context than the clitic-level system. We classified all the errors from our best system (word-based segmentation). The breakdown of the errors listed in Table 3 shows that confusion between ADJ and NOUN is the most common mistake type with a combined 41.1% of the errors followed by mistakes in segmentation. Common reasons for confusion between ADJ and NOUN include:

- Some words can assume either tag. For example, the word "AstrAtyjyp" could mean "strategy" or "strategic".

---

[1] `aljazeera.net`
[2] `code.google.com/archive/p/word2vec/`
[3] `https://github.com/wlin12/JNN`

| System | Truth Segmentation | Farasa Segmentation |
|---|---|---|
| State-of-the-art: MADAMIRA | 95.3 | |
| SVM$^{Rank}$ (Clitic) | 95.9 | 94.9 |
| SVM$^{Rank}$ (Word) | 96.2 | 95.3 |
| bi-LSTM (Clitic) | 94.5 | 93.5 |
| bi-LSTM (Clitic) w/embeddings | 95.0 | 92.4 |
| bi-LSTM (Clitic) w/features | 96.1 | 95.0 |
| bi-LSTM (Clitic) w/features + embeddings | 95.5 | 94.7 |

Table 2: The accuracy of our POS tagger on the WikiNews dataset (Darwish and Mubarak, 2016) against Madamira

- Arabic allows nouns to be omitted and adjectives assume their syntactic roles. For example, the word "AlErby" ("the Arab") could be used in the context of "qAl AlErby ("the Arab said") where it is implied that "the Arab man said", where the word "man" is omitted.

- on some occasions, adjectives may precede the nouns they modify as in the words "¿kbr" ("bigger than").

- the adjective is separated from the noun it modifies by several words.

| Error Type | Percentage |
|---|---|
| ADJ → NOUN | 26.3 |
| Segmentation Errors | 23.0 |
| NOUN → ADJ | 14.8 |
| V → NOUN | 11.2 |
| NOUN → V | 5.5 |
| PREP → PART | 3.0 |
| NUM → ADJ | 2.2 |
| CONJ → PART | 1.8 |
| NUM → NOUN | 1.6 |

Table 3: Most common errors for best SVM$^{Rank}$ configuration

Verbs are often mislabeled as nouns or vice versa. This is more problematic than the confusion between nouns and adjectives, as the mislabeling verbs can have a bigger impact on downstream applications such as parsing. Much of the errors stem from either: words that could assume either POS tag such as "tqy" meaining either "to protect from" or "righteous"; and verbs that were not observed in training, where the tagger would naturally prefer the more common tag of "NOUN". As the results in Table 2 show, using perfect segmentation leads to improved POS tagging accuracy. This is reflected in Table 3 where segmentation errors accounts for 23% of the errors.

## 4.2 bi-LSTM Approach

Similar to the evaluation setup of the SVM$^{Rank}$-based system, we modeled the ATB data into a sequence of clitics and the target was to learn the POS tags. The clitics were obtained using either gold ATB segmentation or from the Farasa Segmenter (Abdelali et al., 2016).

We augmented the input sequence with additional features that included the surface form of the clitic, leading and trailing characters, word meta type, and stem template. In additional experiment, we included the word embeddings learned for aforementioned corpus of Aljazeera.net, that was segmented using the Farasa segmenter. Table 2 shows the results for our bi-LSTM experiments with gold and Farasa segmentation. As expected, bi-LSTM was able to deliver competitive results by capturing complex non-linear and non-local dynamics in sequences (Hochreiter and Schmidhuber, 1997). Results in Table 2 show that:

- Not surprisingly using non-gold segmentation decreased POS tagging accuracy. However, the drop is more pronounced than the drop seen for the SVM$^{Rank}$-based system, particularly when using embeddings where the drop in accuracy was 2.6%.

- Though using either embeddings or features lead to overall improvements, features lead to bigger improvement than embeddings with greater robustness in the presence of segmentation errors.

- Using both features and embeddings together lead to worse results.

- The best bi-LSTM setup edged the SVM$^{Rank}$ clitic setup by 0.1%.

Table 4 summarizes the error types we observed when using the best bi-LSTM system (using features only and Farasa segmentation). The error trends and the reasons for the errors for bi-LSTM are similar to those of the SVM$^{Rank}$. We attempted to extend bi-LSTM to perform word-level tagging, but the results were very low (below 82% accuracy). We plan to investigate the reasons for such a drop.

| Error Type | Percentage |
|---|---|
| Segmentation errors | 21.8 |
| NOUN → ADJ | 17.6 |
| ADJ → NOUN | 15.5 |
| NOUN → V | 9.3 |
| V → NOUN | 7.7 |
| ADJ → NUM | 7.0 |
| NUM → NOUN | 1.6 |
| CONJ → PART | 1.3 |
| NOUN → NUM | 1.0 |

Table 4: Most common errors for best bi-LSTM configuration

## 5 Conclusion

This work presents two open source state-of-the-art POS tagging systems that are trained using standard ATB dataset (Maamouri et al., 2004) and evaluated on the WikiNews test set (Abdelali et al., 2016). In building the system we explored two approaches using Support Vector Machines (SVM) and Bidirectional Long Short-Term Memory (bi-LSTM). While the first is heavily dependent on linguistically engineered features that are modeled on linguistic knowledge, the second approach has the ability to induce latent linguistic features. Our experiments show that generic approaches might reach considerably high results, but using linguistic features may achieve higher results by encoding domain knowledge and nuances that are difficult to induce from the data alone. Further, using embeddings may lead to improved results, but not as much as hand crafted features.

## References


Ahmed Abdelali, Kareem Darwish, Nadir Durrani, and Hamdy Mubarak. 2016. Farasa: A Fast and Furious Segmenter for Arabic. pages 11–16, San Diego, CA, June. Association for Computational Linguistics.

Mohamed Boudchiche, Azzeddine Mazroui, Mohamed Ould Abdallahi Ould Bebah, Abdelhak Lakhouaja, and Abderrahim Boudlal. 2016. Alkhalil morpho sys 2: A robust arabic morpho-syntactic analyzer. *Journal of King Saud University-Computer and Information Sciences*.

Kareem Darwish and Hamdy Mubarak. 2016. Farasa: A New Fast and Accurate Arabic Word Segmenter. In *Proceedings of the Tenth International Conference on Language Resources and Evaluation (LREC 2016)*, Paris, France, may. European Language Resources Association (ELRA).

Kareem Darwish, Ahmed Abdelali, and Hamdy Mubarak. 2014. Using stem-templates to improve arabic pos and gender/number tagging. In *Proceedings of the Ninth International Conference on Language Resources and Evaluation (LREC'14)*, Reykjavik, Iceland, may. European Language Resources Association (ELRA).

Mona Diab. 2009. Second generation amira tools for arabic processing: Fast and robust tokenization, pos tagging, and base phrase chunking. In *2nd International Conference on Arabic Language Resources and Tools*.

Nizar Habash and Ryan M Roth. 2009. Catib: The columbia arabic treebank. In *Proceedings of the ACL-IJCNLP 2009 conference short papers*, pages 221–224. Association for Computational Linguistics.

Nizar Habash, Reem Faraj, and Ryan Roth. 2009a. Syntactic annotation in the columbia arabic treebank. In *Proceedings of MEDAR International Conference on Arabic Language Resources and Tools, Cairo, Egypt*.

Nizar Habash, Owen Rambow, and Ryan Roth. 2009b. Mada+ tokan: A toolkit for arabic tokenization, diacritization, morphological disambiguation, pos tagging, stemming and lemmatization. In *Proceedings of the 2nd international conference on Arabic language resources and tools (MEDAR), Cairo, Egypt*, pages 102–109.

Ahmed Mamdouh A Hassanien. 2016. Sequence to sequence learning for unconstrained scene text recognition. *arXiv preprint arXiv:1607.06125*.

Sepp Hochreiter and Jürgen Schmidhuber. 1997. Long Short-Term Memory. *Neural computation*, 9(8):1735–1780.

Liang Huang, Suphan Fayong, and Yang Guo. 2012. Structured perceptron with inexact search. In *Proceedings of the 2012 Conference of the North American Chapter of the Association for Computational Linguistics: Human Language Technologies*, pages 142–151. Association for Computational Linguistics.

Thorsten Joachims. 2006. Training Linear SVMs in Linear Time. KDD '06, pages 217–226, New York, NY. ACM.

Wang Ling, Tiago Luís, Luís Marujo, Ramón Fernandez Astudillo, Silvio Amir, Chris Dyer, Alan W Black, and Isabel Trancoso. 2015. Finding function in form: Compositional character models for open vocabulary word representation. *arXiv preprint arXiv:1508.02096*.

Mohamed Maamouri, Ann Bies, Tim Buckwalter, and Wigdan Mekki. 2004. The Penn Arabic Treebank: Building a Large-Scale Annotated Arabic Corpus. In *NEMLAR conference on Arabic language resources and tools*, volume 27, pages 466–467.

Ronaldo Messina and Jerome Louradour. 2015. Segmentation-free handwritten chinese text recognition with lstm-rnn. In *Document Analysis and Recognition (ICDAR), 2015 13th International Conference on*, pages 171–175. IEEE.

Tomas Mikolov, Wen-tau Yih, and Geoffrey Zweig. 2013. Linguistic Regularities in Continuous Space Word Representations. In *Proceedings of the 2013 Conference of the North American Chapter of the Association for Computational Linguistics: Human Language Technologies*, NAACL-HLT '13, pages 746–751, Atlanta, GA, USA.

Joakim Nivre, Željko Agić, Lars Ahrenberg, and et al. 2015. Universal dependencies 1.2. LINDAT/CLARIN digital library at the Institute of Formal and Applied Linguistics, Charles University in Prague.

Hamid Palangi, Li Deng, Yelong Shen, Jianfeng Gao, Xiaodong He, Jianshu Chen, Xinying Song, and Rabab Ward. 2016. Deep sentence embedding using long short-term memory networks: Analysis and application to information retrieval. *IEEE/ACM Transactions on Audio, Speech, and Language Processing*, 24(4):694–707.

Arfath Pasha, Mohamed Al-Badrashiny, Mona T Diab, Ahmed El Kholy, Ramy Eskander, Nizar Habash, Manoj Pooleery, Owen Rambow, and Ryan Roth. 2014. MADAMIRA: A Fast, Comprehensive Tool for Morphological Analysis and Disambiguation of Arabic. LREC 2014, pages 1094–1101. European Language Resources Association (ELRA).

Barbara Plank, Anders Søgaard, and Yoav Goldberg. 2016. Multilingual part-of-speech tagging with bidirectional long short-term memory models and auxiliary loss. *Proceedings of the 54th Annual Meeting of the Association for Computational Linguistics*, pages 412–418.

Ilya Sutskever, James Martens, and Geoffrey E Hinton. 2011. Generating text with recurrent neural networks. In *Proceedings of the 28th International Conference on Machine Learning (ICML-11)*, pages 1017–1024.

Peilu Wang, Yao Qian, Frank K Soong, Lei He, and Hai Zhao. 2015. A unified tagging solution: Bidirectional lstm recurrent neural network with word embedding. *arXiv preprint arXiv:1511.00215*.

Heiga Zen and Haşim Sak. 2015. Unidirectional long short-term memory recurrent neural network with recurrent output layer for low-latency speech synthesis. In *2015 IEEE International Conference on Acoustics, Speech and Signal Processing (ICASSP)*, pages 4470–4474. IEEE.

# Toward a Web-based Speech Corpus for Algerian Arabic Dialectal Varieties


**Soumia Bougrine[1]    Aicha Chorana[1]    Abdallah Lakhdari[1]    Hadda Cherroun[1]**
[1]Laboratoire d'informatique et Mathématiques
Université Amar Telidji Laghouat, Algérie
{sm.bougrine,a.chorana,a.lakhdari,hadda_cherroun}@lagh-univ.dz



## Abstract

The success of machine learning for automatic speech processing has raised the need for large scale datasets. However, collecting such data is often a challenging task as it implies significant investment involving time and money cost. In this paper, we devise a recipe for building large-scale Speech Corpora by harnessing Web resources namely YouTube, other Social Media, Online Radio and TV. We illustrate our methodology by building KALAM'DZ, An Arabic Spoken corpus dedicated to Algerian dialectal varieties. The preliminary version of our dataset covers all major Algerian dialects. In addition, we make sure that this material takes into account numerous aspects that foster its richness. In fact, we have targeted various speech topics. Some automatic and manual annotations are provided. They gather useful information related to the speakers and sub-dialect information at the utterance level. Our corpus encompasses the 8 major Algerian Arabic sub-dialects with $4881$ speakers and more than $104.4$ hours segmented in utterances of at least 6 s.


## 1 Introduction

Speech datasets and corpora are crucial for both developing and evaluating Natural Language Processing (NLP) systems. Moreover, such corpora have to be large to achieve NLP communities expectations. In fact, the notion of "More data is better data" was born with the success of modeling based on machine learning and statistical methods.

The applications that use speech corpora can be grouped into four major categories: speech recognition, speech synthesis, speaker recognition/verification and spoken language systems. The need for such systems becomes inevitable. These systems include real life wingspan applications such as speech searching engines and recently *Conversational Agents*, conversation is becoming a key mode of human-computer interaction.

The crucial points to be taken into consideration when designing and developing relevant speech corpus are numerous. The necessity that a corpus takes the within-language variability (Li et al., 2013). We can mention some of them: The corpus size and scope, richness of speech topics and content, number of speakers, gender, regional dialects, recording environment and materials. We have attempted to cover a maximum of these considerations. We will underline each considered point in what follows.

For many languages, the state of the art of designing and developing speech corpora has achieved a mature situation. On the other extreme, there are few corpora for Arabic (Mansour, 2013). In spite that geographically, Arabic is one of the most widespread languages of the world (Behnstedt and Woidich, 2013). It is spoken by more than $420$ million people in $60$ countries of the world (Lewis et al., 2015). Actually, it has two major variants: Modern Standard Arabic (MSA), and Dialectal Arabic. MSA is the official language of all Arab countries. It is used in administrations, schools, official radios, and press. However, DA is the language of informal daily communication. Recently, it became also the medium of communication on the Web, in chat rooms, social media etc. This fact, amplifies the need for language resources and language related NLP systems for dialects.

For some dialects, especially Egyptian and Levantine, there are some investigations in terms of building corpora and designing NLP tools. While,




*Proceedings of The Third Arabic Natural Language Processing Workshop (WANLP)*, pages 138–146,
Valencia, Spain, April 3, 2017. ©2017 Association for Computational Linguistics

very few attempts have considered Algerian Arabic dialect. Which, make us affirm that the Algerian dialect and its varieties are considered as under-resourced language. In this paper, we tend to fill this gap by giving a complete recipe to build a large-size speech corpus. This recipe can be adopted for any under-resourced language. It eases the challenging task of building large datasets by means of traditional direct recording. Which is known as time and cost consuming. Our idea relies on Web resources, an essential milestone of our era. In fact, the Web 2.0, becomes a global platform for information access and sharing that allows collecting any type of data at scales hardly conceivable in near past.

The proposed recipe is to build a speech corpus for Algerian Arabic dialect varieties. For this preliminary version, the corpus is annotated for mainly supporting research in dialect and speaker identification.

The rest of this paper is organized as follows. In the next section, we review some related work that have built DA corpora. In Section 3 we give a brief overview of Algerian sub-dialects features. Section 4 is dedicated to describe the complete proposed recipe of building a Web-based speech dataset. In Section 5, we show how this recipe is narrated to construct a speech corpus for Algerian dialectal varieties. The resulted corpus is described in Section 6. We enumerate its potential uses in Section 7

## 2   Related Work

In this section, we restricted our corpora review to speech corpora dealing with Arabic dialects. We classify them according to two criteria: *collecting method* and *Intra/Inter country dialect collection context*. They can be classified into five categories according to the collecting method. Indeed, it can be done by recording broadcast, spontaneous telephone conversations, telephone responses of questionnaires, direct recording and Web-based resourcing. The second criterion distinguishes the origin of targeted dialects in either Intra-country/region or Inter-country, which means that the targeted dialects are from the same country/region or dialects from different countries. This criterion is chosen because it is harder to perform fine collection of Arabic dialects belonging to close geographical areas that share many historic, social and cultural aspects.

In contrast of relative abundance of speech corpora for Modern Standard Arabic, very few attempts have considered building Arabic speech corpora for dialects. Table 1 reports some features of the studied *DA* corpora. The first set of corpora has exploited the limited solution of telephony conversation recording. In fact, as far as we know, development of the pioneer DA corpus began in the middle of the nineties and it is *CALLFRIEND Egyptian* (Canavan and Zipperlen, 1996). Another part of *OrienTel* project, cited below, has been dedicated to collect speech corpora for Arabic dialects of Egypt, Jordan, Morocco, Tunisia, and United Arab Emirates countries. In these corpora, the same telephone response to questionnaire method is used. These corpora are available via the ELRA catalogue [1].

The *DARPA Babylon Levantine* [2] Arabic speech corpus gathers four Levantine dialects spoken by speakers from Jordan, Syria, Lebanon, and Palestine (Makhoul et al., 2005).

*Appen* company has collected three Arabic dialects corpora by means of spontaneous telephone conversations method. These corpora [3] uttered by speakers from Gulf, Iraqi and Levantine. With a more guided telephone conversation recording protocol, *Fisher Levantine Arabic* corpus is available via LDC catalogue [4]. The speakers are selected from Jordan, Lebanon, Palestine, Lebanon, Syria and other Levantine countries.

TuDiCoI (Graja et al., 2010) is a spontaneous dialogue speech corpus dedicated to Tunisian dialect, which contains recorded dialogues between staff and clients in the railway of Sfax town, Tunisia.

Concerning corpora that gather MSA and Arabic dialects, we have studied some of them. *SAAVB* corpus is dedicated to speakers from all the cities of Saudi Arabia country using telephone response of questionnaire method (Alghamdi et al., 2008). The main characteristic of this corpus is that, before recording, a preliminary choice of speakers and environment are performed. The selection aims to control speaker age and gender and telephone type.

*Multi-Dialect Parallel (MDP)* corpus, a free

---

[1]Respective code product are ELRA-S0221, ELRA-S0289, ELRA-S0183, ELRA-S0186 and ELRA-S0258.

[2]Code product is LDC2005S08.

[3]The LDC catalogue's respective code product are LDC2006S43, LDC2006S45 and LDC2007S01.

[4]Code product is LDC2007S02.

| Corpus | Type | Collecting Method | Corpus Details |
|---|---|---|---|
| **Al Jazeera multi-dialectal** | Inter | Broadcast news | 57 hours, 4 major Arabic dialect groups annotated using crowdsourcing |
| **ALG-DARIDJAH** | Intra | Direct Recording | 109 speakers from 17 Algerian departments, 4.5 hours |
| *AMCASC* | Intra | Telephone conversations | 3 Algerian dialect groups, 735 speakers, more than 72 hours. |
| *KSU Rich Arabic* | Inter | Guided telephone conversations and Direct recording. | 201 speakers from nine Arab countries, 9 dialects + MSA. |
| *MDP* | Inter | Direct Recording | 52 speakers, 23% MSA utterances, 77% DA utterances, 32 hours, 3 dialects + MSA. |
| *SAAVB* | Inter | Selected speaker before telephone response of questionnaire | 1033 speakers; 83% MSA utterances, 17% DA utterances, Size: 2.59 GB, 1 dialect + MSA |
| *TuDiCoI* | Inter | Spontaneous dialogue | 127 Dialogues, 893 utterances, 1 dialect. |
| *Fisher Levantine* | Inter | Guided telephone conversations | 279 conversations, 45 hours, 5 dialects. |
| *Appen's corpora* | Inter | Spontaneous telephone conversations | 3 dialects, Gulf: 975 conver, ⁓ 93 hours; Iraqi: 474 conver, ⁓ 24 hours; Levantine: 982 conver, ⁓ 90 hours. |
| *DARPA Babylon Levantine* | Inter | Direct recording of spontaneous speech | 164 speakers, 75900 Utterances, Size: 6.5 GB, 45 hours, 4 dialects. |
| *OrienTel MCA* | Inter | Telephone response of questionnaire | 5 dialects, # speakers: 750 Egyptian, 757 Jordanian, 772 Moroccan, 792 Tunisian and 880 Emirates. |
| *CALLFRIEND* | Inter | Spontaneous telephone conversations | 60 conversations, lasting between 5-30 minutes, 1 dialect. |

Table 1: Speech Corpora for Arabic dialects.

corpus, which gathers MSA and three Arabic dialects (Almeman et al., 2013). Namely, the dialects are from Gulf, Egypt and Levantine. The speech data is collected by direct recording method.

*KSU Rich Arabic* corpus encompasses speakers by different ethnic groups, Arabs and non-Arabs (Africa and Asia). Concerning Arab speakers in this corpus, they are selected from nine Arab countries: Saudi, Yemen, Egypt, Syria, Tunisia, Algeria, Sudan, Lebanon and Palestine. This corpus is rich in many aspects. Among them, the richness of the recording text. In addition, different recording sessions, environments and systems are taken into account (Alsulaiman et al., 2013).

*Al Jazeera multi-dialectal speech corpus*, a larger scale, based on Broadcast News of Al Jazeera (Wray and Ali, 2015). Its annotation is performed by crowd sourcing technology. It encompasses the four major Arabic dialectal categories.

In an intra country context, there are two cor-

pora dedicated to Algerian Arabic dialect varieties: *AMCASC* (Djellab et al., 2016) and ALG-DARIDJAH (Bougrine et al., 2016). *AMCASC* corpus, based on telephone conversations collecting method, is a large corpus that takes three regional dialectal varieties. While ALG-DARIDJAH corpus is a parallel corpus that encompasses Algerian Arabic sub-dialects. It is based on direct recording method. Thus, many considerations are controlled while building this corpus. Compared to *AMCASC* corpus, the size of ALG-DARIDJAH corpus is restricted.

According to our study of these major Arabic dialects corpora, we underline some points. First, these corpora are mainly fee-based and the free ones are extremely rare. Second, almost existing corpora are dedicated to inter-country dialects. Third, to the best of our knowledge, there is no Web-based speech dataset/corpus that deals with Arabic speech data neither for MSA nor for dialects. While for other languages, there are some investigations. We can cite the large recent collection *Kalaka*-3 (Rodríguez-Fuentes et al., 2016). This is a speech database specifically designed for Spoken Language Recognition. The dataset provides TV broadcast speech for training, and audio data extracted from YouTube videos for testing. It deals with European languages.

## 3 Algerian Dialects: Brief Overview

Algeria is a large country, administratively divided into 48 departments. Its first official language is Modern Standard Arabic. However, Algerian dialects are widely the predominant means of communication. In Figure 1, we depict the main Algerian dialect varieties. In this work, we focus on Algerian Arabic sub-dialects as they are spoken by 75% to 80% of the population. The Algerian dialect is known as Daridjah to its speakers.

Algerian Arabic dialects resulted from two Arabization processes due to the expansion of Islam in the $7^{th}$ and $11^{th}$ centuries, which lead to the appropriation of the Arabic language by the Berber population.

According to both Arabization processes, dialectologists (Palva, 2006), (Pereira, 2011) show that Algerian Arabic dialects can be divided into two major groups: Pre-Hilālī and Bedouin dialects. Both dialects are different by many linguistic features (Marçais, 1986) (Caubet, 2000).

Firstly, Pre-Hilālī dialect is called a sedentary dialect. It is spoken in areas that are affected by the expansion of Islam in the $7^{th}$ century. At this time, the partially affected cities are: Tlemcen, Constantine and their rural surroundings. The other cities have preserved their mother tongue language (Berber).

Secondly, Bedouin dialect is spoken in areas which are influenced by the Arab immigration in the $11^{th}$ century (Palva, 2006) (Pereira, 2011). Marçais (1986) has divided Bedouin dialect into four distinct dialects: i) *Sulaymite* dialect which is connected with Tunisian Bedouin dialects, ii) *Ma'qilian* dialect which is connected with Moroccan Bedouin dialects, iii) *Hilālī* dialect contains three nomadic sub-dialects. *Hilālī-Saharan* that covers the totality of the Sahara of Algeria, the *Hilālī-Tellian* dialect which its speakers occupy a large part of the Tell of Algeria, and the *High-plains of Constantine*, which covers the north of Hodna region to Seybouse river. iv) *Completely-bedouin dialect* that covers Algiers' Blanks, and some of its near sea coast cities. Regarding to

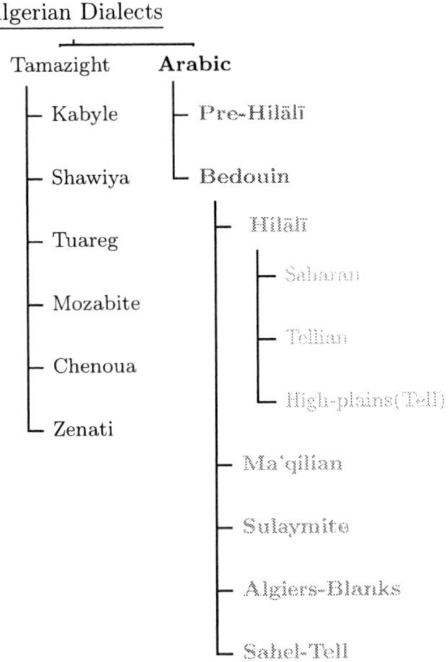


Figure 1: Hierarchical Structure of Algerian Dialects.

some linguistic differences, we have divided this last dialect into two sub-dialects, namely *Algiers-Blanks* and *Sahel-Tell*.

Arabic Algerian dialects present complex linguistic features and many linguistic phenomena can be observed. Indeed, there is many borrowed words due to the deep colonization. In fact, Arabic Algerian dialects are affected by other languages such as Turkish, French, Italian, and Spanish (Leclerc, 30 avril 2012). In addition, code switching is omnipresent especially from French.

Versteegh et al. (2006) used four consonants (the dentals fricative /t, d, d/ and a voiceless uvular stop /q/) to discriminate the two major groups: Pre-Hilālī and Bedouin dialect. In fact, he shows that Pre-Hilālī dialect are characterized by: /q/ is pronounced /k/ and the loss of inter-dentals and pass into the dentals /t, d, d/. For Algerian Bedouin dialect, the four discriminative consonants are characterized by: /q/ is pronounced /g/ and the inter-dentals are fairly preserved. For more details on Algerian linguistic features refer to (Embarki, 2008) (Versteegh et al., 2006) (Harrat et al., 2016).

## 4  Methodology

In this section, we first describe, in general way, the complete recipe to collect and annotate a Web-based spoken dataset for an under-resourced language/dialect. Then, we illustrate this recipe to build our Algerian Arabic dialectal speech corpus mainly dedicated to dialect and speaker identification.

**Global View of the Recipe**

The recipe described in the following can be easily tailored according to potential uses of the corpus and on the specificities of the targeted language resources and its spoken community.

1. *Inventorying Potential Web sources:* First, we have to identify sources that are the most targeted by the communities of the languages/dialects in concerns. Indeed, depending on their culture and preferences, some communities show preference for dealing with some Web media over others. For example, Algerian people are less used to use *Instagram* or *Snapchat* compared with Middle Est and Gulf ones. Moreover, each country has its own most used communication media. For instance, some societies (Arabs ones) are more productive on TVs and Radios, compared with west communities that are more present and productive on social media.

2. *Extraction Process:* In order to avoid crawling useless data, this steps is achieved by three stages

   (a) *Preliminary Validation Lists:* For each chosen Web source, we define the main keywords that can help automatically search video/audio lists. When such lists are established, a first cleaning is performed keeping only the potential suitable data. Sizing such lists depends on the sought scale.

   (b) *Providing the collection script:* For each resource, we fix and implement the suitable way to collect data automatically. Open Source tools are the most suitable. In fact, downloading a speech from a streaming or from YouTube or even from online Tv needs different scripts. The same fact has to be taken into account concerning their related metadata [5] which are very useful for annotation.

   (c) *Downloading:* This is a time consuming task. Thus, it is important to consider many facts such as preparing storage and downloading the related metadata, …

   (d) *Cleaning:* Now, the videos/audios are locally available, a first scan is performed in order to keep the most appropriate data to the corpus concerns. This can be achieved by establishing a strategy depending on the corpus future use.

3. *Annotation and Pre-processing:* For a targeted NLP task, pre-processing the collected speech/video can include segmentation, White noise removing. … Some annotations can simply be provided from the related metadata of the Web-source when they exist. However, this task makes use of other annotation techniques like crowdsourcing where crowd are called to identify the targeted dialect/speaker or/and perform translations.

The method can be generalized to other languages/dialects without linguistic and cultural knowledge of the regional language or dialect by using video/audio search query based on the area (location) of targeted dialect/language. Then use the power of crowdsourcing to annotate corpus.

## 5  Corpus Building

For the context of the Algerian dialects, in order to build a speech corpus that is mainly dedicated to dialect/speaker identification using machine learning techniques, we have chosen several resources.

### 5.1  Web Sources Inventory

The main aim is to allow the richness of the corpus. In fact, it is well known that modeling a spoken language needs a set of speech data counting the within-language/intersession variability, such as speaker, content, recording device, communication channel, and background noise (Li et al., 2013). It is desirable to have sufficient data that include the intended intersession effects.

Table 2 reports the main Web sources that feed our corpus. Let us observe that there are several

---

[5] YouTube video Metadata such as *published_date, duration, description, category…*

speech Topics which allows capturing more linguistics varieties. In fact, this inventory contains "Local radio channels" resources. Fortunately, each Algerian province has at least one local radio (a governmental one). It deals with local community concerns and exhibits main local events. Some of their reports often use their own local dialect. It is the same case for amateur radios. Both, these radio channels and Tvs are Web-streamed live.

In addition, we have chosen some Algerian TVs for which most programs are addressed to large community. So, they use dialects. Finally, we have targeted some YouTube resources such as Algerian PodCasts, Algerian Tags, and channels of Algerian YouTubers.

| Source | Sample | Topics |
|---|---|---|
| Algerian Tv | Ennahar<br>El chorouk<br>Samira, Bina | News<br>News, General<br>Cook |
| Local Radios | 48 departments | Social, local,<br>General |
| On YouTube | | |
| Algerian<br>PodCast | Anes Tina | Politic, Culture,<br>Social |
| Algerian<br>YouTubers | Khaled Fkir<br>CCNA DZ<br><br>Mesolyte | Blogs, Cook<br>Tips, Fun<br>Advices, Beauty<br>Technology, Vlog |
| Algerian TAG | – | Advices, Tips<br>social discussions |

Table 2: Main Sources of Videos

## 5.2 Extraction Process

Now having these Web sources, and as they are numerous, we process in two steps in order to acquire video/audio speech data. First, we drawn up lists by crawling information mainly meta data about existing data related to potential videos/audios that potentially contain Algerian dialect speech. The deployed procedure relies on mainly two different scripts according to the Web resource type.

In order to collect speech data from local radio channels, we refer back manually to the programs of radio to select report and emission lists that are susceptible to contain dialectal speech.

For data from YouTube, the lists are fed by using YouTube search engine through its Data API [6].

---

[6]YouTube Data API, `https://developers.google.com/YouTube/v3/`

In addition, the extraction of related metadata are performed using Python package BeautifulSoup $V4$ dedicated to Web crawling (Nair, 2014).

In order to draw up search queries, we have used three lists. The first one $Dep$, contains the names of the 48 Algerian provinces, spelled in MSA, dialect and French. While the second list $Cat$ contains the selected YouTube categories. Among the actual YouTube categories, we have targeted: *People & Blogs, Education, Entertainment, How-to & Style, News & Politics, Non-profits & Activism categories, and Humor*. The third list $Comm\_Word$ contains a set of common Algerian dialect word (called White Algerian terms) that are used by all Algerians. These chosen set is reported in Table 3. Then, we iterate searching using a search query model that has four keywords. The first and the second ones are from $Dep$ and $Cat$ lists respectively. The remaining two keywords are selected arbitrary from $Comm\_Word$. This query formulation can guarantee that speakers are from the fixed province and the content topics are varied thanks to YouTube topic classification.

Concerning Algerian TVs source, the search queries are drawn up using mainly two keywords. The first one is the name the channel and the second word refers to the report name. In fact, a prior list is filled manually with emission and report names that uses dialects. Easily, videos from Algerian YouTubers/Podcasts channels are searched using the name of the corresponding author.

| | | | | | |
|---|---|---|---|---|---|
| واش | What | مشاكل | Problems | نقاش | Discussion |
| جرنان | Journal | الحقرة | Injure | بلاك | Maybe |
| تريسيتي | Electricity | يصرا | Happen | صاري | Happened |
| دارجة | Colloquial | دزيرية | Algerian | الدشرة | Village |
| النشرة | News | شوف | See | جزايري | Algerian |
| دزاير | Algeria | لولاية | Department | الباك | Baccalaureat |
| بروبليم | Problem | ماكلة | food | وشرايك | Your Opinion |

Table 3: Common Algerian terms used as Keywords

For all YouTube search queries, we selected the first 100 videos (when available). When lists are drawn up, we start the cleaning process that discards the irrelevant video entries. In fact, we remove all list entries whose duration is less than 5s. The videos whose topic shows that it doesn't deal with dialects are also discarded. This is done by analyzing manually the video title then its description and keywords.

In addition, to be in compliance with YouTube Terms of Services, first, we take into account the existence of any Creative Commons license associated to the video.

The whole cleaning process leads us to keep 1182 Audios/videos among 4 000 retrieved ones. Video's length varies between 6s and 1 hour. The cleaning task was carried out by the authors of this paper.

Now, the download process is launched using the resulting cleaned lists. Concerning the data from radio channels, we script a planned recording of the reports from the stream of the radio. Here also the recording amount depends on the desired scale.

Concerning the data from Radios, we deploy, in the download script, mainly the *VLC* Media Player tool [7] with the *cron* Linux command. In order to download videos from YouTube, we have deployed YouTube-dl [8] a command-line program.

### 5.3 Preprocessing and Annotation

A collection of Web speech data is not immediately suitable for exploration in the same way a traditional corpus is. It needs more cleaning and preprocessing. Let us recall, that our illustrative corpus will serve for dialect/speaker identification using machine learning techniques. For that purpose, for each downloaded video, we have applied the following processing:

1. *Audio extraction*: FFmpeg [9] tool is used to extract the audio layer. In addition, the SoX [10] tool, a sound processing program, is applied to get single-channel 16 kHz WAV audio files.

2. *Non-speech segments removal*: such as music or white noise by running a VAD (Voice Activation Detection) tool to remove as many as possible.

3. *Speaker Diarization*: is performed to determine who speaks when, and to assign for each utterance a speaker ID. It is achieved using VoiceID Python library based on the LIUM Speaker Diarization framework (Meignier and Merlin, 2010). The output from VoiceID segmentation is a set of audio files with information about speaker ID, and utterance duration.

| | |
|---|---|
| Number of Dialects | 8 |
| Total Duration | 104.4 hours |
| Clean Speech Ratio | 39, 15 % |
| Number of speakers | 4881 |
| Speech duration by Speaker | 6s – 9hours |

Table 4: Corpus Global Statistics.

For this preliminary version, most manual annotations are made thanks to authors themselves with the help of 8 volunteers. These In Lab annotations concern assigning for each utterance the spoken dialect, validation of speaker gender (previously detected automatically by VoiceID). During these manual annotations, we check that utterances deal with dialect. Otherwise, they are discarded.

## 6 Corpus Main Features

First of all, we note that this preliminary version of our corpus is collected and annotated in less than two months, and the building is still an ongoing process. A sample of our corpus is available online [11]. KALAM'DZ covers most major Arabic sub-dialects of Algeria. Table 4 reports some global statistics of the resulted corpus. *Clean Speech Ratio* row gives the ratio of Speeches that have good sound quality. The remaning portion of speeches present some noise background mainly music or they are recorded in outdoor. However, they can be used to build dialect models in order to represent the within-language variability.

More details on KALAM'DZ corpus are reported in Table 5. Let us observe that some dialects are more represented. This is due to people distribution and Web culture. For instance, Algiers and Oran are metropolitan cities. So their productivity on the Web is more abundant.

In order to facilitate the deployment of KALAM'DZ corpus, we have adopted the same packaging method as TIMIT Acoustic-Phonetic Continuous Speech Corpus (Garofolo et al., 1993).

## 7 Potential Uses

KALAM'DZ built corpus can be considered as the first of its kind in term a rich speech corpus for Algerian Arabic dialects using Web resources. It can be useful for many purposes both for NLP and computational linguistic communities. In fact, it

---

[7]VLC media player V 2.2.4 `https://www.videolan.org/vlc/`

[8]YouTube-dl V3 `http://YouTube-dl.org/`

[9]FFmpeg http://www.ffmpeg.org/ V3.2

[10]SoX `http://sox.sourceforge.net/`

[11]`https://github.com/LIM-MoDos/KalamDZ`

| Sub-Dialect | Departments/Village | # Speakers | Web-sources (h) | | | | |
|---|---|---|---|---|---|---|---|
| | | | Algerian Tv | Local Radios | On YouTube | Total (h) | Good Quality (%) |
| Hilali-Saharan | Laghouat, Djelfa, Ghardaia, Adrar, Bechar, Naâma' South | 1338 | 12.7 | 16.5 | - | 29.4 | 38.5 |
| Hilali-Tellian | Setif, Batna, Bordj-Bou-Arreridj | 605 | 3.6 | - | - | 3.6 | 32.2 |
| High-plains | Constantine, Mila, Skikda | 297 | 2.0 | - | - | 2.0 | 42.7 |
| Ma'qilian | Sidi-Bel Abbas, Saïda, Mascara, Relizane, Oran, Aïn Timouchent, Tiaret, Mostaganem, Naâma' North | 421 | 4.1 | - | 20.7 | 24.8 | 38.3 |
| Sulaymite | Annaba, El-Oued, Souk-Ahras, Tebessa, Biskra, Khanchela, Oum El Bouagui, Guelma, El Taref | 914 | 6.7 | - | 6.9 | 13.6 | 39 |
| Algiers Blanks | Algiers, Blida, Boumerdes, Tipaza | 723 | 5.1 | - | 16.1 | 21.2 | 42.3 |
| Sahel-Tell | Médea, Chlef, Tissemsilt, Ain Defla | 447 | 3.1 | 6.0 | - | 9.1 | 45.5 |
| Pre-Hilālī | Tlemcen Nadrouma, Dellys, Jijel, Collo, Cherchell | 136 | 0.7 | - | - | 0.7 | 34.7 |
| Global | | 4881 | 38.2 | 22.5 | 43.7 | 104.4 | 39.1 |

Table 5: Distribution of speakers and Web-sources per sub-dialect in KALAM'DZ corpus.

| Sub-Dialect | N&P | Edu. | Ent. | H&S | P&B | Hum. |
|---|---|---|---|---|---|---|
| Hilali-Saharan | 29.4 | - | - | - | - | - |
| Hilali-Tellian | 3.6 | - | - | - | - | - |
| High-plains | 2.0 | - | - | - | - | - |
| Ma'qilian | 4.1 | 1.5 | - | 7.4 | 10.2 | 1.6 |
| Sulaymite | 6.7 | - | - | - | 6.9 | - |
| Algiers Blanks | 5.1 | 2.2 | 8.7 | - | 1.4 | 2.8 |
| Sahel-Tell | 9.1 | - | - | - | - | - |
| Pre-Hilālī | 0.7 | - | - | - | - | - |
| Total | 60.7 | 3.7 | 8.7 | 7.4 | 19.5 | 4.4 |

Note: News & Politics (N&P), Educations (Edu.), Entertainment (Ent.), How-to & Style (H&S), People & Blogs (P&B), and Humor (Hum.).

Table 6: Distribution of categories per dialect (in hours).

can be used for building models for both speaker and dialect identification systems for the Algerian dialects. For linguistic and sociolinguistics communities, it can serve as base for capturing dialects characteristic.

All videos related to extracted audio data are also available. This can be deployed to build another corpus version to serve any image/video processing based applications.

## 8 Conclusion

In this paper, we have devised a recipe in order to facilitate building large-scale Speech corpus which harnesses Web resources. In fact, the used methodology makes building a Web-based corpus that shows the within-language variability. In addition, we have narrated this procedure for building KALAM'DZ a speech corpus dedicated to the whole Algerian Arabic sub-dialects. We have been ensured that this material takes into account numerous speech aspects that foster its richness and provides a representation of linguistic varieties. In fact, we have targeted various speech topics. Some automatic and manual annotations are provided. They gather useful information related to the speakers and sub-dialect information at the utterance level. This preliminary KALAM'DZ version encompasses the 8 major Algerian Arabic sub-dialects with 4881 speakers and more than 104.4 hours.

Mainly developed to be used in dialect identification, KALAM'DZ can serve as a testbed supporting evaluation of wide spectrum of NLP systems.

In future work, we will extend the corpus by collecting Algerian sub-dialects uttered by Berber native speakers. As the corpus building is still an ongoing work, its evaluation is left to a future work. In fact, we plan to evaluate the corpus on dialects identification in intra-country context.

## References

Mansour Alghamdi, Fayez Alhargan, Mohammed Alkanhal, Ashraf Alkhairy, Munir Eldesouki, and Ammar Alenazi. 2008. Saudi Accented Arabic Voice Bank. *Journal of King Saud University-Computer and Information Sciences*, 20:45–64.

K. Almeman, M. Lee, and A. A. Almiman. 2013. Multi Dialect Arabic Speech Parallel Corpora. In *Communications, Signal Processing, and their Applications (ICCSPA)*, pages 1–6, Feb.

Mansour Alsulaiman, Ghulam Muhammad, Mohamed A Bencherif, Awais Mahmood, and Zulfiqar Ali. 2013. KSU Rich Arabic Speech Database. *Journal of Information*, 16(6).

Peter Behnstedt and Manfred Woidich. 2013. Dialectology.

S. Bougrine, H. Cherroun, D. Ziadi, A. Lakhdari, and A. Chorana. 2016. Toward a Rich Arabic Speech Parallel Corpus for Algerian sub-Dialects. In *LREC'16 Workshop on Free/Open-Source Arabic Corpora and Corpora Processing Tools (OSACT)*, pages 2–10.

Alexandra Canavan and George Zipperlen. 1996. CALLFRIEND Egyptian Arabic LDC96S49. Philadelphia: Linguistic Data Consortium.

Dominique Caubet. 2000. Questionnaire de dialectologie du Maghreb (d'après les travaux de W. Marçais, M. Cohen, GS Colin, J. Cantineau, D. Cohen, Ph. Marçais, S. Lévy, etc.). *Estudios de dialectología norteafricana y andalusí, EDNA*, 5(2000-2001):73–90.

Mourad Djellab, Abderrahmane Amrouche, Ahmed Bouridane, and Noureddine Mehallegue. 2016. Algerian Modern Colloquial Arabic Speech Corpus (AMCASC): regional accents recognition within complex socio-linguistic environments. *Language Resources and Evaluation*, pages 1–29.

Mohamed Embarki. 2008. Les dialectes arabes modernes: état et nouvelles perspectives pour la classification géo-sociologique. *Arabica*, 55(5):583–604.

J. S. Garofolo, L. F. Lamel, W. M. Fisher, J. G. Fiscus, D. S. Pallett, and N. L. Dahlgren. 1993. DARPA TIMIT Acoustic Phonetic Continuous Speech Corpus CDROM.

Marwa Graja, Maher Jaoua, and L Hadrich-Belguith. 2010. Lexical Study of A Spoken Dialogue Corpus in Tunisian Dialect. In *The International Arab Conference on Information Technology (ACIT), Benghazi, Libya*.

Salima Harrat, Karima Meftouh, Mourad Abbas, Khaled-Walid Hidouci, and Kamel Smaili. 2016. An algerian dialect: Study and resources. *International Journal of Advanced Computer Science and Applications-IJACSA*, 7(3).

Jacques Leclerc. 30 avril 2012. Algérie dans l'aménagement linguistique dans le monde.

M. Paul Lewis, F. Simons Gary, and D. Fenning Charles. 2015. Ethnologue: Languages of the World, Eighteenth edition. Web.

H. Li, B. Ma, and K. A. Lee. 2013. Spoken language recognition: From fundamentals to practice. *Proceedings of the IEEE*, 101(5):1136–1159, May.

J. Makhoul, B. Zawaydeh, F. Choi, and D. Stallard. 2005. BBN/AUB DARPA Babylon Levantine Arabic Speech and Transcripts. Linguistic Data Consortium (LDC). LDC Catalog Number LDC2005S08.

Mohamed Abdelmageed Mansour. 2013. The Absence of Arabic Corpus Linguistics: A Call for Creating an Arabic National Corpus. *International Journal of Humanities and Social Science*, 3(12):81–90.

Philippe Marçais. 1986. *Algeria*. Leiden: E.J. Brill.

Sylvain Meignier and Teva Merlin. 2010. Lium spkdiarization: an open source toolkit for diarization. In *in CMU SPUD Workshop*.

Vineeth G. Nair. 2014. *Getting Started with Beautiful Soup*. Packt Publishing.

Heikki Palva. 2006. Dialects: classification. *Encyclopedia of Arabic Language and Linguistics*, 1:604–613.

C. Pereira. 2011. Arabic in the North African Region. In S. Weninger, G. Khan, M. P. Streck, and J. C. E. Watson, editors, *Semitic Languages. An International Handbook*, pages 944–959. Berlin.

Luis Javier Rodríguez-Fuentes, Mikel Penagarikano, Amparo Varona, Mireia Diez, and Germán Bordel. 2016. Kalaka-3: a database for the assessment of spoken language recognition technology on youtube audios. *Language Resources and Evaluation*, 50(2):221–243.

Kees Versteegh, Mushira Eid, Alaa Elgibali, Manfred Woidich, and Andrzej Zaborski. 2006. Encyclopedia of Arabic Language and Linguistics. *African Studies*, 8.

Samantha Wray and Ahmed Ali, 2015. *Crowdsource a little to label a lot: Labeling a speech corpus of dialectal Arabic*, volume 2015-January, pages 2824–2828. International Speech and Communication Association.

# Not All Segments are Created Equal:
## Syntactically Motivated Sentiment Analysis in Lexical Space


**Muhammad Abdul-Mageed**

School of Library, Archival, and Information Studies
University of British Columbia, Vancouver, BC
muhammad.mageed@ubc.ca



## Abstract

Although there is by now a considerable amount of research on subjectivity and sentiment analysis on morphologically-rich languages, it is still unclear how lexical information can best be modeled in these languages. To bridge this gap, we build effective models exploiting exclusively gold and machine-segmented lexical input and successfully employ syntactically motivated feature selection to improve classification. Our best models achieve significantly above the baselines, with 67.93% and 69.37% accuracies for subjectivity and sentiment classification respectively.


## 1 Introduction

The task of *subjectivity* detection refers to identifying aspects of language that are *objective* (i.e., *I have a meeting at 2:00pm.*) vs. those that express opinions, feelings, evaluations, and speculations (Banfield, 1982; Wiebe, 1994) and hence are *subjective*. Subjective language is further classified based on its *sentiment* into *positive* (e.g., *The new machines are revolutionary!*), *negative* (e.g., *The Syria war is terrifying!*), *neutral* (e.g., *The new models may be released next week.*), or, sometimes, *mixed* (e.g., *I really like this phone, but it is way too expensive!*). The field of subjectivity and sentiment analysis (SSA) is a very vibrant one and there has been a flurry of research on especially the English language (Wiebe et al., 2004; Liu, 2010; Dave et al., 2003; Pang and Lee, 2008; Chaovalit and Zhou, 2005; Zhuang et al., 2006). By now, there is also a fair amount of work on morphologically rich languages (MRL) (Tsarfaty et al., 2010) like Arabic (Abdul-Mageed and Diab, 2011; Abdul-Mageed et al., 2011; Abdul-Mageed

and Diab, 2012; Abdul-Mageed et al., 2014; Aly and Atiya, 2013; Refaee and Rieser, 2014; Nabil et al., 2015; Salameh et al., 2015; Refaee and Rieser, 2016). SSA work on MRLs, however, is still in an early stage as MRLs raise a range of questions on their own. In the current work, we focus on answering the question: "How it is that Arabic can be modeled within lexical space?" More specifically, we investigate the utility of teasing apart lexical input based on grammatical criteria and empirically weigh the contribution of features therein toward SSA. The current work is a follow up on submitted work (Abdul-Mageed, 2017) where we measure both gold and machine-predicted tree-bank style segmentation (Maamouri et al., 2004) on the two tasks of subjectivity and sentiment.

Breaking down surface forms into their component segments is known as *segmentation*. Segmentation is possible when morphological boundaries within a word are identified. In the Penn Arabic Treebank (ATB) (Maamouri et al., 2004), a segment can be a stem, an inflectional affix, or a clitic. For example, the surface word *wbHsnAthm* (Eng. 'and by their virtues') is segmented as *w+b+Hsn+At+hm* with the prefixal clitics (*w* and *b*, Eng. 'and' and 'by'), the stem *Hsn*, the inflection morpheme *At*, and the suffixal pronominal morpheme *hm*. In (Abdul-Mageed, 2017), we have shown how reducing a word to its component segments is a desirable measure for SSA since it reduces the number of observed forms and hence alleviates *sparsity*: The system does not see as many forms at test time that have not been seen at training time. Providing all lexical segmented input to a classifier, however, may or may not be an ideal procedure. In English, usually words like 'a,' 'the,' and 'from' are treated as stop words and hence removed before classification. These tokens are viewed as *functional* words that do not usually contribute to classification accuracy. Are there

147


*Proceedings of The Third Arabic Natural Language Processing Workshop (WANLP)*, pages 147–156,
Valencia, Spain, April 3, 2017. ©2017 Association for Computational Linguistics

ways to break down the lexical space based on relevant, if not comparable, grammatical grounds? That is the question we seek to answer in the current work. Overall, we make the following contributions: (1) We present a new human-labeled ATB dataset for SSA; (2) We introduce a new syntactically motivated feature selection method for SSA on Arabic that can arguably also help classification on other languages of rich morphology; and (3) We present detailed linguistically-motivated (error) analyses of the behavior of the lexical models, against the background of Arabic morphological complexity.

The rest of this paper is organized as follows: In Section 2, we describe our datasets and methods. In Section 3, we present our results. In Section 4, we provide a literature review, and in Section 5 we conclude.

## 2  Dataset and Methods

**Data:** We gold-label a subset from each of the first three parts of the ATB (i.e., the first 70 documents from ATB1V4.1, the first 50 documents from ATB2V3.1, and the first 58 documents from ATB3V3.2) at the sentence level with tags from the set {*OBJ, subjective-positive (S-POS), subjective-negative (S-NEG), subjective-mixed (S-MIXED)*}. The data belong to the newswire genre and were manually labeled by the Linguistic Data Consortium (LDC) for part-of-speech (POS), morphology, gloss, and syntactic treebank annotation. A single annotator, with a Ph.D. in linguistics and a native Arabic fluency, labeled the data after being provided written guidelines and several sessions of training and discussions with the authors. We followed the guidelines in the literature (Abdul-Mageed and Diab, 2011; Abdul-Mageed and Diab, 2012). To ensure quality, 5% of the data (n=250 sentences) was double labeled by a second annotator. Inter-annotator agreement reached 83% without adjudication, and hence the first annotator's decisions were judged sufficient. Table 1 shows class distribution in our data.

**Procedure:** We divide each of the three treebank parts into 80% training, 10% development, and 10% test. The training parts from each Treebank are then added up to build TRAIN, the development parts are added up to build DEV, and the test parts are combined to build TEST. For our experiments, results are reported both on DEV and TEST. Importantly, only the DEV set is used for

| Dataset | OBJ | S-P | S-N | S-M | ALL |
|---|---|---|---|---|---|
| ATB1V4.1 | 582 | 183 | 188 | 39 | 992 |
| ATB2V3.1 | 623 | 151 | 227 | 3 | 1,004 |
| ATB3V3.2 | 1,472 | 462 | 414 | 6 | 2,354 |
| ALL | 2,677 | 796 | 829 | 48 | 4,350 |

Table 1: Data statistics. S-P= *subjective positive* and S-N= *subjective negative*.

tuning classifier performance and error analyses. TEST is used as a fully blind set. We follow a two-stage classification process where the *first stage* is to tease apart the OBJ and SUBJ classes, and the *second stage* is to distinguish the S-POS and the S-NEG classes. For this work, we do not handle the MIXED class, since it is minimal in our data.

**Settings:** We use two settings based on text preprocessing: *Gold* and *machine-predicted*. For the gold setting, human-annotated segmentation and morphosyntactic disambiguation as labeled by LDC are exploited. For the machine-predicted setting, we use the ASMA tool (Abdul-Mageed et al., 2013), which renders state of the art segmentation and morphosyntactic tagging for MSA. For all the subjectivity and sentiment experiments, we use SVMs with a linear kernel.

## 3  Results

### 3.1  Subjectivity with Lexical Filtering

As pointed out earlier, we follow up on previous work (Abdul-Mageed, 2017) where we show the utility of representing lexical input in the form of segments. As such, we cite results from that work with both surface word forms and segmented text and compare the current work to these results. We now set out to answer the question: "Are all segments equally useful to subjectivity and/or sentiment classification?" From a linguistics perspective, segmented lexical input can be viewed as comprised of *content segments* (i.e., those corresponding to verbs or nominals [nouns, adjectives, and adverbs]) and *functional segements* (e.g., definite articles). Content segments are often thought to carry the important semantic content in a sentence, and hence we investigate their utility for SSA. In other words, we employ *lexical filtering*: We filter out functional segments (e.g., clitics and affixes after segmentation) and use content segments exclusively as classifier input. We use the POS tags in Table 2 to identify content segments. Table 3 shows results of subjectiv-

|  |  | Acc | Avg-F | OBJ | | | SUBJ | | |
|---|---|---|---|---|---|---|---|---|---|
|  |  |  |  | Prec | Rec | F | Prec | Rec | F |
| **DEV** | surf | 62.07 | 57.4 | 78.75 | 29.86 | 43.3 | 58.31 | 92.41 | 71.5 |
|  | gold-segs | 68.28 | 65.31 | 87.63 | 40.28 | 55.19 | 62.72 | 94.64 | 75.44 |
|  | asma-segs | 65.98 | 63.02 | 81.19 | 38.86 | 52.56 | 61.38 | 91.52 | 73.48 |
|  | gold-cont | 61.15 | 57.34 | 72.34 | 32.23 | 44.59 | 58.06 | 88.39 | 70.09 |
|  | asma-cont | 62.07 | 58.47 | 73.96 | 33.65 | 46.25 | 58.7 | 88.84 | 70.69 |
|  | gold-cont-M1 | **68.28** | **65.71** | **84.76** | **42.18** | **56.33** | **63.03** | **92.86** | **75.09** |
|  | asma-cont-M1 | 66.9 | 63.92 | 83.84 | 39.34 | 53.55 | 61.9 | 92.86 | 74.29 |
| **TEST** | surf | 60.58 | 60.55 | 90.91 | 44.22 | 59.5 | 46.41 | 91.61 | 61.61 |
|  | gold-segs | 65.03 | 65 | 91.02 | 51.7 | 65.94 | 49.65 | 90.32 | 64.07 |
|  | asma-segs | 66.59 | 66.57 | 93.37 | 52.72 | 67.39 | 50.88 | 92.9 | 65.75 |
|  | gold-cont | 57.68 | 57.63 | 87.14 | 41.5 | 56.22 | 44.34 | 88.39 | 59.05 |
|  | asma-cont | 59.69 | 59.66 | 89.51 | 43.54 | 58.58 | 45.75 | 90.32 | 60.74 |
|  | gold-cont-M1 | 66.15 | 66.12 | 92.26 | 52.72 | 67.1 | 50.53 | 91.61 | 65.14 |
|  | asma-cont-M1 | **67.93** | **67.9** | **94.64** | **54.08** | **68.83** | **51.96** | **94.19** | **66.97** |

Table 3: Subjectivity classification with syntactically motivated feature selection. Th prefixes *gold-* and *asma-* refer to Treebank-acquired and ASMA-acquired segments (i.e., *-segs*), content segments (i.e., *-cont*), and select content segments (i.e., *-cont-M∗*), respectively.

ity classification with both the gold and ASMA syntactically motivated lexical filtering (**gold-cont** and **asma-cont**, respectively) where only content segments are provided as classifier input. For this set of experiments, we use two baselines: 1) performance with surface word forms (surf), and, (in order to compare to performance with both gold- and ASMA-segmented text forms as reported in (Abdul-Mageed, 2017)), 2) **gold-segs** and 3) **asma-segs**, respectively.

As Table 3 shows, for subjectivity classification with gold-cont, no improvement is acquired over the surface word forms (surf). On DEV, gold-cont is 0.92% accuracy below surf. On TEST, gold-cont is at 2.90% accuracy below surf. Similarly, apart from the OBJ class classification on DEV (where 1.29% $F_1$ gain is acquired), gold-cont loses against surf across all evaluation metrics for both the OBJ and SUBJ classes. On TEST, gold-cont is outperformed by surf with 3.28% accuracy. Comparing the results acquired with gold-cont to those acquired without lexical filtering (i.e., with gold-segs and asma-segs) shows that gold-cont causes classification losses on both DEV and TEST. On DEV, gold-cont causes a classification loss with 7.13% accuracy compared to gold-segs and 3.91% accuracy compared to asma-segs. On TEST, gold-cont is outperformed by gold-segs with 7.35% accuracy and also by asma-segs with 6.90% accuracy. In addition, as Table 3

also shows, asma-cont is outperformed by asma-segs and gold-segs on DEV. On TEST, asma-cont is outperformed by surf (with 0.89% accuracy), asma-segs (6.90% accuracy), and gold-segs (5.34% accuracy).

These results show that removing functional segments is not a useful measure for subjectivity classification, regardless whether the segments kept are gold (gold-cont) or ASMA-predicted (asma-cont). As we show in (Abdul-Mageed, 2017), with regard to results acquired using gold-segs and asma-segs as compared to surf, segmented input text helps reduce data sparsity, which partially accounts for classification improvement with these settings. The situation when we remove functional segments as we do here is different: Even though this type of lexical filtering with both gold-cont and asma-cont does reduce sparsity significantly as compared to surf, as is shown in Table 4, performance with these two settings drops. This shows that data sparsity reduction is not the sole deciding factor as to classifier performance, and that the removed functional segments are important input for the subjectivity task. This conclusion is clearly supported by the fact that lexical filtering settings (i.e., gold-cont and asma-cont) are outperformed by their segmentation counterparts (i.e., gold-segs and asma-segs), even though the differences in sparsity rates between the two are minimal.

| VERBS | |
|---|---|
| VERB | verb |
| PSEUDO_VERB | pseudo-verb |
| PV | perfective verb |
| PV_PASS | perfective passive verb |
| IV | imperfective verb |
| IV_PASS | Imperfective passive verb |
| CV | imperative/command verb |
| NOMINALS | |
| NOUN | noun |
| NOUN_NUM | nominal/cardinal number |
| NOUN_QUANT | quantifier noun |
| NOUN.VN | deverbal noun |
| NOUN_PROP | proper noun |
| ADJ | adjective |
| ADJ_COMP | comparative adjective |
| ADJ_NUM | adjectival/ordinal number |
| ADJ.VN | deverbal adjective |
| ADJ_PROP | proper adjective |
| ADV | adverb |
| REL_ADV | relative adverb |
| INTERROG_ADV | interrogative adverb |

Table 2: POS tags for content segments

| | TRAIN | DEV | |
|---|---|---|---|
| | # types | # types | % OOV |
| surf | 13,201 | 3,028 | 44.25% |
| gold-segs | 6,254 | 2,006 | 22.88% |
| asma-segs | 7,053 | 2,159 | 26.40% |
| gold-cont | 6,124 | 1,916 | 23.49% |
| asma-cont | 6,888 | 2,066 | 27.11% |

Table 4: Type statistics and OOV percentages for gold and ASMA-predicted content segments

To further help interpret the results, we perform an investigation of the distribution of functional segments in the TRAIN set for both gold-segs and asma-segs. To help explain the distribution of functional segments, we introduce the concept of *distributional relative frequency* (RF): RF is the frequency of these segments within a given class divided by the total number of data points making up that specific class. The distribution of functional segments is calculated based on RF to cater for the unbalanced class distribution in the TRAIN data where the number of OBJ cases=$1,259$ and the number of SUBJ cases=$3,840$. Also, RF is calculated based on absolute values (i.e., after reducing the segments of frequency $> 1$ to 1 [i.e.,

segments that are repeated multiple times in one sentence are rendered to one occurrence only], to match the presence vs. absence vectors). In acquiring the RF of segments across both the OBJ and SUBJ classes, we use a threshold parameter specifying the number of times a segment occurs in one of the two classes more than the other. This parameter is used with values from the set $\{1, 2, 3, 4\}$.

Functional segments occur with different distributions in the two classes. As extracted from gold-segs TRAIN, there is a total of 160 functional segments out of which 99 occur in gold-segs DEV set. On TRAIN, 60% (n=96) of functional segments occur at least two times in one of the two classes more than the other class, 48.75% (n=78) of them occur at least three times, and 0.05% (n=8) of them occur at least four times. On DEV, 57.57% (n=57) of functional segments occur at least two times in one of the two classes, 49.49% (n=49) of them occur at least three times, and 45.45% (n=45) of them occur at least four times. For ASMA, there is similarly a discrepancy of distribution between the functional segments occurring in the two classes: Within the asma-segs training set, a total of 149 functional segments occur. For a considerable percentage of these segments (%=37.58, n=56), each segment is found to occur with a relative frequency that is four times or more in one of the two classes than its occurrence in the other. When the relative frequency threshold is lowered to three times or more, it is found that 41.61% (n=62) of these functional segments satisfy this lowered threshold of class distribution. When the relative frequency threshold is lowered to two times or more, 57.05% (n=85) of segments satisfy that threshold.

The different distribution of functional segments across the OBJ and SUBJ classes is linguistically motivated, as these segments are related to a host of linguistic phenomena that interact with expression of subjectivity. The following is a number of such phenomena that we find to be used more frequently with the SUBJ class:

**Negation:** Negation is used in natural language for various purposes, including those related to the 'etiquette' of involving in a conversation or politeness (Brown and Levinson, 1987) in discourse. For example, it is usually considered more polite to say that something is 'not good' (and hence employ negation) rather than saying it is 'bad.' Negation is used in newswire discourse in various contexts. For example, politicians use negation when they 'denounce' an action or 'deny' a stance. Often times, contexts where negation is employed would be more SUBJ than OBJ, based on the distribution of negation particles in the TRAIN and DEV data. Examples of negation particles that occur more frequently in the SUBJ class are *lA* (which negates imperfective verbs) *lm* (which negates things in the past) and *ln* (which negates things in the future).

**Restriction:** In situations where it is necessarily to be precise, restrict a statement, stress a position, etc., employment of restriction particles is useful. Restriction particles like <*lA* (Eng., 'except') and <*nmA* (Eng. 'but for') are used more with the SUBJ class in the data. An example sentence where <*lA* is used in a SUBJ-POS context is *lA ysE Al <nsAn <lA <n yqdrhA* (Eng. 'One can only appreciate it').

**Interactional resources:** Writers use a number of linguistic resources, often referred to as interactional resources (Hyland and Tse, 2004), to engage readers in the argument in ways that interact with expression of subjectivity. Interactional resources include self-mentions via first person pronouns, engagement markers like second person pronouns, epistemic modality markers that serve to convey how confident people are about the ideational material they convey (Palmer, 1986) (whether these are hedges like *rbmA* [Eng. 'perhaps'] or boosters like *mwkd* [Eng. 'it is certain']), and attitude markers like *llOsf* (Eng. 'unfortunately'). Self-mentions and engagement markers are, more often than not, expressed via functional segments in Arabic, namely first and second person pronouns. Epistemic modality and attitude markers are either expressed adverbially or as phrases involving functional segments like prepositions. For example, the phrase *mn Almdh$ On* (Eng. 'it is surprising that') acts as an attitude marker. Filtering out functional segments removes these interactional resources which are useful devices for expression of subjectivity, leaving the phrase as *mdh$* (Eng. 'surprising'), which carries less intense polarity. This, in turn, adds to the classification drop.

**Conditionals:** In situations when a writer/speaker needs to describe a hypothetical scenario or condition on occurrence on another, etc., conditionals are used. These, as such, are not as much associated with facts as they are with what the writer/speaker believes is possible, likely, probable, etc. In this way, they can be associated with hedges when they are employed to restrict a claim. Conditionals like <*A* (Eng. 'if') and *lw* (Eng. 'if') are thus distributed more frequently with the subjective class.

## 3.2 Subjectivity with Syntactically Motivated Feature Selection

In order to further investigate the utility of functional segments for subjectivity classification, we perform a set of experiments based on pointwise mutual information (PMI) (Church and Hanks, 1989; Church and Hanks, 1990) feature selection focused at these segments. PMI is a statistical measure of the co-occurrence of two events that captures the discrepancy between the probability of their coincidence given their joint distribution and their individual distributions. The PMI between a functional segment 'fs' and its class 'c' (e.g., the OBJ vs. the SUBJ class) is:

$$PMI(fs|c) = \log_2 \frac{p(fs|c)}{p(fs)p(c)} \qquad (1)$$

PMI is a filter feature selection method that is used to keep only features important to the classification process and filter out the rest. In the current case, only functional segments that occur in one of the two OBJ and SUBJ classes more than the other with a relative frequency (RF) that is $\geq$ a certain threshold are kept for classification (in addition to the content segments) while the rest are filtered out. Experiments with PMI are run with RF different threshold parameters from the set $\{1, 2, 3, 4\}$. It is found that with an RF threshold $\geq 1$, PMI feature selection results in improvements over all previous settings whether gold (i.e., gold-segs and gold-cont) or ASMA-predicted (i.e., asma-segs and asma-cont). Table 3 shows related results. The experiments with only certain functional segments filtered out with gold segmentation are referred to as gold-cont-M1 and those with ASMA are referred to as asma-cont-M1, with the suffix 'M1' standing for 'modified' with a threshold of is $\geq 1$ in both cases.

As Table 3 shows, modified lexical filtering helps improve classification across the board over surf, over comparable lexical filtering (i.e., gold-cont and asma-cont), and over segmentation settings (i.e., gold-segs and asma-segs). On DEV, gold-cont-M1 achieves identical accuracy scores (i.e., 68.28%) as gold-segs. On TEST, gold-cont-M1 improves 1.12% accuracy on gold-segs. For ASMA-predicted settings, asma-cont-M1 improves over asma-segs (with 0.92% accuracy on DEV and 1.34% accuracy on TEST). Results of modified lexical filtering show that some, but not all, functional segments are important for subjectivity classification. In addition to the linguistic analysis provided earlier in this section about the importance of some of the functional segments, it is worth mentioning that filtering out all functional segments also deprives the classifier of any access to multiword expressions (MWE). Although the sentences in the experiments reported above are not represented beyond unigrams and hence MWEs are not explicitly provided to the classifier, there is still a possibility for the classifier to benefit from these expressions when all segments in a sentence are accessible. The following is an example of an MWE carrying SUBJ content and explanations of accompanying filtered out functional segments: In the phrase *wqf fy wjh* (Eng. 'he stood against') removal of functional segment preposition *fy* (Eng. 'face') results in the string *wqf+wjh* (Eng. 'he stood+face'). Again, these resulting CONT segments do not carry SUBJ content themselves.

### 3.3 Sentiment with Lexical Filtering

Table 5 shows results of sentiment classification with both gold lexical filtering (gold-cont) and ASMA lexical filtering (asma-cont). For comparison, earlier results with the segmented unfiltered setting (gold-segs and gold-segs) and results with syntactically motivated feature selection (which we refer to as *gold-cont-M1* and *asma-cont-M1*), as is explained below, are also provided in Table 5. As the Table shows, on both DEV and TEST, syntactically motivated lexical filtering (whether gold-cont or asma-cont) improves classification over surf. On DEV, gold-cont improves 1.98% accuracy and asma-segs improves 3.29% accuracy over surf. On TEST, gold-cont improves 4.51% accuracy and asma-segs improves 2.71% accuracy over surf. Comparing gold-cont to segmented text, however, shows a trend similar to that of subjectivity classification where segmentation without lexical filtering is still competitive: On DEV, gold-cont and asma-cont are both outperformed by segmented text (i.e., both gold-segs and asma-

segs). On TEST, gold-cont outperforms gold-segs. These results show that although lexical filtering is able to outperform surf, it is not consistently useful compared to segmented text. A consideration of the data sparsity in DEV and TEST indicates that there is no consistent correlation between the percentage of OOV segments and performance. For example, although gold-cont has less OOV percentage than gold-segs and asma-segs on DEV, it is still outperformed by these two settings.

Similar to subjectivity classification with lexical filtering, we performed an analysis of the relative frequency (RF) of functional segments as occurring in segmented text across the S-POS and S-NEG classes as is reported in Table 5. The analysis shows a similar trend to that of subjectivity classification where functional segments have different RF distribution across the two classes across both the gold-segs and asma-segs settings.

In order to further investigate the utility of functional segments for sentiment classification, again, we perform a set of experiments based on PMI (Church and Hanks 1989; 1990) feature selection focused at these segments. Similar to subjectivity classification above, all functional segments that occurred in one or another of the two S-POS and S-NEG classes with a PMI value more than that of the other (i.e., with a relative frequency of $\geq$ a threshold from the set $\{1, 2, 3, 4\}$) are kept unfiltered for this set of experiments. The best results are achieved with the RF $\geq$ 1. As is reported in Table 5, with this modified lexical filtering (gold-cont-M1 and asma-cont-M1), an improvement is gained on DEV as compared to surf, segmented text settings (gold-segs and asma-segs), and lexical filtering (gold-cont and asma-cont). The case is different, however, on TEST where no such improvement is possible with the modified lexical filtering settings. Comparing the performance of modified lexical filtering in the case of subjectivity classification as presented earlier to the current performance of modified lexical filtering on sentiment classification shows a discrepancy of the utility of modified/partial lexical filtering. This is the case since the two classification tasks are different, as expression of sentiment itself is different from that of subjectivity. Functional segments are associated with subjective content in general regardless of the specific type of sentiment expressed, for which case these segments do not play as much of a role in distinguishing the S-POS from the S-

|  |  | Acc | Avg- F | S-POS | | | S-NEG | | |
|---|---|---|---|---|---|---|---|---|---|
|  |  |  |  | Prec | Rec | F | Prec | Rec | F |
| **DEV** | surf | 57.89 | 57.71 | 65.33 | 56.32 | 60.49 | 50.65 | 60 | 54.93 |
|  | gold-segs | 65.13 | 64.45 | 69.77 | 68.97 | 69.36 | 59.09 | 60 | 59.54 |
|  | asma-segs | 61.84 | 61.52 | 68.35 | 62.07 | 65.06 | 54.79 | 61.54 | 57.97 |
|  | gold-cont | 59.87 | 59.86 | 69.12 | 54.02 | 60.65 | 52.38 | 67.69 | 59.06 |
|  | asma-cont | 61.18 | 61.19 | 71.21 | 54.02 | 61.44 | 53.49 | 70.77 | 60.93 |
|  | gold-cont-M1 | **66.45** | **66.11** | **72.5** | **66.67** | **69.46** | **59.72** | **66.15** | **62.77** |
|  | asma-cont-M1 | 61.84 | 61.81 | 71.01 | 56.32 | 62.82 | 54.22 | 69.23 | 60.81 |
| **TEST** | surf | 64.86 | 64.85 | 64.91 | 66.07 | 65.49 | 64.81 | 63.64 | 64.22 |
|  | gold-segs | 67.57 | 67.56 | 67.86 | 67.86 | 67.86 | 67.27 | 67.27 | 67.27 |
|  | asma-segs | **69.37** | **69.35** | **71.15** | **66.07** | **68.52** | **67.8** | **72.73** | **70.18** |
|  | gold-cont | 69.37 | 69.17 | 73.91 | 60.71 | 66.67 | 66.15 | 78.18 | 71.67 |
|  | asma-cont | 67.57 | 67.35 | 71.74 | 58.93 | 64.71 | 64.62 | 76.36 | 70 |
|  | gold-cont-M1 | 64.86 | 64.85 | 64.91 | 66.07 | 65.49 | 64.81 | 63.64 | 64.22 |
|  | asma-cont-M1 | 63.96 | 63.97 | 64.29 | 64.29 | 64.29 | 63.64 | 63.64 | 63.64 |

Table 5: Sentiment classification with syntactically motivated feature selection.

NEG classes as they do in distinguishing the OBJ and SUBJ classes. What supports this analysis is the fact that although the distribution of functional segments differs from one class to another, this distribution is not as pronounced with the RF values 2, 3, and 4 as in the case of subjectivity classification. For example, while on TRAIN and DEV combined 58.785% of gold-segs occur with an RF=2 in either the SUBJ or the OBJ classes, only 43.155% of these with the same RF=2 occur in either the S-POS or S-NEG classes (also as derived from TRAIN and DEV combined). The situation is also similar with ASMA functional segments over TRAIN+DEV, where 56.075% occur with an RF=2 in one or the other of subjectivity classes whereas only 42.475% of them occur with the same RF threshold in one or the other of the two sentiment classes.

In order to better understand why it is that full gold lexical filtering yields lower performance than gold segmented data, we perform an error analysis of the gold-cont cases (n=26) that are correctly classified by the gold-segs classifier on the DEV set. The error analysis shows that there is a host of linguistic phenomena that interact with expression of sentiment as follows:

**Negation:** Negation particles belong to functional segments and can cause a change of the polarity of content segments. When negation particles are absent, and hence not accessible to the classifier unlike content segments that potentially carry the opposite of the label of a sentence, clas-

sification errors occur.

**Interactional resources:** Only one category of interactional resources (Hyland Tse, 2004) is found to be most important to sentiment expression: *First person pronouns*. First person singular, but more frequently, plural pronouns are found to be used with higher distribution with the S-POS class. This is specially the case since the data involve discourse where politicians do their best trying to draw a positive image of themselves and/or the political entities they represent and hence cite self. This is an example from the error analysis data: *qAl Alr}ys AlsngAly: 'lA xyAr OmAmnA swy AltjmE'*. (Eng. 'The Senegalese president said: "we have no other choice but uniting".')

The example is human-annotated with S-POS and involves first person plural pronouns (e.g., the possessive pronoun *nA* [Eng. 'our'], the imperfective verb prefixal *n-* [Eng. 'we']) that is filtered out with the lexical filtering setting (both gold-cont and asma-cont) and hence the classifiers do not have access to these as signals of positive sentiment, which results in the erroneous prediction.

The finding that full lexical filtering improves over segmented text on TEST but not on DEV is one that also calls for further investigation. An error analysis of the examples (n=18) gold-cont correctly identifies but gold-segs fails to predict on DEV was performed to better interpret this finding. Among these 18 examples (%=77.77) are human-labeled as S-NEG and hence the gold-cont classifier performs better on the S-NEG class.

This indicates that expression of negative content is more likely to be carried by content segments rather than a combination of both functional and content segments. The addition of certain functional segments (i.e., those that occur with higher RF with the S-POS class) is responsible for misclassification errors. For example, since the first personal plural pronouns mentioned above (i.e., the possessive pronoun *nA* [Eng. 'our'], the imperfective verb prefixal *n-* [Eng. 'we']) are more frequently occurring with the S-POS class, they contribute to causing the gold-segs classifier assigning an S-POS tag to the following S-NEG sentence that was rightly predicted with the gold-cont setting: *mqr bOnh 'ElynA On nEtrf bOn bED jwAnb AlmEAhd p lyst wADHp'*. (Eng. 'Attesting that "we must admit that some aspects of the treaty are not clear".') *-nA* and *n-* have higer RF with the POS class.

A close investigation of the examples wrongly classified by gold-segs also shows that they all carry (very) strong sentiment. Although sentiment intensity is not manually labeled in the data and the current work does not involve predicting degrees of intensity in data, it is worth discussing this aspect as it relates to the current error analysis. Sentiment intensity in Arabic is primarily expressed via content segments and hence these content segments, rather than functional segments, are the important signals in (very) strongly polarized examples. The following example that carries a strong negative sentiment illustrates this point: *wtSwrhA bEbE yEml ElY IhAnp AlnAs wAl-IsA'p IlY Alm$trkyn*. (Eng. 'And portrays it as a monstrous ghost working to humiliate people and wronging participants.'). In this last sentence, the strong sentiment is carried by the content segments *bEbE* (Eng. 'monstrous ghost') and *IsA'* (Eng. 'wronging-related') rather than by any functional segments. This utility of content segments in expressing strong sentiment makes them more crucial for the task and adding functional segments may be 'distractive' to the classifier especially in S-NEG examples as the comparison between the performance of gold-cont and gold-segs shows.

## 4   Related Work

Sentiment analysis has been a popular NLP task, with a lot of work focused at mining movie and product reviews (Dave et al., 2003; Hu and Liu, 2004; Turney, 2002). Recently, there has been a number of SemEval tasks devoted to sentiment (Rosenthal et al., 2014; Rosenthal et al., 2015; Nakov et al., 2016).

For Arabic, early work includes (Abbasi et al., 2008) who detect hostility in Arabic and English web fora and (Abdul-Mageed et al., 2011) who use gold-labeled morphological features and a polarity lexicon from the news domain. This current work differs in that we use automatically predicted morphological features in addition to gold features. (Abdul-Mageed et al., 2014) is also related to our work in that the we also investigate ways to best represent lexical information, yet on newswire data rather than social media. A number of studies have reported models using n-gram features after preprocessing input data (Abdulla et al., 2013; Aly and Atiya, 2013; ElSahar and El-Beltagy, 2015; Mourad and Darwish, 2013; Saleh et al., 2011). The focus of our work is different in that we seek to break the space of lexical input based on syntactic criteria and introduce a method to weigh the informativity of the resulting spaces via feature selection. We also have shown how linguistic phenomena interact with sentiment expression via detailed error analyses of model output.

## 5   Conclusion

In this work, we introduced a new human-labeled ATB dataset for SSA and investigated ways to model subjectivity and sentiment in lexical space in Arabic, a language of rich morphology. We demonstrated how each of these tasks can be performed with both gold and machine-predicted segments under different grammar-based conditions. Our results show that not all lexical input is relevant to the tasks and that some syntactically-defined segments are more relevant to a given task than another, thus motivating our syntactically motivated feature selection method. We found functional segments to be more vehicles for carrying subjective content than devices for communicating positive and negative content. Our detailed error analyses helped uncover a host of linguistic phenomena that interact in intricate ways with both subjectivity and sentiment expression in the Arabic newswire genre. Our results also show that although subjectivity and sentiment are social meaning concepts (i.e., expressed at the levels of semantics and pragmatics), modeling them can benefit from knowledge at lower linguistics levels in lexical space.

## References

A. Abbasi, H. Chen, and A. Salem. 2008. Sentiment analysis in multiple languages: Feature selection for opinion classification in web forums. *ACM Trans. Inf. Syst.*, 26:1–34.

Muhammad Abdul-Mageed and Mona Diab. 2011. Subjectivity and sentiment annotation of modern standard arabic newswire. In *Proceedings of the 5th Linguistic Annotation Workshop*, pages 110–118, Portland, Oregon, USA, June. Association for Computational Linguistics.

Muhammad Abdul-Mageed and Mona Diab. 2012. *AWATIF*: A multi-genre corpus for modern standard arabic subjectivity and sentiment analysis. In *Proceedings of LREC*, volume 12.

Muhammad Abdul-Mageed, Mona Diab, and Mohamed Korayem. 2011. Subjectivity and sentiment analysis of modern standard arabic. In *Proceedings of the 49th Annual Meeting of the Association for Computational Linguistics: Human Language Technologies*, pages 587–591, Portland, Oregon, USA, June. Association for Computational Linguistics.

Muhammad Abdul-Mageed, Mona T Diab, and Sandra Kübler. 2013. Asma: A system for automatic segmentation and morpho-syntactic disambiguation of modern standard arabic. In *RANLP*, pages 1–8.

Muhammad Abdul-Mageed, Mona Diab, and Sandra Kübler. 2014. Samar: Subjectivity and sentiment analysis for arabic social media. *Computer Speech & Language*, 28(1):20–37.

Muhammad Abdul-Mageed. 2017. Modeling subjectivity and sentiment in lexical space. In *Submitted*.

Nawaf Abdulla, N Mahyoub, M Shehab, and M Al-Ayyoub. 2013. Arabic sentiment analysis: Corpus-based and lexicon-based. In *Proceedings of The IEEE conference on Applied Electrical Engineering and Computing Technologies (AEECT)*.

Mohamed A Aly and Amir F Atiya. 2013. Labr: A large scale arabic book reviews dataset. In *ACL (2)*, pages 494–498.

A. Banfield. 1982. *Unspeakable Sentences: Narration and Representation in the Language of Fiction*. Routledge & Kegan Paul, Boston.

P. Brown and S.C. Levinson. 1987. *Politeness: Some universals in language usage*, volume 4. Cambridge Univ Pr.

Pimwadee Chaovalit and Lina Zhou. 2005. Movie review mining: A comparison between supervised and unsupervised classification approaches. In *System Sciences, 2005. HICSS'05. Proceedings of the 38th Annual Hawaii International Conference on*, pages 112c–112c. IEEE.

K.W. Church and P. Hanks. 1989. Word association norms, mutual information and lexicography. In *Proceedings of the 27th Annual Conference of the ACL*, pages 76–83. Association for Computational Linguistics.

Kenneth Ward Church and Patrick Hanks. 1990. Word association norms, mutual information, and lexicography. *Computational linguistics*, 16(1):22–29.

K. Dave, S. Lawrence, and D.M. Pennock. 2003. Mining the peanut gallery: Opinion extraction and semantic classification of product reviews. In *Proceedings of the 12th international conference on World Wide Web*, pages 519–528. ACM.

Hady ElSahar and Samhaa R El-Beltagy. 2015. Building large arabic multi-domain resources for sentiment analysis. In *International Conference on Intelligent Text Processing and Computational Linguistics*, pages 23–34. Springer.

M. Hu and B. Liu. 2004. Mining and summarizing customer reviews. In *Proceedings of the ACM SIGKDD International Conference on Knowledge Discovery and Data Mining*, pages 168–177.

Ken Hyland and Polly Tse. 2004. Metadiscourse in academic writing: A reappraisal. *Applied linguistics*, 25(2):156–177.

B. Liu. 2010. Sentiment analysis and subjectivity. *Handbook of Natural Language Processing,*, pages 978–1420085921.

M. Maamouri, A. Bies, T. Buckwalter, and W. Mekki. 2004. The penn arabic treebank: Building a large-scale annotated arabic corpus. In *NEMLAR Conference on Arabic Language Resources and Tools*, pages 102–109.

Ahmed Mourad and Kareem Darwish. 2013. Subjectivity and sentiment analysis of modern standard arabic and arabic microblogs. In *Proceedings of the 4th workshop on computational approaches to subjectivity, sentiment and social media analysis*, pages 55–64.

Mahmoud Nabil, Mohamed Aly, and Amir F Atiya. 2015. Astd: Arabic sentiment tweets dataset. In *Proceedings of the 2015 Conference on Empirical Methods in Natural Language Processing*, pages 2515–2519.

Preslav Nakov, Alan Ritter, Sara Rosenthal, Fabrizio Sebastiani, and Veselin Stoyanov. 2016. Semeval-2016 task 4: Sentiment analysis in twitter. *Proceedings of SemEval*, pages 1–18.

F. Palmer. 1986. *Mood and Modality. 1986*. Cambridge: Cambridge University Press.

Bo Pang and Lillian Lee. 2008. Opinion mining and sentiment analysis. *Foundations and trends in information retrieval*, 2(1-2):1–135.

Eshrag Refaee and Verena Rieser. 2014. An arabic twitter corpus for subjectivity and sentiment analysis. In *LREC*, pages 2268–2273.

Eshrag Refaee and Verena Rieser. 2016. ilab-edinburgh at semeval-2016 task 7: A hybrid approach for determining sentiment intensity of arabic twitter phrases. *Proceedings of SemEval*, pages 474–480.

Sara Rosenthal, Alan Ritter, Preslav Nakov, and Veselin Stoyanov. 2014. Semeval-2014 task 9: Sentiment analysis in twitter. In *Proceedings of the 8th international workshop on semantic evaluation (SemEval 2014)*, pages 73–80. Dublin, Ireland.

Sara Rosenthal, Preslav Nakov, Svetlana Kiritchenko, Saif M Mohammad, Alan Ritter, and Veselin Stoyanov. 2015. Semeval-2015 task 10: Sentiment analysis in twitter. In *Proceedings of the 9th international workshop on semantic evaluation (SemEval 2015)*, pages 451–463.

Mohammad Salameh, Saif M Mohammad, and Svetlana Kiritchenko. 2015. Sentiment after translation: A case-study on arabic social media posts. In *Proceedings of the 2015 Conference of the North American Chapter of the Association for Computational Linguistics: Human Language Technologies*, pages 767–777.

M Rushdi Saleh, Maria Teresa Martín-Valdivia, Arturo Montejo-Ráez, and LA Ureña-López. 2011. Experiments with svm to classify opinions in different domains. *Expert Systems with Applications*, 38(12):14799–14804.

R. Tsarfaty, D. Seddah, Y. Goldberg, S. Kuebler, Y. Versley, M. Candito, J. Foster, I. Rehbein, and L. Tounsi. 2010. Statistical parsing of morphologically rich languages (spmrl) what, how and whither. In *Proceedings of the NAACL HLT 2010 First Workshop on Statistical Parsing of Morphologically-Rich Languages*, Los Angeles, CA.

Peter D Turney. 2002. Thumbs up or thumbs down?: semantic orientation applied to unsupervised classification of reviews. In *Proceedings of the 40th annual meeting on association for computational linguistics*, pages 417–424. Association for Computational Linguistics.

J. Wiebe, T. Wilson, R. Bruce, M. Bell, and M. Martin. 2004. Learning subjective language. *Computational linguistics*, 30(3):277–308.

J. Wiebe. 1994. Tracking point of view in narrative. *Computational Linguistics*, 20(2):233–287.

Li Zhuang, Feng Jing, and Xiao-Yan Zhu. 2006. Movie review mining and summarization. In *Proceedings of the 15th ACM international conference on Information and knowledge management*, pages 43–50. ACM.

# An enhanced automatic speech recognition system for Arabic


**Mohamed Amine Menacer, Odile Mella, Dominique Fohr**
**Denis Jouvet, David Langlois** and **Kamel Smaili**
Loria, Campus Scientifique, BP 239, 54506 Vandoeuvre Lès-Nancy, France
{mohamed-amine.menacer, odile.mella, dominique.fohr
denis.jouvet, david.langlois, kamel.smaili}@loria.fr



## Abstract

Automatic speech recognition for Arabic is a very challenging task. Despite all the classical techniques for Automatic Speech Recognition (ASR), which can be efficiently applied to Arabic speech recognition, it is essential to take into consideration the language specificities to improve the system performance. In this article, we focus on Modern Standard Arabic (MSA) speech recognition. We introduce the challenges related to Arabic language, namely the complex morphology nature of the language and the absence of the short vowels in written text, which leads to several potential vowelization for each graphemes, which is often conflicting. We develop an ASR system for MSA by using Kaldi toolkit. Several acoustic and language models are trained. We obtain a Word Error Rate (WER) of 14.42 for the baseline system and 12.2 relative improvement by rescoring the lattice and by rewriting the output with the right ء *hamoza* above or below ا *Alif.*


## 1 Introduction

The Arabic language is the fifth most widely spoken language in the world with an estimated 295 million native speakers. It is one of the most morphologically complex languages. Due to this, developing an Automatic Speech Recognition (ASR) system for Arabic is a very challenging task.

Arabic language is characterized by the high number of dialects used in daily communications. There is a significant difference between these dialects and the Modern Standard Arabic (MSA), which is used in newspapers and formal communication. In this article, we will describe our ASR system for MSA implemented using Kaldi toolkit.

Kaldi is a state of the art toolkit for speech recognition based on Weighted Finite State Transducers (WFST) (Povey et al., 2011; Mohri et al., 2008). It includes multiple scripts and recipes for most standard techniques. These recipes are available with many speech corpora and they are frequently updated to support the latest techniques like Deep Neural Networks (DNN).

In this work, several state of the art's modeling techniques are tested, namely the GMM-HMM models, the DNN-HMM models and various techniques like: Maximum Mutual Information (MMI) (Bahl et al., 1986), feature-space Maximum Likelihood Linear Regression (fMLLR) (Povey and Saon, 2006) and Speaker Adaptive Training (SAT) (Anastasakos et al., 1996). The gain obtained after training each model will be reported later on.

Our ASR system is built using several hours of standard Arabic news broadcasts from corpora distributed by ELRA.

Another interesting treatment, proposed in this article, is the auto-correction of ء *hamoza* in the ASR system output in order to rectify the orthography confusion of this symbol above or below ا *Alif.* The approach used is inspired from various techniques proposed in the literature for detection and correction of spelling errors. The particularity of our approach is the use of the vector representation of words to retrieve the context and to correct misspelled words.

In the next section, an overview about Arabic language issues and some works proposed in the literature to deal with those problems is presented. Section 3 describes the different corpus used to train the acoustic and language models, as well as the data normalization process. Section 4 details




*Proceedings of The Third Arabic Natural Language Processing Workshop (WANLP)*, pages 157–165,
Valencia, Spain, April 3, 2017. ©2017 Association for Computational Linguistics

the acoustic and language models. Finally, the experimental results are discussed in Section 5.

## 2   Related works

Even though classic techniques for ASR systems can be efficiently applied to Arabic speech recognition, it is necessary to take into account language specificities to improve the system performance. Arabic is a morphologically rich language. By concatenating prefixes and suffixes to stems, other words are obtained. The stem can be also decomposed into a root (generally a sequence of three consonants) and a pattern of vowels and, possibly, additional consonants. For example: the word وبكتبهم *wabikutubihim*[1] *"and with their books"* is composed of the two prefixes و *w "and"* and ب *b "with"*, the stem كتب *kutub "books"*, which is derived from the root كتب *ktb "to write"* and the suffix هم *hum "their"*. This explains the high out-of-vocabulary (OOV) rate compared with English language which consequently leads to the increase of the Word Error Rate (WER). To deal with this issue, (Afify et al., 2006; Xiang et al., 2006; Diehl et al., 2009; Ng et al., 2009) propose to use morphological segmentation. They shown that the results obtained with a large lexicon could be achieved with a reduced one if morphological decomposition is applied.

Another interesting approach investigates language models based on morphological analysis. Choueiter et al. (2006) used a morpheme-based language modeling by exploiting a statistical segmentation algorithm (Lee et al., 2003) to decompose data. An automaton of type finite state acceptor was used to allow legal sequences of morphemes. With this approach, a 2.4% absolute WER improvement was achieved by using a medium vocabulary (less than 64k words) and a morpheme n-gram model compared to a conventional word-based model. However, by using a large vocabulary (800k words), an absolute improvement of only 0.2% was achieved.

Likewise, the Factored Language Models (FLMs) (Bilmes and Kirchhoff, 2003) was used to improve the WER. In (El-Desoky et al., 2010), the morphological decomposition was combined with FLM to iron out the Arabic complex morphology. A good improvement was shown by rescoring the

---

[1]We use Buckwalter transliteration to represent Arabic words.

n-best list with a FLM based on partially decomposed words.

One more idiosyncrasy of the Arabic language is that it is a consonantal language. It just has three vowels, each of which has a long and short form. Formal texts are generally written without short vowels, consequently a single grapheme word could have several possible pronunciations. For example, the word كتب *ktb* could be pronounced like: كَتَبَ *kataba "write"*, كُتُبٌ *kutubN "books"* or كُتِبَ *Kutiba "written by"* and it also has other potential diacritizations. This ambiguity is solved by using the contextual information of words. Even though the short vowels make easy the pronunciation modeling, their use increases the number of the entries in the vocabulary and consequently the size of the language model. In fact, El-Desoky et al. (2009) showed that the best WER value is achieved by applying a morphological decomposition on a non-diacritized vocabulary. However, a nice improvement was shown in (Kirchhoff and others, 2002) by using short vowels in data training transcripts.

Besides short vowels, another problem to be taken into account in pronunciation modeling is the geminated consonants. In fact, there are cases where the consonant pronunciation should be stressed, and this can frequently happen with the prefix ال *Al "the"*. The solar consonants after this prefix should be doubled (the solar consonants are: ت *t*, ث *v*, د *d*, غ *g*, ر *r*, ز *z*, س *s*, ش *$*, ص *S*, ض *D*, ط *T*, ظ *Z*, ل *l*, ن *n*). The matter of geminated consonants was investigated in some studies. In (Lamel et al., 2009), it has been shown that modeling explicitly geminates improved a little bit the system performance.

Another issue in Arabic concerns the omission of the symbol ء *hamoza* which is pronounced but often not written. This leads to a pronunciation ambiguity. For example: the word العب *AlEb* could be pronounced ألعب *>aloEab "I play"* if the *hamoza* is above *Alif* أ or إلعب *<ilEab "play"* if it is below *Alif* إ.

## 3   Data resources

The data presented in this section are utilized to train acoustic and language models, to estimate the

158

different parameters and to test the performance of the system.

## 3.1 Acoustic data

To train the acoustic model, a collection of spoken transcribed data-set is required. In our case, we used two corpora: Nemlar[2] and NetDC[3] distributed by ELRA. They consist of several hours of Standard Arabic news broadcasts recorded in linear PCM format, 16 kHz and 16 bits.

The data was splitted into three parts: one part for training (Train), the second for tuning (Dev) and the last one for evaluating the performance of our system (Test). Table 1 illustrates some statistics about the acoustic data.

| Corpus | Train | Dev | Test | Total |
|--------|-------|-----|------|-------|
| Nemlar | 33(83%) | 3(08%) | 3(9%) | 40 |
| NetDC | 19(82%) | 3(10%) | 2(8%) | 23 |
| Total | 52(83%) | 6(09%) | 5(8%) | 63 |

Table 1: The acoustic data (hours).

The data splitting was done randomly by keeping 52 hours for the Train, which is equivalent to 83% of data. 6 hours (9% of data) are used in the Dev set and the rest (5 hours) is used in the Test set. In order to balance the data selection between the two corpora, two-thirds of the data is selected from Nemlar corpus.

## 3.2 Textual data

The language model is trained by using two corpora: GigaWord[4] Arabic corpus and the acoustic training data transcription.

GigaWord corpus was collected from nine sources of information with a total of 1,000 million word occurrences. The transcription of the acoustic training data contains about 315k words.

As regards the lexicons, the Nemlar and NetDC corpora are provided with phonetic lexicons in Arabic SAMPA format, which has 34 phonemes (3 vowels, 3 long vowels and 28 consonants). We used them in the training task in order to specify the pronunciation of each word in the transcription of acoustic training data. The two lexicons have

79k pronunciation variants and 77k unique vowelized words, which is equivalent to an average of 1.02 pronunciation variants per word. The number of pronunciation variants per word is weak because all data transcripts and lexicons are written with short vowels and thus each word will not have various pronunciations.

In the recognition task, we used non-diacritized data for training language model, therefore another lexicon without short vowels is used. This lexicon will be described in Section 4.2.

## 3.3 Data normalization

Several issues were encountered while processing the textual corpora due to the Arabic spelling, which is often ambiguous. Therefore, a normalization step is necessary when processing the Arabic text.

Most of the orthographical errors were treated by using regular expression rules. In following, some processing necessary for reducing the ambiguity of spelling and pronunciation are presented:

- All email addresses, url paths, special characters (<, & ...), punctuations and non-Arabic texts are removed.

- All diacritics representing short vowels or consonant stressing are striped.

- All numbers are normalized and they are converted into literal words.

- The prefix و *wa "and"* is separated from words by using Farasa toolkit (Abdelali et al., 2016) and all other prefixes: ب *b*, ف *f*, ال *Al*, ك *k*, ل *l* and س *s* are concatenated to words.

- The stretched words are reduced to their original form. For example: الرجاااال is replaced by الرجال *"men"*.

- A space is inserted after all words end by a ة *ta marobuTa* if it is attached to the next word. For example: نهايةالقرن is replaced by نهاية القرن *nihAyat Aloqaron "century end"*.

- The time is literally written such as in the following example: 15:30 is replaced by الثالثة و ثلاثون دقيقة *Alv~livap wa valAvwn daqyqap*.

[2] http://catalog.elra.info/product_info.php?products_id=874

[3] http://catalog.elra.info/product_info.php?products_id=13&language=fr

[4] https://catalog.ldc.upenn.edu/LDC2011T11

- Some abbreviations are replaced by their corresponding meaning (see Table 2 for some examples).

| Abbre | Word | English gloss |
| --- | --- | --- |
| % | في المائة | Percent |
| ت غ | توقيت غرينتش | GMT |
| ت | تاريخ | Date |
| هـ | هجري | Islamic Calendar |
| د.ك | دولار كندي | canadian dollar |
| س | ساعة | Hour |
| د | دقيقة | Minute |
| ث | ثانية | Second |

Table 2: Abbreviations and their corresponding meaning.

## 4 Modelization

In this section, the different steps involved in the development of the DNN acoustic model is presented. Afterwards, the language modeling aspects and the various models developed are detailed.

### 4.1 Acoustic model

The development of the acoustic model is based on the Kaldi recipe. Our purpose here is to train a DNN model, which perform well with respect to the WER. For this, six different acoustic modeling systems are developed. For three of them, the emission probability of the HMM states is modeled by Gaussian Mixture Models (GMM) and for the others, it is modeled by DNN models.

The acoustic features used are the Mel-Frequency Cesptral Coefficients (MFCC) with first and second order temporal derivatives. Therefore, the feature vector dimension is 39.

Three GMM-HMM models are successively trained. The first acoustic model (triphone1) is trained using directly the MFCC features. A Linear Discriminative Analysis (LDA) followed by a Maximum Likelihood Linear Transform (MLLT) are applied to train the second acoustic model (triphone2). For the third model (triphone3), the Speaker Adaptive Training (SAT) transformation with feature-space Maximum Likelihood Linear Regression (fMLLR) are used to make the system independent of speakers.

In order to take into account the influence of the context on the acoustic realization of the phones, all these models are triphone based models. The last model (triphone3) has 100k Gaussians for 4,264 states.

The DNN-HMM systems are trained using the frame-level cross entropy, sMBR criterion, the senone generated from the last GMM-HMM model (triphone3) and corresponding fMLLR transforms. In total, three DNN models are trained.

- DNN1 classifies frames into triphone-states, i.e it estimates Probability Density Functions (PDFs). DNN1 training is based on the cross-entropy criterion.

- DNN2 and DNN3 are based on sMBR sequence-discriminative training. The difference between the two models is the number of iterations used to train the model. The sMBR sequence-discriminative training is used to train the neural network to jointly optimize for whole sentences instead of a frame-based criterion.

The DNN models have 6 hidden layers and 2048 nodes per layer. The input layer has 440 nodes (40-dimensional fMLLR features spliced across 5 frames on each side of the central frame) and the output has 4,264 nodes. The number of parameters to estimate is about 30.6 millions.

Figure 1 summarizes all the acoustic models of our ASR system.

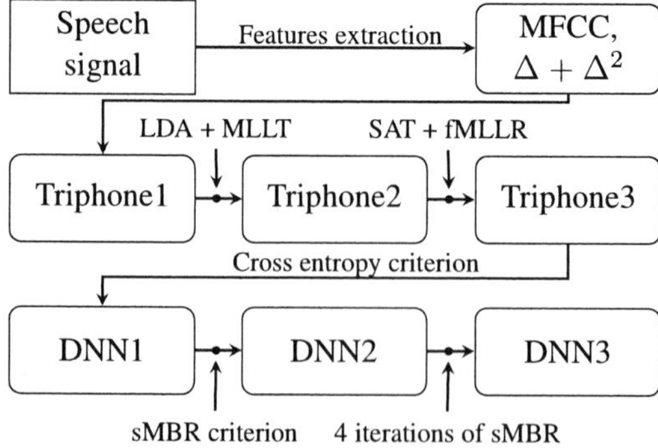


Figure 1: Acoustic model flow diagram.

### 4.2 Language modeling

A 2-gram Language Model (LM) is used to generate the lattice and a 4-grams LM is used to rescore this lattice. As the two text corpora available (Gi-gaWord and transcripts of Train corpus) are unbalanced, a conventional training process is used. A LM is first trained on each data set (one on GigaWord and one on transcripts). They are then merged through a linear interpolation, where the optimal weights are determined in order to maximize the likelihood of the transcripts of the Dev set, which has a size of about 31k words.

For the 4-gram LM, which is used to rescore the lattice, 10 LMs are interpolated. Nine of them are trained on the different sources of GigaWord corpus and the last one is trained on the transcripts of the Train data. The interpolation coefficients are again estimated on the transcripts of the Dev data set.

The recognition vocabulary (lexicon) was generated by first keeping the 109k most frequent words from GigaWord corpus and the words that appear more than 3 times in the transcripts of the Train corpus. Afterwards, only the words for which pronunciation variants are in the Nemlar, NetDC lexicons and the lexicon used in (Ali et al., 2014) were kept. This process has generated a lexicon having 95k unique grapheme words and 485k pronunciation variants, that is an average of 5.07 pronunciation variants per word. The high number of pronunciation variants per word is due to the fact that the lexicon entries do not contain the indication of the short vowels. Hence several pronunciation variants are possible for each word. This lexicon was used as the vocabulary to train the language models.

The SRILM toolkit (Stolcke, 2002) was used to train the different LMs and all of them use Good-Turing (Katz) (Katz, 1987) smoothing technique. It is known that the Kneser-Kney smoothing (Chen and Goodman, 1996) performs better than the Katz technique. However, in (Chelba et al., 2010), the authors showed through different experimental setup that the Katz smoothing performs much better than the Kneser-Kney smoothing for aggressive pruning regimes, which is the case in our system. In fact, due to memory constraints while compiling the automaton used by Kaldi for speech decoding, we used 2-grams pruned language models to generate the lattice. The pruning was done by keeping the n-grams with probability greater than $10^{-9}$. The 4-grams language model was also pruned according two approaches. The first approach is the same as the one used to prune the

2-grams LM and the second is based on stolcke pruning technique (Stolcke, 2000). This second pruned 4-grams LM is presented in Section 5.2.

The n-gram number and the perplexity calculated on the transcripts of the Dev data for various models before and after pruning are presented in Table 3.

| *n*-gram | unpruned | pruned | Stolcke pruning |
|---|---|---|---|
| *1*-gram | 95 589 | | |
| *2*-grams | 69 307k | 20 164k | 2 449k |
| *3*-grams | 327 302k | 22 283k | 1 395k |
| *4*-grams | 586 722k | 4 967k | 192k |

(a) Number of *n*-grams in the interpolated language models.

| *n*-gram | Perplexity |
|---|---|
| *2*-gram | 246.8 |
| *2*-grams (pruned) | 258.2 |
| *4*-grams | 178.5 |
| *4*-grams (pruned) | 189.5 |
| *4*-grams (stolcke pruning) | 214.6 |

(b) 2 and 4-grams models perplexity.

Table 3: Statistics about LMs used to generate and to rescore the lattice.

## 5 Evaluations

This section presents the speech recognition results obtained with a 95k word lexicon for the baseline system, and after rescoring the lattice. We also proposed an approach to auto-correct the ء *hamoza* above or below ا *Alif* to improve the performance.

### 5.1 Baseline system

Speech recognition engines determine the word sequence $W$ which maximises the combination of two scores: the acoustic score $P(O|W)$ and the linguistic one $P(W)$. However, these two scores are calculated on different data which leads to a different scale of probabilities. In fact, the language model score is greater than the one provided by the acoustic model. The probabilities are adjusted as follows:

$$\hat{W} = \arg\max_{W} P(O|W)P(W)^{LM} \qquad (1)$$

where $LM$ is a fudge factor.

In order to estimate the best value of $LM$, we used the transcripts of the Dev corpus. Figure 2 presents the evolution of the WER with respect to the language model weight $LM$ for each acoustic model.

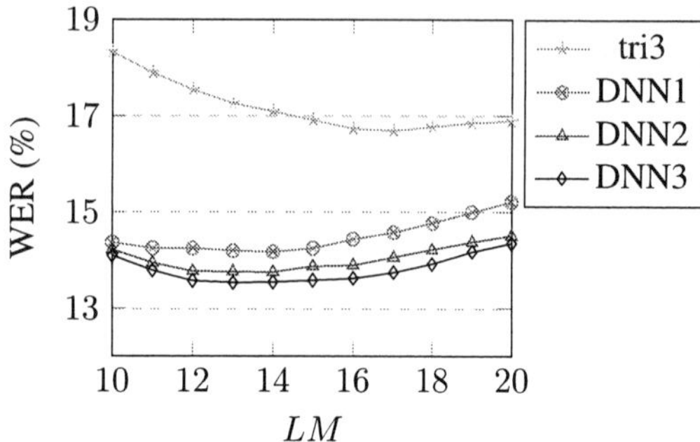

Figure 2: WER evolution with respect to the language model weight.

In Table 4, the best values of $LM$ for each acoustic model are presented, as well as the WER calculated on the Dev (31,314 running words) and the Test (31,726 running words) sets. Note that the lattice, in this baseline system, is generated by using the pruned 2-grams language model.

| Model | $LM_w$ | Dev WER | Test WER |
|---|---|---|---|
| tri3 | 17 | 16.69 | 17.65 |
| DNN1 | 14 | 14.18 | 15.23 |
| DNN2 | 14 | 13.76 | 14.61 |
| DNN3 | 13 | 13.54 | 14.42 |

Table 4: WERs (%) for baseline systems (without rescoring and by using the 2-grams LM).

As expected, DNN-HMM models perform better than the GMM-HMM models. The best WER value is 14.42 obtained by using the DNN3 model, which is based on four iterations of sMBR sequence-discriminative training. It should be noted that another GMM-HMM model is trained by applying the Maximum Mutual Information (MMI) criterion. By this, the WER decreased from 17.65 to 16.86 (a relative improvement of 4%). By using the DNN model, a relative reduction in WER of 14% has been achieved with respect to GMM-HMM model.

It should be also noted that OOV rate is about 2.35% for the Dev part and 2.54% for the Test.

## 5.2 Rescoring

Let's recall that Kaldi is based on Weighted Finite State Transducers (WFST) for decoding. Because of this constraint, the decoding is done with a 2-grams LM. One can expect that a rescoring using a more detailed LM (e.g., 4-grams) would improve performance. Thus, we applied a 4-grams rescoring, but only on the DNN3 hypotheses.

WFST is an automaton, which has a set of states and a unique start state. These states are interconnected by arcs, where each arc has an input label, an output label and a weight. To accomplish the language model rescoring, Kaldi generally first subtract the old language model cost from the global score and then add in the new language model cost to avoid modifying the other parts of the global score.

When using this approach, it is more accurate to replace a 4-grams model by another 4-grams LM. For this, we pruned the full 4-grams LM by using stolcke pruning technique (Stolcke, 2000). This technique is based on minimizing the relative entropy between the full and the pruned model. We get a model which represents only 30% of the original model and consisting of $4 \times 10^6$ n-grams. It should be noted that the pruning is done by using the pocolm toolkit[5]. We used this new model to produce the lattice. Afterward, this lattice is rescored by using a full 4-grams LM.

As in the baseline system, we estimate the impact of the LM weight on the Dev data. The variation of the LM weight is illustrated in Figure 3. We can remark that the smallest value of WER is obtained for $LM = 14$.

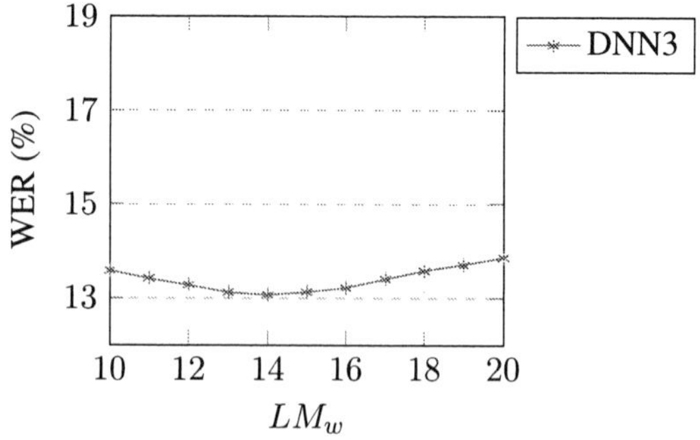

Figure 3: WER with respect to the language model weight after rescoring the lattice.

The evolution of the WER with or without rescoring is given in Table 5.

---

[5]https://github.com/danpovey/pocolm

| Model | Dev WER | Test WER |
| --- | --- | --- |
| DNN3 | 14.65 | 15.32 |
| DNN3+rescoring | 13.07 | 14.02 |

Table 5: WERs (%) before and after rescoring the whole lattice produced by using the 4-grams pruned LM.

Rescoring the whole lattice with the 4-gram LM leads to an absolute improvement of 1.58% on the Dev set and 1.3% on Test corpus in comparison to the system, where the lattice is produced using the pruned 4-grams language model (the LM with $4 \times 10^6$ n-grams).

We can also remark that producing the lattice by using a pruned 2-grams LM gives better results than using a 4-grams LM pruned with an aggressive pruning regimes. This is justified by the number of n-grams in each model (the number of n-grams in the 2-grams LM is 5 times greater than the number of n-grams in the pruned 4-grams LM).

## 6  Auto-correction of *hamoza*

The ء *hamoza* symbol is widely used in Arabic; by analyzing the errors of our ASR system on the Dev corpus, we noticed that one of the main errors concerns the presence or not of this symbol above or below ا *Alif*. Therefore, it seems interesting to auto-correct the *hamoza* spelling.

Our approach is inspired from techniques proposed in the literature to detect and auto-correct the spelling errors. This issue is a common problem to all languages. In Arabic, the most frequently occurring errors are editing errors and semantic spelling errors. The first error type occurs when a correctly spelled word is replaced by a non-word, while in the semantic spelling errors, the word is replaced by another correctly spelled word (Alkanhal et al., 2012).

Several works have been proposed for spelling auto-correction in Arabic. Most of these works are based on the three steps described below.

**Error detection:** Techniques used in the literature for detecting Arabic spelling errors are essentially based on two approaches: the language rules (AlShenaifi et al., 2015; Shaalan et al., 2010; Hassan et al., 2014) or a dictionary (Attia et al., 2014; Zerrouki et al., 2014; Alkanhal et al., 2012). For the first technique, detecting whether a word is misspelled or not depends on morphological analyzers. While the dictionary based technique depends on a large word list that covers the most frequently used words in the language.

The technique which we used to detect *hamoza* error is the dictionary lookup, where the input word is considered such as a non-word if it is not found in the dictionary. The word list size used in our case is 9.2 million fully inflected Arabic word entries. It is developed by Attia et al. (2012) by amalgamating various Arabic resources.

**Production of hypotheses:** The most common used technique to produce candidates is based on an edition distance, which measures the difference between two sequences by calculating the number of required edits to transform a word into another. As we just want to correct *hamoza* error, it is not necessary to use an edition distance in our case. In fact, to produce correction hypotheses, we just considered words in the Arabic word list, which have the same spelling as the wrong word except for the *hamoza* above or below ا *Alif* (أ and إ). For example: consider the misspelled word امر *Aamara "to order"*, the candidate list contains the two words أمر *>amara "to order"* and آمر *|miro "commander"*. It is clear that the misspelled word has the same spelling as candidates except the two letters أ *>* and آ *|*.

**Error correction:** for error correction i.e. selecting the best solution among the list of candidates, we tried to retrieve the words context by using word2vec (Mikolov et al., 2013). In fact, we used the GigaWord corpus to train a *cbow* model and to obtain word vectors, which are positioned in a 200-dimensional space such that words that share common contexts in the corpus are located in close proximity to one another in the space. Afterwards, we used the cosine similarity to retrieve the most similar word among the candidates.

Table 6 shows the results before and after correcting the *hamoza* in the ASR system output.

| Model | Dev WER | Test WER |
| --- | --- | --- |
| Baseline | 13.54 | 14.42 |
| Correction | 13.03 | 14.14 |
| Rescoring | 13.07 | 14.02 |
| Rescoring+correction | **12.26** | **13.45** |

Table 6: WERs (%) before and after correcting the *hamoza*.

From Table 6, note that the WER for the baseline system is 14.42. It should be noted that the lattice in this system is generated by using the 2-grams LM. Correcting the *hamoza* errors in the output of the baseline ASR system improves the WER by 2%. Rescoring the lattice of the baseline ASR system with a pruned 4-grams LM improves the WER by 3% (14.02). The best WER (13.45) is achieved by combining the two methods.

## 7 Conclusion

In this article, we described an ASR system for MSA developed by using Kaldi toolkit. We presented the different acoustic models trained and the text pre-processing done before training the LMs. The best results are achieved by rescoring the lattice, which is generated by using the DNN-HMM model, a 4-grams pruned LM and a lexicon of 95k words. This way we have obtained 3% relative improvement. In order to improve the system output, we proposed an approach based on the dictionary lookup to auto-correct the *hamoza* spelling above or below *Alif*. Applying this approach, we achieved an improvement of 12% relative in comparison to the baseline model.

## References


Ahmed Abdelali, Kareem Darwish, Nadir Durrani, and Hamdy Mubarak. 2016. Farasa: A fast and furious segmenter for arabic. In *HLT-NAACL Demos*, pages 11–16. Association for Computational Linguistics, San Diego, California.

Mohamed Afify, Ruhi Sarikaya, Hong-Kwang Jeff Kuo, Laurent Besacier, and Yuqing Gao. 2006. On the use of morphological analysis for dialectal arabic speech recognition. In *Interspeech*.

Ahmed Ali, Yifan Zhang, Patrick Cardinal, Najim Dahak, Stephan Vogel, and James Glass. 2014. A complete kaldi recipe for building arabic speech recognition systems. In *Spoken Language Technology Workshop (SLT), 2014 IEEE*, pages 525–529, Dec.

Mohamed I. Alkanhal, Mohamed A. Al-Badrashiny, Mansour M. Alghamdi, and Abdulaziz O. Al-Qabbany. 2012. Automatic stochastic arabic spelling correction with emphasis on space insertions and deletions. *IEEE Transactions on Audio, Speech, and Language Processing*, 20(7):2111–2122.

Nouf AlShenaifi, Rehab AlNefie, Maha Al-Yahya, and Hend Al-Khalifa. 2015. Arib@ qalb-2015 shared task: A hybrid cascade model for arabic spelling error detection and correction. In *ANLP Workshop 2015*, page 127.

Tasos Anastasakos, John McDonough, Richard Schwartz, and John Makhoul. 1996. A compact model for speaker-adaptive training. In *Spoken Language, 1996. ICSLP 96. Proceedings., Fourth International Conference on*, volume 2, pages 1137–1140. IEEE.

Mohammed Attia, Pavel Pecina, Younes Samih, Khaled Shaalan, and Josef van Genabith. 2012. Improved spelling error detection and correction for arabic. In *The International Conference on Computational Linguistics (COLING)*, pages 103–112, Mumbai, India, 14 December.

Mohammed Attia, Mohamed Al-Badrashiny, and Mona Diab. 2014. Gwu-hasp: Hybrid arabic spelling and punctuation corrector. In *Proceedings of the EMNLP 2014 Workshop on Arabic Natural Langauge Processing (ANLP)*, pages 148–154.

L. R. Bahl, Peter F. Brown, Peter V. De Souza, and Robert L. Mercer. 1986. Maximum mutual information estimation of hidden markov model parameters for speech recognition. In *proc. icassp*, volume 86, pages 49–52.

Jeff A. Bilmes and Katrin Kirchhoff. 2003. Factored language models and generalized parallel backoff. In *Proceedings of the 2003 Conference of the North American Chapter of the Association for Computational Linguistics on Human Language Technology: companion volume of the Proceedings of HLT-NAACL 2003–short papers-Volume 2*, pages 4–6. Association for Computational Linguistics.

Ciprian Chelba, Thorsten Brants, Will Neveitt, and Peng Xu. 2010. Study on interaction between entropy pruning and kneser-ney smoothing. pages 2422–2425.

Stanley F. Chen and Joshua Goodman. 1996. An empirical study of smoothing techniques for language modeling. In *Proceedings of the 34th annual meeting on Association for Computational Linguistics*, pages 310–318. Association for Computational Linguistics.

Ghinwa Choueiter, Daniel Povey, Stanley F. Chen, and Geoffrey Zweig. 2006. Morpheme-based language modeling for arabic lvcsr. In *2006 IEEE International Conference on Acoustics Speech and Signal Processing Proceedings*, volume 1, pages I–I. IEEE.

Frank Diehl, Mark J. F. Gales, Marcus Tomalin, and Philip C. Woodland. 2009. Morphological analysis and decomposition for arabic speech-to-text systems. In *Interspeech*, pages 2675–2678.

Amr El-Desoky, Christian Gollan, David Rybach, Ralf Schlüter, and Hermann Ney. 2009. Investigating the use of morphological decomposition and diacritization for improving arabic lvcsr. In *Interspeech*, pages 2679–2682.

Amr El-Desoky, Ralf Schlüter, and Hermann Ney. 2010. A hybrid morphologically decomposed factored language models for arabic lvcsr. In *Human Language Technologies: The 2010 Annual Conference of the North American Chapter of the Association for Computational Linguistics*, pages 701–704. Association for Computational Linguistics.

Youssef Hassan, Mohamed Aly, and Amir Atiya. 2014. Arabic spelling correction using supervised learning. *arXiv preprint arXiv:1409.8309*.

Slava Katz. 1987. Estimation of probabilities from sparse data for the language model component of a speech recognizer. *IEEE transactions on acoustics, speech, and signal processing*, 35(3):400–401.

Katrin Kirchhoff et al. 2002. Novel speech recognition models for arabic. In *Johns-Hopkins University summer research workshop*.

Lori Lamel, Abdelkhalek Messaoudi, and Jean-Luc Gauvain. 2009. Automatic speech-to-text transcription in arabic. *ACM Transactions on Asian Language Information Processing (TALIP)*, 8(4):18.

Young-Suk Lee, Kishore Papineni, Salim Roukos, Ossama Emam, and Hany Hassan. 2003. Language model based arabic word segmentation. In *Proceedings of the 41st Annual Meeting on Association for Computational Linguistics-Volume 1*, pages 399–406. Association for Computational Linguistics.

Tomas Mikolov, Ilya Sutskever, Kai Chen, Greg Corrado, and Jeffrey Dean. 2013. Distributed representations of words and phrases and their compositionality. *arXiv preprint arXiv:1310.4546*.

Mehryar Mohri, Fernando Pereira, and Michael Riley. 2008. Speech recognition with weighted finite-state transducers. In *Springer Handbook of Speech Processing*, pages 559–584. Springer.

Tim Ng, Kham Nguyen, Rabih Zbib, and Long Nguyen. 2009. Improved morphological decomposition for arabic broadcast news transcription. In *2009 IEEE International Conference on Acoustics, Speech and Signal Processing*, pages 4309–4312. IEEE.

Daniel Povey and George Saon. 2006. Feature and model space speaker adaptation with full covariance gaussians. In *Interspeech*.

Daniel Povey, Arnab Ghoshal, Gilles Boulianne, Lukas Burget, Ondrej Glembek, Nagendra Goel, Mirko Hannemann, Petr Motlicek, Yanmin Qian, Petr Schwarz, Jan Silovsky, Georg Stemmer, and Karel Vesely. 2011. The kaldi speech recognition toolkit. In *IEEE 2011 Workshop on Automatic Speech Recognition and Understanding*. IEEE Signal Processing Society, December. IEEE Catalog No.: CFP11SRW-USB.

Khaled Shaalan, Rana Aref, and Aly Fahmy. 2010. An approach for analyzing and correcting spelling errors for non-native arabic learners. In *Informatics and Systems (INFOS), 2010 The 7th International Conference on*, pages 1–7. IEEE.

Andreas Stolcke. 2000. Entropy-based pruning of backoff language models. *arXiv preprint cs/0006025*.

Andreas Stolcke. 2002. SRILM-an extensible language modeling toolkit. In *Interspeech*, volume 2002, page 2002.

Bing Xiang, Kham Nguyen, Long Nguyen, Richard Schwartz, and John Makhoul. 2006. Morphological decomposition for arabic broadcast news transcription. In *2006 IEEE International Conference on Acoustics Speech and Signal Processing Proceedings*, volume 1, pages I–I. IEEE.

Taha Zerrouki, Khaled Alhawaity, and Amar Balla. 2014. Autocorrection of arabic common errors for large text corpus. *ANLP 2014*, page 127.

# Universal Dependencies for Arabic

**Dima Taji, Nizar Habash and Daniel Zeman**[†]
Computational Approaches to Modeling Language (CAMeL) Lab,
New York University Abu Dhabi
[†]Faculty of Mathematics and Physics, Charles University
{dima.taji,nizar.habash}@nyu.edu, zeman@ufal.mff.cuni.cz

## Abstract

We describe the process of creating NUDAR, a Universal Dependency treebank for Arabic. We present the conversion from the Penn Arabic Treebank to the Universal Dependency syntactic representation through an intermediate dependency representation. We discuss the challenges faced in the conversion of the trees, the decisions we made to solve them, and the validation of our conversion. We also present initial parsing results on NUDAR.

## 1 Introduction

Parsers have been used in many Natural Language Processing (NLP) applications, such as automatic summarization, question answering, and machine translation. This motivates the creation of treebanks on which these parsers can be trained. Treebanks have two main different syntactic representations. On one hand, there are phrase structure (constituency) treebanks such as the Penn Treebank (Marcus et al., 1993), and its sister treebanks such as the Penn Arabic Treebank (PATB) (Maamouri et al., 2004) and the Penn Chinese Treebank (Xue et al., 2005). On the other hand, there are dependency treebanks, such as Columbia Arabic Treebank (CATiB) (Habash and Roth, 2009), and the Prague Dependency Treebank (PDT) (Hajič et al., 2001). Other treebanks that followed the style of PDT are the Slovene (Džeroski et al., 2006) and the Croatian (Berović et al., 2012) treebanks, as well as the Prague Arabic Dependency Treebank (PADT) (Smrž et al., 2002; Hajič et al., 2004; Smrž et al., 2008).

Having these different syntactic representations makes it difficult to compare treebanks, and parsing results (Nilsson et al., 2007). This motivated the creation of the Universal Dependency (UD) syntactic representation, that aims to create cross-linguistically consistent annotation guidelines that facilitate the creation of treebanks that are built with the same label sets and structural basis (Nivre, 2014; Pyysalo et al., 2015). In this paper, we present the *New York University Abu Dhabi Universal Dependency Arabic Treebank*, a UD treebank for Arabic, which we dub NUDAR.[1]

## 2 Related Work

In this section we present the Universal Dependency syntactic representation, as well as some of the most prominent previous efforts on Modern Standard Arabic (MSA) treebanks.

### 2.1 Universal Dependencies

UD is an open community effort. It builds on the existing treebank structure of the Stanford dependencies (De Marneffe et al., 2006; De Marneffe and Manning, 2008; De Marneffe et al., 2014), as well as the universal Google dependency scheme (McDonald et al., 2013). In addition, it makes use of the Google Universal Parts-of-Speech (POS) Tagset (Petrov et al., 2011), and the morphosyntactic tag set of the *interset interlingua* (Zeman, 2008).

The aim of UD is to facilitate the creation of treebanks in different languages that are consistent in their syntactic representation, while still allowing the extension of the relations to accommodate for language-specific constructs. The target of UD is to facilitate the development of multilingual learning systems, and multilingual NLP, as well as allow for comparative linguistic studies and evaluation (Nivre et al., 2016).

In its last release of version 1.4, the UD treebank collection contained 64 different treebanks,

---

[1]The noun Nudar نُضَار *nuDAr* is Arabic for 'pure gold'.



*Proceedings of The Third Arabic Natural Language Processing Workshop (WANLP)*, pages 166–176,
Valencia, Spain, April 3, 2017. ©2017 Association for Computational Linguistics

with over 10 other treebanks scheduled for release in the upcoming version 2.0. The treebanks are in 47 languages, including Swedish (Nivre, 2014), Danish (Johannsen et al., 2015), Finnish (Pyysalo et al., 2015), Estonian (Muischnek et al., 2014), Norwegian (Øvrelid and Hohle, 2016), Croatian (Agić and Ljubešić, 2015), Persian (Seraji et al., 2016), Bulgarian (Osenova and Simov, 2015), Catalan and Spanish (Alonso and Zeman, 2016), as well as the Prague Arabic Universal Dependency Treebank (PAUDT), among others.

## 2.2 Arabic Treebanks

A number of treebanks exist for MSA. These treebanks vary in terms of their syntactic representation (constituency vs. dependency), richness of annotation, and source of data. We discuss next four treebanks that are relevant to this paper.

**PATB:** The Penn Arabic Treebank (Maamouri et al., 2004; Maamouri et al., 2009) is a Linguistic Data Consortium (LDC) project, for which there are currently 12 parts for MSA. PATB consists of constituency trees, the sources of which are newswire articles from a variety of news sources.

**CATiB:** Columbia Arabic Treebank (Habash and Roth, 2009) is a dependency treebank effort that allows for faster annotation and uses "intuitive dependency structure representation and relational labels inspired by traditional Arabic grammar" (Habash, 2010). The basic CATiB treebank uses six POS tags, and eight relational labels. It contains 273K tokens that have been annotated directly in the CATiB representation, as well as the entire PATB parts 1, 2, and 3 that were automatically converted into CATiB representation.

**PADT and PAUDT:** The Prague Arabic Dependency Tree 1.0 (Smrž et al., 2008) was published in the LDC in 2004 (Hajič et al., 2004) and consisted of about 114K tokens. The data in PADT comes from part of the PATB parts 1 and 2, and the Arabic Gigaword (Graff et al., 2006). Variants of that dataset were released for the CoNLL 2006 (60K tokens) and CoNLL 2007 (116K tokens, improved morphology) shared tasks. An extended dataset (282K tokens) was incorporated in the HamleDT collection, where 30 treebanks were first harmonized in the Prague annotation style, later in Stanford dependencies (Rosa et al., 2014). Finally, this dataset was converted to Universal

Dependencies and it has been part of UD releases since UD 1.2, labeled simply "UD Arabic".[2]

The annotation guidelines of PADT 1.0 were derived from the Prague Dependency Treebank (Czech), with some necessary adjustments to account for the differences between Arabic and Czech. The original morphological and syntactic disambiguation was done manually but the subsequent conversion steps were automatic.

Word forms in PADT are fully diacritized; in PAUDT we preserve the diacritized as a useful extra attribute, but the main form is undiacritized, to provide more natural training material for parsers. Morphological tags were converted to the UD tags and features, dependency relation types were translated to the UD label set. Occasionally the translation of labels relied on other sources such as part of speech or even lemma. For example, the PADT relation AuxM *(modifying expression)* is used for prepositions (which are attached as `case` or `mark` in PAUDT), for negative particles *lA, lam, lan*[3] (which ended up as `neg` in UD v1 and as `advmod` in UD v2), for future particles *sa, sawfa* (which are `aux` dependents in PAUDT) and also for the negative copula *laysa* (`cop` in PAUDT).

Unlike UD, the Prague treebanks do not distinguish whether the dependent is a nominal or a clause (`nsubj` vs. `csubj`, `obj` vs. `ccomp` etc.) Heuristics have to be used here. At present, only phrases headed by verbs are considered clausal; clauses with non-verbal predicates without a copula are attached as if they were bare nominals. On the other hand, when a copula is involved, we reattach it as a dependent of the non-verbal predicate (in PADT, if the copula is present, it heads the clause). Similarly, prepositions head prepositional phrases in the Prague style but they are attached as modifiers of their nouns in PAUDT.

Finally, coordination in the Prague style is al-

---

[2]In this paper we use UD to refer to the general shared concept of Universal Dependency representation. For language specific decision and treebanks we will use the name of the treebanks, i.e. PAUDT or NUDAR.

[3]All Arabic transliterations are provided in the Habash-Soudi-Buckwalter transliteration scheme (Habash et al., 2007b). This scheme extends Buckwalter's transliteration scheme (Buckwalter, 2002) to increase its readability while maintaining the 1-to-1 correspondence with Arabic orthography as represented in standard encodings of Arabic, i.e., Unicode, CP-1256, etc. The following are the only differences from Buckwalter's scheme (which is indicated in parentheses): Ā آ (|), Â أ (>), ŵ ؤ (&), Ă إ (<), ŷ ئ (}), ħ ة (p), θ ث (v), ð ذ (*), š ش ($), Ď ظ (Z), ς ع (E), γ غ (g), ý ى (Y), ã ً (F), ũ ٌ (N), ĩ ٍ (K), á ٰ (`).

ways headed either by a conjunction, or, if no conjunction is present, by a punctuation symbol. All conjuncts are at the same tree level. In PAUDT these structures are transformed so that the first conjunct is the head and all subsequent conjuncts are attached to it.

**Why Another Arabic Universal Dependency Treebank?** PAUDT is based on PADT, which is a small treebank, compared to the existing PATB treebank. Our aim is to make use of the automatic conversion of PATB, parts 1, 2, and 3, into a richer version of CATiB, and use it to create NUDAR. This would allow us in the future to convert the remaining parts of PATB, both in MSA and dialectal Arabic (such as Egyptian (Maamouri et al., 2012)), as well as extend the existing CATiB treebank that has no parallel in PATB's constituency representation.

## 3 NUDAR: NYUAD Universal Dependency Arabic Treebank

In this section we describe the creation of NUDAR, starting with the PATB. The conversion strategy we adopt is to transform the constituency PATB trees into the rich CATiB++ dependency representation (Section 3.2). We then apply morphological and syntactic transformations on these trees – Section 3.3, and Section 3.4 respectively.

### 3.1 A Note on Tokenization and Datasets

The datasets that are currently included in NUDAR are the PATB part 1, v4.1 (Maamouri et al., 2010a), part 2, v3.1 (Maamouri et al., 2011), and part 3, v3.2 (Maamouri et al., 2010b). The tokenization followed in NUDAR is the same tokenization scheme followed in PATB, which tokenizes all the clitics, with the exception of the definite article +ال Al+ 'the' (Pasha et al., 2014). The treebank contains 19K sentences, containing 738K tokens. For our parsing experiment, we followed the guidelines detailed by Diab et al. (2013), to split the treebanks into TRAIN, DEV, and TEST. The details of the sizes of the different datasets are shown in Table 1.

### 3.2 From Constituency to Dependency

Our conversion pipeline starts from PATB, converting it to a richer version of the Columbia Arabic Treebank which we refer to as CATiB++. We use the Columbia Arabic Conversion Tool v0.7

(Habash and Roth, 2009),[4] that converts PATB trees to the CATiB representation, with the addition of the semantic dashtags and the PATB complete morphological tags (BW) (Buckwalter, 2004). We supplement the trees with additional feature-value pairs representation in the style used in the MADAMIRA morphological analyzer and disambiguator (Pasha et al., 2014).

We chose to convert the treebanks through this methodology to allow for the conversion of the existing CATiB treebank that has no parallel in PATB's constituency representation. In the future, we envision enriching the CATiB treebank with the morphosyntactic features it lacks, using techniques described by Alkuhlani et al. (2013).

### 3.3 Morphological Transformation

The mapping of the morphological features from CATiB++ to NUDAR includes mapping the NUDAR POS tag, as well as the set of features that appear with each token. The mapping of POS tags is done through a lookup that takes the CATiB POS tag and the gold BW tag of the token stem, and maps them to the equivalent NUDAR POS tag. The lookup map is shown in Table 2. The mapping of the morphological features uses another lookup map, that is shown in Table 3.

### 3.4 Syntactic Transformation

UD and CATiB representations share a number of similarities, both being dependency representations. However there are differences between them that primarily arise from the basic focus on what a dependency is, and affect the structure of the trees. CATiB tries to represent a structure closer to traditional Arabic grammar analysis, which is more interested in modeling the assignment of *case*. This results in function words tending to head their phrase structures more. In contrast, UD tends to get closer to the meaning, and minimize differences between different languages that have different morphosyntactic structures (Nivre, 2016).

The CATiB and NUDAR representations use a different set of labels that refer to very similar concepts, although they use different forms. This results in having a number of similar constructs where we only need to map the labels without modifying the structure.

---

[4]For more information on this tool, contact the second author.

| | DEV | | TRAIN | | TEST | | ALL | |
|---|---|---|---|---|---|---|---|---|
| | Tokens | Sentences | Tokens | Sentences | Tokens | Sentences | Tokens | Sentences |
| **PATB1** | 16,881 | 447 | 16,586 | 487 | 133,813 | 3,585 | 167,280 | 4,519 |
| **PATB2** | 16,972 | 264 | 17,128 | 228 | 135,219 | 2,099 | 169,319 | 2,591 |
| **PATB3** | 40,092 | 1,275 | 40,411 | 1,248 | 321,787 | 10,105 | 402,290 | 12,628 |
| **Total** | 73,945 | 1,986 | 74,125 | 1,963 | 590,819 | 15,789 | 738,889 | 19,738 |

Table 1: The tokens and sentences in the current NUDAR Treebank, based on PATB parts 1, 2, and 3

### 3.4.1 Verbal Constructs

Verbal constructs representation in CATiB and NUDAR are the same, except for the choice of label. The verb heads the optional subject, zero or more objects, and other modifiers. The label used for the attachment between the subject and the verb is `SBJ` in CATiB, and `nsubj` in NUDAR. Any object is attached to the verb using the `OBJ` relation in CATiB. In NUDAR, the first object takes the label `obj`, and any other objects take the label `iobj`. An example of a verbal sentence is demonstrated in Figure 1.

In the case of passive verbs, the subject of the passive verb takes the relation `nsubj:pass`. CATiB marks passive verbs using the POS tag **VRB-PASS**, and uses the relation `SBJ` for the subject.

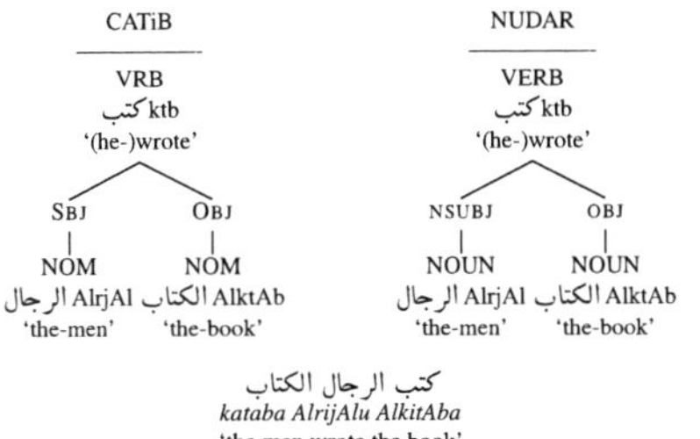

Figure 1: Verb-Subject-Object Construct

### 3.4.2 Adjectival Constructs

A noun followed by an adjectival modifier maintains the same structure in both CATiB and NUDAR, with the noun heading the adjectival modifier. The label that this relation takes in NUDAR is `amod`, as in the example in Figure 2.

### 3.4.3 Idafa Constructs

The *Idafa* construct can be used to mark the genitive possessor, objects of preposition-like nominal adverbs, and some quantification constructs (Habash et al., 2009). Each of these cases is

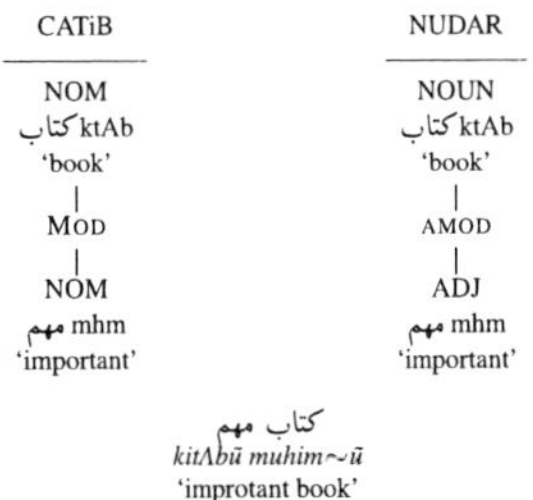

Figure 2: Adjectival Modifier Construct

treated differently. For the case of possessive constructs, such as in Figure 3, we extend the existing `nmod` UD label to the language-specific `nmod:poss` label.

Figure 3: *Idafa* Construct: the genitive possessor

Nominal adverbs (e.g., أمام *AmAm* 'front', خلف *xlf* 'behind') are connected to their parents with an *Idafa* relation (`IDF`) in CATiB. Since these nominal-adverbs are tagged with the **ADV** POS tag in NUDAR, this relation gets directly mapped to `advmod`, as demonstracted in Figure 4.

The case of *Idafa* in quantification constructs (Figure 6) will be discussed next with the other number constructs.

### 3.4.4 Number Constructs

Number constructs take different relational labels in the CATiB representation. A number[5] heads the

---

[5]The numbers we discuss in this section are three and above. The number *one* in Arabic (واحد *wAHd*) is an ad-

| CATiB POS | BW' POS | UD POS |
|---|---|---|
| NOM | *SUFF_DO | PRON |
| NOM | ABBREV | NOUN |
| NOM | ADJ | ADJ |
| NOM | ADJ_COMP | ADJ |
| NOM | ADJ_NUM | ADJ |
| NOM | ADV | ADV |
| NOM | DEM_PRON | DET |
| NOM | DIALECT | X |
| NOM | FOREIGN | X |
| NOM | INTERJ | INTJ |
| NOM | INTERROG_ADV | ADV |
| NOM | INTERROG_PRON | PRON |
| NOM | LATIN | X |
| NOM | NOUN | ADV if *nom-prep* |
| NOM | NOUN | NOUN if not *nom-prep* |
| NOM | NOUN_NUM | NUM |
| NOM | NOUN_PROP | PROPN |
| NOM | NOUN_QUANT | NOUN |
| NOM | POSS_PRON | PRON |
| NOM | PRON | PRON |
| NOM | REL_ADV | ADV |
| NOM | REL_PRON | PRON |
| NOM | TYPO | X |
| PROP | !! | PROPN |
| PNX | NUMERIC_COMMA | PUNCT |
| PNX | PUNC | PUNCT |
| PRT | CONJ | CCONJ |
| PRT | CONNEC_PART | PART |
| PRT | DET | DET |
| PRT | FOCUS_PART | PART |
| PRT | FUT_PART | AUX |
| PRT | INTERJ | INTJ |
| PRT | INTERROG_PART | PART |
| PRT | JUS_PART | PART |
| PRT | NEG_PART | PART |
| PRT | PART | PART |
| PRT | PREP | ADP |
| PRT | PSEUDO_VERB | CCONJ |
| PRT | RC_PART | PART |
| PRT | RESTRIC_PART | PART |
| PRT | SUB_CONJ | SCONJ |
| PRT | VERB_PART | AUX |
| PRT | VOC_PART | PART |
| UNK | DIALECT | X |
| UNK | LATIN | X |
| UNK | TYPO | X |
| VRB | !! | VERB |
| VRB-PASS | !! | VERB |

Table 2: Part-of-Speech mapping from CATiB POS and BW POS to NUDAR. BW' denotes the complete or partial match of the full BW tag set. Entries marked with !! under BW' POS means that the relevant information is taken from the CATiB POS tag only. Entries starting with * under the BW means that there are multiple tags the contain this partial tag, and that they all map to the same UD POS. *nom-prep* is a function that determines if the word falls under the list of nominal adverbs, which are specified words that are tagged as nominals in CATiB and PATB, but behave like adverbs.

| MADAMIRA | UD |
|---|---|
| asp | Aspect |
| cas | Case |
| stt | Definite |
| gen | Gender |
| mod | Mood |
| num | Number |
| per | Person |
| vox | Voice |
| pos | PronType, NumForm |
| bw | Polarity |

Table 3: Morphological features mapping from CATiB to NUDAR

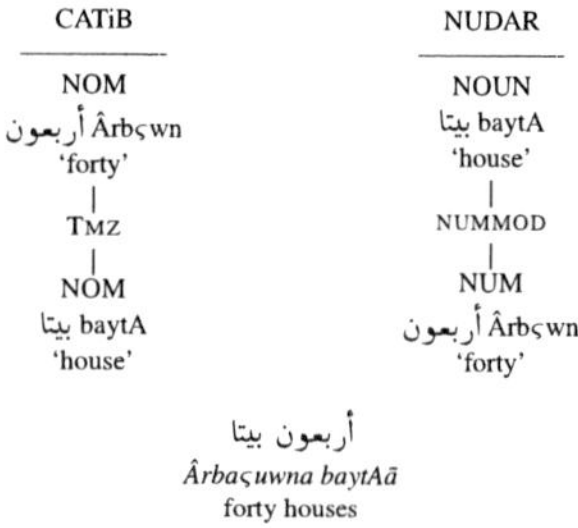

Figure 4: *Idafa* Construct: the object of a preposition-like nominal adverb

word it modifies. The relation between the number and the noun is either *Tamyiz* - if the number is between 11 and 99, as in Figure 5 or *Idafa* otherwise, as in Figure 6. In NUDAR the noun heads the number, and the relation is `nummod` in both cases.

Figure 5: *Tamyiz* Consrtuct: the numeral modifier of numbers between 11 and 99

The relations between numbers in compound number structures in CATiB are similar to the

jective, and will always be headed by the word it modifies. Number *two* (اثنان *AvnAn*) can also be an adjective that attaches low to the word it modifies, or it can be part of the noun's morphology.

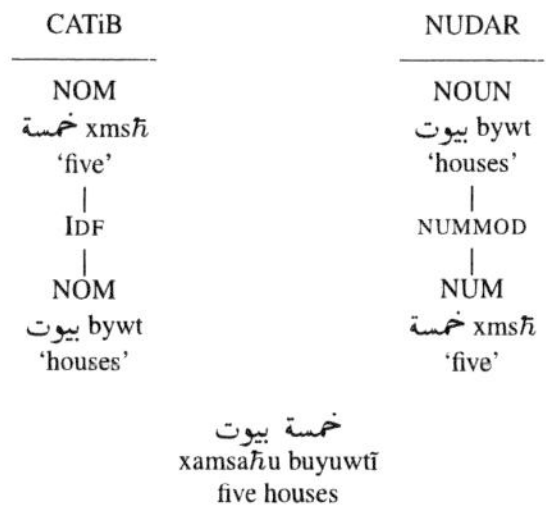

Figure 6: *Idafa* Construct: the numeral modifier

relations between numbers and the nouns they modify. In this example, as shown in Figure 7, الف *Alf* 'thousand' would be headed by أربعون *Ârbϛwn* 'forty' with the *Tamyiz* relation (TMZ) in CATiB. However, in NUDAR, the subtree would be headed by *Alf*, and *Ârbϛwn* would be attached to it with a `compound` relation.

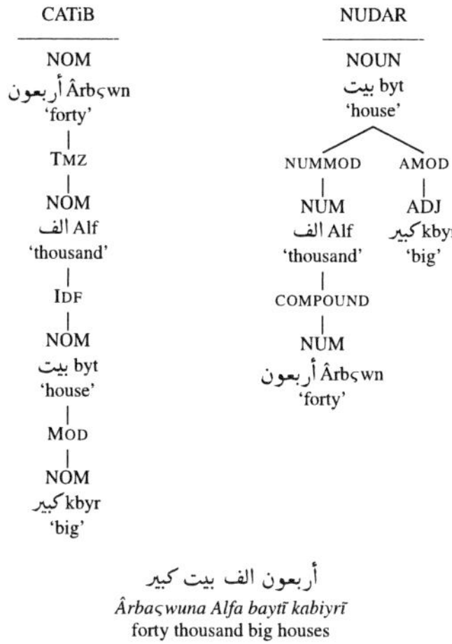

Figure 7: Compound Number Construct

### 3.4.5 Coordination Constructs

In CATiB, the coordinating conjunction heads the sub-tree of the following phrase in a cascading structure. In NUDAR, however, the construct is flat, with all the coordinating conjunctions and conjuncts being headed by the first conjunct of the coordination construct. The coordinating conjunctions take the relation `cc`, and the conjuncts take the relation `conj`. The difference between the two tree structures in illustrated in Figure 8.

It is also common for the coordinating conjunctions in Arabic to be sentence-initial discourse connectives (واو ابتدائية/واو استئنافية) or interruptives (واو اعتراضية) (Habash et al., 2009). In these cases, the coordinating conjunctions are dependent on the root predicate of the sentence with the relation `cc`.

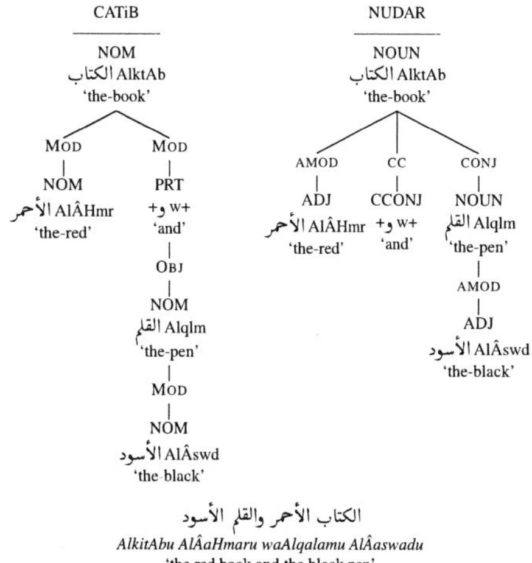

Figure 8: Coordination Construct

### 3.4.6 Proper Name Constructs

Proper nouns having two or more nominal elements have these elements linked using the language-specific relation `flat:name` in NUDAR. If a proper noun has more than two nominal elements, they all are headed by the first element of the proper name, unlike CATiB, where each element is headed by the one that precedes it, as seen in Figure 9.

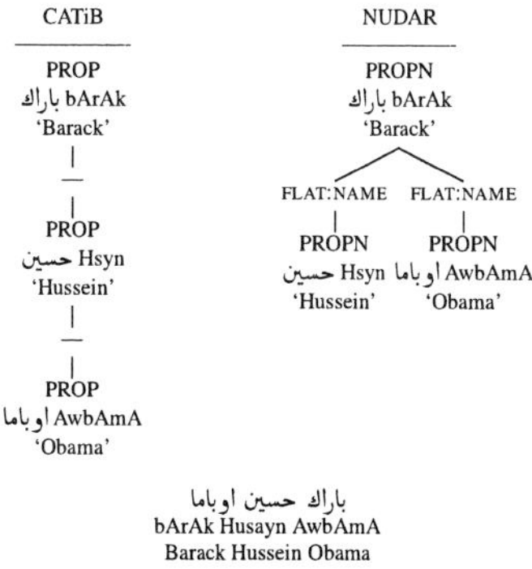

Figure 9: Proper Name Construct

Apposition is marked by the relation `appos` in NUDAR, as in Figure 10, opposed to the MOD relation it takes in CATiB.

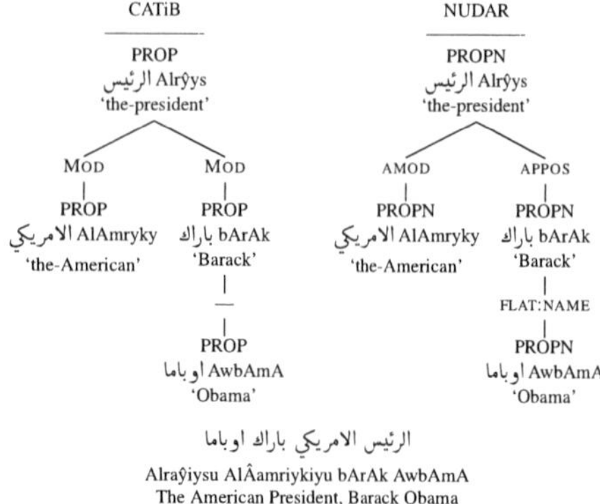

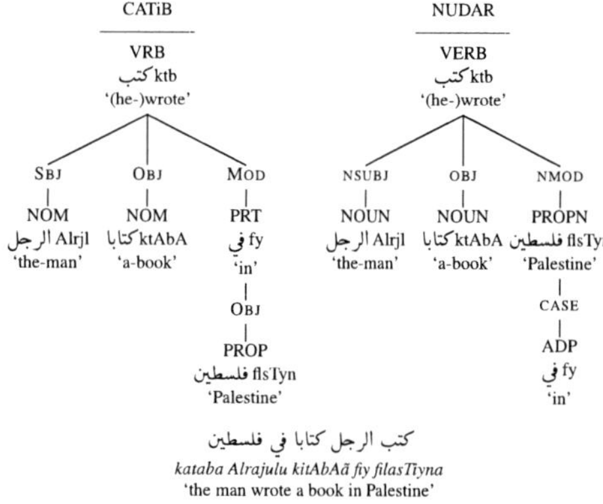

Figure 10: Apposition Construct

### 3.4.7 Preposition Constructs

Prepositions in NUDAR are case-marking elements that are dependent on the element they introduce. They attach low, unlike the CATiB structure. The label this relation takes is `case`, as can be seen in Figure 11.

Figure 11: Prepositional Construct

### 3.4.8 Copular Constructs

The basic copular construct in Arabic does not include copular verbs. It has the same tree structure in both CATiB and NUDAR. The predicate heads the relation, and the subject attaches to it with the label `SBJ` in CATiB and `nsubj` in NUDAR, as seen in Figure 12.

Some so-called *incomplete verbs* in Arabic, such as كان kAn 'to be', and verb-like particles, such as إِن Ăn 'indeed/verily' act like the copula verb *be* in English. Since copula verbs cannot be the heads of clauses, they attach to their predicates with the relation `cop`, like the example in Figure 13.

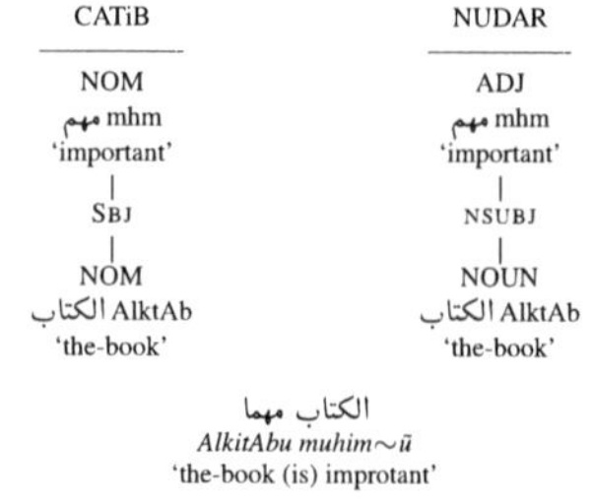

Figure 12: Basic Copular Construct

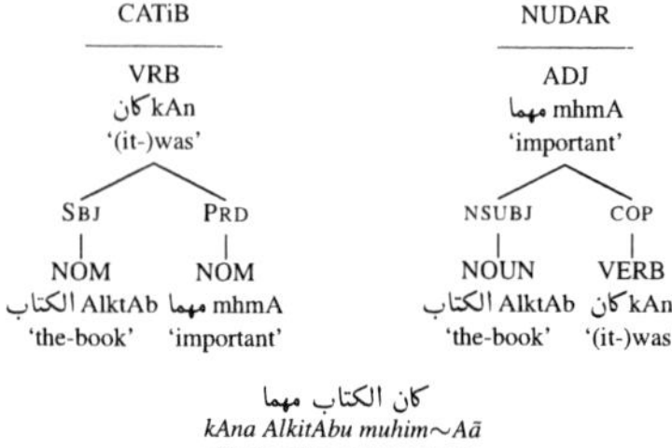

Figure 13: Copular Construct with Copular Verb

### 3.4.9 Subordinating Conjunction Constructs

Subordinating conjunctions introduce a finite clause that is subordinate to another clause. As with copula, they cannot head a clause. The subordinating clause's predicate becomes the parent of the subordinating conjunction, as shown in Figure 14.

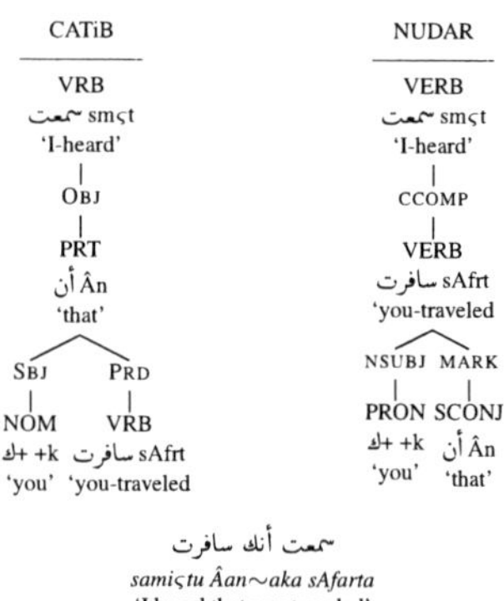

Figure 14: Subordinating Conjunction Construct

### 3.4.10 Clausal Complement Constructs

Clauses that are a core argument of a verb are attached to that verb with a `ccomp` or an `xcomp` relation. The `ccomp` relation is used for clauses that have their own subject, while `xcomp` refers to clauses with a subject that is the same as the subject of the verb that heads them. An example of a clause attaching with a `ccomp` relation is in Figure 15.

### 3.5 Validation

During our conversion process, we selected a random subset of 17 sentences, containing 608 tokens, from the TRAIN set. We manually created a gold reference for this set, and we used it to fine tune our convertor. After we froze the conversion, we converted a randomly selected subset of 82 sentences, containing 2,685 tokens, from the TEST set, that we automatically converted into NUDAR, and manually checked and fixed to create a gold test set. This gold subset was used to test the performance of the final version of the convertor. The scores that we got in both subsets against the gold were very high. We show the Labeled and Unlabeled Attachment Scores (LAS and UAS respectively) and Label Accuracy Score (LAcc) in Table 4.

|          | LAS    | UAS    | LAcc   |
|----------|--------|--------|--------|
| **Dev**  | 98.5%  | 98.8%  | 99.3%  |
| **Test** | 98.0%  | 99.1%  | 98.3%  |

Table 4: Conversion scores against manually created gold trees

An error analysis shows that the majority of the errors originated from the gold annotations of the PATB treebank. These errors are caused by either having the wrong dashtag, or attachment in the PATB trees (Habash et al., 2007a). A small number of errors were caused either by bugs in the conversion rules, or by missing rules.

### 3.6 Comparing PAUDT and NUDAR

A direct comparison between PAUDT and NUDAR proved hard to perform. Even though both treebanks follow the UD guidelines in general, there were many differences originating from the data sources, as well as from the interpretation of the guidelines. The data in PAUDT comes from portions of PATB parts 1 and 2, and from Arabic Gigaword. The data in the current NUDAR treebank comes from PATB parts 1, 2, and 3. In total, NUDAR contains 1,834 documents, and PAUDT contains 874 documents. The two treebanks overlap in 207 documents (based on document IDs). Within these shared documents, we find a number of differences such as PAUDT's

inclusion of article titles and full stop sentence segmentation, compared with missing article titles and occasional trees covering multiple sentences in NUDAR. Even among sentences that are similarly segmented, we find many tokenization differences: dates and times are tokenized differently (e.g., *11-5* vs *11 - 5*), as well as specific Arabic words that are treated differently (e.g., فيما *fyma* or في ما *fy mA* 'in that'). Out of the shared 207 documents, only 335 sentences had the same tokenization, and these had additional differences in POS choice as well as tree structures and labels. We plan a more detailed comparison in the future to help consolidate the two treebanks.

## 4 Parsing Experiment

We conducted some experiments to benchmark the parsing scores in the NUDAR treebank. We also compare the result of parsing directly in NUDAR space to parsing in CATiB space then converting to NUDAR representation.

For our parsing experiments, we used the MaltParser (Nivre et al., 2006) to train an Arabic dependency parser in the space of both CATiB and NUDAR. We compared the output of the NUDAR parser, to the results of converting the output of the CATiB parser to NUDAR using the system described in Section 3.

For the CATiB parser, we used the optimized settings described by Shahrour et al. (2016), and were able to achieve comparable results. We used the gold CATiBex POS tags (Marton et al., 2013), and gold morphological features derived from gold BW tags, to train the parser on the TRAIN dataset of PATB parts 1, 2, and 3. We tested on the TEST dataset of the same treebank parts. The output of the parser was then converted to NUDAR representation.

For the NUDAR parser, we ran the MaltOptimizer (Ballesteros and Nivre, 2012) on the full TRAIN dataset of NUDAR. We used the optimized settings to train and run our parser.

The results of these experiments are shown in Table 5. The first row shows the result of training the MaltParser on the NUDAR training dataset with the optimized settings. The second row shows the results of training the MatlParser on the CATiB training dataset, with the optimized settings from Shahrour et al. (2016). Finally, the last row shows the results of converting the output of the CATiB parser to NUDAR representation.

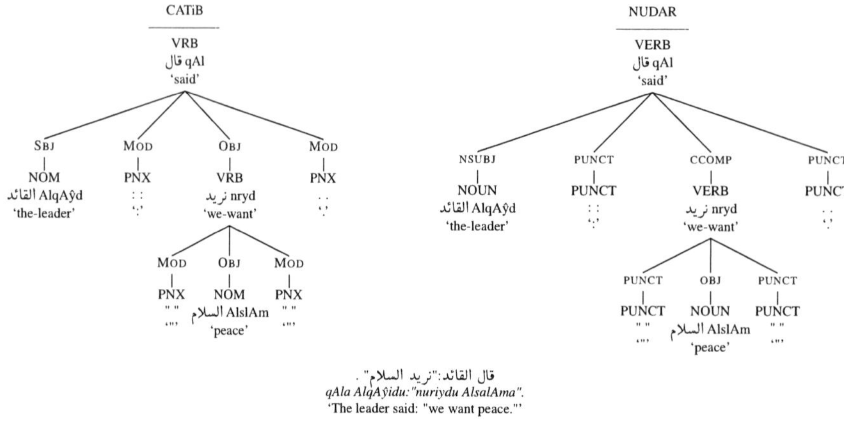



Figure 15: Clausal Complement Construct

Our results show that training a parser in NUDAR space produces better results than training a parser in CATiB space and converting the output to NUDAR representation. This can be attributed to the fact that the output of the CATiB parser does not produce the dashtags that are present in CATiB++, which help in the conversion process.

We also observe that the scores of the NUDAR parser are slightly lower than the scores of the CATiB parser. Although it is not possible to directly compare both parsers because of the different structures, we hypothesize that the larger label set in NUDAR (more than 40 labels compared to the eight labels of CATiB), and factors related to the structures, such as the longer distance between words and their parents in NUDAR (4.4 on average compared to 3.5 in CATiB) may be harder for a parser. We offer these insights as possible explanations, with the assumption that measuring and confirming these hypotheses need more research. It is also possible that further optimization will help increase the scores achieved by the NUDAR parser.

| System | REF | LAS | UAS | LAcc |
|---|---|---|---|---|
| *NUDAR-Parser* | *NUDAR-GOLD* | 81.9% | 83.7% | 93.8% |
| *CATiB-Parser* | *CATiB-Gold* | 83.1% | 85.0% | 94.3% |
| *CATiB-Parser+converted* | *NUDAR-GOLD* | 75.3% | 80.0% | 88.3% |

Table 5: Scores for the NUDAR and CATiB parsing and conversion experiments

## 5 Conclusion and Future Work

In this paper, we presented a fully automated converter from PATB to the UD syntactic representation. The conversion includes converting the POS tags and other morphological features, as well as the dependency relations and tree structures to UD, through a pipeline of conversion rules. The work was validated through a manually checked test set. We also present the results of an initial parsing experiment. This treebank will be made available as part of the UD v2.0 release as "UD Arabic-NYUAD".

In the future, we plan to improve the conversion process, and to convert the remaining available PATB parts, in both MSA and dialectal Arabic into the UD syntactic representation. We also plan on converting other Arabic dependency treebanks, such as the CATiB treebank, and the Quranic treebank (Dukes and Habash, 2010) into UD. This will require enriching these treebanks with additional morphosyntactic features, as per the techniques described by Alkuhlani et al. (2013). More experiments on optimizing the parsing process are planned, to make use of the available features to improve the parsing results. Finally, we plan on exploiting the NUDAR treebanks and parsers for use in other areas of NLP such as machine translation.

## Acknowledgments

The work done by the third author was supported by the grant 15-10472S of the Czech Science Foundation.

## References

Željko Agić and Nikola Ljubešić. 2015. Universal dependencies for croatian (that work for serbian, too).

In *The 5th Workshop on Balto-Slavic Natural Language Processing (BSNLP 2015)*.

Sarah Alkuhlani, Nizar Habash, and Ryan Roth. 2013. Automatic morphological enrichment of a morphologically underspecified treebank. In *HLT-NAACL*, pages 460–470.

Héctor Martínez Alonso and Daniel Zeman. 2016. Universal dependencies for the ancora treebanks. *Procesamiento del Lenguaje Natural*, 57:91–98.

Miguel Ballesteros and Joakim Nivre. 2012. Maltoptimizer: an optimization tool for maltparser. In *Proceedings of the Demonstrations at the 13th Conference of the European Chapter of the Association for Computational Linguistics*, pages 58–62. Association for Computational Linguistics.

Daša Berović, Željko Agić, and Marko Tadić. 2012. Croatian dependency treebank: Recent development and initial experiments. In *Seventh International Conference on Language Resources and Evaluation (LREC 2012)*.

Tim Buckwalter. 2002. Buckwalter Arabic Morphological Analyzer Version 1.0. Linguistic Data Consortium, University of Pennsylvania, 2002. LDC Catalog No.: LDC2002L49.

Tim Buckwalter. 2004. Buckwalter Arabic Morphological Analyzer Version 2.0. LDC catalog number LDC2004L02, ISBN 1-58563-324-0.

Marie-Catherine De Marneffe and Christopher D. Manning. 2008. The stanford typed dependencies representation. In *Coling 2008: proceedings of the workshop on cross-framework and cross-domain parser evaluation*, pages 1–8. Association for Computational Linguistics.

Marie-Catherine De Marneffe, Bill MacCartney, Christopher D. Manning, et al. 2006. Generating typed dependency parses from phrase structure parses. In *Proceedings of LREC*, volume 6, pages 449–454. Genoa.

Marie-Catherine De Marneffe, Timothy Dozat, Natalia Silveira, Katri Haverinen, Filip Ginter, Joakim Nivre, and Christopher D. Manning. 2014. Universal stanford dependencies: A cross-linguistic typology. In *LREC*, volume 14, pages 4585–92.

Mona Diab, Nizar Habash, Owen Rambow, and Ryan Roth. 2013. LDC Arabic treebanks and associated corpora: Data divisions manual. *arXiv preprint arXiv:1309.5652*.

Kais Dukes and Nizar Habash. 2010. Morphological Annotation of Quranic Arabic. In *Proceedings of the Language Resources and Evaluation Conference (LREC)*, Malta.

Sašo Džeroski, Tomaž Erjavec, Nina Ledinek, Petr Pajas, Zdenek Žabokrtsky, and Andreja Žele. 2006. Towards a slovene dependency treebank. In *Proc. of the Fifth Intern. Conf. on Language Resources and Evaluation (LREC)*.

David Graff, Ke Chen, Junbo Kong, and Kazuaki Maeda. 2006. *Arabic Gigaword*. Linguistic Data Consortium, Philadelphia, second edition.

Nizar Habash and Ryan M. Roth. 2009. CATiB: The Columbia Arabic Treebank. In *Proceedings of the ACL-IJCNLP 2009 Conference Short Papers*, pages 221–224. Association for Computational Linguistics.

Nizar Habash, Ryan Gabbard, Owen Rambow, Seth Kulick, and Mitchell P. Marcus. 2007a. Determining case in Arabic: Learning complex linguistic behavior requires complex linguistic features. In *EMNLP-CoNLL*, pages 1084–1092.

Nizar Habash, Abdelhadi Soudi, and Tim Buckwalter. 2007b. On Arabic Transliteration. In A. van den Bosch and A. Soudi, editors, *Arabic Computational Morphology: Knowledge-based and Empirical Methods*. Springer.

Nizar Habash, Reem Faraj, and Ryan Roth. 2009. Syntactic Annotation in the Columbia Arabic Treebank. In *Proceedings of MEDAR International Conference on Arabic Language Resources and Tools*, Cairo, Egypt.

Nizar Habash. 2010. *Introduction to Arabic natural language processing*, volume 3. Morgan & Claypool Publishers.

Jan Hajič, Eva Hajičová, Petr Pajas, Jarmila Panevová, Petr Sgall, and Barbora Vidová-Hladká. 2001. Prague Dependency Treebank 1.0. LDC catalog number LDC2001T10, ISBN 1-58563-212-0.

Jan Hajič, Otakar Smrž, Petr Zemánek, Petr Pajas, Jan Šnaidauf, Emanuel Beška, Jakub Kráčmar, and Kamila Hassanová. 2004. Prague Arabic dependency treebank 1.0. LDC2004T23. web download.

Anders Johannsen, Héctor Martínez Alonso, and Barbara Plank. 2015. Universal dependencies for danish. In *International Workshop on Treebanks and Linguisic Theories (TLT14)*, page 157.

Mohamed Maamouri, Ann Bies, Tim Buckwalter, and Wigdan Mekki. 2004. The Penn Arabic Treebank: Building a Large-Scale Annotated Arabic Corpus. In *NEMLAR Conference on Arabic Language Resources and Tools*, pages 102–109, Cairo, Egypt.

Mohamed Maamouri, Ann Bies, Sondos Krouna, Fatma Gaddeche, and Basma Bouziri, 2009. *Penn Arabic Treebank Guidelines*. Linguistic Data Consortium.

Mohamed Maamouri, Ann Bies, Seth Kulick, Fatma Gaddeche, Wigdan Mekki, Sondos Krouna, Basma Bouziri, and Wadji Zaghouani. 2010a. Arabic treebank: Part 1 v 4.1 ldc2010t13.

Mohamed Maamouri, Ann Bies, Seth Kulick, Sondos Krouna, Fatma Gaddeche, and Wadji Zaghouani. 2010b. Arabic treebank: Part 3 v 3.2 ldc2010t08.

Mohamed Maamouri, Ann Bies, Seth Kulick, Fatma Gaddeche, Wigdan Mekki, Sondos Krouna, Basma Bouziri, and Wadji Zaghouani. 2011. Arabic treebank: Part 2 v 3.1 ldc2011t09.

Mohamed Maamouri, Sondos Krouna, Dalila Tabessi, Nadia Hamrouni, and Nizar Habash. 2012. Egyptian Arabic Morphological Annotation Guidelines.

Mitchell P. Marcus, Beatrice Santorini, and Mary Ann Marcinkiewicz. 1993. Building a large annotated corpus of English: The Penn treebank. *Computational Linguistics*, 19(2):313–330, June.

Yuval Marton, Nizar Habash, and Owen Rambow. 2013. Dependency parsing of modern standard Arabic with lexical and inflectional features. *Computational Linguistics*, 39(1):161–194.

Ryan T. McDonald, Joakim Nivre, Yvonne Quirmbach-Brundage, Yoav Goldberg, Dipanjan Das, Kuzman Ganchev, Keith B Hall, Slav Petrov, Hao Zhang, Oscar Täckström, et al. 2013. Universal dependency annotation for multilingual parsing. In *ACL (2)*, pages 92–97.

Kadri Muischnek, Kaili Müürisep, Tiina Puolakainen, Eleri Aedmaa, Riin Kirt, and Dage Särg. 2014. Estonian dependency treebank and its annotation scheme. In *Proceedings of 13th Workshop on Treebanks and Linguistic Theories (TLT13)*, pages 285–291.

Jens Nilsson, Sebastian Riedel, and Deniz Yuret. 2007. The conll 2007 shared task on dependency parsing. In *Proceedings of the CoNLL shared task session of EMNLP-CoNLL*, pages 915–932. sn.

Joakim Nivre, Johan Hall, and Jens Nilsson. 2006. MaltParser: A data-driven parser-generator for dependency parsing. In *In Proc. of LREC-2006*, pages 2216–2219.

Joakim Nivre, Marie-Catherine de Marneffe, Filip Ginter, Yoav Goldberg, Jan Hajic, Christopher D. Manning, Ryan McDonald, Slav Petrov, Sampo Pyysalo, Natalia Silveira, Reut Tsarfaty, and Daniel Zeman. 2016. Universal dependencies v1: A multilingual treebank collection. In Nicoletta Calzolari (Conference Chair), Khalid Choukri, Thierry Declerck, Sara Goggi, Marko Grobelnik, Bente Maegaard, Joseph Mariani, Helene Mazo, Asuncion Moreno, Jan Odijk, and Stelios Piperidis, editors, *Proceedings of the Tenth International Conference on Language Resources and Evaluation (LREC 2016)*, Paris, France, may. European Language Resources Association (ELRA).

Joakim Nivre. 2014. Universal dependencies for Swedish. In *Proceedings of the Swedish Language Technology Conference (SLTC)*.

Joakim Nivre. 2016. Universal dependencies: Dubious linguistics and crappy parsing? COLING Keynote Talk.

Petya Osenova and Kiril Simov. 2015. Universalizing bultreebank: a linguistic tale about glocalization. *BSNLP 2015*, page 81.

Lilja Øvrelid and Petter Hohle. 2016. Universal dependencies for norwegian.

Arfath Pasha, Mohamed Al-Badrashiny, Mona Diab, Ahmed El Kholy, Ramy Eskander, Nizar Habash, Manoj Pooleery, Owen Rambow, and Ryan M. Roth. 2014. MADAMIRA: A Fast, Comprehensive Tool for Morphological Analysis and Disambiguation of Arabic. In *Proceedings of the Language Resources and Evaluation Conference (LREC), Reykjavik, Iceland*.

Slav Petrov, Dipanjan Das, and Ryan McDonald. 2011. A universal part-of-speech tagset. *arXiv preprint arXiv:1104.2086*.

Sampo Pyysalo, Jenna Kanerva, Anna Missilä, Veronika Laippala, and Filip Ginter. 2015. Universal dependencies for finnish. In *Proceedings of the 20th Nordic Conference of Computational Linguistics, NODALIDA 2015, May 11-13, 2015, Vilnius, Lithuania*, number 109, pages 163–172. Linköping University Electronic Press.

Rudolf Rosa, Jan Mašek, David Mareček, Martin Popel, Daniel Zeman, and Zdeněk Žabokrtský. 2014. HamleDT 2.0: Thirty dependency treebanks stanfordized. In Nicoletta Calzolari, Khalid Choukri, Thierry Declerck, Hrafn Loftsson, Bente Maegaard, and Joseph Mariani, editors, *Proceedings of the 9th International Conference on Language Resources and Evaluation (LREC 2014)*, pages 2334–2341, Reykjavík, Iceland. European Language Resources Association.

Mojgan Seraji, Filip Ginter, and Joakim Nivre. 2016. Universal dependencies for persian.

Anas Shahrour, Salam Khalifa, Dima Taji, and Nizar Habash. 2016. Camelparser: A system for arabic syntactic analysis and morphological disambiguation.

Otakar Smrž, Jan Šnaidauf, and Petr Zemánek. 2002. Prague Dependency Treebank for Arabic: Multi-Level Annotation of Arabic Corpus. In *Proceedings of the International Symposium on Processing of Arabic*, pages 147–155, Manouba, Tunisia.

Otakar Smrž, Viktor Bielický, Iveta Kouřilová, Jakub Kráčmar, Jan Hajič, and Petr Zemánek. 2008. Prague Arabic dependency treebank: A word on the million words. In *Proceedings of the Workshop on Arabic and Local Languages (LREC 2008)*, pages 16–23, Marrakech, Morocco. European Language Resources Association.

Naiwen Xue, Fei Xia, Fu-Dong Chiou, and Marta Palmer. 2005. The penn chinese treebank: Phrase structure annotation of a large corpus. *Natural language engineering*, 11(02):207–238.

Daniel Zeman. 2008. Reusable tagset conversion using tagset drivers. In *LREC*.

# A Layered Language Model based Hybrid Approach to Automatic Full Diacritization of Arabic

**Mohamed Al-Badrashiny, Abdelati Hawwari, Mona Diab**
Department of Computer Science
The George Washington University
{badrashiny,abhawwari,mtdiab}@gwu.edu

## Abstract

In this paper we present a system for automatic Arabic text diacritization using three levels of analysis granularity in a layered back off manner. We build and exploit diacritized language models (LM) for each of three different levels of granularity: surface form, morphologically segmented into prefix/stem/suffix, and character level. For each of the passes, we use Viterbi search to pick the most probable diacritization per word in the input. We start with the surface form LM, followed by the morphological level, then finally we leverage the character level LM. Our system outperforms all of the published systems evaluated against the same training and test data. It achieves a 10.87% WER for complete full diacritization including lexical and syntactic diacritization, and 3.0% WER for lexical diacritization, ignoring syntactic diacritization.

## 1 Introduction

Most languages have an orthographical system that reflects their phonological system. Orthographies vary in the way they represent word pronunciations. Arabic orthography employs an alphabetical system that comprises consonants and vowels. Short vowels are typically underspecified in the orthography. When present they appear as diacritical marks. Moreover, other phonological phenomena are represented with diacritics, such as letter doubling, syllable boundary markers, elongation, etc. In this paper, we are interested in restoring most of these diacritics, making them explicit in the written orthography. This process is referred to as diacritization/vowelization, or "tashkeel" in Arabic. Absence of these diacritics from the orthography renders the text extremely ambiguous. Accordingly, the task of diacritization is quite important for many NLP applications such as morphological analysis, text to speech, POS tagging, word sense disambiguation, and machine translation.

Moreover, from a human processing perspective, having the orthography reflect the diacritics explicitly makes for better readability comprehension and pronunciation.

## 2 Linguistic Background

Unlike English, Arabic comprises an alphabet list of 28 letters. Short vowels are not explicitly marked in typical orthography as stand alone letters. The Arabic orthographic system employs a list of diacritics to express short vowels. The Arabic writing system maybe conceived to comprise two levels: consonantal letters including consonants and long vowels; and diacritics indicating short vowels and other pronunciation markers which are typically written above and/or below such consonantal letters.

The Arabic diacritics relevant to our study can be characterized as follows:[1]

- Short vowels *(a, i, u)*:[2], corresponding to the three short vowels (fatha 'a', kasra 'i', damma 'u'). They can occur word medially and/or word finally;

- Nunation "Tanween" *(F, K, N)*: these occur word finally only and they correspond to either an *an* 'F' , *in* 'K', or an *un* 'N' sound. They indicate indefinite nominals as well as

---

[1]There are other diacritics that we don't consider in the context of this work.

[2]We use Buckwalter (BW) transliteration scheme to represent Arabic in Romanized script throughout the paper. http://www.qamus.org/transliteration.htm



*Proceedings of The Third Arabic Natural Language Processing Workshop (WANLP)*, pages 177–184,
Valencia, Spain, April 3, 2017. ©2017 Association for Computational Linguistics

they could mark adverbials and some frozen expressions.

- Gemination (~), aka "shaddah": indicating doubling of the preceding character;

- Sukoun *o*: marks the absence of a vowel, typically appears between syllables, as well as word finally to indicate jussive syntactic mood for verbs.

Diacritization reflects morphological (including phonology) and grammatical information. Accordingly, in this paper we make a distinction between the two types of diacritization as follows:

**A) Morphological Diacritization:** Reflect the manner by which words are pronounced, not including the word final diacritization except the last letter diacritization. Morphological diacritization could be further subdivided into:

- Word structure or lexical diacritization: this represents the internal structure of words, that distinguish different possible readings of a phonologically ambiguous word (homograph) when the diacritics are missing. For instance, the Arabic word *mlk* could have the following readings: *malik* (king), *malak*(angel/he possessed), *mulok*(kingdom/property), *milok*(ownership), or *mal ak* (gave possession to another);

- Inflectional diacritization: this represents the morphophonemic level of handling affixations (prefixes, suffixes and clitics), how morphemes interact with each other, making possible morphophonemic changes which are reflected in the phonological and orthographic systems. For example the Arabic word *qAblthm* could be *qAbalatohum* (I met them), *qAbalotahum* (you_masc. met them), *qAbalatohum* (she met them) or *qAbalotihim*(you_fem. met them).

**B) Syntactic Diacritization:** Syntactic functions are represented by adding one of short vowels or nunation to the end of most of Arabic words, indicating the word's grammatical function in the sentence. For example, in a sentence like "*zAra Alwaladu zamiylahu*" (the boy visited his colleague), the diacritization of the last letters in the words *Alwaladu* and *zamiyla* indicate the syntactic roles of grammatical subject **u**, and grammatical object **a**, respectively.

## 2.1 Levels of Diacritization

Although native speakers of Arabic can read the majority of Arabic script without explicit diacritical marks being present, some diacritic symbols in some cases are crucial in order to disambiguate/pronounce homographical words. Historically, diacritics were invented by Arabic grammarians more than 200 years after the emergence of the Arabic writing system which was primarily consonantal. In Modern Standard Arabic (MSA) script, there are several levels of possible diacritization:

- **No Diacritization**: This level is completely underspecified. The script is subject to ambiguity, especially with homographical words;

- **Full Diacritization**: The reverse where there is complete specification, namely where each consonant is followed by a diacritic. This level is used more in classical and educational writing;

- **Partial Diacritization**: This level is anywhere in between the two previous levels, typically writer dependent. In this case, the writer adds diacritics where s/he deems fit (Zaghouani et al., 2016).

## 2.2 Challenges

There are a number of challenges in Arabic diacritization, we can list some of them as follows:

- **Morphological aspects**: Some Arabic words serve as a phrase or full sentence such as *waS alatohA* (she delivered her), *waS alotuhA* (I delivered her), and *waS alotihA* (you_feminine drove her);

- **Syntactic aspects**: Arabic is a free word-order language, syntactic functions are realized on the morphological level via word final diacritization in most cases. However, we note changes to the penultimate orthographic realization of the consonants due to syntactic position. For example, *>abonA&uhu*, *>abonA}ihi*, and *>abonA'ahu*, all corresponding to "his sons" but reflect different syntactic case: nominative, genitive, accusative, respectively.

- **Phonological aspects**: The phonological system exhibits assimilation in cases of affixation word finally. For example the word final possessive suffix *h* meaning "his" in the following word takes on the same vowel/diacritic as that of the lexeme it is attached to: *kitAbi+hi* (his book) and *kitAbu+hu* (his book). It is important to note that the short vowel diacritic attached to the *h* suffix has no semantic or syntactic interpretation, it is a pure assimilation vowel harmony effect.

## 3 Approach

Figure 1 illustrates the system architecture of our proposed solution for MSA Full diacritization. Our approach relies on having fully diacritized data for building various types of language models at training time: a word level language model (WLM), a morpheme level language model (MLM), a character+diacritic level language model (CLM). The WLM is created in the diacritized untokenized surface level words. We experiment with 1-5 gram WLMs. The MLM are created using the same WLMs but after tokenizing them into prefix, stem, and suffix components where each is fully diacritized. Thus each 1 gram in the WLM is equivalent to 3 grams in the MLM, i.e. this renders MLMs of 3, 6, 9, 12, and 15, corresponding to the WLM of 1, 2, 3, 4, 5, respectively. Finally for CLMs, we are using the WLMs but after segmenting them into characters+associated diacritics. The maximum gram size we managed to build is 20 grams. Thus, each 1 gram in the word level WLM is equivalent to 4 grams in the character level, given that the smallest word in Arabic is two consonants long which is equivalent to 4 characters, i.e. each consonant is associated with at least one diacritic. This means that the LMs we are experimenting with for the character level are of sizes 4, 8, 12, 16, and 20 grams.

At test time, the undiacritized input text goes through the following pipeline:

**a) Word-Level Diacritization:** In this step, we leverage the WLM created at train time using all possible diacritizations for each word in the input raw text using the training data. If there are new words (out of vocabulary [OOV]) that have not been seen in the training data, they are tagged as unknown (UNK). A lattice search technique (for example: Viterbi or A* search) is then used to select the best diacritization for each word based on context.

**b) Morpheme Level Diacritization:** The output from the first step is being morphologically analyzed using SAMA (Maamouri et al., 2010). We only keep the morphological analyses that match the diacritization from the WLM. But if there is any word that is tagged as UNK, we keep all of its morphological analyses if they exist. If SAMA failed to find a possible morphological solution for any word (ex: non-Arabic word), it is marked as UNK. The MLM is used via a lattice search technique to pick the best morphological solution for each word; hence the best diacritization.

**c) Character-Level Diacritization:** If there are still some UNK words after steps (a) and (b), the CLM is used to find a plausible solution for them.

## 4 Experimental Setup

### 4.1 Data

Several studies have been carried out on the problem of full automatic diacritization for MSA. Five of these studies, that also yield the most competitive results despite approaching the problem in different ways, use and report on the same exact data sets. These studies are Zitouni et al. (2006), Habash and Rambow (2007), Rashwan et al. (2011), Abandah et al. (2015), and Belinkov and Glass (2015). We will use the same data which is LDC's Arabic Treebank of diacritized news stories-Part 3 v1.0: catalog number LDC2004T11 and ISBN 1-58563-298-8. The corpus includes complete Full diacritization comprising both morphological and syntactic diacritization. This corpus includes 600 documents from the Annahar News Text. There are a total of 340,281 words. The data is split as follows into two sets:

- Training data comprising approximately 288K words;

- Test data (TEST): comprises 90 documents selected by taking the last 15% of the total number of documents in chronological order dating from "20021015 0101" to "20021215 0045". It comprises approximately 52K words.

But having a single set TEST serving as both test and dev data is not correct which is what previous studies have done. Therefore, we split the data into three parts instead of two. We split off 10% of the training data and use it as a development set, rendering our training data (TRAIN) to

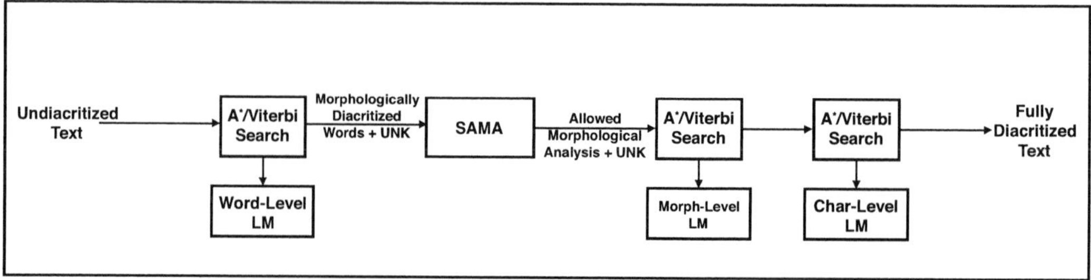

Figure 1: System Architecture.

comprise only 90% of the original training data. We keep the same exact test data, TEST, as the previous studies however. Accordingly, the new current training data for this paper is roughly 259K words and the development set (DEV) comprises approximately 29K words. DEV is used for tuning our system.

In all of our experiments, we use TRAIN to train and build our models and DEV to find the best configuration parameters. TEST is used as held out data. It is only evaluated using the resulting best models on DEV.

### 4.2 Evaluation Metrics

We adopt the same metrics used by Zitouni et al. (2006), Habash and Rambow (2007), Rashwan et al. (2011), Abandah et al. (2015), and Belinkov and Glass (2015). These are word error rate (WER) and character error rate (CER). CER compares the predicted words to the gold words on the character level. WER compares the predicted diacritized word as a whole to the gold diacritized word. If there is one error in a word, the whole word is considered incorrect. All words are evaluated including digits and punctuation. In the case of morphological diacritization, word final diacritics are ignored. In the case of syntactic diacritization only word final diacritics are considered. Finally in the Full diacritization case, both morphological and syntactic diacritization are considered.

### 4.3 Baselines

We compare our approach against the following baselines:[3]

- Zitouni et al.: The best published results by Zitouni et al. (2006);

- Habash et al.: The best published results by Habash and Rambow (2007);

- Rashwan et al.: The best published results by Rashwan et al. (2011);

- Abandah et al.: The best published results by Abandah et al. (2015);

- Belinkov and Glass: The best published results by Belinkov and Glass (2015).

## 5 Evaluation

Table 1 illustrates the morphological and Full (morphological+syntactic) diacritization performance on DEV using the lattice search on the word, morpheme, and character levels. The language models are all built using the TRAIN dataset.

The table shows five experiments using A* search using 1, 2, 3, 4, and 5 grams LMs.[4] And two experiments using Viterbi search because the implementation we have for the Viterbi search supports 2 grams as a maximum size. The best performance is yielded by the Viterbi algorithm and 2-grams LMs (i.e. 2-grams for WLM, 6-grams for MLM, and 8-grams for CLM). It yields 6.11% WER for Full diacritization (FULL), corresponding to 2.61% WER for morphological diacritization (MORPH), i.e. by ignoring word final syntactic diacritics.

Table 2 compares the performance of our system to the baselines systems. It shows that our system is outperforming all of the published CER and WER on "MORPH" level. On "FULL" level, we outperform all of the baselines except (Abandah et al., 2015). They are doing better on the syntactic level diacritization. Their system is based

---

[3]The descriptions of these baselines systems are in section: 7-Related Work

[4]Note: every 1-gram in word level is equivalent to 3-grams morphological level and 4-grams in characters level

| Lattice Search Method | LM-Size | FULL | | MORPH | |
|---|---|---|---|---|---|
| | | WER | CER | WER | CER |
| Viterbi | 1 | 6.67% | 1.14% | 3.13% | 0.61% |
| **Viterbi** | **2** | **6.11%** | **1.06%** | **2.61%** | **0.55%** |
| A* | 1 | 6.51% | 1.09% | 3.01% | 0.57% |
| A* | 2 | 6.28% | 1.04% | 2.77% | 0.53% |
| A* | 3 | 6.26% | 1.04% | 2.74% | 0.53% |
| A* | 4 | 6.26% | 1.04% | 2.74% | 0.53% |
| A* | 5 | 6.18% | 1.03% | 2.66% | 0.51% |

Table 1: System performance on DEV. The best setup is by using the Viterbi algorithm via 2 grams LMs.

on a deep bidirectional long short-term memory (LSTM) model. These kinds of models can exploit long-range contexts; which could yield the better performance on the syntactic diacritization level. It is also worth mentioning that they are using a post-processing correction layer that applies some rules to fix some of the diacritization errors after the LSTM.

It should be highlighted, that in contrast to the previous studies, TEST remained a complete held out data set that was not explored at all during the tuning phase of the system development, where for the previous studies TEST was used as both a development and test set.

## 6 Error Analysis

By reviewing the errors rendered by our system and comparing them to the gold data we discovered several issues in the training and test data that affected the performance and evaluation results. We list them as follows:

**Undiacritized words:** There are many cases in both the training and test data where the words are completely undiacritized. Since we rely on fully diacritized texts to build our various language models, this type of error affects our system in two ways:

- Errors in the training data affect the quality of the language models that are built;

- Errors in the test data decrease the accuracy of our system because such cases are being counted as incorrect even if they are correctly diacritized by our system. Upon manual inspection, for example, our system renders the correct diacritization for the words: *xal af* "left behind/gave birth" and *bAruwd* "gun powder" are counted as errors because

they are not diacritized at all in the gold test data set).

**Missing Case marker:** 25.2% of the syntactic diacritization errors are due to missing syntactic diacritization from the gold TEST words. Table 3 illustrates some examples of that.

## 7 Related Work

Many research efforts addressed the problem of automatic full Arabic diacritization, especially for MSA.

Gal (2002) developed a statistical system using HMM to restore Arabic diacritics and applied it on the Holy Quran as a corpus. Their approach did not include any language-specific knowledge. This system achieved a WER of 86% for morphological diacritization without syntactic diacritization.

El-Imam (2004) developed a comprehensive set of well-defined language-dependent rules, that are augmented by a dictionary, to be used in the transcription of graphemes into phonemes.

Nelken and Shieber (2005) developed a probabilistic model for Arabic diacritization using a finite state transducer, and trigram word and character based language models. Their approach used the ATB and achieved 7.33% WER without case endings (morphological diacritization) and 23.61% WER with case ending.

Ananthakrishnan et al. (2005) leveraged a word-level trigram model combined with a four-gram character language model. The authors used ATB as training data and used the LDC TDT4 Broadcast News data set as test data. The reported word accuracy using this model was 80.21%.

Zitouni et al. (2006) presented a statistical model based on a Maximum Entropy framework. Their approach integrates different sources of

| | | FULL | | MORPH | |
|---|---|---|---|---|---|
| **Training Data** | **System** | **WER** | **CER** | **WER** | **CER** |
| TRAIN+DEV | Zitouni et al. | 18.00% | 5.50% | 7.90% | 2.50% |
| TRAIN+DEV | Habash et al. | 14.90% | 4.80% | 5.50% | 2.20% |
| TRAIN+DEV | Rashwan et al. | 12.50% | 3.80% | 3.10% | 1.20% |
| TRAIN+DEV | Abandah et al. | **9.07%** | **2.72%** | 4.34% | 1.38% |
| TRAIN | Belinkov and Glass | N/A | 4.85 | N/A | N/A |
| TRAIN | Our System | 10.90% | 1.60% | **3.10%** | **0.60%** |
| TRAIN+DEV | Our System | 10.87% | 1.60% | **3.00%** | **0.59%** |

Table 2: Our System performance against baselines

| **Word** | **POS** |
|---|---|
| *AlHumayoDiy~* | DET+NOUN_PROP |
| *mud~ap* | NOUN+NSUFF_FEM_SG |
| *waragom* | CONJ+NOUN |
| *Eam~An* | NOUN_PROP |
| *gayor* | NOUN |
| *IixorAj* | NOUN |

Table 3: Examples for the missing syntactic diacritics in TEST

knowledge including lexical, segment-based and POS features. They achieved a CER of 5.5% and a WER of 18.0% for morphological and syntactic diacritization. By ignoring case endings, they obtained a CER of 2.5% and a WER of 7.9%.

Elshafei et al. (2006) proposed a diacritic restoration system which uses HMM for modeling and a Viterbi algorithm to select the most probable diacritized form of a sentence. The result was 4.1% errors in the diacritical marking of letters.

Habash and Rambow (2007) proposed a diacritization system that is based on a lexical resource, combining a tagger and a lexeme language model. The system gets a list with all potential analysis for each word, then applies a series of Support Vector Machine (SVM) classifiers to several morphological dimensions, then combines the various values for the dimensions to decide on the final analysis chosen from among the various possible analyses provided by an underlying morphological analyzer such as BAMA. They achieved a CER of 5.5% and a WER of 14.9% for morphological and syntactic diacritization. And CER of 2.2% and a WER of 5.5% by ignoring case endings.

Shaalan et al. (2009) proposed a hybrid approach that relies on lexicon retrieval, a bigram word level language model, and SVM classification. The system achieves a reported WER of 12.16% for combined morphological and syntactic diacritization.

Rashwan et al. (2011) developed a hybrid approach with a two-layer stochastic system. They split the input sentence into smaller segments, where each segment is consisting of at leas one word. Then they use a WLM to diacritize the segments that all of its words can be found in the unigrams of the WLM. Another MLM is used to diacritize the segments that are out of vocabulary from the point of view if the WLM. The final output is the combination of the all segments. They achieved 12.5% WER and 3.8% for combined morphological and syntactic diacritization. And 3.1% WER and 1.2% CER by ignoring the case ending.

Hifny (2012) developed a diacritic restoration system which uses dynamic programming (DP), n-gram language model, and smoothing. The author reported a WER of 3.4% for morphological diacritization and a WER 8.9% for combined morphological and syntactic diacritization.

MADAMIRA (Pasha et al., 2014) is a morphological analysis and disambiguation tool of Arabic. It applies SVM and language models to predict the word's morphological features. The diacritization accuracy of MADAMIRA is 86.3% on MSA and 83.2% on the Egyptian dialect.

Abandah et al. (2015) trained a recurrent neural network (RNN) to transcribe undiacritized Arabic text with fully diacritized sentences. After that they used some post-processing correction rules to correct the output from the RNN. For example, if the undiacritized word can be found in the training data but its diacritization by the the RNN does not exist, they replace the output diacritization by the variant from the training data leveraging a minimum edit distance algorithm. They achieved a CER of 2.72% and a WER of 9.07% for morphological and syntactic diacritization. And CER of 1.38% and a WER of 4.34% by ignoring case endings.

Belinkov and Glass (2015) developed a recurrent neural network with long-short term memory (LSTM) layers for predicting diacritics in Arabic text. They achieved a CER of 4.85% for morphological and syntactic diacritization.

Although the system of Rashwan et al. (2011) looks close to our system, but there is a significant difference between the two systems. The method they used of splitting the input sentence into smaller segments and diacritizing each segment separate from others, results in information loss yielding a suboptimal solution. Unlike, their approach, we do not split the sentences at the OOV words. Instead, we pass on the probability values of the unknowns. Therefore, even if there are one or more words that are OOV from the point of view of any of our LMs, the searching technique remains able to benefits from surrounding words.

## 8 Conclusion

In this paper we introduce a hybrid approach to full Arabic diacritization that leverages three underlying language models on different levels of linguistic representation with a filtering step that relies on a morphological analyzer to find the most probable diacritization for undiacritized surface form Arabic text in context. The results show that the presented approach outperforms all published systems to date using the same training and test data.

## References


Gheith A. Abandah, Alex Graves, Balkees Al-Shagoor, Alaa Arabiyat, Fuad Jamour, and Majid Al-Taee. 2015. Automatic diacritization of arabic text using recurrent neural networks. *International Journal on Document Analysis and Recognition (IJDAR)*, 18(2):183–197.

Sankaranarayanan Ananthakrishnan, Srinivas Bangalore, and Shrikanth S. Narayanan. 2005. Automatic diacritization of arabic transcripts for automatic speech recognition. In *Proceedings of the International Conference on Natural Language Processing (ICON)*, Kanpur, India, December.

Yonatan Belinkov and James Glass. 2015. Arabic diacritization with recurrent neural networks. In *Proceedings of the 2015 Conference on Empirical Methods in Natural Language Processing*, pages 2281–2285, Lisbon, Portugal, September. Association for Computational Linguistics.

Yousif A. El-Imam. 2004. Phonetization of arabic: rules and algorithms. *Computer Speech and Language*, 18(4):339 – 373.

Moustafa Elshafei, Husni Al-muhtaseb, and Mansour Alghamdi. 2006. Statistical methods for automatic diacritization of arabic text. In *Proceedings of Saudi 18th National Computer Conference (NCC18)*, Riyadh, Saudi Arabia.

Ya'akov Gal. 2002. An hmm approach to vowel restoration in arabic and hebrew. In *Proceedings of the ACL-02 Workshop on Computational Approaches to Semitic Languages*, SEMITIC '02, pages 1–7, Stroudsburg, PA, USA. Association for Computational Linguistics.

Nizar Habash and Owen Rambow. 2007. Arabic diacritization through full morphological tagging. In *Human Language Technologies 2007: The Conference of the North American Chapter of the Association for Computational Linguistics; Companion Volume, Short Papers*, NAACL-Short '07, pages 53–56, Stroudsburg, PA, USA. Association for Computational Linguistics.

Yasser Hifny. 2012. Higher order n-gram language models for arabic diacritics restoration. In *Proceedings of the 12th Conference on Language Engineering (ESOLEC 12)*, Cairo, Egypt.

Mohamed Maamouri, Dave Graff, Basma Bouziri, Sondos Krouna, Ann Bies, and Seth Kulick. 2010. Ldc standard arabic morphological analyzer (sama) version 3.1.

Rani Nelken and Stuart M. Shieber. 2005. Arabic diacritization using weighted finite-state transducers. In *Proceedings of the ACL Workshop on Computational Approaches to Semitic Languages*, Semitic '05, pages 79–86, Stroudsburg, PA, USA. Association for Computational Linguistics.

Arfath Pasha, Mohamed Al-Badrashiny, Mona Diab, Ahmed El Kholy, Ramy Eskander, Nizar Habash, Manoj Pooleery, Owen Rambow, and Ryan M. Roth. 2014. MADAMIRA: A Fast, Comprehensive Tool for Morphological Analysis and Disambiguation of Arabic. In *Proceedings of LREC*, Reykjavik, Iceland.

M. A.A. Rashwan, M. A.S.A.A. Al-Badrashiny, M. Attia, S. M. Abdou, and A. Rafea. 2011. A stochastic arabic diacritizer based on a hybrid of factorized and unfactorized textual features. *Trans. Audio, Speech and Lang. Proc.*, 19(1):166–175, January.

Khaled Shaalan, Hitham M. Abo Bakr, and Ibrahim Ziedan. 2009. A hybrid approach for building arabic diacritizer. In *Proceedings of the EACL 2009 Workshop on Computational Approaches to Semitic*

*Languages*, Semitic '09, pages 27–35, Stroudsburg, PA, USA. Association for Computational Linguistics.

Wajdi Zaghouani, Houda Bouamor, Abdelati Hawwari, Mona Diab, Ossama Obeid, Mahmoud Ghoneim, Sawsan Alqahtani, and Kemal Oflazer. 2016. Guidelines and framework for a large scale arabic diacritized corpus. In Nicoletta Calzolari (Conference Chair), Khalid Choukri, Thierry Declerck, Sara Goggi, Marko Grobelnik, Bente Maegaard, Joseph Mariani, Helene Mazo, Asuncion Moreno, Jan Odijk, and Stelios Piperidis, editors, *Proceedings of the Tenth International Conference on Language Resources and Evaluation (LREC 2016)*, Paris, France, may. European Language Resources Association (ELRA).

Imed Zitouni, Jeffrey S. Sorensen, and Ruhi Sarikaya. 2006. Maximum entropy based restoration of arabic diacritics. In *Proceedings of the 21st International Conference on Computational Linguistics and the 44th Annual Meeting of the Association for Computational Linguistics*, ACL-44, pages 577–584, Stroudsburg, PA, USA. Association for Computational Linguistics.

# Arabic Textual Entailment with Word Embeddings

**Nada Almarwani** and **Mona Diab**
Department of Computer Science
The George Washington University
{nadaoh;mtdiab}@gwu.edu

## Abstract

Determining the textual entailment between texts is important in many NLP tasks, such as summarization, question answering, and information extraction and retrieval. Various methods have been suggested based on external knowledge sources; however, such resources are not always available in all languages and their acquisition is typically laborious and very costly. Distributional word representations such as word embeddings learned over large corpora have been shown to capture syntactic and semantic word relationships. Such models have contributed to improving the performance of several NLP tasks. In this paper, we address the problem of textual entailment in Arabic. We employ both traditional features and distributional representations. Crucially, we do not depend on any external resources in the process. Our suggested approach yields state of the art performance on a standard data set, ArbTE, achieving an accuracy of 76.2 % compared to current state of the art of 69.3 %.

## 1 Introduction

Recently, there have been a number of studies addressing the problem of Recognizing Textual Entailment (RTE). The core problem is to recognize semantic variability in textual expression, which can potentially have the same meaning (Dagan et al., 2010). Modeling this phenomenon has a significant impact on various NLP applications, such as question answering, machine translation, and summarization. Textual Entailment (TE) can be defined as a directional entailment relation between a pair of text fragments; if the meaning of the Hypothesis (H) can be inferred from the Text (T) (Dagan et al., 2006). Since the first PASCAL RTE challenge (Dagan et al., 2006) to date, different approaches have been proposed. A popular trend is the use of supervised machine learning approaches that rely on extracting a set of features based on the underlying syntactic/semantic/lexical relation between the TH pair. Most of the approaches have been applied and tested on English TE.

Arabic, on the other hand, has relatively fewer studies for entailment detection. It is one of the most complex languages to process due to its morphological richness and relatively free word order as well as its diglossic nature (where the standard and the dialects mix in most genres of data). Moreover, Arabic still lacks the large scale hand-crafted computational resources that have come in very handy for English such as a large Word-Net (Miller, 1995) or a resource such as VerbOcean (Chklovski and Pantel, 2004). Hence building a reliable RTE system for Arabic poses more challenges than those faced when dealing with English. Accordingly, in this paper, we propose an approach that does not rely on such external resources but rather on modeling word relations derived from large scale corpora.

The rest of this paper is organized as follows: Section 2 provides an overview of textual entailment works in both English and Arabic, Section 3 describes the basic features and word distributional representation based features, Results and an evaluation of the system are presented in Section 4, and we conclude in Section 5.

## 2 Related Work

Since the start of the PASCAL RTE challenges in 2005 up until 2011, a large number of methods and approaches have been proposed. The



*Proceedings of The Third Arabic Natural Language Processing Workshop (WANLP)*, pages 185–190,
Valencia, Spain, April 3, 2017. ©2017 Association for Computational Linguistics

entailment judgment is typically cast as a classification decision: *true* entailment if the relation holds and *false* otherwise. Therefore, most of the proposed systems have been based on machine learning approaches which model the entailment relation over a variety of conventional features varying from basic lexical features to deep semantic features (Inkpen et al., ; Pakray et al., 2011; Zanzotto and Moschitti, 2006; Malakasiotis and Androutsopoulos, 2007). External semantic resources such as WordNet and VerbOcean have been extensively used to capture the semantic relationships between words in the H and T, and also to further enhance the entailment recognition system (Iftene and Moruz, 2009; Mehdad et al., 2009). Using such resources, the authors explicitly model lexical and semantic features (Zanzotto et al., 2009; Sammons et al., 2009; Clinchant et al., 2006; Mehdad et al., 2009; Wang and Neumann, 2008; Moschitti, 2006). Other methods rely on dependency tree representations using different computations ranging from basic common edge count (Malakasiotis and Androutsopoulos, 2007) to syntactic dependency analysis on corresponding text pairs (Wang and Neumann, 2007).

Recent advances in modeling word representations are shown to be useful for many NLP tasks. Zhao et al., (2015) investigated the effectiveness of word embeddings in different tasks including TE. The focus of this work is Arabic TE, which to the best of our knowledge, has few studies in the entailment literature. In 2011, Alabbas (2011) develops the ArbTE system to assess existing TE techniques when applied to Arabic TE. Later work proposed the use of extended tree edit distance with subtrees resulting in a more flexible matching algorithm to identify TE in Arabic (Alabbas and Ramsay, 2013). Moreover, others have looked closely at negation and polarity as additional features (AL-Khawaldeh, 2015) both of which resulted in better Arabic TE recognition performance, 61% and 69% accuracy, respectively.

## 3 Approach

Similar to previous approaches to the RTE, we cast the problem as a binary classification task. Namely, we identify if a T entails an H. We model the problem within a supervised framework. We rely on the following set of features in our modeling.

### 3.1 Features

1. Length: entailment is a directional relation and in general T may include more information, therefore, in most cases T and H are similar in their length or H is shorter than T. Therefore, the following set of features are used to record the length information of a given pair using the following measures: $|B - A|, |A \cap B|, \frac{(|B|-|A|)}{|A|}, \frac{(|A|-|B|)}{|B|}, \frac{|A \cap B|}{|B|}$, where $|A|$ represents the number of unique instances in A, $|B - A|$ refers to the number of unique instances that are in B but not in A, and $|A \cap B|$ represents the number of instances that are in both A and B. We applied them at the token, lemma, and stem levels.

2. Similarity score: A similar pair is more likely to share more words and hence the entailment relation holds. Therefore, a two typical similarity measures Jaccard (Jaccard, 1901) and Dice (Dice, 1945) have been used to measure the similarity between the TH pair at the token, lemma, and stem levels. In particular: $Jaccard(A, B) = \frac{|A \cap B|}{|A \cup B|}$; and $Dice(A, B) = \frac{2|A \cap B|}{|A| + |B|}$.

3. Named Entity: Recognizing the similarity and differences between name entity instances in the pair plays an important role in recognizing entailment. Therefore, we use NERAr (Gahbiche-Braham et al., 2014) to extract the following entities: Organization, Person, and Location, then we represent each of them as a bag of words and we use the length based feature explained in 1 resulting in 5 features for each named entity in the extracted categories. For example, if a location name in T appears as "The United State of America" and in H appears as "United States" or "America". Then the length feature $\frac{|A \cap B|}{|B|}$ from 1 gives the percentage of NEs overlapping between T and H; i.e. if "United States" is the NE found, then the percentage overlap between the T and H is 40%, and if the NE is "America" then the percentage overlap is 20%.;

4. Word Embeddings: Word embeddings capture word meaning and paraphrases which should overcome the lack of explicit lexical overlap between the TH pair. We derive word vector representations for about 556K words

using the Word2vec (w2v) (Mikolov et al., 2013) model built using the standard implementation,[1] Namely, we use commonly set parameters: the skip-gram architecture with 300 dimensions for the vectors, window size set to 10. We use inverse document frequency (IDF) scores as dimension values for the input matrix to the w2v. For each TH pair, we obtain the following features: 1. The cosine distance between the T and H vectors which consider both matched and unmatched words; and, b) The cosine distance between the T-H and H-T vectors which consider unmatched words only; specifically, they represent the words in T that are not in H and vice versa, respectively. The latter provides for additional evidence for the distance between T and H. Each vector is calculated as follows:

$$Vector = \sum_{i=1}^{n} IDF(Wi) \cdot w2v(Wi)$$

For example, given the following TH pair:[2]

**T**: lys bEAlm Algyb AlA Allh.
**H**: lA ydrk Algyb AlA Allh.
**English Translation of Both T and H**: Only God knows the unseen.

The T-H vector in the above example is the sum of two vectors: "lA" and "ydrk", which are the words in T and that are not in H, each multiplied by its IDF score.

## 4 Experiments and Result

### 4.1 Data

We use the annotated data used in previous studies, ArbTE (Alabbas, 2013), which comprises 600 TH pairs in Modern Standard Arabic (MSA). The ArbTE has been collected from news websites and annotated for entailment manually (Alabbas and Ramsay, 2012). For the word embedding models we use Arabic Gigaword (Parker et al., 2011), the Arabic Treebank (ATB) (Maamouri et al., 2008) and Wikipedia.[3]

All the data, ArbTE and the data used for deriving the word embeddings, are preprocessed in the same manner using the following preprocessing steps: SPLIT (Al-Badrashiny et al., 2016) is used to check if the word is a number, date, URL, or punctuation. Then all URLs and punctuation are removed and numbers and dates are normalized to Num and Date, respectively. Next, Alef and Yaa characters are normalized each to a single form which is typical in large scale Arabic NLP applications. For tokenization, lemmatization and stemming we use MADAMIRA (Pasha et al., 2014). We apply the D3 tokenization scheme which segments determiners as well as proclitics and enclitics; i.e. the D3 tokenization scheme is similar to the ATB scheme with the extra tokenization of the determiner Al. Finally, we remove stop words based on a list,[4] however, we keep negation words as we believe they are important for TE. As a side note, the resulting word vectors cover almost all the words in the ArabTE except for about 30 OOV words most of which are NE and we ignore them during vector calculation.

### 4.2 Experimental Setup

Our system is a supervised model, therefore, we experiment with multiple supervised frameworks: an SVM classifier (LIBSVM), Logistic Regression (LR) using specifically the LIBLINEAR classifier, and Random Forest (RF). All experiments are implemented using the WEKA software package (Witten and Frank, 2005). All classifiers yield relatively similar performance with the LR classifier obtaining the best results, which is expected since both the feature space and the dataset are relatively small. Therefore, we report results using LR only.

We report results on a development tuning set, DEV, and a TEST set. We devised 3 training protocols: DEV1, DEV5, and DEV10. Given the size of the labeled data, we run our experiments varying the training protocol and tuning steps while keeping the TEST as a held out data set constant for set ups DEV1 and DEV5. The tuning data, DEV1, comprises 10% of the data, our TRAIN1 data corresponds to 80%, and TEST (held out) is 10% of the data. In the second set up, for DEV5 we calculate the average performance as measured across 5-fold cross validation on 90% of the data. In DEV10 we carry out our experiments with 10-fold cross validation on the entire dataset so as to

---

[1] http://code.google.com/p/word2vec
[2] examples are presented using the Buckwalter transliteration system (Buckwalter, 2002)
[3] https://dumps.wikimedia.org/arwiki/20161120/

[4] https://pypi.python.org/pypi/many-stop-words

| System | DEV1 | DEV10 | DEV5 | TEST |
|---|---|---|---|---|
| BOW1 | 58.75 | 59.07 | 59.3 | 65 |
| BOW2 | 72.71 | 72.96 | 73 | 65 |
| ETED1 (Alabbas, 2013) | | 60 | | |
| ETED2 (Alabbas, 2013) | | 65.7 | | |
| ETED+ABC (Alabbas, 2013) | | 67.3 | | |
| ATE (AL-Khawaldeh, 2015) | | 61.7 | | |
| SANATE (AL-Khawaldeh, 2015) | | 69.3 | | |
| LR-WE | 67.5 | 64.67 | 65.56 | 61.67 |
| LR-TYP | 76.66 | 74.33 | 74.44 | 68.33 |
| LR-ALL | **79.16** | **76.2** | **76.48** | **71.67** |

Table 1: Performance Accuracy % of our system on ArbTE datasets, along with results yielded by comparative state of the art systems

compare to previous work. We report the results: with typical features (length and similarity score, named entity), specifically, without word embeddings, as **TYP**; with word embeddings features alone, as **WE**; the last setting is with all features combined, as **ALL**, both TYP and WE combined.

We report results on two baselines based on the percentage of common words or lemmas between T and H. BOW1 and BOW2 represent these baselines in Table 1. In BOW1, we represent the overlap score as binary score (0 or 1) according to a predefined threshold of 75% overlap.[5] In the second baseline, BOW2, the word overlap score is used but, different from BOW1, we use the classifier to determine the optimal threshold based on the training data. As can be seen, BOW2 is higher than BOW1 where a threshold is manually set; this is an artifact of the nature of this dataset where there is a high correlation between overlap percentage and the entailment relation, and the cutting point for the entailment learned by the classifier is optimal for this dataset. Therefore, we include both as baselines for the system.

Beside the baselines, Table 1 illustrates the results obtained by previous studies on the same data set. We only have the 10 fold (DEV10) results from other systems. As illustrated, **LR-ALL** condition yields the best results for all test conditions consistently across all data sets improving over the baselines by a significant margin and outperforms **LR-TYP** and **LR-WE**. Other systems (ETED1, ETED2, ETED+ABC, ATE, and SANATE) have approached the Arabic TE in a dif-

ferent way, wherein ETED systems the main focus was on the impact of Tree Edit Distance (TED) on the Arabic TE using different model extension, and in ATE and SANATE systems the focus was on the effect of negation and polarity on the Arabic TE. Our system outperforms these systems significantly. Moreover, **LR-TYP** significantly outperforms **LR-WE** and achieves the best performance among all runs and all three setups.

These results indicate that word embedding based features enhance the accuracy by about 2% increase from the **TYP** based system. The 10 fold cross validation experimental set up is carried out to compare our performance against previous studies, namely, employing the same experimental setups in Alabbas (2013). We can see that our result outperforms other works when using **TYP** and **ALL** which shows that not only the word embedding but also the basic similarity features that have been heavily implemented on the English system have improved the result over the Arabic entailment state of the art, along with explicit NE modeling as a bag of words and the calculation of similarity measures over it. On the other hand, the word embedding based features alone yield comparable results to the other systems.

### 4.3 Error Analysis and Discussion

In our system, we use the text as a bag of words and ignore their order. Also, we follow a simple basic assumption: that is if the overlap between the TH pair is high then the positive entailment relation holds, and that it fails to hold otherwise. As can be seen from the baseline in Table 1 this assumption works very well in this dataset. When inspecting the dataset, it turns out that the

---

[5]This is empirically determined in pervious studies in the English RTE system and it has been also used as baseline in the Arabic systems.

Arabic dataset has this as a dominant phenomenon meaning higher overlap induces entailment and vice versa. Furthermore, the word embedding features in our model help in the semantic interpretation of the unmatched words which results in a performance boost of the result as the pair become closer or far apart in the vector space. Thus, the type of errors inspected are for the more complicated pairs. For example, our system failed to detect the lack of entailment relation in the following example:

**T**: AlElmA' yHtArwn fy ASAbp AlnwE Algryb mn bktryA <y kwlAy Alty Zhrt fy AlmAnyA ntyjp AsthlAk xyAr mn AsbAnyA llnsA' AlbAlgAt Akvr mn gyrhn

**T-English-Translation**: Scientists are confused about a strange kind of E.coli that has emerged in Germany as the result of the consumption of cucumbers from Spain, which affects adult women more than others.

**H**: bktryA AlxyAr fy AlmAnyA tSyb AlnsA' Akvr mn AlrjAl

**H-English-Translation**: Cucumbers bacteria in Germany affects women more than men.

In this example, the H has a specific piece of information which is not in the text, yet our system labels it as a true entailment. Furthermore, NE features in our model are basic features that do not apply any preprocessing or normalization to, for example, map abbreviations, which leads to some errors in our model. In addition, there are different NLP phenomena we did not handle such as co-reference resolution and syntactic parsing, which we believe could improve the performance.

## 5   Conclusion

This paper shows our work to address the entailment relation in under-resourced languages, specifically Arabic. We have shown that the use of word representation based features provides a reasonable result when compared with other basic surface level matching features. The key characteristic of these features is the fact that they do not depend on external language resources, but are induced in the latent space, namely using a word2vec model that can be easily generated in any language, i.e. an advantage over the required use of external resources. While we have only studied the effect of such features on Arabic, they can easily be applied to other languages. Although the set we evaluated on was limited in size and to types of phenomena that are usually related to entailment, it was sufficient to confirm that, indeed, word embeddings can be used to enhance textual entailment in such languages. Finally, the current system still has limitations including various ways in which word embeddings could be incorporated.

## References

Mohamed Al-Badrashiny, Arfath Pasha, Mona Diab, Nizar Habash, Owen Rambow, Wael Salloum, and Ramy Eskander. 2016. Split: Smart preprocessing (quasi) language independent tool. In *10th International Conference on Language Resources and Evaluation (LREC'16)*, Portoro, Slovenia. European Language Resources Association (ELRA).

Fatima T. AL-Khawaldeh. 2015. A study of the effect of resolving negation and sentiment analysis in recognizing text entailment for arabic. *World of Computer Science and Information Technology Journal (WCSIT)*, 5(7):124–128.

Maytham Alabbas and Allan Ramsay. 2012. Dependency tree matching with extended tree edit distance with subtrees for textual entailment. In *FedCSIS*, pages 11–18.

Maytham Alabbas and Allan Ramsay. 2013. Natural language inference for arabic using extended tree edit distance with subtrees. *Journal of Artificial Intelligence Research*, 48:1–22.

Maytham Alabbas. 2011. Arbte: Arabic textual entailment.

Maytham Abualhail Shahed Alabbas. 2013. Textual entailment for modern standard arabic.

Tim Buckwalter. 2002. Arabic transliteration. *URL http://www. qamus. org/transliteration. htm.*

Timothy Chklovski and Patrick Pantel. 2004. Verbocean: Mining the web for fine-grained semantic verb relations. In *EMNLP*, volume 4, pages 33–40.

Stéphane Clinchant, Cyril Goutte, and Eric Gaussier. 2006. Lexical entailment for information retrieval. In *Advances in Information Retrieval*, pages 217–228. Springer.

Ido Dagan, Oren Glickman, and Bernardo Magnini. 2006. The pascal recognising textual entailment challenge. In *Machine learning challenges. evaluating predictive uncertainty, visual object classification, and recognising tectual entailment*, pages 177–190. Springer.

Ido Dagan, Bill Dolan, Bernardo Magnini, and Dan Roth. 2010. Recognizing textual entailment: Rational, evaluation and approaches–erratum. *Natural Language Engineering*, 16(01):105–105.

Lee R. Dice. 1945. Measures of the amount of ecologic association between species. *Ecology*, 26(3):297–302.

Souhir Gahbiche-Braham, Hélène Bonneau-Maynard, and François Yvon. 2014. Traitement automatique des entités nommées en arabe: détection et traduction. *TAL*, 54(2):101–132.

Adrian Iftene and Mihai-Alex Moruz. 2009. Uaic participation at rte5. *Proceedings of TAC*.

Diana Inkpen, Darren Kipp, and Vivi Nastase. Machine learning experiments for textual entailment.

Paul Jaccard. 1901. *Etude comparative de la distribution florale dans une portion des Alpes et du Jura.* Impr. Corbaz.

Mohamed Maamouri, Ann Bies, and Seth Kulick. 2008. Enhancing the arabic treebank: a collaborative effort toward new annotation guidelines. In *LREC*.

Prodromos Malakasiotis and Ion Androutsopoulos. 2007. Learning textual entailment using svms and string similarity measures. In *Proceedings of the ACL-PASCAL Workshop on Textual Entailment and Paraphrasing*, pages 42–47. Association for Computational Linguistics.

Yashar Mehdad, Alessandro Moschitti, and Fabio Massiomo Zanzotto. 2009. Semker: Syntactic/semantic kernels for recognizing textual entailment. In *Proc. of the Text Analysis Conference, Gaithersburg, MD*. Citeseer.

Tomas Mikolov, Ilya Sutskever, Kai Chen, Greg S. Corrado, and Jeff Dean. 2013. Distributed representations of words and phrases and their compositionality. In *Advances in neural information processing systems*, pages 3111–3119.

George A. Miller. 1995. Wordnet: a lexical database for english. *Communications of the ACM*, 38(11):39–41.

Alessandro Moschitti. 2006. Efficient convolution kernels for dependency and constituent syntactic trees. In *Machine Learning: ECML 2006*, pages 318–329. Springer.

Partha Pakray, Sivaji Bandyopadhyay, and Alexander Gelbukh. 2011. Textual entailment using lexical and syntactic similarity. *International Journal of Artificial Intelligence and Applications*, 2(1):43–58.

Robert Parker, David Graff, Ke Chen, Junbo Kong, and Kazuaki Maeda. 2011. Arabic gigaword fifth edition ldc2011t11. *Philadelphia: Linguistic Data Consortium.*

Arfath Pasha, Mohamed Al-Badrashiny, Mona T. Diab, Ahmed El Kholy, Ramy Eskander, Nizar Habash, Manoj Pooleery, Owen Rambow, and Ryan Roth. 2014. Madamira: A fast, comprehensive tool for morphological analysis and disambiguation of arabic. In *LREC*, volume 14, pages 1094–1101.

Mark Sammons, V.G. Vinod Vydiswaran, Tim Vieira, Nikhil Johri, Ming-Wei Chang, Dan Goldwasser, Vivek Srikumar, Gourab Kundu, Yuancheng Tu, Kevin Small, et al. 2009. Relation alignment for textual entailment recognition. In *Text Analysis Conference (TAC)*.

Rui Wang and Günter Neumann. 2007. Recognizing textual entailment using a subsequence kernel method.

Rui Wang and Guenter Neumann. 2008. An divide-and-conquer strategy for recognizing textual entailment. In *Proc. of the Text Analysis Conference, Gaithersburg, MD*.

Ian H. Witten and Eibe Frank. 2005. *Data Mining: Practical machine learning tools and techniques.* Morgan Kaufmann.

Fabio Massimo Zanzotto and Alessandro Moschitti. 2006. Automatic learning of textual entailments with cross-pair similarities. In *ANNUAL MEETING-ASSOCIATION FOR COMPUTATIONAL LINGUISTICS*, volume 44, page 401.

Fabio Massimo Zanzotto, Marco Pennacchiotti, and Alessandro Moschitti. 2009. A machine learning approach to textual entailment recognition. *Natural Language Engineering*, 15(04):551–582.

Jiang Zhao, Man Lan, Zheng-Yu Niu, and Yue Lu. 2015. Integrating word embeddings and traditional nlp features to measure textual entailment and semantic relatedness of sentence pairs. In *2015 International Joint Conference on Neural Networks (IJCNN)*, pages 1–7. IEEE.

# Author Index